TUTORIAL ON
Software Maintenance

GIRISH PARIKH & NICHOLAS ZVEGINTZOV

IEEE CATALOG NO. EHO201-4
LIBRARY OF CONGRESS NO. 82-83405
IEEE COMPUTER SOCIETY ORDER NO. 453
ISBN NO. 0-8186-0002-0

COMPUTER
SOCIETY
PRESS Φ.

Φ IEEE COMPUTER SOCIETY

Φ THE INSTITUTE OF ELECTRICAL AND ELECTRONICS ENGINEERS INC.

Order from: IEEE Computer Society
Post Office Box 80452
Worldway Postal Center
Los Angeles, CA 90080

IEEE Service Center
445 Hoes Lane
Piscataway, NJ 08854

Published by IEEE Computer Society Press
1109 Spring Street
Suite 300
Silver Spring, MD 20910

IEEE Catalog Number EHO201-4
Library of Congress Number 82-83405
IEEE Computer Society Order Number 453
ISBN Number 0-8186-0002-0

Order from: IEEE Computer Society   IEEE Service Center
            Post Office Box 80452   445 Hoes Lane
            Worldway Postal Center   Piscataway, NJ 08854
            Los Angeles, CA 90080

 The Institute of Electrical and Electronics Engineers, Inc.

Abstract

Software maintenance, the work done on a software system after it becomes operational, consumes at least half of all technical and management resources expended in the software area. This Tutorial approaches maintenance not only as an essential element in the life of a software system but also as a process with its own rules and techniques.

The Tutorial explores maintenance in six parts. Part I, *The world of software maintenance*, explores empirical and observational data on maintenance activity. Part II, *Understanding software*, deals with techniques for deriving or reconstructing the development framework (goals, requirements, specifications, design, etc.) from an operational system. Part III, *The modification of software*, describes tools and techniques for modifying the function of a system. Part IV, *The evolution of software*, describes the lifetime of a software system in terms of growth, renewal, and survival. Part V, *The death of software*, deals with the disappearance of software systems—scheduled, premature, and frustrated. Finally, Part VI deals with *The management of software maintenance*. Each part contains an explanatory introduction and selected reprints.

In all, the Tutorial includes thirty-one papers by thirty-seven leading authorities on software maintenance—papers most often requested from their authors, papers in hard-to-find sources, papers that are the foundations of modern thinking in the topic, and papers that extend the frontiers of research. The editors introduce each paper and each author to give the reader entrance into the invisible network of people and ideas which forms the emerging field of software maintenance. Also included in this Tutorial are an introduction, an epilogue, an annotated bibliography, and name and topic indexes.

Acknowledgements

We thank the authors of the papers in this Tutorial. Their original work changed software maintenance from a black art to an intellectual reality. The authors also provided us the background information giving them and their work an historical context. We also thank the publishers and authors for reprint permissions.

We thank Dr. Bruce Berra and Dr. Ez Nahouraii of the IEEE Computer Society Press Advisory Committee, the reviewers for their critical scrutiny, and Mr. C. G. Stockton, Ms. Margaret Brown, and all the staff of the IEEE Computer Society Press for transforming our manuscript into a book.

We thank our own publishers (Little, Brown and Company for Parikh, and McGraw-Hill Book Company for Zvegintzov) for letting this project go ahead.

We thank Viido Polikarpus for Figure VI-2, which is used by permission.

We thank the free-lance copy editor, Barbara Wittig, for the excellent editing of our text.

Parikh thanks Swami Bhashyananda of Vivekananda Vedanta Society, Chicago, for reviewing the material on "Life Cycle of the Hindu Universe." He is grateful to Gerald M. Weinberg, his programming guru, and the original publisher of his first book *Techniques of Program and System Maintenance*. Weinberg, and his works have been a constant inspiration to him. He thanks Ken Orr for reviewing introductions to three papers. He also thanks Mr. Lem Ejiogu, Director, Lemcomm Softech, and Mr. Dinesh Patel, a computer programmer, both of Chicago, for their kind help with two papers. Ejiogu also persuaded Parikh that "no non-fiction book should be without an index"! Mr. Patel also helped in preparing the index. Parikh thanks Zvegintzov for patiently interpreting and refining his part of the manuscript, which he had written in longhand; and for entering it into his word processor. He also thanks Edward Yourdon, his structured programming guru, whose lively introductions to the papers in *Classics in Software Engineering* (Yourdon Press, 1979) provided examples. He thanks Dr. Helmut Epp, Chairman of the Computer Science Department, DePaul University, Chicago, for giving him an opportunity to teach a graduate course in software maintenance. Finally, he thanks his wife Hasu for her patience and encouragement.

Zvegintzov thanks Laszlo Belady, Peter Freeman, Geoffrey Hegeman, Susanna Ryburn Hegeman, Girish Parikh, Charles Stewart, Diana Zvegintzov, and Serge Zvegintzov for their faith and support. Harlan Ellison gave him a vision of the True Editor.

Preface

This Tutorial draws together original material and selected reprints on software maintenance—work done on a software system after it becomes operational—to give the reader a basic grasp of the theory and practice in this emerging field of software engineering.

It can be used in the following contexts:

- As a workbook for an in-house or public technical development seminar.

- As course material for a senior or graduate level college course in a software engineering or computer science curriculum.

- As self-study material for the experienced programmer or manager with responsibility for software, both operational and under development.

- As a guide for the manager to further resources available in the maintenance field.

Introduction

The topic of this book is software maintenance, which we define as *Work done on a software system after it becomes operational.* Thus, software maintenance includes: understanding and documenting existing systems; extending existing functions; adding new functions; finding and correcting bugs; answering questions for users and operations staff; training new systems staff; rewriting, restructuring, converting, and purging software; managing the software of an operational system; and many other activities that go into running a successful software system.

Various objections have been made to calling these activities maintenance, chiefly on the grounds that they do not resemble the activities of physical maintenance and should not be called by the same name. Maintenance of physical systems consists chiefly of repairing deteriorated equipment whereas software does not deteriorate; maintainers of physical systems are usually less skilled than builders of physical systems, whereas maintainers of software are not; and so on.

Nevertheless, the term "software maintenance" seems to be well accepted in the sense we defined it, and we shall stick with it. There are well accepted statistics about the extent and content of maintenance defined in this sense.

- Half of all programming resources are expended for software maintenance.
- More than half of these resources are used for adding new functions and capabilities.
- More than half of the programmer's task is in understanding the system.

These statistics shape our approach in this Tutorial.

Three premises

We approach software maintenance as a promising career path for practitioners and as a challenging research topic for theorists. We hold to three premises about the nature of maintenance.

Our first premise is *Maintenance is an essential element in the life of a software system.*

Software systems exist to support human activities (business, government, research, and so on) or to embody subsystems within them. These activities existed before there was software; they go ahead, for better or worse, whether the software systems are ready or not. Software development is the process of bringing software into a state where it can take part in human activities; it is a necessary process, often a difficult

one, but it is in some sense a sheltered process. The software is on probation; it is tested against dummy data and artificially frozen goals. Only when the software is operational is it productive; only then is it tested against real human activities. Maintenance begins.

The function of maintenance is to keep the software targeted on real goals. These goals are moving targets. A significant proportion of the functionality of a software system is created in the maintenance phase. The software, like the human manager, must handle "today's business today" and "tomorrow's business tomorrow," even if these are quite incompatible.

Our second premise is *Maintenance is a process with its own rules and techniques.*

The inescapable challenge for the maintainer is that a system exists already. This provides an additional complexity not faced in traditional development theory. The developer learns the user's requirements and then synthesizes the system. The maintainer listens to the user's request, learns the user's view of the system, analyzes the system, plans and implements a change, and brings the changed system on line with a smooth transition.

The softness of software is an opportunity for the system synthesist, but it is a pitfall for the maintainer. The maintainer's chief skill, like the surgeon's, is not in making desirable changes but in avoiding undesirable ones. (Any fool can take out an appendix; the trick is to take it out without killing the patient.)

The maintainer must also match the resources of the change to the apparent size of the change, not to the size of the system as a whole. The user may be willing to wait six months for a mailing list data base system, but not for a "simple" change like going from a five digit to a nine digit zip code. The maintainer must somehow reduce the complexity of the system to the complexity of the part to be modified; often such reductions are simple in retrospect ("simple when you know how") but are a major challenge when they arise.

In any case, this challenge is not going away. Our third premise is: *The era of mature software is here.*

Many day-to-day human activities are already computerized. The costs were high; the results are not always as satisfactory as they might be; but society will not incur those costs again. There is no question of writing an infinite number of payroll systems or language compilers. Existing systems will be restructured and new functions will be built on top of them, but the era of wholesale software creation is past.

In the 1980's, software is mature. It needs mature practitioners. This is the professional and intellectual challenge of software maintenance.

Outline

In the light of the three premises, we identify the major problems of maintenance as follows:

- Grasping, and retaining, intellectual control of the system; understanding and documenting systems; and protecting the maintenance team against decay due to staff turnover, forgetting, and functional change.
- Controlling the implementation of a continuing stream of requirements changes.
- Minimizing the structural decay of systems due to adding functions not envisaged in the original design.

We have chosen thirty-one papers that illuminate these problems. (There are actually thirty-three sources, because the Overton paper in Part I is extracted from three sources.) These are the papers most often requested from their authors, papers in hard-to-find sources, papers that are the foundations of modern thinking in the topic, and papers that extend the frontiers of research. One paper, by Gilb, appears here for the first time. We have organized and distributed these papers into six parts.

Part I, *The world of software maintenance*, explores empirical and observational data on maintenance activity. It answers the questions: How much maintenance is there? What are its objectives? What do maintainers do?

Part II, *Understanding software*, deals with techniques for deriving or reconstructing the development framework (goals, requirements, specifications, design, etc.) from an operational system. The aim is to put the maintenance team into a relationship with the system that enables it to make changes correctly.

Part III, *The modification of software*, describes tools and techniques for modifying the function of a system. We defined maintenance as "work done on a software system after it becomes operational;" Part III deals with the specifics of that work.

Part IV, *The evolution of software*, describes the lifetime of a software system in terms of growth, renewal, and survival. "Evolution" has been used by several writers to express the unfolding or development of a system as it adapts to its environment. The papers in Part IV consider evolution both passively, as a way of measuring system change, and actively, as a way of guiding it.

Part V, *The death of software*, deals with the disap-

pearance of software systems—scheduled, premature, and frustrated. It concludes that software systems are hardy and perverse creatures; often they survive when they should perish. Most computer education does not prepare the student for this reality.

Part VI deals with *The management of software maintenance*. Like all management problems, it is half technical and half political. How can the manager balance the paradoxical demands of users for both stability and change against the finite abilities of the staff to control a complex system?

We conclude the text of the Tutorial with an *Epilogue: songs for unsung heroes* in which we point out that the challenge that maintainers face is large and the ability of computer science and software engineering to help is still small. Our Tutorial helps to bridge some of the gap between practice and theory, but it is only a beginning.

Beyond the text there are two sections which make the Tutorial a solid reference source—the annotated bibliography and the indexes.

The *Annotated bibliography*, prepared by Girish Parikh, provides a guide to the periodicals which have been most helpful to date in the field of maintenance, and a bibliographic listing, with brief annotations, of 45 books, papers, and reports. It includes eight books which deal principally with maintenance, 13 books which give valuable side-lights on maintenance, and a selection of important papers that we could not include in the body of the Tutorial.

The indexes, prepared by Girish Parikh and Dinesh Patel, comprise a *Topic index* and a *Name index*. Both indexes cover the entire Tutorial—our introductory texts, the included papers, and the annotated bibliography. Thus the indexes provide a unique resource which welds the Tutorial into an integrated survey of the current state of maintenance. The name index supplies extra depth to the references, since it points to citations within the introductions, the included papers, and the annotated bibliography.

Thirty-seven soothsayers

In 1967 Harlan Ellison edited an anthology of science fiction stories, *Dangerous visions* (Doubleday & Company, Inc.), on topics that had hitherto been taboo. Predicting, correctly, that the anthology would become a classic, he wrote a personal introduction to each story and its author so that the reader would understand that the book was not a random collection of independent pieces but was the product of an invisible community of writers, whose history and culture twined among themselves and with the reader, writers who had made the field what it was. Ellison titled his first introduction "Thirty-two soothsayers." (Zvegintzov was one of those soothsayers, writing under the pseudonym Jonathan Brand.)

When we began to organize this Tutorial we had the same feeling—that we were collecting papers on hitherto taboo topics, that we are on the cusp of a fundamental change in the field of software engineering, and that the reader deserves an insight into an invisible community that is responsible for that change. Therefore we decided to introduce each paper and each of our thirty-seven writers. We asked the authors such questions as: How did you get into computing? What were you doing when you wrote the paper? and What are you doing now? Some interesting trends emerged. (The following proportions are presumably low, because we did not get answers on all questions from all authors.)

First, these authors have extensive experience. We are aware that at least Hamlen, Overton, Gilb, Weinberg, Warnier, Bucher, and Holt have been in computing since the 1950's. Virtually all the authors have been in computing since the 1960's. In retrospect, it is no surprise that experience in computing makes one appreciate the problems of maintenance.

Second, a surprising number of the authors are associated with operating systems programming. Bucher worked on the development of the Computer Sciences Teleprocessing System. Spier, Van Vleck, and Clingen all worked on the development of Multics. Spier also designed and programmed Europe's first commercial time-sharing system. Holt worked on the Generalized Programming System for the Univac I. Cashman is working on the National Software Works distributed operating system. Parnas, Belady, Van Horn, and Denning have written major research papers on operating systems design. The reason, perhaps, is that operating systems, at least successful ones, are unique testbeds for maintenance problems—they are large, long-lived, and subjected to hard use by demanding users.

Third, many of the authors in the maintenance field work for themselves or control their own companies. Parikh, Zvegintzov, Overton, Higgins, Hetzel, Gilb, Weinberg, Miller, and Warnier are in this category. Perhaps this only reflects that consultants have the leisure to be able to write, and the hunger to want to!

We are glad to report that, as we go to press in early 1983, all the authors are alive and well and still working. However, one soothsayer has passed on. Walt Cameron initiated a five-day course at IBM Systems Science Institute (since 1982, IBM Information Systems Management Institute) on "Application test and maintenance." He told us slyly that he always asked his incoming students to "bring with you a copy of your company's maintenance procedure manual." "They never did!" he said, laughing. Though not one of our authors, it was Cameron who first gave us a copy of the Fjeldstad and Hamlen report reprinted in Part I. He died in 1981. We miss him.

Invitation to the network

A network consists of people in different locations, different jobs, and different specialties who find they have ideas to share. A network is exchanging phone calls, letters, first drafts, and publications. A network is planning business trips or conference sessions to meet distant colleagues. A network is what sometimes reassures you—"I'm *not* the only crazy one!" A network is what every emerging field needs and creates. If you have ideas to share, data to contribute, experiences to tell, or even complaints to make, put yourself on the network. Contact us. We look forward to it.

Girish Parikh
Shetal Enterprises
1787 B West Touhy
Chicago IL 60626
312-262-1133

Nicholas Zvegintzov
141 St Marks Place #5F
Staten Island NY 10301
212-981-7842

Table of Contents

Part I: The world of software maintenance

The papers in Part I deal with software maintenance, not as it ought to be, not as it might be, but as it *is*. The authors either have practiced maintenance or questioned those who practice it or have observed those who practice it. They write with the wisdom of the street, not of the ivory tower. They give clear and consistent answers to three questions:

- How much maintenance is there?
- What are its objectives?
- What do maintainers do?

How much maintenance is there?

In recent years there have been three studies in which the managers of programming groups have been questioned on their attitudes and activities with respect to maintenance. Two of these questionnaire studies are reported in this part—one by Fjeldstad and Hamlen and the other by Lientz and Swanson. The third such study, the "Federal agencies' maintenance of computer programs: expensive and undermanaged" (AFMD-81-25), was published by the U.S. General Accounting Office in 1981.

All three studies conclude that about half of the respondents' resources is applied to maintaining existing systems, and the other half is applied to developing new systems. This "half and half" answer has been consistent since at least 1969. Figure I-1 plots fourteen published references to the proportion of computing resources that are applied to maintenance; the O's are the three questionnaire studies, and the X's are other individual opinions.

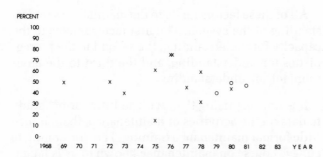

PERCENT

Figure I-1 MAINTENANCE AS A PROPORTION OF PROGRAMMING RESOURCES

The 50% figure measures the proportion of resources a typical computing *organization* puts into maintenance versus development. A similar question has sometimes been asked about a typical *system*:

How much of the resources applied to it was for maintenance and how much was for development? Such a question can be answered for a particular system but not for a "typical" system, for no system is typical. Some systems are "throwaway" and incur no maintenance at all, and some systems are immensely long-lived.

In the long-lived category are some of the most used software systems ever written—the operating systems of the major mainframes. This Tutorial, for instance, includes papers relating to the maintenance of IBM's OS operating system, Computer Sciences Corporation's CSTS, and Honeywell's Multics, all of which were developed in the 1960's and seem to be in little danger of being superseded. At the other end of the spectrum, every installation and every programmer has programs that are written, run once, stored, backed into archival storage (or desk drawers), and never used again.

All we can say about maintenance resources is that, taking all personnel over all systems, about half of all resources goes into maintenance.

What are the objectives of maintenance?

The answers of the questionnaire studies are also clear and consistent about the objectives of maintenance, which are listed in the order of resources expended.

- New features and enhancements.
- Adaptation to new data or hardware.
- Corrections and fixes.
- "Other."

Figure I-2 gives representative data from the Lientz and Swanson study.

Especially consistent is the data on enhancements versus corrections. Over half of the maintenance effort goes toward enhancement of program function or the handling of new data, and less than a fifth goes toward the correction of errors:

	% ENHANCE- MENTS	% CORREC- TIONS
Lientz and Swanson	64	17
Fjeldstad and Hamlen	88	12
U.S. General Accounting Office	51	19

EHO201-4/83/0000/0001$01.00 © 1983 IEEE

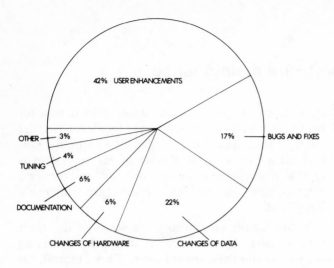

Data from:
Lientz, B.P., Swanson, E.B.
   Software maintenance management—a study of the maintenance of computer application
software in 487 data processing organizations.
Reading, MA: Addison-Wesley Publishing Company, 1980.

**Figure I-2   APPLICATIONS MAINTENANCE
AREAS** (487 DPMA member organizations)

It should not be inferred that all software is equally reliable and requires only 20% of the maintainers' time for trouble-shooting. These three studies deal only with heavily used software . Presumably, usage and errors vary inversely: the less a system is used, the more errors it contains; the more errors a system contains, the less it is used.

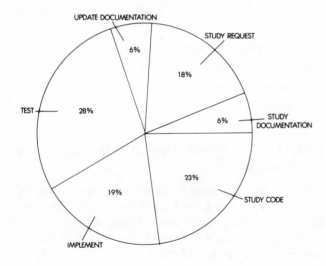

Data from:
Fjeldstad, R.K., Hamlen, W.T.
   Application program maintenance study—report to our respondents.
IBM Corporation, DP Marketing Group, White Plains, NY, 1979.

**Figure I-3   MAINTENANCE PERSONNEL
ACTIVITIES—ENHANCEMENTS**
(25 IBM installations)

What do maintainers do?

The published data on the activities of maintainers is scanty, but again it is clear and consistent. Maintainers spend at least half of their time trying to *understand*—the system code, the system documentation, and the requests or complaints from the users. Figure I-3 shows data from the Fjeldstad and Hamlen study on the activities of maintainers in performing an enhancement: maintainers spend 47% of their time studying. (When correcting errors, they spend 62% of their time studying.)

Fjeldstad and Hamlen comment:

> [U]nderstanding the intent and style of implementation of the original programmer was the major cause of time and difficulty in making the change.

The other studies did not ask about maintainer activities, but the Lientz and Swanson managers cited "quality of application system documentation" as a pressing problem in maintenance.

The only major research study of maintenance programmers at work was done by Overton et al. and reported in three U.S. Government studies that are excerpted in this part. The aim of Overton's group was to discover the factors that make it difficult for a maintainer to do an effective job, and to recommend tools or techniques to lessen the difficulty. Overton's group found the following three factors:

- The limited rate at which a person can perceive relevant clues in a mass of material.
- The human tendency to require more clues to a situation than are "logically" necessary to understand it.
- The human liability to distraction and procrastination.

All of these factors relate to the maintainer's understanding of the system. The first factor relates to the capacity for understanding, the second to the prerequisites for understanding, and the third to the environment for understanding.

It is not surprising that, with so little formal study to date on the activities of maintenance, there is also little formal maintenance training. The first complete college course on maintenance known to us is taught at the National Technical Institute for the Deaf at Rochester Institute of Technology. It is a hands-on course in which the students perform assigments in conversion, debugging, documentation, and enhancement; many of the assignments are based on real problems handled by the data center staff. An account of this course by its originator, Donald Beil, concludes Part I of this Tutorial.

Conclusions

The world of software maintenance is a world in which programmers spend half of all their time. In this world, the main programming objective is to enhance an existing system to perform new functions or handle new data. The major professional challenge is to understand and conquer the complexity of the system as it is. This world, this objective, and this challenge must shape the manager's or educator's approach for increasing the productivity of the software professional.

Introduction

Parikh, G. "The world of software maintenance." In: Parikh, G., ed., *Techniques of program and system maintenance*, Boston, MA: Little, Brown and Company, 1982, 9-13. [The following introduction was written by Nicholas Zvegintzov.]

The extract that you are about to read is the first reprint in this tutorial volume, and it is by my coeditor, Girish Parikh. He originally wrote it for the first American book ever published on software maintenance, *Techniques of program and system maintenance*, which he also edited. I will not summarize the piece, except to say that it sets software maintenance in its place in the whole field of software engineering. Instead, I would like to give you some personal glimpses into how that first American book came into being. I think the story teaches an important lesson about the field of computing.

Girish Parikh (pronounced PAREEK) is the son of a high school teacher, and a native of the western state of India called Gujarat, the same region that produced Mahatma Gandhi, leader of the peaceful separation of India from Britain. In 1959 Parikh graduated from Gujarat University with a B.E. in civil engineering. His first love was writing. During his years in India he wrote short stories, poems, plays, and essays in his native language. He won a government prize for a collection of children's poems, and he edited a multi-lingual engineering college annual.

In February 1967, after working seven years in engineering, he sold his house in Bombay and came to the United States to study computer technologies (hardware oriented) at the Milwaukee School of Engineering. A FORTRAN course from an inspiring professor, and a *Fortune* article, "Help wanted: 50,000 programmers," caused the first change in his professional outlook. He no longer wanted to be a civil engineer or to work on hardware: he wanted to become a computer programmer.

He continued to study data processing at a business school in Milwaukee, and in early 1968 he moved to Chicago and began to look for a job—and found that he could not get one without experience. At one point he was down to his last twenty-five cent bag of potato chips. Finally, he entered the data processing field—as a tab operator on the night shift at a large corporation. Later that year, he moved to a smaller company as a computer operator with some programming responsibilities. In this, and in subsequent jobs, he underwent the second change in his professional outlook. He found himself maintaining undocumented programs. "If my teachers had mentioned the painful maintenance," he told me, "I might have had second thoughts about entering data processing!"

However, he did love programming, and he continued as a programmer for 13 years, hopping jobs every eighteen months or so "like a typical programmer." In 1976, "while working on some of the most depressing maintenance assignments of my career," he decided to work on an original book on software maintenance. Before writing his own book, he decided to consult the books of others. There were none. So he started to track down the items on maintenance that were scattered through the academic and trade literature.

In this period, he acknowledges three influences. The first was Cris Miller, a manager at one of his programming jobs. Miller pointed out that the so-called "structured technologies" can only become completely effective when there is a way to bring them to bear on the mass of existing code. The second influence was Gerald M. Weinberg, whose pioneering 1971 book, *The psychology of computer programming*, starts off, not with writing programs, but with reading them. The third was the work of Lientz and Swanson, whose early reports on their questionnaire studies cited many of the existing articles on maintenance. All of these authors are represented in this Tutorial.

After reviewing the existing work, Parikh linked new and reprinted articles, plus an index and annotated bibliography, into a book of readings on maintenance. This was (as seems to be traditional with classics) rejected by major publishers but was finally brought out in March 1980 by Ethnotech, Inc., the training and consulting company founded by Gerald M. Weinberg. Thus did a computer programmer from India and a small company in Nebraska become the author and publisher, respectively, of the first American book on software maintenance. Now the subject is picking up its own momentum; Parikh's book is out in a handsome new edition from Little, Brown and Company, and there are, at the time of this writing (May 1982), four other American books on maintenance, as well as one each from Britain, France, and Germany, which the reader will find in Parikh's updated annotated bibliography at the end of the Tutorial.

The lesson of Parikh's story is this: The field of computing is a vast one, comprising a universe of machines and people and specialties. If you, too, feel that you are aware of some world of computing that nobody has stopped to analyze or explain—you are probably right.

The World of Software Maintenance

Girish Parikh

Welcome to the world of software maintenance!

Let me ask you: Do you really like the world of software maintenance? If you know this world already, I'm confident your answer is a definite no. A few of you may be exceptions, however, you who can see maintenance as a challenge (usually unappreciated), or as job security (though it's a myth), or even find it easier than new development (once you know the system). Whether you like maintenance or not, it's a fact of life in data processing. Someone, perhaps you, must do that dirty work— until the mess is cleared and replaced by more maintainable systems developed using structured technologies. Maintainable systems make maintenance programming a decent job.

This chapter focuses on software maintenance as an important part of software engineering. It outlines different aspects of software maintenance, and presents a case for collection and development of "software maintenance technologies."

Software engineering and its functions

Software engineering, simply defined, is a collection of methodologies, both technical and managerial, for development and maintenance of software. (Canning 1978) The word "maintenance" is used here in its broadest sense, to include error corrections, changes (also called modifications or amendments), enhancements, and improvements to the existing software.

The field of software engineering includes technical as well as managerial functions for the equally important functions of software development and software maintenance, as shown in figure 1.

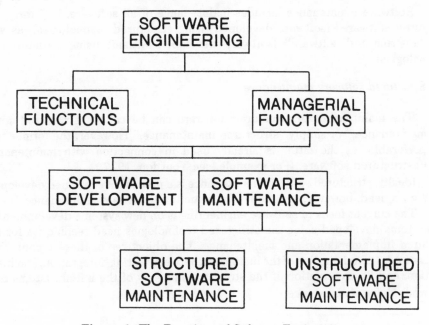

Figure 1. The Functions of Software Engineering

The two branches (or functions) of software engineering, i.e. software development and software maintenance, can also be called "software development engineering" and "software maintenance engineering." However, the shorter terms are already in use, and it appears that their use will continue.

We can further divide software maintenance into "systems software maintenance" and "applications software maintenance." However, in this article, software maintenance includes maintenance of both.

Software maintenance includes both "structured software maintenance" and "unstructured software[1] maintenance." We will take a closer look at them later in this chapter.

Software maintenance: extremely important but neglected topic

Traditionally, computing literature has focused on software development. Software maintenance has been almost always neglected.[2] This imbalance is like trying to fly with only one wing!

According to one study, about 45% of the overall hardware-software dollar is *currently* going into software maintenance. The same study further reveals that this number is likely to grow to about 60% by 1985; and is expected to continue to grow for a long time as we add new code to our inventory faster than we discard the old code. (Boehm, 1976) The on-going maintenance, where most programmers spend 50%, and in some cases 80% of their time, is clearly a significant burden to the DP industry.

The structured technologies and maintenance in the future

The proper use of structured technologies (comprising structured analysis, structured design, structured programming; and the productivity techniques such as top-down design and development, walkthroughs, team operations, development support libraries) during software development helps produce more maintainable systems and programs, reducing the future burden of software maintenance.

Software maintenance

Software maintenance includes maintenance of all software, including "structured software" (software developed using structured technologies), as well as "unstructured software" (software developed without using structured technologies).

Structured software maintenance

The maintenance of structured software can be called "structured software maintenance," or simply "structured maintenance." However, the former term is preferable, as the latter is already used in connection with maintenance of unstructured software. (For example, see Yourdon, 1977.)

Ideally, structured software maintenance is a process of continued development. We do need, however, techniques for structured software maintenance.

The current focus in software engineering is on new systems development. The systems developed using the structured technologies need techniques for structured implementation and maintenance. The objectives of these techniques are twofold: 1) minimization of the distinction between testing, integration, and installation, and 2) preservation of the structural integrity of the initial systems design, while doing maintenance.

Unstructured software maintenance

The maintenance of unstructured software can be called "unstructured software

8

maintenance," or simply "unstructured maintenance;" however, the former term is preferable.

Until unstructured software is given a partial or full "face-lift," (described later in this chapter), or, partially or completely rewritten using structured technologies, it may continue to be a major burden. The need for collecting (and even developing) techniques to handle such software maintenance is even greater than that for structured software.

Some techniques common to both kinds of software maintenance

Many techniques may be different for the two kinds of software maintenance. It is likely that some techniques are common to both kinds of maintenance. For example, the techniques for face-lift can be applied to the structured software also.

The collection of techniques for both kinds of software maintenance can be called software maintenance technologies.

Maintainability of unstructured software

The maintainability of unstructured software can vary in degrees, from easily maintainable to almost unmaintainable. Several factors such as the structure of the unstructured software, the quality of available documentation, the experience and application knowledge of maintenance programmers, the extensiveness and types of maintenance, and the management attitude, should be considered in estimating the maintainability of software. Again, maintainability may be relative to the criteria established, and it may vary for the different components of the same software package.

Types of maintenance

Maintenance can be classified into three types: "Corrective maintenance" to take care of processing, performance, or implementation failures; "adaptive maintenance" to satisfy changes in the processing or data environment; and "perfective maintenance" for enhancing performance or maintainability. (Swanson, 1976)

Techniques for unstructured software maintenance

Little has been written on "how to" aspects of unstructured software maintenance. Nevertheless, while each such system may have its own problems, some common techniques, based on experience and study, can be collected and/or developed.

Some of the structured technologies, such as a human librarian, walkthroughs, chief programmer teams, can also be used to maintain unstructured software.[3]

Techniques for a software face-lift

These techniques essentially improve the appearance of software. Reformatting of programs (which can be automated) may dramatically improve maintenance programming productivity.

The restructuring of programs (possibly automated) can also increase maintenance programming productivity; however, it may have limitations depending on the structure of the original software.

Software tools in maintenance

Available software packages, such as automated libraries, preprocessors including reformatting packages and structuring engines, file compare utilities, and online testing and debugging packages, can be efficiently used to increase maintenance programming productivity. This subject needs to be explored.[4]

Conclusion

Software maintenance technologies, collected and organized, can help manage maintenance better, and help reduce some of its burden. I hope that this chapter, briefly covering the range of software maintenance ideas, generates further interest in this vital subject.

Notes

[1]The term "unstructured software" in this chapter is used to represent the software developed without using structured technologies. However, the qualifying term "unstructured" might be misleading, since there is more of a continuum between the two polar extremes of structured and unstructured, and very little work is *completely* unstructured. The term, though imprecise, is used in this chapter (instead of "software developed without using structured technologies"), since it seems that it is currently in use to represent such software (e.g., see the use of the term "unstructured program", Yourdon 1979:3).

[2]In recent programming literature, however, software maintenance has been receiving increased attention. See, for example, *High Level COBOL Programming* by Gerald M. Weinberg, *et al,* containing a whole chapter on maintenance, and *Techniques of Program Structure and Design* by Edward Yourdon.

[3]See Girish Parikh, "Improved Maintenance Techniques" in the series "Programmer Productivity Reports," (Chicago: Shetal Enterprises).

[4]For a study of COBOL preprocessors in maintenance (and new developments) see Girish Parikh, "How to Increase COBOL Programming Productivity Using a Preprocessor" in the series "Programmer Productivity Reports," (Chicago: Shetal Enterprises).

References

Boehm, B.W. "Software engineering." *IEEE Transactions on Computers,* C-25, 12, 1226-1241.

Canning, R., ed. "Progress in software engineering: Part 1." *EDP Analyzer* (February 1978).

Canning, R., ed. "Progress in software engineering: Part 2." *EDP Analyzer* (March 1978).

Swanson, E.B. "The dimensions of maintenance." IEEE Computer Society, *2nd International Conference on Software Engineering,* 1976, 492-497.

Yourdon, E. "Structured maintenance—Part 1: Approach trains user to read 'alien' code." *Computerworld* (September 12, 1977), 38.

Yourdon, E. "Structured maintenance—Part 2: Cost to reshape user system can be forecast." *Computerworld* (September 19, 1977), 33.

Yourdon, E. "Choosing a pilot project." *The Yourdon Report* (February/March 1979), 3-4, 7.

Introduction

Fjeldstad, R.K., Hamlen, W.T. "Application program maintenance study—report to our respondents." IBM Corporation, DP Marketing Group, 1979, also reprinted in *Proc. GUIDE 48*, Philadelphia, PA, 1979.

The following report is one of the three questionnaire studies summarized in the introduction to this part of the Tutorial. The authors, Bob Fjeldstad (pronounced FYELSTAT) and Bill Hamlen, are both veteran IBM-ers—they joined the company in 1966 and 1950 respectively. In 1978, the DP Marketing Group (the computing side of IBM) directed them to investigate the problems and needs of customers in software maintenance as an aid to long-range planning of products in this area.

Their study took about six months and involved visits and interviews at 25 sites in which medium and large IBM mainframes were used for applications systems. Their final report and recommendations were made confidentially to the company; the following article is a summary of the results sent as a courtesy to their respondents, and it was also delivered to the GUIDE users group conference in 1979. It is reprinted here for three reasons:

- Because it broadly corroborates the other studies on maintenance.
- Because of its clarity and straightforward style.
- Because it deserves a wider audience.

The report gives numerical data on the proportion of maintenance in the total work load, on the types of maintenance changes that are made, and on the interesting question of what maintainers actually *do*. In the last section the authors discuss maintenance problems from the programmer's and manager's point of view and report, not surprisingly, that "[r]espondents most often said that understanding the original programmer's intent was the most difficult problem." They also conclude that "we found no evidence of an easy solution!"

The authors remain closely associated with IBM's applications programming products. Fjeldstad has been a Systems Engineering Manager in New York City since 1980, and Hamlen has had oversight of user requirements in the area of application development languages since 1981. They report a steady demand for copies of this report.

Terminology note for non-IBM-ers: MVS, VS1, and DOS (mentioned in charts 3, 4, and 5) are operating systems, and "IPTs" are "improved programming technologies," which comprise six techniques: structured programming, top-down development, chief programmer teams, development support libraries, structured walkthroughs, and HIPO.

APPLICATION PROGRAM MAINTENANCE STUDY

REPORT TO OUR RESPONDENTS

Purpose of the Study

During the past several months, twenty-five data processing installations have been visited in order to understand better the problems encountered in maintenance of application programs. Our purpose was first to define an acceptable structure of the tasks or activities involved in all application programming, thereby to determine those considered maintenance.

Then, in the area of maintenance, we further examined the process of maintaining programs and the variety of activities involved. Included was a profile of programs being maintained and the various systems of control being exercised over the people and process.

From these interviews, we have identified many maintenance problems and have organized them into common areas. An examination of these problems suggests several areas for potential improvement.

Programming Definitions and Activities

To ensure a common understanding between members of the study team and those interviewed, we first defined the dividing line between development and maintenance. For an application programming effort to be considered development, it must be possible to take an independent approach or design for a DP solution, without having to follow an existing programming procedure for the application. Maintenance is the change to an existing program, using or modifying an existing approach or design, then understanding and modifying or expanding existing program logic. In addition, because the maintainer of an existing production program is often the most knowledgeable of its function, he is called on to spend non-productive programming time to help others in operations or user departments in their work.

Respondents found our definitions to be reasonable and a framework within which they were able to allocate resources. Few defined development and maintenance as we did. The most widely used definition considered small tasks as maintenance and large as development. The dividing line varied from a man-week to a man-year. Rewrites were considered development by some, maintenance by others. One customer considered rewrites for technological reasons to be maintenance, those initiated by users to be development.

We gathered statistics on resource allocation of application programmers based on our definitions. In the systems programming area, we separated resources into four areas of activity: new development, changes or corrections, conversions to new versions or releases and the management or maintenance of data base and communications environments.

Programming Resources by Type of Activity

Chart 1 shows the breakdown of total programming resources for the year 1977 as reported by our respondents. The percentage of systems programmers among all programmers varied from under 5% to over 20%. Two-thirds grouped between 8 and 14%, averaging 12% for all respondents. Variations in this ratio were not related to system size, operating system or any other attribute we examined.

CHART 1

ALLOCATION OF TOTAL PROGRAMMER RESOURCE

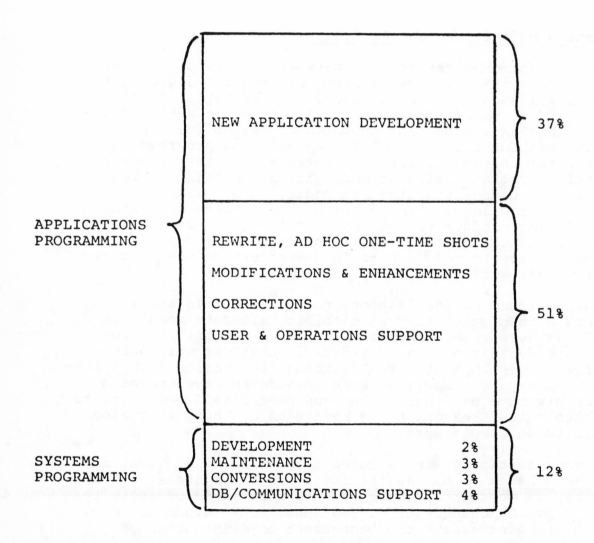

Chart 2 shows the percentage breakdown for application programmers only. It should be noted that although we collected data for time spent changing programs as a result of system conversion, this time was too small to include on the chart. Only two customers reported significant application program conversion. Many said that system conversions were made for use of new function by new applications and that existing programs were converted only when the program or application was completely rewritten.

CHART 2

ALLOCATION OF APPLICATION PROGRAMMER RESOURCE

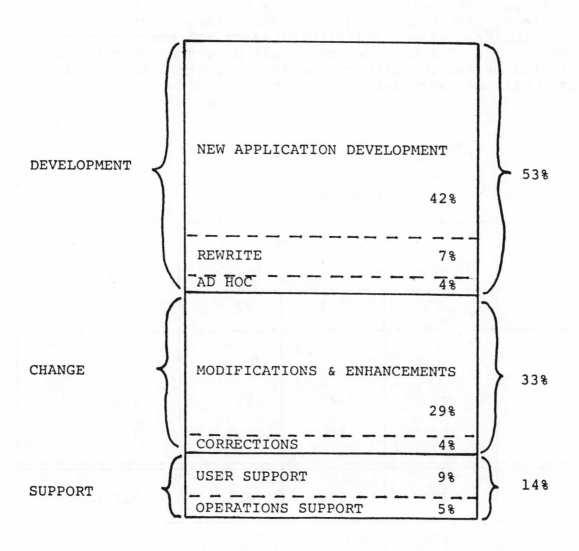

We requested respondents to report separately activity on re-writes and ad hoc one-shot programs. Had we not, two-thirds would have considered rewrites as development. Half of our respondents thought of ad hoc one-time programs as maintenance activity, usually because they viewed any small job as maintenance.

By our definitions, the study group reported 53% of their resource on development type work, 33% on modifications, enhancements and corrections, and 14% on support of non-programming activity.

Production Library Profile

Questions were asked concerning the number, size, and age of the programs being maintained as well as the language used and the number of programs developed using advanced programming techniques.

75% of the programs being maintained by the first line managers we interviewed were over three years old. (See Chart 3). One customer library averaged under three years and one was over eight years old. The average age of all programs was over five years in the production library. Only two installations had programs which averaged less than four years old.

CHART 3

PROGRAM AGE

	% OF PROGRAMS YEARS IN PROGRAM LIBRARY			AVERAGE PROGRAM AGE
	< 3	3-7	>7	
MVS	23%	47%	30%	5.7 YEARS
VS1	31	54	15	4.7
DOS	33	58	9	4.3
TOTAL	25%	50%	25%	5.3 YEARS

70% of the programs being maintained were coded in COBOL and 15% in ASSEMBLER. (See Chart 4). 35% of our respondents had half or more of their programs coded in ASSEMBLER while 50% had virtually all their library in COBOL. The remaining libraries were a mixture of several languages, only two of them having the majority of their programs in PL/1.

CHART 4

PROGRAM LANGUAGE

| | % OF PROGRAMS | | | OTHER |
	ASSEMBLER	COBOL	PL/1	
MVS	11%	65%	13%	11%
VS1	20	78	1	1
DOS	23	75	.5	1.5
TOTAL	15%	70%	8%	7%

Less than 25% of the programs being maintained had been developed using advanced programming techniques. Only 20% reported a majority of the library developed with structured or modular techniques.

The first line managers estimated the number of programs they
were responsible to maintain and the number of people on maintenance activity. Each manager had responsibility for approximately 700 programs and each maintenance programmer averaged
143 programs in his responsibility. (See Chart 5).

CHART 5

MAINTENANCE PROGRAMMER ACTIVITY

	AVERAGE # PROGRAMS MAINTAINED	AVERAGE # MAINTENANCE PROGRAMMERS	AVERAGE # PROGRAMS PER PROGRAMMER	MAINTENANCE PROJECTS PER MAN-YEAR *
MVS	2490	19.5	128	80
VS1	1570	10	157	68
DOS	1275	6.6	193	35
TOTAL	1930	13.5	143	69

*   STATISTICS ON MAINTENANCE PROJECTS INITIATED EACH YEAR
     WERE AVAILABLE ONLY FROM A FEW RESPONDENTS AND DO NOT
     REPRESENT THE GROUP AS A WHOLE.

S/168 MVS establishments averaged 128 programs per maintenance
person, whose program age averaged 5.7 years. S/158 VS1 maintenance people averaged 157 programs of 4.7 years in the library.
The relatively small group of DOS/VS customers averaged 193
programs per maintenance programmer, with their age 4.3 years.

"Productivity" Measure

No generally accepted measure of maintenance productivity was reported by our respondents. However, several installations tracked the processing of changes, were able to identify those delayed in the process and later reported statistically their results.

While size and complexity of both programs and changes to them may vary between installations, we did compile a measure of "Productivity" based on number of changes per maintenance programmer per year. About half of our respondents were able to provide the number of changes processed per month. When compared to the manpower assigned to maintenance resulting from these requests for change, the average maintenance programmer processed 69 jobs each year. (See Chart 5)

S/158 VS1 respondents, all of whom have a high percentage of COBOL programs in their libraries, were grouped closely around this "Productivity" level. The S/168 MVS respondents averaged slightly better, 80 projects per man-year. Although the samples are small and many other factors may have greater effect, PL/1 maintenance programmers appear to process more changes than COBOL programmers and assembler maintenance results in the lowest "Productivity."

System of Control or Management

Formal written requests were used by 80% as a means of providing management control of the maintenance process, but most made exceptions for small tasks or unscheduled corrections. 55% of the customers responding charged back their users for services as performed. Time was recorded for these customers, the most popular increment being to the tenth of an hour. One customer resorted to charging for phone calls as a means of discouraging undue support activity.

50% of the installations had instituted formal coordinators, all but one assigned to user departments. These coordinators handled a variety of activities in development and maintenance areas, but appeared for the most part to be most effective in defining user priorities and determining relative business cases. Where applied to maintenance, they tended to reduce the incidence of shifting priorities and, to some degree, the amount of user support required. Maintenance managers felt more in control with fewer problems where they were relieved of priority decision making. Productivity comparisons are not possible in terms of work accomplished versus man-months applied, but the study teams were impressed that those who managed the programming activity as the application of a scarce resource, removing as many peripheral tasks as possible from maintenance programmer responsibility, had maintenance under control.

Standards and Techniques

The customers contacted included those who had few formal standards for maintenance or development, those who had relatively elaborate ones but which were not stringently applied, and those who implemented standards, new techniques to support them as well as procedures to assure compliance.

It was not possible to get conclusive evidence on the effect of standards on productivity, but we sensed consensus that improvement was or should be significant. In one case, where modular techniques were adopted and the existing library was being reformatted, an early estimate was 25% improvement. In another, where new tools to help in implementing, testing, and documentation were being enforced, there was feeling of significant improvement without figures to substantiate it.

Generally, it was felt that IPTs were not being employed in the maintenance area to the same extent as in development functions. This may not be surprising in view of the small number of customers (20%) reporting more than 50% of their library developed with IPTs.

Programming Resources in the Maintenance Process

As we defined it, the maintenance process consisted of modification, enhancement, and correction of programs in the production library. In each of these activities of change to existing programs, understanding the intent and style of implementation of the original programmer was the major cause of time and difficulty in making the change.

CHART 6

CHANGE PROCESS

	MODIFICATIONS & ENHANCEMENTS (%)	CORRECTIONS (%)
DEFINE & UNDERSTAND THE CHANGE	18	25
REVIEW DOCUMENTATION	6	4
TRACE LOGIC	23	33
IMPLEMENT CHANGE	19	15
TEST	28	20
UPDATE DOCUMENTATION	6	3

Chart 6 shows an analysis of the time spent in the change
process. Lack of confidence in documentation is the reason
that little time is spent in its review. The cause of the
lessening value of a program's documentation over time is
shown in the small increment of time given to updating it
after the change. Maintenance programmers are not technical
writers, dislike documentation, and the next maintenance job
gets priority over recording the status of the previous change.

Therefore, the status of program design and implementation
must be deduced from the logic listing itself. What must be
changed and how best to make the change requires knowledge
of original design and implementation.

Testing to assure the intended change results in expected
new function without inadvertantly disturbing other parts
of the application is part of this iterative process.
Tracking logic, implementing the change, and testing the
results consume about 70% of the maintenance resource regardless of the type of change.

Despite the large amount of time spent in the testing process,
most of our respondents were dissatisfied with the difficulty
of devising an adequate test. They seldom could afford the
time and cost involved in full testing before the changed
program had to be returned to production.

The larger S/168 MVS installations spent a greater percentage of time on testing than VS1 or DOS accounts.

CHART 7

PROGRAM AREAS AFFECTED

	MODIFICATIONS & ENHANCEMENTS	CORRECTIONS
	%	%
FILE AND DATA DEFINITION	18	12
APPLICATION LOGIC	57	75
BUSINESS FACTORS	25	13

21

We asked how much effort in the change or correction of programs was due to each program area. Chart 7 shows that errors in program logic consume the most time. However, a significant 25% of the time was involved in planned change to business factors. We defined business factors as literals or constants which in the past often were imbedded in the logic, but which increasingly are being structured as external tables to ease the problem of locating and changing them.

Major Maintenance Problem Areas

o   Complexity of Existing Program Logic

Respondents most often said that understanding the original programmer's intent was the most difficult problem facing the person asked to change the function of the program.

Among the causes is inflexibility of the original design, sometimes because future change was not considered, but often because the nature of future business needs could not be forecast. It is the greatest cause of program rewrite.

The multiplicity of coding styles residing in the program library is another cause of difficulty. Languages were designed to be flexible, programming standards were few, programs were shoe-horned into small and costly memory, and a programmer often left his signature in his work.

Finally, in many installations, there reside different programs in different languages, a cause of extra time and difficulty when an infrequent one must be changed.

o   Testing is Difficult

Testing poses a problem proportionally greater and costlier with maintenance than with program development, and is therefore, more often skipped or skimped. In development, testing is a preplanned part of the process, needed to prove to the user and operations that the program is ready to be transferred to production status. Not so in maintenance. Here the program is already operational and changes constitute only additional function. Almost always, there is no residual test data and it is often necessary to create both test data and environment for the original program as well as testing the validity of the change. Test time and availability are at a premium and turnaround slow.

The ripple effects of change within the program and affecting other programs are not easy to predict or detect. Diagnosis of abends in testing is often as difficult as those in operational programs. The cost of doing a thorough job of testing is often considered prohibitive and not done.

o   <u>Documentation is Lacking or Inadequate</u>

Programmers are not technical writers and do not want to
be. If proper documentation would take significant additional time over that spent on making the change, and
another job waits to be started, they find it hard to
justify the cost or establish the value of doing the documentation. Documentation is often already incomplete,
difficult to understand, and organized so that changing it
is a major job.

In short, a maintenance programmer is neither motivated
nor trained for the job of documentation, and from a programming view, it is non-productive activity.

o   <u>Improvement of Knowledge and Skill</u>

An attendant problem is how to accelerate the acquisition
of knowledge and skill. From a professional standpoint,
customers expressed the need for classes on methods and
techniques as well as concepts and facilities, the how
with the what. Special mention was made of the need for
means to increase the ability of their best programmers
in advanced programming techniques.

Areas for Potential Improvement

Our respondents readily described problems facing them in maintaining their programs, but none anticipated quick solutions.
Some thought there was little a vendor such as IBM could do
to provide more resources, help them foresee future problems
or increase the expertise of their people. Others suggested that
IBM help, leadership or new tools and function would be welcome
in both the development and maintenance areas. A few had set
out to develop for themselves these tools and techniques and
also to install the requisite management control to assure they
were used consistently and well.

o   <u>Program Development</u>

The great majority of the managers we interviewed felt
that a better way to develop programs, designed for future
change and anticipating future problems held out the best
hope for improvement in maintenance. Many mentioned
aspects of new, more formalized and disciplined approaches.
Modular design could make future change simpler to incorp-
orate into the overall application structure. Use of
common modules of reusable code, isolation of business
factors in tables separate from logic and the discipline
of structured programming with attendant walkthroughs
would ease later understanding of program logic and simplify
future location and changing of data and function.

It was suggested that IBM should define the best way for
a customer to convert from old programming methods to new
structured techniques. Many of our respondents had used
one or more of the techniques and a few had defined and
were implementing a new approach to development with improved maintenance a principal design point.

o   Testing

An automatic way of developing adequate test data, especially when all program conditions are not known, was most
often expressed as the greatest testing need. With original
data quickly discarded, designing the test, parameters for
data selection or generation, simulation of a production
environment, a facility to verify results and restoration of
data after the test all were difficult and time consuming.

On-line test increased the problem especially in isolating
the test in a real environment, in protecting both production
and the data base from invasion and in validation of results.

Turnaround time problems, often requiring programmers to be
working on multiple programs simultaneously, increase the
test burden. Suggestions were made for tools to aid in
testing. One involved a step function test tool to allow
on-line limited testing. Another was for a compressed in-
terpretive dump which would aid in understanding test abends
in maintenance and development but also could help with production programs.

o   Documentation

The inadequate state of existing documentation was seen by
all as a contributor to the difficulty of determining the
intent or methods used by the original developer of a program when it was scheduled later for a change in function.
Yet documentation as conceived today is not viewed by all
as worth the effort it takes to keep it up to date.

The timing, it should be done immediately after the change
is made, the priority, programmer and manager face pressure
of change backlog, the inclination, distasteful to programmer
to do and manager to enforce, all combine to work against
proper update if done at all. Its value is difficult to
assess and its need in the future easy to disregard. It was
a universal hope that some way could be found to produce
needed documentation automatically as a result of the change
process, preferably as a part of the change specification and
the program logic.

While a few respondents felt that documentation was over valued, others diverted significant resources to bring it to a current status. Various methods were used to enforce compliance, the most successful requiring quality assurance by a librarian, before the program itself was accepted for production status. In some cases, use of a Data Dictionary was planned to alleviate the lack of accurate documentation. In others, user documentation was required for specification of change, assuring its reflection of current conditions of the program.

Many customers expressed the need to have a rational approach defined for documentation, the relation between data flow and logic modules and standards for what to maintain and how to do it.

o   Support

There appeared to be an increasing determination to place responsibility on the user for crisp problem and change definition as well as for priority decisions on choice of work to be done. Along with user willingness to accept these responsibilities was an attendant need for DP knowledge and skill to perform the tasks and provide the DP interface.

One customer has successfully installed in user departments, a terminal based job scheduler for set up as well as initiation and some limited modification of his jobs. Applying specification for program change on user documentation tends to increase user knowledge of program function while he assumes the documentation update function.

In several installations increasing user interaction and responsibility simplified the maintenance job while minimizing the need for non-productive support.

o   Interactive Maintenance

When asked what recent new techniques or facilities have added to maintenance productivity in the past four years, very few respondents mentioned the use of interactive terminal based operation. We believe this reflects a slower growth in interactive maintenance than in development.

Those who did mention interactive mode, generally were positive about its influence on productivity. One respondent said it could increase an average maintenance programmers' productivity between 50 and 100% and he felt the interactive edit facility and attendant function could do far better than that for the highly skilled person.

o   Management and Control

     As with other activities, a major influence on maintenance
     productivity is good management and the means used to con-
     trol both what is to be done and how it is done. Time and
     again the theme was reiterated, it is useless to institute
     new techniques or standards unless the means and the will
     to enforce and control them are also employed.

     One customer gave as much emphasis to devising means to
     account for and control the use of new tools as to the
     tools themselves. Another postponed implementing a new
     technique until compliance could be assured.

     The management method to assure all maintenance is "good"
     maintenance (that needed for business benefit) is a most
     important productivity technique. The way that programmers'
     time is protected against unnecessary user/operations sup-
     port can be a major influence on productivity. Phased and
     monitored project control can have a major impact on the
     maintenance process itself.

     There were many requests for management education courses
     in support of project estimation and other techniques in
     the management of maintenance, preferably of the workshop
     or forum type.

Summary

Those of us who took part in the interviews of this study were
impressed with the competence of the people interviewed and
appreciate their cooperation in sharing their knowledge of the
application maintenance process with us.

Of the total application programming resource represented by our
respondents, slightly more than half was employed on development
tasks. Those on maintenance work spent 70% of their time on
making changes to existing programs with the remaining 30% given
to non-programming support of user and operations tasks.

There appeared to be a trend toward making users more self-suffi-
cient, with greater user participation in establishing priority
for maintenance projects as well as scheduling jobs and making
some changes themselves.

We believe that one of the major means of improving maintenance
productivity will result from use of improved techniques in the
development process. This will provide maintenance programmers
with clearer specification of program design and logic flow.
Separating tables of oft-changed factors will allow them to be
found and attended to more simply.

At the same time our respondents had a heavy percentage of older programs in their production libraries with little inclination to rewrite or replace them until absolutely necessary. Productivity improvement may be brought to the maintenance of these programs by introducing improved techniques to the maintenance programmer, as well as the developer, with an interactive editor based facility.

Our respondents reported using tools to aid in many maintenance activities. Tools are available to help analyze the flow of data and logic, to retrieve or generate test data and to help in the test process itself. Dictionary facilities can help to identify and locate data requiring change. Respondents pointed to additional function that would be valuable to them. Neither we nor the users were able to place a value on the use of these tools in maintenance activity, but several claimed a productivity improvement resulted.

Finally, we found no evidence of an easy solution. Management commitment has as much or more influence as any factor in the productivity equation. We noted a growing feeling among those with whom we talked of the importance of managing the scarce resource of the maintenance programmer.

R. K. Fjeldstad/W. T. Hamlen
IBM Corporation
DP Marketing Group
January 23, 1979

Introduction

Lientz, B.P., Swanson, E.B. "Problems in application software maintenance." *Comm. ACM*, 24, 11 (November 1981), 763-769.

Bennet Lientz (pronounced LENTS) and Burton Swanson are on the faculty of the Graduate School of Management at UCLA. They became interested in research on software maintenance through the work of a Ph.D. student, G.E. Tompkins, who questioned 69 applications managers for his 1977 thesis. Using Tompkins' work as a pilot project, Lientz and Swanson mailed a questionnaire to 2000 managers randomly selected from members of the Data Processing Management Association. They received 487 usable responses, making theirs by far the largest body of data on software maintenance ever assembled and analyzed. The questionnaire and its results are published in their book, *Software maintenance management* (Addison-Wesley Publishing Company, 1980).

Like the authors of the preceding paper, Lientz and Swanson asked quantitative questions on maintenance activities and then asked the respondents to score a list of 26 potential maintenance problems. The activity data is briefly summarized on the first page of this paper; it matches the other data cited in the introduction to this part of the Tutorial. The rest of the paper provides a careful statistical analysis of the "problem" responses.

Two major trends emerge. First, whatever the other characteristics of the respondents' problems, they are nearly unanimous in citing as their worst problem "User demands for enhancements and extensions to the application system." These managers do not doubt that enhancement is the core of maintenance.

Second, by far the greatest discriminator among the respondents is a factor of "user knowledge," represented by scores on the problems of "lack of user understanding" and "inadequate user knowledge."

Thus all maintenance managers have the same problem of coping with user demands, but some managers are additionally burdened by apparently uncomprehending users. (This perception, as the authors wisely note, is from the data processor's, not the user's, viewpoint.) It suggests that the first activity for a manager who inherits a bad maintenance situation is to establish closer liaison with users.

The concentration on the users' problems of understanding contrasts with the Fjeldstad and Hamlen data in the previous reprint which notes the *programmers'* problems with understanding. In the Lientz and Swanson report, "programmer effectiveness" is a secondary factor in the discrimination of maintenance environments. However, an important finding is the association between high experience of the programmers with the system being maintained and low maintenance effort and even lower maintenance problems in general. This parallels the observation of Barry Boehm that, in development, "the level of personnel/team capability far outweighs any of the other factors influencing software productivity" ("Keeping a lid on software costs," *Computerworld*, January 18, 1982). The second line of attack for the manager with maintenance problems is to improve the staff's control and understanding of the system being maintained.

The importance of Tompkins, Lientz, and Swanson's pioneering surveys of maintenance managers is to bring such intuitive managerial decisions into explicit focus.

Applications:
Operations and Management

Howard L. Morgan*
Editor

Problems in Application Software Maintenance

Bennet P. Lientz and E. Burton Swanson
UCLA

The problems of application software maintenance in 487 data processing organizations were surveyed. Factor analysis resulted in the identification of six problem factors: user knowledge, programmer effectiveness, product quality, programmer time availability, machine requirements, and system reliability. User knowledge accounted for about 60 percent of the common problem variance, providing new evidence of the importance of the user relationship for system success or failure. Problems of programmer effectiveness and product quality were greater for older and larger systems and where more effort was spent in corrective maintenance. Larger scale data processing environments were significantly associated with greater problems of programmer effectiveness, but with no other problem factor. Product quality was seen as a lesser problem when certain productivity techniques were used in development.

Key Words and Phrases: application software maintenance, maintenance problem factors

CR Categories: 3.50, 4.6

Introduction

What are the principal problems in application software maintenance and how do these problems vary according to the application system maintained and the data processing environment in which maintenance takes

* Former editor of Applications: Operations and Management, of which Alan Merten is the current editor.

This work was partially supported by the Information Systems Program, Office of Naval Research under Contract N00014-75-C-0266, Project Number NR 049-345.

Author's Present Address: Bennet P. Lientz and E. Burton Swanson, Graduate School of Management, University of California, Los Angeles, CA 90024

Reprinted with permission from Communications of ACM, Volume 24, Number 11, November 1981, pages 763-769. Copyright © 1981 by The Association of Computing Machinery.

place? This paper reports research results which provide some answers to these questions.

The results are based on a sample survey of 2000 managers of data processing organizations. Each manager was randomly selected from the membership of the Data Processing Management Association (DPMA) and mailed a questionnaire on application software maintenance. A total of 487 responses were received, a return rate of 24 percent, considered good given the demanding nature of the questionnaire.

The overall purpose of the survey was to explore five sets of issues associated with maintenance: (i) conceptual issues (the meaning of maintenance), (ii) scale-of-effort issues (resource level and allocation), (iii) organizational issues (task definition and assignment), (iv) productivity aid issues (impact on maintenance), and (v) problem area issues (relative importance in maintenance). These issues were developed from a review of the literature on maintenance [1].

Basic descriptive results of the survey are reported in [2]. Among the more important findings: (i) departments tend to spend about half of their applications staff time on maintenance; (ii) over 40 percent of the effort in supporting an operational application system is typically spent on providing user enhancements and extensions; (iii) the average application system is between three and four years old, consists of about 55 programs and 23,000 source statements, and is growing at a rate in excess of 10 percent per year; (iv) about half a man-year of effort is allocated annually to maintenance of the average system. (See also [3], [7].)

The present paper concentrates on issues associated with problems of maintenance, as assessed by data processing managers in responding to one item of the questionnaire. Analysis of the responses considered in conjunction with responses to other questionnaire items provides insight into both the factors underlying the maintenance problems and the variables that serve as determinants. These insights provide us with some essential building blocks for the development of a theory of software maintenance.

The Problem Items

The questionnaire sought the data processing manager's judgment of the problems in maintaining a selected application system. A list of 26 potential problems was provided and we requested that each be evaluated on a 1 to 5 point scale ranging from "no problem at all" to "major problem." The list of potential problems was identical to that used in a preliminary survey [4], with the exception of the last three items which were added on the basis of comments received in this first attempt.

A summary of the descriptive results is presented in Table I. The computation of means and variances is based upon the assumption of interval item scales. (For a summary of the same results, based upon ordinal item

Table I. Distributions of Maintenance Problem Items.

Item	Label	Mean	Standard dev	Cases
1	Maintenance personnel turnover	2.2332	1.3356	446
2	Documentation quality	3.0000	1.3103	446
3	System hardware and software changes	2.0404	1.1739	446
4	Demand for enhancements and extensions	3.2018	1.1745	446
5	Skills of maintenance programmers	2.0807	1.1564	446
6	Quality of original programming	2.5897	1.3256	446
7	Number of maintenance programmers available	2.5762	1.3348	446
8	Competing demands for programmer time	3.0336	1.3395	446
9	Lack of user interest	1.8677	1.2171	446
10	System run failures	1.8677	0.9706	446
11	Lack of user understanding	2.6076	1.2670	446
12	Program storage requirements	1.9776	1.2158	446
13	Program processing time requirements	2.5538	1.2562	446
14	Maintenance programmer motivation	1.9170	1.1076	446
15	Forecasting maintenance prog. requirements	2.4552	1.2239	446
16	Maintenance programming productivity	2.0359	1.0866	446
17	System hardware and software reliability	1.8094	1.0438	446
18	Data integrity	1.9036	1.0840	446
19	Unrealistic user expectations	2.5516	1.2616	446
20	Adherence to programming standards	2.1143	1.0905	446
21	Management support	1.8453	1.1141	446
22	Adequacy of system design specs	2.4233	1.2606	446
23	Budgetary pressures	1.9798	1.2075	446
24	Meeting scheduled commitments	2.6861	1.2435	446
25	Inadequate user training	2.7623	1.2387	446
26	Turnover in user organization	2.3610	1.2351	446

scaling, see [2].) Problem items are listed in the order they appeared on the questionnaire. User demands for enhancements and extensions emerged as the leading problem, a result which validates the findings of the preliminary study [1].

The Problem Factors

A factor analysis of the responses to the 26 problem items was performed in order to explore the underlying dimensionality and to facilitate further analysis. The principal factor with iteration option was employed, with varimax rotation [5]. A classical factor analysis based on inferred factors was performed. The method of rotation was the commonly used one.

The factor analysis produced six factors that accounted for about half the total variance in the 26 problem items. These factors are summarized in Table II. The labels attached to the factors are the result of an interpretation of the factor loadings (not shown to conserve space).

On the whole, the results of the factor analysis were striking. The dimensions emerged with unexpected clarity and the dominance of the oft-cited user problem is remarkable. It is not simply that user problems are common to all; it is that user problems account for the major variance in the problems common to all. Particularly noteworthy is that problem item 4, user demand for enhancements and extensions, while it is the major problem item among all those cited, is *not* a significant component in the user knowledge factor which accounts for 59.5 percent of the common variance. The major contributors to the latter are lack of user understanding and inadequate user training.

For purposes of subsequent analysis, the six problem factors were formalized as indices, computed on the basis of problem items with factor coefficients of absolute value 0.200 or greater. Normalized values of the problem item scores were used in the indices [5]. A summary of the six factor indices and their problem item components is presented in Table III.

In interpreting these results and those that follow, the reader should keep in mind that the problems identified

Table II. Summary of Maintenance Problem Factors.

Factor	Label	Eigenvalue	Percent of Var	Cum Percent
1	User knowledge	7.25414	59.4	59.5
2	Programmer effectiveness	1.45230	11.9	71.4
3	Product quality	1.16047	9.5	80.9
4	Programmer time availability	0.97415	8.0	88.9
5	Machine requirements	0.76567	6.3	95.2
6	System reliability	0.58859	4.8	100.0

Table III. Problem Factor Indices and Their Item Components.

Factor Index	Item Component
1. User Knowledge	11. Lack of user understanding (0.363)
	25. Inadequate user training (0.237)
2. Programmer Effectiveness	16. Maintenance programming productivity (0.369)
	14. Maintenance programming motivation (0.349)
	5. Skills of maintenance programmers (0.227)
3. Product Quality	22. Adequacy of system design specs (0.404)
	6. Quality of original programming (0.321)
	2. Documentation quality (0.272)
4. Programmer Time Availability	8. Competing demands for programmer time (0.785)
5. Machine Requirements	12. Program storage requirements (0.476)
	13. Program processing time requirements (0.471)
6. System Reliability	17. System hardware and software reliability (0.440)
	18. Data integrity (0.223)

Note: Factor score coefficients shown in parentheses.

here are those expressed by data processing management. User perceptions may or may not accord, a point that we will return to in the Conclusions.

Problem Determinants

What are the determinants of the problems of application software maintenance? The relationships between the problem factors and other maintenance variables were investigated. Among the potential determinants were application system size and age, magnitude and allocation of the maintenance effort, relative development experience of the maintainers of the system, use of productivity techniques in system development, use of a database management system, programming language, use of organizational controls, and the data processing environment. In the sections that follow, the results of the investigation are summarized for each variable.

Application System and Age

Five measures of application system size were obtained in the survey: number of programs, number of source statements, number of files, number of database bytes, and number of predefined user reports. Where parametric analyses were performed, natural logarithm transformations of these measures were judged necessary to meet normality assumption requirements.

Larger systems proved to be significantly associated with greater problems in maintenance. Of 30 first-order Pearson correlation coefficients computed between the six problem factors and the five measures of system size, 26 were positive of which 22 were significant at the $s \leq 0.100$ level and 14 were of magnitude $r \geq 0.100$. Programmer effectiveness demonstrated a notable positive association with all five measures of system size. Product quality was positively associated with four of the five size measures.[1]

The age of the application system, measured in terms of the number of months since the system became operational, was also obtained from the questionnaire. As with system size, first-order Pearson correlation coefficients between the six problem factors and system age were computed.

Older systems tended to be perceived as having greater problems in maintenance. In particular, system age was positively and notably associated with problems of product quality ($r = 0.142$, $s = 0.001$) and programmer effectiveness ($r = 0.128$, $s = 0.003$). The other correlations were not notable, however.

Though system size and age are seen to be strongly associated with the problems of maintenance, this association was shown in subsequent analysis to be explainable in terms of other, intervening variables, viz. magnitude and allocation of the maintenance effort and the relative development experience of maintainers of the system.

Magnitude and Allocation of the Maintenance Effort

The magnitude and allocation of the maintenance effort on the application system described were also included among the data obtained. Two measures of the magnitude of effort were obtained: the total number of individuals assigned (in whole or in part) to maintenance of the system, and the total number of man-hours expended annually. The allocation of the maintenance effort was indicated by a percentage breakdown of annual man-hours according to eight categories: (i) emergency program fixes, (ii) routine debugging, (iii) accom-

---

[1] Because of the sample size, many correlation coefficients of small magnitude were nonetheless statistically significant. The term "notable" refers here to coefficients of absolute magnitude $r \geq 0.100$ which was found to be an effective cutoff level for the focus of research attention among the many "significant" results.

modation of changes to data inputs and files, (iv) accommodation of changes to hardware and system software, (v) enhancements for users, (vi) improvement of program documentation, (vii) recoding for efficiency in computation, and (viii) others. The categories chosen were based on the classification system originally proposed by [6]. Within this system, emergency program fixes and routine debugging comprise *corrective maintenance*; accommodations of change represent *adaptive maintenance*; and user enhancements, improved documentation, and recoding for efficiency make up *perfective maintenance*.

As with the measures of application system size, natural logarithm transformations of the two measures of the magnitude of the maintenance effort were judged necessary for parametric analysis purposes.

The problems of maintenance were perceived to be greater, the larger the magnitude of the effort in maintenance. The first-order Pearson correlation coefficients are shown in Table IV. All twelve coefficients are positive, eleven of which are statistically significant at the $s \leq 0.100$ level and eight of which are of notable magnitude $r \geq 0.100$. The correlations between number of maintenance man-hours and the problems of programmer effectiveness ($r = 0.263$) and product quality ($r = 0.240$) are particularly striking.

Problems of maintenance were also perceived to be greater, the more relative time spent in corrective maintenance. Of twelve first-order Pearson correlation coefficients relating the six problem factors to relative time spent in emergency fixes and routine debugging, eleven were positive of which nine were statistically significant

and five were notable. Relative time in emergency fixes was positively associated with problems of product quality ($r = 0.200$, $s = 0.001$); user knowledge ($r = 0.130$, $s = 0.002$); and programmer effectiveness ($r = 0.117$, $s = 0.005$). Relative time in routine debugging was positively associated with problems of product quality ($r = 0.204$, $s = 0.001$) and programmer effectiveness ($r = 0.132$, $s = 0.002$).

Two other relationships involving the allocation of the maintenance effort with problem factors were of notable significance and magnitude. The problem of machine requirements was positively associated with both recoding for computational efficiency ($r = 0.164$, $s = 0.001$) and accommodating system hardware and software changes ($r = 0.106$, $s = 0.010$). Both these relationships are easily understood.

Interestingly, no notable findings related the percent time spent in providing user enhancements to any of the problems of maintenance, including that of user knowledge.

Relative Development Experience of Maintainers of the System

The questionnaire asked how many of the individuals currently assigned to the maintenance of the application system had previously worked on the development of this same system. The number who had, divided by the total, thus served as a measure of the relative development experience of the maintainers with respect to the system being maintained.

The computation of first-order Pearson correlation coefficients showed relative development experience to be significantly related to perceived problems in maintaining the application system. The most significant relationships indicate greater development experience to be associated with lesser problems with product quality ($r = -0.270$, $s = 0.001$) and lesser problems with programmer effectiveness ($r = -0.171$, $s = 0.001$). Lesser problems with user knowledge and programmer time availability were also indicated for higher levels of relative development experience but correlation coefficients were not of magnitude $r \geq 0.100$. Greater problems with machine requirements were indicated ($r = 0.104$, $s = 0.011$) for which there is no obvious interpretation. No relationship to the problem of system reliability existed.

To summarize thus far, system age and size, magnitude of the maintenance effort, relative allocation of effort to corrective maintenance, and the relative development experience of the maintainers are all shown to be associated with the problems of maintenance. However, these variables proved themselves to be interrelated; thus their impact upon the problems of maintenance must be considered jointly. To examine these effects, a series of multiple regression analyses were performed. Results confirmed that the magnitude of the effort in maintenance, the allocation of this effort to corrective maintenance, and relative development experience are all of importance in explaining the problems of mainte-

Table IV. Maintenance Problem Factors and Magnitude of Maintenance Effort: First-order Pearson Correlation Coefficients.

	Annual man-hours	Persons assigned
PFactor1 (User knowledge)	0.1158* (451) P = 0.007	0.0965 (461) P = 0.019
PFactor 2 (Programmer effectiveness)	0.2625** (447) P = 0.000	0.2088** (456) P = 0.000
PFactor3 (Product quality)	0.2404** (499) P = 0.000	0.1099* (459) P = 0.009
PFactor (Programmer time availability)	0.1445* (453) P = 0.001	0.0879 (462) P = 0.029
PFactor5 (Machine requirements)	0.0949 (452) P = 0.022	0.0502 (462) P = 0.141
PFactor6 (System reliability)	0.1372* (4452) P = 0.002	0.1186* (461) P = 0.005

Asterisk key: ** indicates |r| ≥ 0.200; * indicates 0.100 ≤ |r| < 0.200

nance. In particular, the number of maintenance man-hours accounts for a substantial portion of the problem of programmer effectiveness and the relative development experience of the maintainers and the percent time on corrective maintenance (which includes both emergency fixes and routine debugging) are of similar significance in accounting for the problem of product quality.

However, results also indicate that system size and age have little influence upon the problems of maintenance, apart from their established impact upon the magnitude and allocation of the maintenance effort, and the relative development experience of the maintainers. When the latter variables have been entered first into the regression equations, measures of system size have notable influence only upon the problems of machine requirements and system reliablity, which together account for only 11.1 percent of the common problem variance. System age has no notable influence whatsoever.

The network of causal effects that appear to bear directly upon the problems of maintenance is shown in Figure 1.

Use of Productivity Techniques in System Development

The questionnaire also asked which of a variety of tools, methods, and techniques were employed in the development of the application system described. Included in the checklist were decision tables, database dictionary, test data generators, structured programming, automated flowcharting, HIPO (Hierarchy plus Input-Process-Output), structured walk-through, and chief programmer team. Provision for "others" to be indicated was also included.

One-way analyses of variance of the six problem factors according to the use of the productivity tools were performed. The results showed the problem of product quality to vary significantly according to the use of five of the eight tools listed. Specifically, the software product is perceived to be of better quality (in terms of the three components from which the factor is derived: system design specifications, programming, and documentation) where test data generators, structured programming, HIPO, structured walk-through, or the chief programming team have been employed. These results should be heartening to advocates of these techniques. However, it is also noteworthy that the problems of user knowledge and programmer effectiveness which together account for 71.4 percent of the common problem variance, are little affected through the use of these same techniques.

Use of a Database Management System

Whether the application system made use of a database management system was also asked in the questionnaire. Analyses of variance of the six problem factors according to the use of a database management system were thus performed. No significant variances were found and it may be concluded that management's assessment of the problems in maintenance is likely to be the same, on average, for application systems supported by a DBMS as for unsupported application systems.

Programming Language

The variances in the six maintenance problem factors according to the principal language in which the application system was programmed were also examined. Employing one-way analyses of variance, two problem factors were seen to vary significantly according to the programming language used: programmer effectiveness ($s = 0.010$) and system reliability ($s = 0.080$). In the case of programmer effectiveness, problems tend to be slightly greater than average when assembler languages are used and notably greater than average when Fortran or PL/1 is used. When Cobol is used, problems of programmer effectiveness are about average and when RPG is used, notably less than average. It appears at first that the use of certain languages is associated with greater problems in programmer effectiveness.

However, the interpretation of a direct causal relationship between the programming language and the problem of programmer effectiveness proves to be unwarranted. Other analysis suggests that the scale of the data processing environment may largely account for the apparent relationship, since language use varies according to the size of the data processing department which itself is associated with the problems of maintenance (as will be discussed shortly.) Specifically, a two-way analysis of variance of the problem of programmer effectiveness was conducted, controlling for the size of the data processing equipment budget, in addition to the programming language used. Results indicated that the main effects of programming language are not significant at the $s \leq 0.100$ level, when the size of the equipment budget is controlled. Thus, the apparent relationship between programming language and the problem of programmer effectiveness is explained in terms of the data processing environment in which programming takes place. It may be that larger installations are characterized by more complex applications for which certain languages are better suited, and which, at the same time, present greater challenges to effective programming. However, other explanations are also possible.

In the case of system reliability, one-way analysis of variance showed the problem to be greater than average

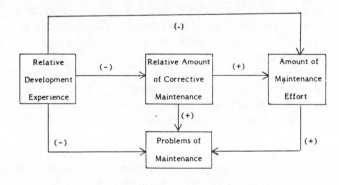

Fig. 1. Some Relationships Involving the Problems of Maintenance.

when Fortran is used, and less than average when RPG is used. For the other languages, the problem is about average. Since other analysis indicates the problem of system reliability does not vary significantly with the scale of the data processing environment, the present apparent relationship may not be explained in the same way as programmer effectiveness. Any interpretation is tenuous. It may be that RPG software is seen as more reliable for certain application programming than Fortran. Alternatively, since Fortran tends to be associated with the older application systems, the reliability problem may simply reflect this age differential.

Use of Organizational Controls

Also included on the questionnaire was a checklist of organizational controls which might be established for the maintenance of the application system. Listed were: (*i*) logging and documentation of user requests, (*ii*) cost justification of user requests, (*iii*) logging and documentation of troubles in operational processing, (*iv*) logging and documentation of changes to programs, (*v*) formal retest procedure for program changes, (*vi*) batching of program changes according to a predetermined schedule, (*vii*) periodic formal audit, (*viii*) equipment cost charge-back system, (*ix*) personnel cost charge-back system. Respondents were asked to indicate which of the above controls were used in the maintenance of the application system described.

One way analyses of variance of the six problem factors according to the use of organizational controls were first performed. A total of 16 relationships were established at significant levels ranging from $s < 0.001$ to $s = 0.070$. Of these, 13 relationships were positive, suggesting at first that the use of organizational controls is associated with *greater* problems in maintenance.

However, further analysis showed these results to be explainable in terms of previously established relationships. When these relationships are taken into consideration, the use of organizational controls proves to be little related to the problems of maintenance. Specifically, multiple regression analysis indicated that when the effects of the magnitude and allocation of the maintenance effort and the relative development experience of the maintainers were first accounted for, few significant associations between the problems of maintenance and the use of organizational controls exist. An exception is the periodic audit which emerges as significantly associated with lesser problems of user knowledge and product quality.

The Data Processing Environment

The first part of the questionnaire sought to establish the data processing environment in which the maintenance of the application system took place. The industry served by the data processing department was identified. The scale of the department was specified, in terms of both personnel and annual equipment budget, and the overall organization and allocation of staff time between maintenance and new system development activities was indicated. The demands of maintenance on the data processing manager's own time was assessed as was the current level of departmental staffing.

The scale of the data processing department as measured by the annual equipment budget proved to be strongly related to the perceived problems in maintaining the application system described. Specifically, analysis of variance showed the problem of programmer effectiveness to be perceived as greater, the larger the scale of the department ($s < 0.001$, linearity also significant at the $s < 0.001$ level). No significant variances in the other five problem factors were found. Thus, the perceived problems of maintenance vary by the size of the organization along the single dimension of programmer effectiveness. Two interpretations are suggested for consideration. The straightforward interpretation is that smaller organizations do have greater programmer effectiveness, possibly because the simplicity of work coordination outweighs the lack of technical specialization. An alternative interpretation is that programmer effectiveness does not vary but awareness of the "problem" is heightened according to the visibility of the data processing budget. Other interpretations may also be possible.

Maintenance problem factors were also correlated to the percent time spent on maintenance in the organization as a whole. As might be expected, problems are seen to be more severe, the more of the organization's time is allocated to maintenance. Four of the six problem factors, accounting together for 88.9 percent of the problem variance, are of notable significance and magnitude: programmer effectiveness ($r = 0.191$, $s = 0.001$); product quality ($r = 0.158$, $s = 0.001$); user knowledge ($r = 0.113$, $s = 0.006$); and programmer time availability ($r = 0.101$, $s = 0.013$). System reliability is also positively related, although the magnitude is not notable. The problem of machine requirements is unrelated.

Finally, analyses of variance of the six problem factors by the perceived level of staffing sufficiency and the demands of maintenance on the manager's own time were performed. It was found that four problem factors varied significantly by perceived level of staffing sufficiency: user knowledge ($s = 0.007$), programmer effectiveness ($s < 0.001$), product quality ($s < 0.001$), and programmer time availability ($s < 0.001$). In each case, linearity was also significant at the $s = 0.003$ level or better and it may be concluded that each problem tends to be perceived as greater, as the staffing level is regarded as less sufficient. These are strong results, though not particularly surprising.

In the case of the demands of maintenance on the manager's own time, four problem factors also varied significantly: user knowledge ($s = 0.005$), programmer effectiveness ($s = 0.055$), product quality ($s < 0.001$), and system reliability ($s = 0.076$). Again, linearity was also significant in each case, here at the $s = 0.016$ or better level and it may be concluded that each problem tends to be perceived as greater, the more of the manager's own time is absorbed by the demands of maintenance. As before, these results are what might be expected.

Conclusions

User knowledge has been seen to account for the majority of the variance in data processing management's assessment of the problems in maintenance. This result provides further evidence of the importance of the relationship between the users and the providers of information systems in the determination of system success or failure.

Lack of user understanding and inadequate user training are the two components of user knowledge and both suggest an estrangement of the users from the systems intended to serve them. It is this aspect of the oft-cited user problem which distinguishes systems with relatively lesser maintenance problems from those with greater maintenance problems.

User demands for enhancements and extensions is seen as the most severe problem item overall. This item is *not* a component of the user knowledge factor, although it may be somewhat related. It does not account for variance in the problems of maintenance. Rather, it is the most common complaint. That it is such is perhaps understandable when it is recalled that user demand is not controllable by data processing management, but has substantial implications for its resource allocation decisions.

The potential determinants investigated proved most strongly related to problems of programmer effectiveness and product quality. When the nature of these determinants is considered, this result is, in part, understandable. The determinants consist primarily of the characteristics of the software, the programming staff, the programming effort, and the programming environment. Characteristics of the user environment were not included. Such characteristics would presumably be more strongly related to the problem of user knowledge.

The direction for future research seems clearly indicated. Attention should be focused on the users of data processing applications. Characteristics of user environments in which relatively successful applications exist should be identified. These characteristics should then be related to their impact upon the maintenance of the application software as performed by the data processing department.

A likely approach would be to study the problems of ongoing systems from the viewpoints of users as opposed to data processing professionals. Problem factors from the users' perspective might be identified and correlated to the corresponding problem factors as seen by data processing management. An interesting question is whether the user knowledge problem factor would be recognized by the users themselves. If not, how would the users see the problem? Further, what characteristics of user environments would explain the variance in their problem perceptions?

By approaching the user problem from both sides, a more enlightened understanding of the problems of application software maintenance should ultimately be expected.

The development of a unifying theory of software maintenance remains a long-term prospect. In the present paper we have taken some initial inductive steps in this direction. Variables of importance have been identified, and certain relationships established. The picture is by no means complete; much remains to be done. However, a number of building blocks for the theory have been provided.

Received 8/79; revised 9/80; accepted 5/81

References
1. Lientz, B.P., and Swanson, E.B. Discovering issues in software maintenance. *Data Management, 16*, 10, (Oct 1978), 15–18.
2. Lientz, B.P., and Swanson, E.B. Software maintenance: A user/management tug-of-war. *Data Management, 17*, 4, (April 1979), 26–30.
3. Lientz, B.P., and Swanson, E.B. Impact of development productivity aids on application system maintenance. Proceedings of a Conference on Application Development Systems, *Data Base, 11*, 3, (Winter–Spring 1980), 114–120.
4. Lientz, B.P., Swanson, E.B., and Tompkins, G.E. Characteristics of application software maintenance. *Comm. ACM, 21*, 6, (June 1978), 466–471.
5. Nie, N.H., Hull, C.H., Jenkins, J.G., Steinbrenner, K., and Bent, D.H. *SPSS: Statistical Package for the Social Sciences.* 2nd Ed., McGraw Hill, New York, 1975.
6. Swanson, E.B. The dimensions of maintenance. *Proc. 2nd Int. Conf. on Software Engineering.* San Francisco, October 13–15, 1976.
7. Lientz, B. P., and Swanson, E. B. *Software Maintenance Management.* Addison-Wesley, Reading, MA, 1980.

Introduction

CIRAD, Inc. (Overton, R.K., et al.) "A study of fundamental factors underlying software maintenance problems: final report." Deputy for Command and Management Systems, Electronic Systems Division, Hanscom Air Force Base, Bedford, MA., 1971. NTIS numbers: AD 739479 (report), AD 739872 (appendices). [Excerpted.]

Overton, R.K., et al. "Research toward ways of improving software maintenance: RICASM final report." Deputy for Command and Management Systems, Electronic Systems Division, Hanscom Air Force Base, Bedford, MA, 1973. NTIS number: AD 760819. [Excerpted.]

Overton, R.K., et al. Developments in computer aided software maintenance. Deputy for Command and Management Systems, Electronic Systems Division, Hanscom Air Force Base, Bedford, MA, 1974. NTIS number: AD/A005 827. [Excerpted.]

The most extensive study of the maintenance programmer at work was performed by a research team directed by Richard K. Overton from 1971 to 1974. The original reports are cited above and are available through NTIS (National Technical Information Service, Springfield, VA), but this is the first time, as far as we know, that this material has been excerpted in the open literature.

Overton received a doctorate in psychology from the University of Texas in 1956; he comments that in those days he was as much a mathematician as he was a psychologist. Like many authors in this Tutorial, he has had many years of computing experience. In 1959 he authored a book, *Thought and action: a physiological approach* (Random House, 1959), in which he blended the then known facts about neurophysiology and computer control to speculate on the mechanisms of the brain; this book was an early example of what is now known as artificial intelligence.

In 1970 he put together some consulting resources to bid on a U.S. Air Force contract to investigate maintenance, and his bid was successful. The first excerpt, taken from the Appendices volume of the 1971 report, is the Statement of Work of that first contract. It was written by John B. Goodenough, who told us that he found himself in charge of an Air Force research budget, some of which he decided to apply to the neglected topic of maintenance problems. His Statement of Work is relevant today as an agenda for maintenance research.

STATEMENT OF WORK

Computer Aided Software Maintenance Study

1.0 Introduction: Systems programmers must often maintain programs that someone else wrote. To do so, they must first learn about these programs by consulting the written documentation prepared by the original programmer. Such documentation commonly consists of flowcharts at various levels of detail, narrative descriptions, and ultimately, program symbolics. Even for only moderately complex systems, it is difficult to use these materials efficiently to remedy defects that show up in use or to evaluate proposed system changes.

In this procurement, the Contractor will focus on problems faced by programmers who must maintain programs someone else wrote. He will identify and study the factors which inhibit the effectiveness of current maintenance programming aids, and as a result of this study, he will propose new kinds of computer aids for use by maintenance programmers. The emphasis in this study will be on the development of principles underlying the effective use of such aids, although some effort will be devoted to initial development and test of promising aids.

2.0 Scope

2.1 Objective: The objective of this procurement is to study problems of maintaining complex programs in order to develop more effective, computer aids for software maintenance. It is intended that these methods be especially useful to programmers who must maintain programs that someone else wrote.

2.2 Approach: Contractor will investigate fundamental problems limiting the effectiveness of maintenance programmers and will propose and study new techniques for increasing their effectiveness. He will identify inadequacies in current methods and identify reasons for these inadequacies. He will develop case studies illustrating principles and problems encountered in software maintenance, together with some estimate of the importance of the principles and problems. He will specify and carry out a research program for developing further information that must be known in order to create useful maintenance programming aids, and he will specify and investigate new methods to help maintenance programmers. He will investigate the role of graphics consoles in maintenance programming. At the end of the study, he will present a balanced view of realities vs. possible techniques, together with a plan for further study of these problems and techniques.

Excerpted from "A Study of Fundamental Factors Underlying Software Maintenance Problems: Final Report," *Hanscom Air Force Base Report NTIS Numbers: AD 739479 (report) and AD 739872 (appendices)*, 1971, pages I-1—I-4. U.S. Government work. Not protected by U.S. copyright.

3.0 Areas of Consideration

3.1 Use of Graphics Terminals: Contractor's study should emphasize the use of on-line interaction with a graphics console.

3.2 Case Studies: The Contractor will develop and evaluate his ideas with respect to the maintenance or modification of particular compilers, operating systems, data management systems, or other sets of existing complex programs with which he is familiar. From this source of material, the Contractor will draw examples of the kinds of problems one faces in maintaining or modifying programs that someone else wrote. The Contractor will evaluate his proposed techniques with respect to these specific real-world examples. Preferably the system of programs that serves as a test environment and as a source of case studies will be a system that is already being maintained or modified by the Contractor. Note that it is not necessary and not expected that any software modifications or software maintenance be carried out. The Government only desires that the research be accomplished with respect to actual problems that have arisen in connection with existing systems of programs.

3.3 Extent of Programming Effort: Contractor shall test his techniques by thoughtful, scientific study; he shall not embark on an extensive programming effort before fundamental limitations have been carefully identified. The Contractor is encouraged to test his ideas on actual computers only if a relatively small amount of programming is required for a meaningful test.

3.4 Possible Problem Area (example): One of the inherent deficiencies in current documentation methods is the presentation of information only in a static format. A programmer who must analyze program flow for complex test cases may have considerable difficulty in relating the test case to the actions described in the flowcharts. Hence means might be provided to show the actual program flow (on-line) for test cases specified by the programmer, and thus the programmer might learn the structure and function of the program more quickly and more thoroughly.

3.5 Interdisciplinary Approach: The Contractor is encouraged to include on his research team a person with background in the behavioral sciences as well as persons experienced in computer sciences. Such a person will be expected to help devise suitable methods for scientifically assessing the general advantages and limitations of the techniques to be developed under this Contract. He would be expected to provide useful insight into the cognitive processes and the inherent human limitations and requirements of maintenance programmers.

4.0 Task to be Accomplished

4.1 Phase I - Overall Analysis:

4.1.1 Step 1: The contractor will identify problems interhent in (and especially those peculiar to) maintenance programming where the maintenance programmer is not the original programmer. The maintenance programmer is assumed to be an experienced systems programmer, and the system being maintained is to be considered fairly complex (e.g., any system which would normally be programmed by more than one programmer).

4.1.2 Step 2: A set of case studies, based on actual systems maintenance problems (see 3.2 above) will be developed to illustrate the fundamental principles and the problems inherent in maintenance programming. (The case studies are to serve as paradigms of system maintenance problems, and hence should represent problems which are in some sense typical of the problems faced by maintenance programmers.)

4.1.3 Step 3: A number of possible maintenance programming computer aids will be proposed. Each proposed aid will be characterized in terms of (1) its relation to fundamental factors underlying systems maintenance problems; (2) the kind of research that must be accomplished to assess the probable utility (e.g., what information must be known to make this assessment, and how could this information be developed) of the proposed aid; and (3) the amount of work that would be required to test the proposed aid's effectiveness. (The solutions proposed in this part of Phase I, together with the case studies, will be used by the Air Force to determine the extent and value of initiating a broader, more intensive, research effort on maintenance problems). Solutions proposed as part of this step will range from conservative to highly speculative, since the purpose of the Step is, in part, to stimulate thought on solutions to maintenance programming problems.

4.1.4 Step 4: The contractor will next select a small set of problems, factors, and/or proposed solutions to be investigated more thoroughly in the remainder of the contract (Phase II). The rationale for this selection and a plan of research for gaining a deeper understanding of the selected issues will be furnished (see 4.2 and 4.3 below).

4.2 Phase I - Report: The results of the Phase I study will be presented in a Technical Report consisting of two parts. Part I will contain the results of Steps 1, 2, and 3 of Phase I. Part II will contain the information developed in Phase I, Step 4.

4.3 Phase II - Intensive Study of Selected Problems/Solutions: A scientific study of selected problems or proposed solutions to software maintenance will be undertaken as specified in Part II of the Phase I report (see 4.2). The purpose of this study is to examine more carefully the feasibility of these approaches and especially, the underlying fundamental problems that might impede the effectiveness of proposed techniques. The emphasis of the study will be the development and evaluation of principles concerning the nature of software maintenance so that the effectiveness of possible programmer aids can be more accurately assessed in advance of implementation or actual tests. Limited evaluation of proposed programmer aids will be accomplished (see 3.2). Extensive programming will not be undertaken in this phase. Instead, scientific study and pilot experiments together with judicious hand-simulation or analysis of proposed computer implementations will be used insofar as possible to assess the probable effectiveness of proposed techniques and to examine underlying problems. (Some programming effort will undoubtedly be necessary, but since the emphasis of this contract is the study of principles underlying the effectiveness of proposed maintenance programmer aids rather than the implementation of immediately useful aids, it is expected that a relatively small amount of programming effort will be required.)

4.4   Final Report: At the conclusion of Phase II (4.3), a Final Report will be prepared consisting of 1) Part I of the Phase I report, revised as necessary to reflect knowledge gained in the Phase II studies; and 2) a presentation of results obtained in Phase II.

4.5   Part II of the Phase I report (4.2) will serve as a working paper defining the work to be accomplished during the remainder of the contract (Phase II). Work on Phase II will not proceed until receipt of Government approval. A decision on whether or not the proposed plan is approved, with or without modifications, will be rendered within seven (7) calendar days of the receipt of Part II.

The Overton team began their inquiry with a search of the literature, including some unpublished reports collected in the 1971 Appendices. They questioned experienced maintenance programmers, and requested "thoughts for the future" and "scenarios" of the ideal maintenance programming environment.

From this inquiry they distilled three "fundamental inhibiting factors" on maintenance programmers:

- The limited rate at which a person can perceive relevant clues in a mass of material.

- The human tendency to require more clues to a situation than are "logically" necessary to understand it.

- The human liability to distraction and procrastination.

They ranked the problems arising from these factors intuitively by (a) how much they inhibit maintenance, and (b) how easy they might be to answer. They outlined nine research projects that scored high on both dimensions (see their 1971 report, 46-79). Most of these projects were never funded or completed; they remain promising targets for the maintenance researcher today.

Toward the end of the first contract the Overton team chose three topics to study:

- Metrics for Maintainability: Consider factors which affect programmers' ability to make "relevance tests." Categorize "distant referents"—elements in a system which are related but are not close together. How can programmers deal with them?

- Conceptual Groupings: How do programmers group or "chunk" code?

- Path Analysis Feasibility Study: How do good programmers find their way through code? Where do ineffective or inexperienced programmers go astray?

The following single page, taken from the 1971 report, defines the Conceptual Groupings study. The next six pages, taken from the 1973 study, give the results. The Overton group found that programmers *do* use small groupings of code that can be distinguished by a fairly simple scanner. In the 1974 report, they give programs to scan FORTRAN and PL/I code, and mark off the groupings with blank lines and asterisks. They showed in a small pilot study that such visual groupings were almost as effective as human-written comments in helping programmers understand alien code.

SECTION 9 – CONCEPTUAL GROUPINGS PILOT STUDY

9.1   Introduction

When a programmer is actually working with a listing -- changing it to instal a modification, or explaining it to someone who is going to help him work with it -- he does not just repeat or read the listing, one statement at a time. He says (to himself, or perhaps to someone else): "...Now this gets you into a big old DO-loop; and it does so-and-so; and along the way you go to this other little routine which stores the results; and later you go to a print routine..." Generally, each of the clauses in his thinking covers more than a single programming-language statement.

The moral of this story is that (1) there <u>are</u> some units in which people think about the details of the program, and (2) those units are not limited to statements.

Beyond this moral, another assumption is made: When programmers are studying or explaining a program for their own benefit, they use the explanatory units which best <u>clarify the program</u>. But when they are just meeting the requirements of documenting a program, they choose the units which <u>minimize the work of documentation</u>.

Obviously, it would be valuable to define the units which best clarify the logic of a program. (Reasons why were summarized in Section 5.3.) The discovery of such optimally-clarifying units is the general objective which extends beyond this pilot study.

Excerpted from "A Study of Fundamental Factors Underlying Software Maintenance Problems: Final Report," *Hanscom Air Force Base Report NTIS Numbers: AD 739479 (report) and AD 739872 (appendices)*, 1971, page 115. U.S. Government work. Not protected by U.S. copyright.

4.1 PERCEPTION OF GROUPS

The authors' activities included experimentation aimed at gaining additional data on the characteristics of the perceptual groups which are most useful to programmers doing maintenance work. Data and observations were collected relating to three topics:

1. The level of groupings, associated with level of discourse, which programmers find easiest to use in explanations.

2. The types of conceptual groups which programmers seem to perceive most naturally.

3. The sizes of those groups.

Results of these topics are described below.

Also described are certain comments of interest by the programmers. Finally, the merits of this and an alternative kind of research are discussed.

4.1.1 Level of Groups

Observations on this interesting topic were largely subjective, but they were very consistent.

Five programmers were asked to pick a program of their own (in either FORTRAN or COBOL), and then to explain it to one of the authors, assuming that we were going to have to maintain the program. All of the five were very consistent in explaining their programs at the <u>functional</u> level rather than at the <u>detailed</u> or code level. That is, the programmers seemed to have very firm, "atomic" conceptual groups which they did not like to "split" further; and their explanations were volunteered.

The authors then "pushed" the programmers by questions like the following: "Remember, I'm going to be maintaining this program: don't I need to understand it at a more detailed level?"

The response of the experimental programmers to this "pushing" was either to:

1. Inquire as to whether or not we were really competent with the language involved; or

2. Go through the code on a statement-by-statement basis which seemed desultory, without apparently making any attempt to pair logically-coupled statements.

Excerpted from "Research toward Ways of Improving Software Maintenance: RICASM Final Report," *Hanscom Air Force Base Report NTIS Number AD 760819*, 1973, pages 36–41. U.S. Government work. Not protected by U.S. copyright.

There was no experimentation with assembly- or machine-language programs. However, opinions on this topic were obtained from a large maintenance programming installation concerned with avionics programs. Most of those opinions are described elsewhere in this volume, but one is relevant here:

Opinion: Two levels of documentation will generally suffice.

a. The upper level emphasizes "signal flow." It tells, for example, what steps executes before a load can be jettisoned.

b. The lower level tells what each subroutine does, ignoring the rest of the system.

c. If still lower level, explaining individual commands. becomes necessary, it can be incorporated into the subroutine level commentary.

4.1.2 Types of Groups

The CASMS final report implied that the following are some, but certainly not all, of the kinds of material which statistically tend to mark the existence of perceptual groups:

1. Tags or equivalents.

2. Conditional transfers not followed by certain "unimportant" tests.

3. Unconditional transfers.

4. PERFORM or equivalent statements, and RETURNs.

5. CALLS, but only when a certain number appear together.

In the experimentation of the present study, 130 different groups were observed. Table 4.1 breaks these down into eight different categories, and reports the frequency of occurrence of each type.

The different categories are named immediately below and then discussed.

1. I/O: This group consists of input/output and closely related statements.

2. DO: A group starting with a DO statement and ending with the last executable statement within the range of the loop.

3. IF: A conditional statement primarily involved in an if statement.

4. GO TO: Ending with an unconditional transfer.

5. ASSIGN: A group of statements, mostly FORTRAN assignment statements.

6. DEC: Consists of FORTRAN declaration statements.

7. DESCRIP: Consists of COBOL description statements (data or file).

8. Misc: All groups not falling into one of these categories.

TYPE	# OBSERVED	% TOTAL
I/O	30	23.1
DO	22	16.9
IF	21	16.2
GOTO	30	23.1
ASSIGN	6	4.6
DECLARATION	3	2.3
DESCRIPTION	10	7.7
Misc	8	6.2
	130	100.1

Table 4.1: Observed Groups by type

Probably the most interesting facet of the data is that more than 80% of the blocks marked by the programmers belong to one of only 5 general types. This was not an entirely expected result and, furthermore, after these categories were established and additional data were obtained, they covered new instances as well. In spite of the thinness of the data overall, this suggests that a) one might be able to rather easily identify meaningful groups automatically and b) provide a fair amount of assistance to maintainers by working only with these groups.

We do not believe that extremely precise definition of conceptual groups is possible from our data, nor that it is necessary to do so in order to effectively use them. However, we can provide a bit more description of the categories outlined above:

1. I/O: In FORTRAN these groups usually consist of READ, WRITE, PRINT, ENCODE, or DECODE statements with their associated FORMAT statements. In some instances, assignment statements that were used to prepare control parameters for the I/O operation were included. In COBOL, in addition to WRITE and READ sentences, OPEN and CLOSE sentences, paragraphs relating solely to I/O (regardless of the type of sentences), and MOVE sentences dealing with I/O setup are the natural candidates.

2. DO-loops: These are the easiest to define and seem to be generally used by most programmers. It has been informally observed many times that FORTRAN programmers explicitly block off their DO-loops when debugging a program. This would suggest that something so simple as automatically spacing off and perhaps indenting DO-loops (by the compiler) might be a big aid.

3. IF groups: By definition, a conditional defines two groups of code: those statements to be executed if the condition is true and those to be executed if it is false. The actual groups used by maintainers are not so clearly defined due to the possible forms of conditionals. In COBOL with a full form conditional, the groups usually consist of both sets of clauses. In both COBOL and FORTRAN, the use of GOTO (perhaps implicit in the case of FORTRAN arithmetic conditionals) serves as a delimiter by providing an upper bound (the target of the GOTO) for the group started by the conditional statement itself. In FORTRAN an arithmetic conditional often forms the end of a block with the beginning being less well defined in general (but usually relating in some way to statements relating to the condition to be tested at the end).

4. GO TO: These are usually rather simply defined. They end with an unconditional transfer and usually begin with the first preceeding labelled statement.

5. ASSIGNMENT: In scientific programs, it was observed that related groups of assignment statements were sometimes blocked. In particular, a common programmer tendancy was to group statements that either(a) had basically identical syntactic structure (with different variables) or (b) involved a large number of variables common to each.

If one asks why these groupings exist, and not others, an answer given in the CASMS report still seems to provide a partial explanation. Quoted below (from page 121), it made the following interpretation:

"The principal lesson learned subjectively from the study relates to the concept of "pay-off". In particular programmers' explanations tended to focus on what the programmers seemed to think were pay-off points. That is, explanatory units tended to build toward points at which the program either produced the desired outputs, or stored the results necessary for the desired outputs to be printed later, or overcame barriers to the desired outputs."

"For example, a check-writing program had to calculate a deduction; the calculation was treated as an explanatory unit. The program had to cause a number of X's to be printed before a number; the set-up of these X's formed an explanatory unit."

"More generally, a simulation program had to update certain parameters; each cyclic updating of each parameter tended to be an explanatory unit. It also had to determine if subsequent events had taken place; this determination was a small unit of explanation."

"In what seemed a very common kind of situation, a resource allocation program had to determine certain requirements by calling certain subroutines. Since the calls seemed to be steps toward pay-offs, they tended to be cited in brief explanatory units."

"More generally, anything that completed a <u>stage</u> of a
project might represent a pay-off. Once he has his "tools"
at hand, a worker (or programmer) might think, he has
successfully completed one stage of his work .... even
though he might not have begun the work <u>per se</u>."

4.1.3 <u>Sizes of Groups</u>

In the course of performing their various maintenance tasks,
the programmers explicitly marked off a total of 130 blocks or groupings
on the 33 listings used in those tasks. Those 130 blocks encompassed
1,258 lines of code. (Lines, rather than statements, were used in
counting; although in most cases they were synonymous.)

In terms of the sizes of these explicit groupings, the
findings were: The groupings were
1. Small, but
2. Skewed in distribution toward the larger sizes.

In particular, the modal (or most frequent single) size of
explicit group contained only two lines of code. The median size
was 5 lines, and the arithmetic mean was 9.68 lines. Also, 12.3%
of the groupings were longer than 20 lines.

By comparison, a study during the CASMS contract found a median
group size of 6 <u>statements</u> versus the 5 <u>lines</u> found here. Also, about
11% of those groupings were longer than 16 statements. Thus, the results
of the two experiments are in general agreement.

(It should be noted that the people who actually collected the
data in the present experiments had not participated in the CASMS studies
and the principal investigator deliberately did not give them the CASMS
results. So the data were really obtained independently.)

An additional activity of the present study was the analysis of
four listings to yield information concerning the <u>implicit</u> code groupings
set up by the original authors of the programs. The findings from the
four generally correspond to the findings from the explicit groupings.
Observations on the four are summarized below:

1. FORTRAN simulation program. Maintained by P5. A great
deal of regularity in the spacing of statement numbers was
noted. Taking as conceptual groups all the statements beginning with a numbered statement, we found 68 blocks with a 266 block
total. This yields a mean of 3.91 statements/group. The
median was 3 statements and the mode was 2.

2. Scientific FORTRAN program. Maintained by P4. Comments
seemed to be spaced throughout the program in a consistent and
complete manner. Using comment cards as the boundary of a
conceptual group, we found 12 groups covering the 210 statements of the program. This corresponds to 17.5 statements/
group. The median was 6 statements and the mode was undefined.

3. COBOL program for simple office accounting. Maintained by P3. Paragraphs appeared to be grouped regularly. There were 33 paragraphs covering 174 statements. Mean is 5.29 statements/group; median is 6; mode is 6.

4. FORTRAN program to produce a population density map. maintained by P1. Comments were carefully inserted and were taken to delimit groups. There were 19 groups covering 153 statements. Mean is 8.05; median is 7; mode is 6.

In discussing these results, it should be noted that the "firmest" data relating to conceptual groupings are those on the size of conceptual groups used by maintainers. Since size was taken over all the blocks observed, the figures reported should be indicative of what would be observed in other situations as well.

As noted above, there are big blocks (larger than 15 or 20 statements) and small blocks (around 8 lines or statements) with the preponderance of those observed being small. It appears that the larger blocks are not groups that form perceptual groupings, rather they are due to syntactic definitions that the programmer finds useful or compelling. For example, some DO-loops (an outer loop) may be quite large and be marked as a group along with smaller loops. We suspect, however, that these large groups are used more as structural delimiters than as manageable conceptual groups useful for aiding understanding of the detail of the program.

The size of the small groups strongly suggests a correlation with the known parameters of short term memory (Overton, 1961). This correlation may exist, but it should be noted that some of the structure of groups arises from the syntax of the language and really doesn't provide us with a useful indication of how to deal with conceptual groups (other than to keep them small).

We also noted that the one program which was most carefully commented also had one of the least skewed distribution of sizes. Compared with the experimentally-generated explicit groupings this one program had a mode of 6 and a mean of 8.05, versus a mode of 2 and a mean of 9.68. (The well-commented program was the one in FORTRAN for producing population density maps.)

We suspect that in general the discipline of creating good comments might reduce the variance of groupings, at least at any given level of analysis.

Overton, R.K., "Some data and comments on brain and computer memory capacities." Proceedings, San Diego Symposium on Biomedical Engineering, San Diego: 1961.

After the end of the 1974 contract, Overton went on to other commercial ventures, and neither the U.S. Air Force nor any other agency has sponsored comparable research since then. Why did this research die? Not because it was complete; Overton's team was no more able to write a "final report" on maintenance than Columbus could write a "final report" on America. It was certainly true that personnel had changed at the sponsoring agency (John Goodenough moved to SofTech, Inc., in 1972), that there was a cutback on government research funds in the mid-1970's, and that the researchers cut themselves off from a wider audience by not publishing in the open literature.

More salient, we believe, is that maintenance has been, and to some extent still is, a taboo activity. Researchers prefer to believe that the next programming technology will be the magic mushroom that will make maintenance unnecessary or costless. In the mid-1970's the magic mushroom was "software engineering" and "Improved Programming Prac-tices." Now, perhaps, it is "Fourth Generation Languages." It is easier to believe in magic mushrooms than to confront the uncompromising problems of our existing software.

Overton was a rare—and unpopular—pioneer in insisting on two principles:

- Studying maintenance means studying maintainers.
- Maintainability is not a quality of a system alone, but of a system and those who maintain it.

Overton has returned in recent years to human factors research. In 1982 he began to work on the U.S. Air Force's ICAM (Integrated Computer Assisted Manufacturing) project. We are trying to persuade him to publish a more extensive retrospective of his maintenance research in the open literature. We hope it will rekindle interest in this dangerously neglected topic.

Introduction

Beil, D.H. "A course in program maintenance." *ACM Special Interest Group on Computer Science Education SIGCSE Bulletin*, 11, 2 (June 1979), 19-22.

The following paper is the first, and as far as we know, the only report of a college course in software maintenance. The course is offered at the National Technical Institute for the Deaf, which is a college within the Rochester Institute of Technology, and is a required course in the second year of a three-year Associate degree in Data Processing.

The course was originated in 1976 by the author of this paper, Donald Beil (pronounced BEEL), after Donald Stabley of Kodak, a member of the Institute's DP Advisory Committee, suggested that the students should be exposed to the problems of modifying software. The course has been taught every spring since 1976; it has been taught for the last few years by instructor Robert Berl. The current class, due to graduate in 1983, has 23 students. Beil was appointed Chairperson of the Data Processing Department in 1979.

This software maintenance course has a real-world, project-oriented character rather than a theoretical orientation. The students work in teams of two on problems of conversion, program library control, reading and writing documentation, system enhancement, and system testing. Projects are selected from problems actually encountered by the data processing staff at the Institute and at other local computing centers. The mix of projects has evolved over the years. The current set of projects is based on a large existing payroll system; the students handle the conversion to different hardware, the updating of tax tables, and modifications based on government flyers that inform employers about legal and regulatory changes.

The course is given in sign language. Instructors Beil and Berl are not themselves hearing-impaired; like other instructors, they started their careers at the Institute with intensive courses in signing. The course is not presently offered to other students at the Rochester Institute of Technology, which is the larger institution which includes the National Technical Institute for the Deaf, but the author has received many requests for copies of the following paper since its publication by the Association for Computing Machinery's Special Interest Group on Computer Science Education.

This was the only college course on software maintenance known to us until one of us (Parikh) initiated a graduate course at DePaul University, Chicago, in the Fall of 1982. Why was maintenance taught to the hearing-impaired and not to other software engineering students? We speculate that computer people are temperamentally and professionally optimistic, concentrating on the perfection of a system as it will be when it is completed rather than on its inevitably imperfect, present state. Perhaps hearing-impaired students are more realistic; having a physical handicap, they are willing to give up the mental handicap of wishful thinking.

A COURSE IN PROGRAM MAINTENANCE

Donald H. Beil

National Technical Institute for the Deaf, 60-1055
Rochester Institute of Technology
One Lomb Memorial Drive
Rochester, NY 14623

This paper describes a course in program maintenance, entitled Business Data Processing Project I, (called Project I throughout this paper), currently offered in the Associate degree program of the Business Careers Department of the National Technical Institute for the Deaf, which is a college within the Rochester Institute of Technology. The catalog description for the course follows:

> Business Data Processing Project I (#0802-288)
>
> Project I students will concentrate on maintenance programming activities. Students, working with programs written by others, will test, modify, and document working programs and will complete partially finished programs. Students will convert programs from one computer system to another. By maintaining programs, students will have an opportunity to become aware of programming habits that ease the maintenance task. (3 class hours, 3 credit hours)

This course is offered at the end of the second year of a three year Associate degree (AAS) program. Students enrolled will have successfully completed the following technical course prerequisites (refer to the Technical Course Matrix below):

- A Summer Vestibule Program, a six week program of career sampling and counseling, which affords students the opportunity to learn about careers in this field before formally choosing Data Processing as a major.

- A three quarter sequence, Problem Solving with Computers I, II, and III, which introduces students to the logical problem solving tools available to computer programmers in the area of report preparation.

- A two quarter sequence, Data Files I and II, which concentrates on the programming techniques used to create, update, and process information kept on computer based files.

- Three courses in the operations area, Computer Operations I, II, and III, in which students are given hands-on experience with a variety of central computer systems and peripherals plus classroom work on the basics of job control language (JCL), console operation and operating systems.

- One industry work experience in which students have worked in a computer operations area full-time for approximately 10 weeks.

While students take the Project I course in program maintenance, they also take Systems Design. Students then must complete a second successful 10 week work experience in computer programming followed by a course in basic assembly language (BAL). This is followed by a second project class in which students work individually or as a team member in implementing a computer based system of programs.

This technical course sequence is summarized below. Note the Project I course occurring in the Spring quarter of the second year.

Reprinted from *ACM Special Interest Group on Computer Science Education SIGCSE Bulletin*, Volume 11, Number 2, June 1979, pages 19-22. Published by The Association of Computing Machinery.

TECHNICAL COURSE MATRIX
DATA PROCESSING
AAS LEVEL GRADUATES

Fall	Winter	Spring	Summer
			Summer Vestibule Program
FIRST YEAR			
PSC*I Operations I	PSC*II Operations II	PSC*III Operations III**	Operations Work Experience
SECOND YEAR			
Data Files I	Data Files II	Project I (Maintenance) Systems Design	Programming Work Experience
THIRD YEAR			
Assembly Language (BAL)	Project II DP Seminar**		

* PSC: Problem Solving with Computers
** Optional

This placement of Project I serves in the short run to prepare students for the programming work experience which follows it. Project I provides them with experiences similar to those which they may encounter on that work experience. In the long run, the classroom activity serves to strengthen students' knowledge in the areas of program maintenance, testing, documenting, and conversion.

All programming is done in COBOL on the central computer, a Xerox Sigma 9, of the Rochester Institute of Technology. Each student has sufficient permanent disk memory and access to terminals which allow the student to program on-line.

The current course goals, and explanations of the associated student activities for each goal, are presented below.

PROGRAM CONVERSION

Goal:

Students, when given a COBOL program written for an IBM computer, will be able to successfully implement that program on a Xerox Sigma 9 computer.

Student Activities

Students convert four programs during the quarter.

Program 1 is a very short program (approximately 75 lines including job control language, JCL), which permits students to concentrate on learning the JCL differences between the two systems. Few changes, other than JCL, are required.

Program 2 (approximately 200 lines) requires many changes in the COBOL source code as well as in the JCL.

Program 3 is longer (over 1400 lines), and is a program which accompanies an accounting problem set used in another course at the National Technical Institute for the Deaf. It was written for an IBM compiler and came to us on cards. Students are required to implement, test, and prepare user documentation (see the PROGRAM DOCUMENTATION goal below) for the program. The source deck contained minor errors when obtained.

Program 4 (approximately 100 lines) is a source program obtained from another system on which a pre-compiler and program library maintenance system were in use. This provides an opportunity for classroom discussion of both of these topics. This source code was accompanied by sample output which indicates to students that this program was also incomplete as obtained.

PROGRAM DOCUMENTATION

Goals:

A. Students, when given a COBOL program listing of a PROCEDURE DIVISION that does not follow structured programming concepts, will prepare an accurate flowchart of the procedure.

B. Students, when given a listing of a COBOL program and a copy of a COBOL programming standard, will be able to identify and correct all violations of the standard that appear in the program.

C. Students, when given a program, will prepare user documentation for the program.

Student Activities

A. Students prepare flowcharts for one or more of the programs described under the PROGRAM CONVERSION goal. Students' previous programming work has been done with concepts of structured programming. These programs provide their first classroom exposure to non-structured technique.

B. Students are given a source listing and a COBOL standard and asked to note all violations. The COBOL standard used is "COBOL Under Control," offered by Henry F. Ledgard and William C. Cave [1].

C. Students prepare departmental documentation for Program 3 as discussed above under PROGRAM CONVERSION.

PROGRAM LIBRARIES

Goals:

A. Students, when working with tape or disk, will be able to add or delete files from the volume.

B. Students, when given IBM JCL (including expanded catalog procedures) or Xerox UCL, will draw a system flowchart to correspond to the JCL. This JCL may include several separate programs or include assemblies which may be linked later.

Student Activities

A. Students are provided with tapes and required to manipulate files between tapes and their disk storage. Students also compute storage requirements for various files

B. Students draw system flowcharts of the expansion of a number of multi-step catalog procedures from IBM/OS JCL.

READING MANUALS

Goals:

A. Students, when given the command syntax notation of COBOL, will be able to determine if a COBOL statement meets the syntax. Students, when given a series of errors and the error message manual, will locate and correct the errors.

B. Students, when given a COBOL program and specifications containing a requirement calling for the addition of a language feature unknown to them, will implement the addition using only the manual and compilations; i.e., without support from instructor or others.

Student Activities

A. Students are given a series of COBOL statements and must decide if they are valid statements based on the command syntax notation for those sentences. If they are valid sentences, students write the appropriate generating syntax by selecting from the notation.

B. At the present time, this particular goal has not been implemented as an assignment.

PROGRAM MAINTENANCE

Goals:

A. Students, when given a COBOL program containing an apparent error, the cause of which is known or unknown, will correct the error.

B. Students, when given a COBOL program and specifications for changes of any type (including edits, changes to tables and searches, etc.), will modify the program.

C. Students, when given one COBOL program and the specifications for a second similar program, will modify the first program to create the second.

Student Activities

A. Students are given output from a lengthy invoice program which all have written during the previous quarter. The program aborted for "unknown" reasons. Students must find the cause of the problem and then suggest both a short-term solution, which will allow the program to run successfully on this run, and a long-term solution which will prevent this problem from recurring.

B. & C. Both are self-explanatory as recorded above.

PROGRAM TESTING

Goals:

Students, when given a COBOL program, will be able to develop a set of test data and subsequently correct any inadequacies in the program uncovered by the test data.

Student Activity

Students test the invoice program referred to above under PROGRAM MAINTENANCE, Student Activities, A. Students must develop a variety of test data which cause errors or other problems in the program. Each set must be run and then suggestions for eliminating the problem must be presented.

This course meets a number of the goals listed in the Curriculum Recommendations and Guidelines for the Community and Junior College Career Program in Computer Programming [2]. These include:

Modify an existing program or program module to accomplish requested changes in requirements.

Verify and thoroughly test the accuracy and completeness of computer programs by preparing sample data and by using debugging techniques and software aids.

Prepare appropriate documentation of computer programs....

Use...job control language, utilizing associated reference manuals and documentation. [2]

This course will be taught for the third time during the current academic year (1978-79). For that offering, development is expected under the goals of READING MANUALS and PROGRAM TESTING. Under READING MANUALS, goal B should be implemented as an assignment. Under PROGRAM TESTING, development may include assignments involving the use of the COBOL DEBUG package.

Acknowledgments

The author gratefully acknowledges Donald Stabley, Eastman Kodak Company, Rochester, New York, a member of our Standing Curriculum Advisory Committee, who provided the central idea for this course; John Sweeney, Richard Walton, and Robert Berl, all instructors of Data Processing at the National Technical Institute for the Deaf, for their careful reading of the paper; and George Schnellman, Data Processing Department, City of Rochester, New York, who provided a number of the programs used in the course.

References

1. Ledgard, Henry F. and William C. Cave, "COBOL Under Control," Communications of the ACM 19,11 (Nov. 1976), 601-607.

2. Little, Joyce Currie, Richard H. Austing, Harice Seeds, John Maniotes, and Gerald L. Engel, "Curriculum Recommendations and Guidelines for the Community and Junior College Career Program in Computer Programming," ACM SIGCSE Bulletin 9,2 (June 1977), 17-36.

Part II: Understanding software

The most common activities of maintenance programmers are these three:

- Thumbing through listings and/or paging through display screens.
- Talking to colleagues, users, or operations staff.
- Staring into space.

Assuming that these are more than idle activities, what are they for and how do they help in maintaining an operational system?

In Part I of this Tutorial, we presented questionnaire data indicating that maintainers spend at least half of their time trying to understand—the request, the existing system, and its documentation. We infer that these activities are part of the effort of understanding the system, where understanding is defined as: *A relationship between the maintenance staff and the system that enables maintenance staff to make changes and explain the system, correctly.*

If this definition is to be more than circular ("You handle the system correctly because you understand it; I know you understand it because you handle it correctly"), we need some analysis of the processes of understanding, some guide to appropriate tools and techniques, and some criteria for adequate performance. These needs are extraordinarily difficult to meet, and the selected papers in Part II represent work at one of the frontiers of software engineering.

One way to develop a perspective on the understanding of software is to ask the classic WHO? - WHAT? - WHEN? - HOW? - WHY? questions.

WHO should understand software?

Each element of a software system—the code, the data, the procedures—has a primary "understander." When the system operates, the code is "understood" by the processors, the data is "understood" by the storage devices or data base systems, and the procedures are "understood" by the users and operations staff. This is the minimum level of understanding necessary for the system to run at all. If the understanding goes no further, the system will continue to run only if nothing ever changes. When the system changes, the staff concerned with change—which includes maintenance programmers, development programmers, operations staff, quality assurance staff, and all their respective managers—must demonstrate understanding that goes beyond the existing documents.

In the first selection in Part II, Zvegintzov approaches understanding from an activist point of view. How do programmers or managers make decisions through understanding? How do they gain understanding through making decisions?

WHAT should be understood?

A large system is beyond the capacity of any one person to understand, even if that person dedicates an entire lifetime to it. The manager must assign parts of the understanding to individuals to achieve a collective understanding and a group coverage of the system. The manager must decide how the system should be partitioned for the best coverage.

The most common criteria for partitioning are the following:

- Distinct units of the system as viewed by the users (the functional classification).
- Units that are most often changed.
- Units that give the most trouble.

There is much commonality in these classifications because the functions as the user sees them are the functions in which the most changes are demanded, and the functions in which the most changes are made are often those that give the most problems.

Significantly, three papers in Part II remind the reader to concentrate on the externals of the system—the inputs and outputs as perceived by the user. Heninger's paper deals with specifications ("Specify external behavior only"), and the Parikh and Higgins papers deal with the Warnier/Orr methodology, which explicitly advises that the structure of a program should follow the structure of its output. The logic of concentrating on the outside of a system as a path to understanding its inside is not paradoxical:

- The external environment of a system has a simplicity which is limited by the constraints, conventions, rules, and habits of the real world.
- No system need be more complex than the operations it embodies.
- The necessary simplicities of a system's function can be exploited to cut through the accidental complexities of that system's implementation.

WHEN should software be understood?

When you need to put out a fire, you have no time to dig a well! You must understand the system before you attempt to change it. The manager must be committed to familiarizing the staff with the system. Several methods can be used to achieve this:

- Long-term dedication of the staff to the system ("the elite team").
- Scheduled walk-throughs, presentations, seminars, etc., in which staff members cover the system on a rotational basis.
- A one-time intensive initialization (such as the redocumentation of an existing system described by Heninger).
- The demand mode, in which an analyst "scopes" a section of the system from the narrow point of view of executing a particular change.

These methods form a continuum from the most broadly strategic approach to the most narrowly tactical. The manager or programmer can achieve the swiftest and smoothest performance at the top end of the continuum, but real-world circumstances, particularly staff reassignments, often put these strategies beyond reach. The wise manager uses the short-term methods when necessary, meanwhile developing long-term experience in the team by installing a policy of maintenance reviews, change logs, and system walk-throughs.

HOW should software be understood?

A person understands a system by:

- Knowing the different levels, points of view, and constituencies from which the behavior of the system can be described.
- Knowing the objects and activities that characterize each level.
- Being able to relate the objects and activities of one level to those of another.

The best theoretical account of this process as it is applied to a software system is Brooks' behavioral theory of program comprehension, reprinted as the last paper in Part II. Zvegintzov's "Eureka Countdown" gives a catchy 5-4-3-2-1 checklist for the activities that support this process. The other papers describe the most promising tools and techniques for systematizing the process.

WHY should software be understood?

If a system is not understood, it is out of control. Its users have only the alternatives of accepting it entirely, which is slavery, or rejecting it entirely, which is revolution. The maintainers stand as a bridge between these costly alternatives, allowing the system and its users the freedom to evolve. In software, as in politics, the price of freedom is vigilance.

Further readings

Gerald M. Weinberg was the first author to highlight the importance of reading a program as opposed to writing one. Chapter 1 of his *The psychology of computer programming* (Van Nostrand Reinhold Company, 1971) is "Reading programs." Weinberg, Wright, Kauffman, and Goetz's *High level COBOL programming* (Little, Brown and Company, 1977) contains a chapter on "Critical program reading." Linger, Mills, and Witt's *Structured programming: theory and practice* (Addison-Wesley Publishing Company, 1979) includes a chapter on "Reading structured programs." Shneiderman's *Software psychology: human factors in computer and information systems* (Little, Brown and Company, 1980) contains much material and many references on software comprehension.

Among forthcoming books, Mills' *Software productivity* (Little, Brown and Company) will include a chapter on "Reading programs as a managerial activity," and Parikh's *The guide to software maintenance* (also to come from Little, Brown and Company) will include sections on "Program reading for managers," "Program reading for programmers," and the "R^2/A^2 formula of W. Clement Stone."

The activity of understanding is a relationship between people and people as well as between people and systems. An indispensable reference on interpersonal techniques in software management is Freedman and Weinberg's *Handbook of walkthroughs, inspections, and technical reviews* (Little, Brown and Company, 3rd edition, 1982).

Introduction

Zvegintzov, N. "The Eureka Countdown." *Datamation* (April 1982), 172-178. [The following introduction was written by Girish Parikh.]

Nicholas Zvegintzov, my coeditor and the author of the next paper, suggested that we give hints in these introductions on pronouncing uncommon names. He wishes it to be known that his name is pronounced just as it is written, with the accent on the second syllable: ZVEGÍNTZOV.

His "Eureka Countdown" is named after what Archimedes is supposed to have shouted ("Eureka! I figured it out!") after realizing in his bath that a floating body displaces exactly its own mass of liquid. The Eureka Countdown is a five step process for displacing ignorance and replacing it with your own brainpower:

5 The Five Questions

4 The Four Actions

3 The Three Places to Work

2 The Two Products

1 The One Golden Rule

Zvegintzov tells me that he conceived the Eureka Countdown when challenged by the statistic that maintainers spend at least half their time trying to understand. If this is true and if we are trying to explain or teach maintenance, what are we doing to explain or teach understanding? He tried to answer the question at a level above tools and methodologies. He assumes that you, the engineer, will use the sharpest tools of analysis and documentation available to you; how do you as a tool-user make progress to understanding?

Zvegintzov's approach to understanding is action-oriented. It is significant that immediately after "the five questions" are "the four actions," which in his paper are

REVIEW

REFLECT

RECORD

REACT

They remind me of the "R^2/A^2 Formula" of W. Clement Stone, the dynamic founder of Combined Insurance Company of America, Chicago, for whom I worked as a senior programmer. R^2/A^2 means *Recognize, Relate/Assimilate, Action*. I describe the R^2/A^2 Formula in my forthcoming *The guide to software maintenance* (Little, Brown and Company) this way:

- *Recognize* the problem, i.e., identify the problem. Discovering the cause behind the symptoms is winning half the battle.

- *Relate* the problem to other similar problems solved or encountered. Think... Recall your past experience and stretch it beyond your experience in the present company. Have you solved such problems before? Have your co-workers tackled such problems?

  Here, the documentation of previous problems—solved and unsolved—comes to aid. Dig that treasure if available, and you may get a clue to the present problem.

- *Assimilate*, digest the information regarding the problem, past experience and data on such problems. Let it sink in your subconscious.

  Also, learn from experience—assimilate the experience for future use.

- And then... Take *Action*. Unless you take action, the previous steps do not mean anything. Formulate a plan of action, then ACT.

Finally, I should like to point out that the writing of Zvegintzov's article—content, style, and presentation—is superb. On this point, the author commented:

I wrote 'The Eureka Countdown' in a week when the hard-copy printer on my word processor was down. There is nothing that concentrates your style as much as viewing your work through a 72 character by 24 line window!

How to understand a software system, in five steps.
Also includes the secret of the magic box.

THE EUREKA COUNTDOWN

by **Nicholas Zvegintzov**

Understanding a system means knowing what to do when things go wrong, knowing how to seize the advantage when things go right, and knowing how to make changes to keep things going in your favor. Knowledge is power—in management, government,

love, war . . . and software systems.

How do you understand a software system? There are textbooks and courses to teach you everything else— how to design, document, test, buy, and sell a system. But how to understand? Isn't that a bit "philosophical?" Maybe a skilled programmer can understand a system, but isn't

that a luxury the typical manager can't afford? Isn't it something you have to know already, something that can't be learned?

No, on all counts. Understanding is not philosophical; it is a practical, hands-on, tab-A-in-slot-B skill. Understanding is not just for skilled programmers, nor is it a luxury for

Understanding is not a sequence of once-and-for-all phases, but a continual repetition and interweaving of four different actions.

the manager. In fact, programmers are notorious for their incoherence in explaining systems and their unwillingness to distinguish the forest from the trees. Understanding is the key to taking the right action at the right time, which is the essence of the manager's job. And finally, understanding *can* be learned and taught.

The path to understanding is what this author calls the Eureka Countdown, named after the Greek word for "I figured it out!"—what Archimedes shouted in his bath when he realized that a body exactly displaces its own mass of water. The Eureka Countdown will help you displace ignorance with your own brainpower. Here's how it works:

Five: the five questions to ask.

Four: the four actions to take with the answers.

Three: the three places to work. These are the places to penetrate the system.

Two: the two products—what you do with your knowledge.

One: the one golden rule to remember if you forget everything else.

The five questions are WHAT? WHY? HOW? WHERE FROM? WHERE TO? They are visualized in Fig. 1. This figure shows one jigsaw piece. Pieces like it lock onto each other to form a "knowledge network."

The WHAT? pieces can fit either UP/DOWN in a WHY?/HOW? pair or LEFT/RIGHT in a WHERE FROM?/WHERE TO? pair. Fig. 2 shows some pieces fitted together.

For example, in an accounts receivable program, the HOW? of GET INCOME is answered by the invoice sequence ending with the alternatives RECEIVE PAYMENT or PURSUE DEADBEAT. Correspondingly, the WHY? of the invoice sequence is answered by GET INCOME. In the invoice sequence, WRITE INVOICE leads to TRACK INVOICE.

The WHAT?s in your system include any functions important enough to have names. Find out what names your people use, and you'll know what things your people are dealing with. This principle is as old as language itself—people name the things they are interested in.

Where do you find these names?
- The organization chart. The units that people work in have names: "Financial Services Division," "Disbursements Unit."
- The main actors or participants in the organization. Some important categories of people—"Customers," "Auditors," "Data Entry Clerks"—are not localized in any particular unit, but they are the *reasons* for the organizational units. They can be found by asking WHY? about organizational units.
- Job descriptions. The tasks that people work on have names, like "the payroll edit."
- The main functions or products of the organization. Some important categories of action—"Make sale," "New hire," "Service

call"—are not really tasks but rather the *reasons* for the tasks. They can be found by asking WHY? about tasks.
- Objects that move around the system. These are often forms or standard memoranda. Their names, though cryptic to the outsider, are often household words to the insider.
- The software. The Job Control Language gives the names of files and programs, and the programs themselves give the names of the fields and processes used.

Database and data dictionary systems are closely related to this naming process. They provide a way of mechanically storing, controlling, and manipulating the names of files, fields, and processes. They are the di-

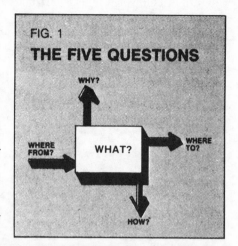

FIG. 1

THE FIVE QUESTIONS

WHY?

WHERE FROM? WHAT? WHERE TO?

HOW?

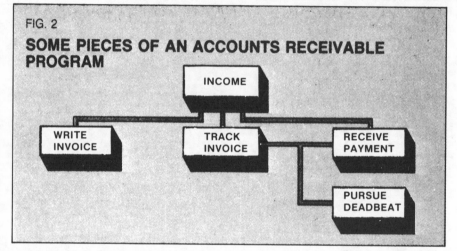

FIG. 2

SOME PIECES OF AN ACCOUNTS RECEIVABLE PROGRAM

INCOME

WRITE INVOICE   TRACK INVOICE   RECEIVE PAYMENT

PURSUE DEADBEAT

rect source of the names you need. But if you do not have them in place, your main prerequisite for installing them is to search out, simplify, and standardize names, i.e., perform the first phase of understanding the system. This illustrates that understanding a system is part of controlling it.

LEARN ABOUT THE WHAT?S

The names become the WHAT?s in your system. Your aim is to discover enough about them to relate them to each other either by the WHY?/HOW? (vertical) connection or by the WHERE FROM?/WHERE TO? (horizontal) connection. Things that relate to each other by subordination (e.g., organizational hierarchies) or in a parts-of-a-whole relationship are naturals for the UP/DOWN connection. Things that move are naturals for the LEFT/RIGHT connection. While the UP/DOWN and LEFT/RIGHT connections may not adequately describe all the relationships that can arise, they are a useful simplification for working on a flat paper or screen. When advanced systems allow the manager to see and diagram in seven dimensions, it will be time to introduce a seven-way classification.

The four actions to get and use the

answers are shown in the RECYCLE (Fig. 3). All the actions start with RE, to remind you to do them over and over, again and again. Understanding is not a sequence of once-and-for-all phases, but a continual repetition and interweaving of four different actions which supplement and illuminate each other.

In the REVIEW action you look, listen, and perceive what is going on. You should both ask what people are doing and watch them doing it. You should both ask what is in a program or a procedure and look yourself. You should scan any existing documentation, even if it is out of date or incomplete, because its value will usually outweigh its imperfections.

The REFLECT action involves using your intelligence to simplify, correlate, and evaluate. Simplifying is reducing material to its essentials—a bulky manual to its table of contents, a lengthy procedure to its essential function.

Correlating includes finding parallels and/or discrepancies between your findings. Parallels help in simplification; they reveal the regularity and routinization in the organization. Discrepancies, e.g., between what people say and what they do, or between a manual and a procedure, usually re-

Understanding is not a passive state, but a component of action.

veal recent changes. An organization will often change its function to react to outside requirements quicker than it will change its image of itself.

In evaluation, you assign priority or value to information. Not everything that you see and hear can be taken at its face value; it may have to be discounted according to context. For instance, in the classic example of a sales-oriented organization, the announced design aims and methods of the product group would need to be discounted by the external market influences.

The RECORD action in the RECYCLE forces you to use your fingers to put marks on paper or on a screen to supplement your memory. This is surprisingly hard work—there is a great difference between thinking you know something and being able to express what you know.

There are three ways to supplement your memory—diagrams, lists or tables, and text. Diagrams depict an aspect of your system. They can use one of the WHAT?, WHY?, HOW?, WHERE FROM?, WHERE TO? jigsaw pieces described above, or any other symbology you prefer. A diagram should be limited to the amount the eye can scan or the brain handle in one sweep. A piece of paper or a screen is limited in size as well as dimensions. Do not continue a diagram over the edge of the paper onto another sheet. If there is too much material, either discard some or put the extra material on another sheet—but also start a higher-level sheet that indexes the two.

Lists or tables are for large groups of similar items such as files, fields, or forms. Keep them in easily retrievable order, e.g., alphabetically. This type of material can also be derived mechanically from the software by cross-referencers, indexers, or data dictionaries, and can be printed and formatted on a word processor.

Text can introduce, link, or comment on the diagrams and the lists or tables. You won't generally have to write extensive chapters—just notes that enable you to make these introductions, links, or comments if needed. In fact, the text might be so abbreviated as to go conveniently into WHAT?, WHY?, HOW?, WHERE FROM?, WHERE TO? diagrams.

In the REACT segment of the RECYCLE, you use your own position and power in the system to change it. This part of the cycle reminds you that understanding is not a passive state, but a component of action. Furthermore, gaining understanding is an action in itself; like light shone on photographic film, understanding changes the object it illuminates. Be ready to cause changes in the behavior that you observe, and, if you have the authority, to order changes. For instance, one classic method of discovering whether a report or a procedure is redundant is to de-

stroy it, hide it, or abolish it—and see if anybody misses it.

And remember that the RECYCLE really is a cycle—after you react, go on to review, reflect, record, and react again.

THREE PLACES TO WORK

The system is inevitably too large to grasp in a single session. You cannot work on all of it at the same time. The three places to work are the top, the problem, and the edges (Fig. 4).

The first place to work is at the top—a statement of purpose (i.e., the answer to a WHY?) broad enough to include you, your aims, and as much of the organization as you intend to understand. In a strict hierarchical theory of your role, this purpose need be no higher than your immediate boss's job de-

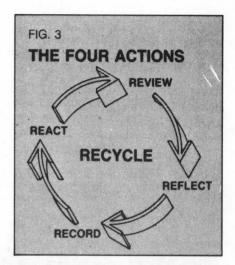

FIG. 3
THE FOUR ACTIONS

REVIEW
REACT
RECYCLE
REFLECT
RECORD

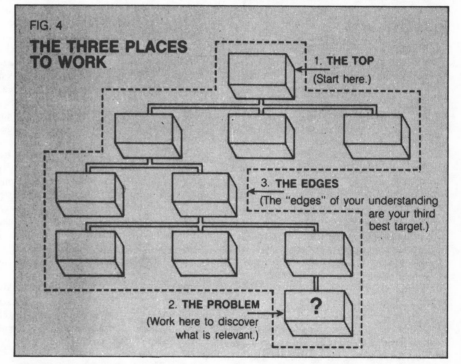

FIG. 4
THE THREE PLACES TO WORK

1. THE TOP (Start here.)

3. THE EDGES (The "edges" of your understanding are your third best target.)

2. THE PROBLEM (Work here to discover what is relevant.)

scription, since your aims are supposed to be totally determined by your boss's. In practice, you will want to start from a higher point. You cannot effectively work for your boss without an understanding of his or her context in the organization—and your personal aims may reach much farther in the hierarchy.

In any case, the reasons for working on your understanding from the top are:
• The simplest and most succinct descriptions of the system are at the top.
• The same top-level explanation can be used as part of many different low-level explanations.
• If you have to choose between learning to speak the language of your boss or the language of your subordinates, it is always in the

interest of your career to choose your boss's.

The second place to work is where the problem is—that is, on whatever prompted you to try to understand the system. Such a problem might be a function that you have been told to change, improve, or eliminate. This is a well-known technique called "working backwards"—studying a system from where you want to arrive back to where you are now. It does not guarantee a solution, but it often works. Also, it steers you away from irrelevancies and it is the best highlighter of what *is* relevant.

This is why, when studying a programming language, it is important both to read the manual and to do problems. Techniques in the language only make sense in the context of problems, and the problems can

**The things that you partially understand—the "edges"
of your knowledge—are the best targets for study.**

only be done by remembering techniques in the language.

The third place to work is at the edges—that is, from what you know already toward presently unfilled areas. At a given point in your inquiry there will be things you understand completely, partially, and not at all. The things you understand completely need no work, and the things you do not understand at all offer too little to get started on. Therefore, the things that you partially understand—the "edges" of your knowledge—are the best targets.

Something you partially understand is connected to the rest of your knowledge in some but not all directions. You may know how something is done but not why, or why and not how. Ask the missing question. It may link up with something you already know and significantly simplify your quest. Or it may link to something new, extending the edge of your understanding. In either case, your questions are concrete because they build on what you know already.

In the priority order, the three places to work are the top, the problem, and the edges. Nevertheless, you should work at all of them for two reasons: you can become boxed-in or blocked at some point. Or, paradoxically, you can make too much progress at some point and become compulsive about something like writing down all the files and their fields—to the detriment of other, more neglected areas.

Therefore, it may be wise to act like a timesharing monitor and deliberately apportion your time among the areas. This technique is consciously used by many managers.

TWO PRODUCTS RESULT

The two products of understanding are ACTION and READINESS. Understanding isn't measured by having a manual on the shelf, or passing a course, or getting high grades on a test. The true measure of understanding is whether your actions in relation to the system are appropriate and productive. Therefore, the visible payoff is effective action, and the invisible payoff is readiness for effective action.

It is critical to know the answers to the five questions because they are the questions that arise when you have to act. For each function in responsibility, you must know:

1. WHAT it is, so when someone names it, you can channel your attention properly.

2. WHY it is, so you can defend it.
3. HOW it works, so you can implement, supervise, or change it.
4.-5. WHERE its inputs come FROM, and WHERE its outputs go TO, so you can ensure that it fulfills its function.

You can think of understanding as software that runs in your head. The importance of software is not the state it puts the computer into, nor the code with which it is written, but its action or potential for action on the environment. Similarly, understanding is not a state of mind nor a heap of documentation, although both are by-products of it.

In fact, the status of documentation as a by-product of understanding accounts for its awkward position in the data processing world: many people admire it, some people need it, but few people either write or read it. Current action is *never* impaired by lack of documentation, because if the participants don't already have that knowledge, it is too late to consult the documentation. It is readiness to act in the long run that is impaired by lack of documentation, but readiness is not a salient goal for a manager unless change is imminent.

Thus adequate documentation is usually a by-product of change. It is usually out of date quickly because it is documentation of the old or changing system. The new system will probably be understood by key managers and participants, but it will only be adequately documented when it too is about to be changed.

The Eureka Countdown can be integrated with other methodologies and tools. For example, while following the countdown you can use automated tools that derive standardized documentation from your software, word processing to format your documentation, or a database system to store and analyze your knowledge of the system.

The rule for tools is: if it exists, and you have it or can procure it, and you know how it can help you—use it! No one tool will be sufficient; different tools help with different parts of the problem. The only limitation is that where there are alternatives, as the rival methods of diagramming, you may want to standardize so that different people working on the project can link their work.

The Eureka Countdown is not so much a method as an attitude. It does not tell you what records to keep or what tools to use,

but how to approach the problem. In fact, as the following Chinese story reminds us, it's not snake oil that keeps you fit, it's elbow grease:

A farmer who believed in magic was near to ruin. His stock was depleted, his harvests were sparse, and his garden was barren. He went to the Sage and said: "Sell me magic to make me prosperous."

For a large sum, the Sage sold him a box and told him: "The magic is in this box. Do not open it—but every day for a year carry it to every corner of your farm."

Every day for a year the farmer carried the box to every corner of his farm. At the end of the year his stock was numerous, his harvest ample, and his garden fertile. He took the box back to the Sage, and said:

"That is certainly a powerful magic in the box. May I see it now?"

The Sage said: "Before you see the magic, tell me what you saw when you carried it around your land."

"I saw fences down, so that my stock escaped. I saw terraces eroded, so that my harvest parched. I saw weeds in my garden, so that the fruit was choked."

The Sage said: "Now you can look in the box."

The farmer looked in the box, and saw that it was empty.

The Sage said: "The magic of making your farm prosper is not in the box. It is in you."

The Sage was an early consultant (and an unusually honest one). His empty but much-traveled box brings us to the last stop on the Eureka Countdown, the one golden rule:

Never give up.

The aim of studying your system is not to understand it perfectly and then make the one perfect decision. The aim is to make satisfactory decisions today on the basis of partial understanding and to learn a little. As you learn, you will understand better, and make better decisions.   ✳

Nicholas Zvegintzov is a Staten Island, N.Y., writer and teacher who specializes in the renovation, redocumentation, and enhancement of software systems. He is the author of *Applications Software Maintenance*, forthcoming from McGraw-Hill.

Introduction

Heninger, K.L. "Specifying software requirements for complex systems: new techniques and their application." *IEEE Trans. Software Engineering*, SE-6, 1 (1980), 2-13.

The essential difference between maintenance and development is that the maintainer must confront the complexity of an existing software system. Thus much of the activity of the maintainer—particularly the understanding activity discussed in this Part—consists of analysis and investigation of the existing system. When documentation is inadequate, the maintainer often climbs the development path in the reverse direction:

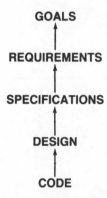

In the following paper, Kathryn Heninger (since 1981, Kathryn Heninger Britton) reports on a unique project to derive a specifications document (the function of the system as opposed to its internal mechanisms) from an operational system as a basis for reprogramming. This project was part of a wider one which was:

> to produce a complete description of the A-7 program requirements in a form that would facilitate the development of the new program and that could be updated easily as the requirements continue to change.

The system in question is a 12,000 line assembly language program running as part of the avionics system of the A-7, a U.S. Navy airplane. The resources for its respecification were

- The program itself—"some questions could not be answered without experimentation with the existing system."
- Several shelves of documentation—"none of the available documents was entirely accurate."
- The systems staff:—"no single person knew the answers to all our questions; some questions were answered differently by different people."

Sound familiar? The outstanding value of Heninger's paper is that she describes remedies for this situation. With clarity and conviction, she lays out costs, benefits, and techniques for creating requirements documentation. You will find objectives and design principles for such documentation, techniques for documenting interfaces to real-time devices, techniques for specifying software functions without specifying implementation, advice on distinguishing hard requirements from future change areas, and tabular techniques to promote completeness and correctness ("it is much easier for a reviewer to recognize an error than an omission"). Some specific techniques are directed at the real-time embedded software environment, but much is applicable to any programming environment.

The benefit of the project is a document used to understand the existing system, to guide enhancements, and to serve as a basis for an intended reprogramming. The costs were significant: 17 person-months for a 500-page document. They can be compared with the other scanty statistics on documentation bulk in the literature—particularly Capers Jones' measurement of English words per line of code for IBM systems of various sizes (*Tutorial—Programming productivity: issues for the eighties*, IEEE Computer Society, 1981, p. 225). Jones reports 4.5 words per line of code for systems of 8,000 lines and six words per line of code for systems of 16,000 lines.

Heninger estimated for us that the A-7 specifications document runs less than 100 words per page, because of presentation techniques such as forms, tables, etc., for a total of about 50,000 words, which is less than 4.2 words per line of code. The document that she describes is only a requirements document; there is more documentation for the module structure, module interfaces, and so on. Nevertheless, it is encouraging that Heninger's and Jones' statistics are in the same range.

The manager oppressed by the documentation problem should note that Heninger started out with *more* documentation ("several shelves"); part of the problem was therefore pruning—errors, overlaps, vagueness, obsolescence. The documentor, like the maintainer, must search for simplicity under complexity.

In this introduction we have stressed the lessons to be learned from Heninger's paper about restoring documentation where it is deficient or absent. In commenting on an early draft of this introduction, Heninger pointed out to us that the purpose of the paper was to argue that the requirements documentation should be done during development; doing it after the fact is a poor second. It is more expensive, it takes more resources, and the reasons for development decisions cannot be reconstructed.

The overall project was the redesign of the software, Heninger told us:

> When the project first started, we had no particular intentions of making a contribution in the software requirements area...
>
> However we needed a precise definition of what our new system had to do in order to be functionally equivalent to the existing system.

The redesign project is still in progress in 1982; the software requirements document has been actively used and maintained since it was completed. Several hundred copies have been distributed all over the world. Since 1981 Heninger has been at IBM, working on specifications of Systems Network Architecture.

IEEE TRANSACTIONS ON SOFTWARE ENGINEERING, VOL. SE-6, NO. 1, JANUARY 1980

Specifying Software Requirements for Complex Systems: New Techniques and Their Application

KATHRYN L. HENINGER

Abstract—This paper concerns new techniques for making requirements specifications precise, concise, unambiguous, and easy to check for completeness and consistency. The techniques are well-suited for complex real-time software systems; they were developed to document the requirements of existing flight software for the Navy's A-7 aircraft. The paper outlines the information that belongs in a requirements document and discusses the objectives behind the techniques. Each technique is described and illustrated with examples from the A-7 document. The purpose of the paper is to introduce the A-7 document as a model of a disciplined approach to requirements specification; the document is available to anyone who wishes to see a fully worked-out example of the approach.

Index Terms—Documentation techniques, functional specifications, real-time software, requirements, requirements definition, software requirements, specifications.

I. INTRODUCTION

MUCH software is difficult to understand, change, and maintain. Several software engineering techniques have been suggested to ameliorate this situation, among them modularity and information hiding [11], [12], formal specifications [4], [9], [10], [13], [16], [20], abstract interfaces [15], cooperating sequential processes [2], [18], [21], process synchronization routines [2], [8], and resource monitors [1], [6], [7]. System developers are reluctant to use these techniques both because their usefulness has not been proven for programs with stringent resource limitations and because there are no fully worked-out examples of some of them. In order to demonstrate feasibility and to provide a useful model, the Naval Research Laboratory and the Naval Weapons Center are using the techniques listed above to redesign and rebuild the operational flight program for the A-7 aircraft. The new program will undergo the acceptance tests established for the current program, and the two programs will be compared both for resource utilization and for ease of change.

The new program must be functionally identical to the existing program. That is to say, the new program must meet the same requirements as the old program. Unfortunately, when the project started there existed no requirements documentation for the old program; procurement specifications, which were originally sketchy, are now out-of-date. Our first step was to produce a complete description of the A-7 program requirements in a form that would facilitate the development of the new program and that could be updated easily as the requirements continue to change.

Writing down the requirements turned out to be surprisingly difficult in spite of the availability of a working program and experienced maintenance personnel. None of the available documents were entirely accurate; no single person knew the answers to all our questions; some questions were answered differently by different people; and some questions could not be answered without experimentation with the existing system. We found it necessary to develop new techniques based on the same principles as the software design techniques listed above to organize and document software requirements. The techniques suggested questions, uncovered ambiguities, and supported crosschecking for completeness and consistency. The techniques allowed us to present the information relatively concisely, condensing several shelves of documentation into a single, 500-page document.

This paper shares some of the insights we gained from developing and applying these techniques. Our approach can be useful for other projects, both to document unrecorded requirements for existing systems and to guide software procurers as they define requirements for new systems. This paper introduces the techniques and illustrates them with simple examples. We invite anyone interested in more detail to look at the requirements document itself as a complete example of the way the techniques work for a substantial system [5].

First this paper addresses the objectives a requirements document ought to meet. Second it outlines the general design principles that guided us as we developed techniques; the principles helped us achieve the objectives. Finally it presents the specific techniques, showing how they allowed us to achieve completeness, precision, and clarity.

II. A-7 PROGRAM CHARACTERISTICS

The A-7 flight program is an operational Navy program with tight memory and time constraints. The code is about 12 000 assembler language instructions and runs on an IBM System 4 PI model TC-2 computer with 16K bytes of memory. We chose this program because we wanted to demonstrate that the run-time overhead incurred by using software engineering principles is not prohibitive for real-time programs and because

Manuscript received February 12, 1979; revised March 12, 1979.
The author is with the Naval Research Laboratory, Washington, DC 20375.

the maintenance personnel feel that the current program is difficult to change.

The A-7 flight program is part of the Navigation/Weapon Delivery System on the A-7 aircraft. It receives input data from sensors, cockpit switches, and a panel with which the pilot keys in data. It controls several display devices in the cockpit and positions several sensors. Twenty-two devices are connected to the computer; examples include an inertial measurement set providing velocity data and a head-up display device. The head-up display projects symbols into the pilot's field of view, so that he sees them overlaying the world ahead of the aircraft. The program calculates navigation information, such as present position, speed, and heading; it also controls weapon delivery, giving the pilot steering cues and calculating when to release weapons.

III. REQUIREMENTS DOCUMENT OBJECTIVES

For documentation to be useful and coherent, explicit decisions must be made about the purposes it should serve. Decisions about the following questions affect its scope, organization, and style: 1) What kinds of questions should it answer? 2) Who are the readers? 3) How will it be used? 4) What background knowledge does a reader need? Considering these questions, we derived the following six objectives for our requirements document.

1) *Specify external behavior only.* A requirements document should specify only the external behavior of a system, without implying a particular implementation. The user or his representative defines requirements using his knowledge of the application area, in this case aircraft navigation and weapons delivery. The software designer creates the implementation, using his knowledge of software engineering. When requirements are expressed in terms of a possible implementation, they restrict the software designer too much, sometimes preventing him from using the most effective algorithms and data structures. In our project the requirements document must be equally valid for two quite different implementations: the program we build and the current program. For our purposes it serves as a problem statement, outlining what the new program must do to pass acceptance tests. For those maintaining the current program, it fills a serious gap in their documentation: they have no other source that states exactly what the program must do. They have pilot manuals, which supply user-level documentation for the entire avionics system, of which the program is only a small part. Unfortunately, the pilot manuals make it difficult to separate the activities performed by the computer program from those performed by other devices and to distinguish between advice to the pilot and restrictions enforced by the program. The maintainers also have implementation documentation for the current program: mathematical algorithm analyses, flowcharts, and 12 000 lines of sparsely commented assembler code. But the implementation documents do not distinguish between the aspects that are dictated by the requirements and those that the software designer is free to change.

2) *Specify constraints on the implementation.* In addition to defining correct program behavior, the document should describe the constraints placed on the implementation, especially the details of the hardware interfaces. As is usually the case with embedded systems,[1] we are not free to define the interfaces to the system, but must accept them as given for the problem. A complete requirements description should therefore include the facts about the hardware devices that can affect the correctness of the program.

3) *Be easy to change.* Because requirements change, requirements documentation should be easy to change. If the documentation is not maintained during the system life cycle, control is lost over the software evolution; it becomes difficult to coordinate program changes introduced by maintenance personnel.

4) *Serve as a reference tool.* The primary function of the document is to answer specific questions quickly, rather than to explain in general what the program does. We expect the document to serve experienced programmers who already have a general idea about the purpose of the program. Precision and conciseness are valued. Indispensable reference aids include a glossary, detailed table of contents, and various indices. Since tutorial material has different characteristics, such as a narrative style, it should be developed separately if it is needed.

5) *Record forethought about the life cycle of the system.* During the requirements definition stage, we believe it is sensible to exercise forethought about the life cycle of the program. What types of changes are likely to occur [22]? What functions would maintainers like to be able to remove easily [17]? For any software product some changes are easier to make than others; some guidance in the requirements will help the software designer assure that the easy changes correspond to the most likely changes.

6) *Characterize acceptable responses to undesired events.* Undesired events [14], such as hardware failures and user errors, should be anticipated during requirements definition. Since the user knows the application area, he knows more than the software designer about acceptable responses. For example, a pilot knows better than a programmer whether a particular response to a sensor failure will decrease or increase his difficulties. Responses to undesired events should be stated in the requirements document; they should not be left for the programmer to invent.

IV. REQUIREMENTS DOCUMENT DESIGN PRINCIPLES

Our approach to requirements documentation can be summarized by the three principles discussed below. These principles form the basis of all the techniques we developed.

1) *State questions before trying to answer them.* At every stage of writing the requirements, we concentrated first on formulating the questions that should be answered. If this is not done, the available material prejudices the requirements investigation so that only the easily answered questions are asked. First we formulated the table of contents in Fig. 1 in order to characterize the general classes of questions that should be answered. We wrote it before we looked at the A-7

---

[1] An embedded system functions as a component of a significantly larger system. Parnas [15] has a discussion of embedded system characteristics.

Chapter	Contents
0 Introduction	Organization principles; abstracts for other sections; notation guide
1 Computer Characteristics	If the computer is predetermined, a general description with particular attention to its idiosyncrasies; otherwise a summary of its required characteristics
2 Hardware Interfaces	Concise description of information received or transmitted by the computer
3 Software Functions	What the software must do to meet its requirements, in various situations and in response to various events
4 Timing Constraints	How often and how fast each function must be performed. This section is separate from section 3 since "what" and "when" can change independently.
5 Accuracy Constraints	How close output values must be to ideal values to be acceptable
6 Response to Undesired Events	What the software must do if sensors go down, the pilot keys in invalid data, etc.
7 Subsets	What parts of the program should be easy to remove
8 Fundamental Assumptions	The characteristics of the program that will stay the same, no matter what changes are made
9 Changes	The types of changes that have been made or are expected
10 Glossary	Most documentation is fraught with acronyms and technical terms. At first we prepared this guide for ourselves; as we learned the language, we retained it for newcomers.
11 Sources	Annotated list of documentation and personnel, indicating the types of questions each can answer

Fig. 1. A-7 Requirements table of contents.

at all, basing it on our experience with other software. Then we generated questions for the individual sections. Like any design effort, formulating questions requires iteration: we generated questions from common sense, organized them into forms, generated more questions by trying to fill in the blanks, and revised the forms.

2) *Separate concerns.* We used the principle of "separation of concerns" [3] to organize the document so that each project member could concentrate on a well-defined set of questions. This principle also serves the objective of making the document easy to change, since it causes changes to be well-confined. For example, hardware interfaces are described without making any assumptions about the purpose of the program; the hardware section would remain unchanged if the behavior of the program changed. The software behavior is described without any references to the details of the hardware devices; the software section would remain unchanged if data were received in different formats or over different channels.

3) *Be as formal as possible.* We avoided prose and developed formal ways to present information in order to be precise, concise, consistent, and complete.

The next two sections of the paper show how these principles are applied to describe the hardware interfaces and the software behavior.

V. TECHNIQUES FOR DESCRIBING HARDWARE INTERFACES

Organization by Data Item

To organize the hardware interfaces description, we have a separate unit, called a *data item*, for each input or output that changes value independently of other inputs or outputs. Examples of input data items include barometric altitude, radar-measured distance to a point on the ground, the setting of the inertial platform mode switch, and the inertial platform ready signal. Examples of output data items include coordinates for the flight path marker on the head-up display, radar antenna steering commands, and the signal that turns on and off the computer-failed light. The A-7 computer receives 70 input data items and transmits 95 output data items.

In order to have a consistent approach, we designed a form to be completed for each data item. We started with an initial set of questions that occurred to us as we read about the interfaces. How does the program read or write these data? What is the bit representation of the value? Can the computer tell whether a sensor value is valid? As we worked on specific data items, new questions occurred to us. We added these questions to the form, so that they would be addressed for all data items. The form is illustrated in Figs. 2 and 3 at the end of this section.

Symbolic Names for Data Items and Values

The hardware section captures two kinds of information about data items: *arbitrary details* that might change if a device were replaced with a similar device, and *essential characteristics* that would be shared by similar devices. The bit representation of a value is an arbitrary detail; the semantics of the value is an essential characteristic. For example, any barometric altitude sensor provides a reading from which barometric altitude can be calculated—this information is essential. But the resolution, representation, accuracy, and timing might differ between two types of barometric altitude sensors—this information is arbitrary.

Essential information must be expressed in such a way that the rest of the document can use it without referencing the arbitrary details. For example, each data item is given a mnemonic name, so that it can be identified unambiguously in the rest of the document without reference to instruction sequences or channel numbers. If a data item is not numerical and takes on a fixed set of possible values, the values are given mnemonic names so that they can be used without reference to bit encodings. For example, a switch might be able to take the values "on" and "off." The physical representation of the two values is arbitrary information that is not mentioned in the rest of the document in case it changes. The names allow the readers and writers of the rest of the document to ignore the physical details of input and output, and are more visually meaningful than the details they represent.

We bracket every mnemonic name in symbols indicating the item type, for example /input-data-items/, //output-data-items//, and $nonnumeric-values$. These brackets reduce confusion by identifying the item type unambiguously, so that the reader knows where to find the precise definition. Moreover, the brackets facilitate systematic cross referencing, either by people or computers.

Templates for Value Descriptions

The values of the numerical data items belong to a small set of value types, such as angles and distances. At first we described each data item in an ad hoc fashion, usually imitating the descriptions in the documents we referenced. But these documents were not consistent with each other and the descriptions were not always complete. We made great progress when we developed informal templates for the value descriptions, with blanks to be completed for specific data items. For example, the template for angles might read:

angle (?) is measured from line (?) to line (?) in the (?) direction, looking (?)

For example, magnetic heading is measured from the line from the aircraft to magnetic north to the horizontal component of the aircraft X axis, in the clockwise direction looking down.

Although templates were not used as hard-and-fast rules, their existence made values easier to describe, made the descriptions consistent with each other, and helped us apply the same standards of completeness to all items of the same type.

Input Data Items Described as Resources, Independent of Software Use

When describing input data items, we refrain from mentioning how or when the data is used by the software, to avoid making any assumptions about the software function. Instead, we describe the input data items as if taking inventory of the resources available to solve a problem. We define numerical values in terms of what they measure. For example, the value of the input data item called /RADALT/ is defined as the distance above local terrain as determined by the radar altimeter. Many nonnumerical inputs indicate switch positions; these are described without reference to the response the pilot expects when he changes the switch, since the response is accomplished by the software. For example, when the pilot changes the scale switch on the projected map display, he expects the map scale to change. Since the response is achieved by the software, it is not mentioned in the input data item description, which reads, *"/PMSCAL/ indicates the position of a two-position toggle switch on the projected map panel. This switch has no hardware effect on the projected map display."*

Example of an Input Data Item Description

Fig. 2 shows the completed form for a nonnumerical input data item. The underlined words are the form headings. Value encoding shows how the mnemonic value names used in the rest of the document are mapped into specific bit representations. "Switch nomenclature" indicates the names of the switch positions as seen by the pilot in the cockpit. Instruction sequence gives the TC-2 assembler language instructions that cause the data to be transmitted to or from the computer. We are not usurping the programmer's job by including the instruction sequence because there is no other way to read in this data item—the instruction sequence is not an implementation decision for the programmer. The channel number is a cross reference to the computer chapter where the general characteristics of the eight channels are described. Data representation shows the location of the value in the 16-bit input word. Notice how the Comments section defines the value assumed by the switch while the pilot is changing it. This is an example of a question we asked about all switches, once it had occurred to us about this one.

Output Data Items Described in Terms of Effects on External Hardware

Most output data items are described in terms of their effects on the associated devices. For example, the description of the output data items called //STEERAZ// and //STEEREL// shows how they are used to communicate the direction to point the antenna of the radar. This section does not explain how the software chooses the direction. For other output data items we define the value the peripheral device must receive in order to function correctly. For example, the description of the output data item called //FPANGL// shows that the radar assumes the value will be a certain angle which

Input Data Item: IMS Mode Switch

Acronym: /IMSMODE/

Hardware: Inertial Measurement Set

Description: /IMSMODE/ indicates the position of a six-position rotary switch on the IMS control panel.

Switch nomenclature: OFF; GND ALIGN; NORM; INERTIAL; MAG SL; GRID

Characteristics of Values

Value Encoding:		
	$Offnone$	(00000)
	$Gndal$	(10000)
	$Norm$	(01000)
	$Iner$	(00100)
	$Grid$	(00010)
	$Magsl$	(00001)

Instruction Sequence: READ 24   (Channel 0)

Data Representation: Bits 3-7

Comments: /IMSMODE/ = $Offnone$ when the switch is between two positions.

Fig. 2. Completed input data item form.

Output Data Item: Steering Error

Acronym: //STERROR//

Hardware: Attitude Direction Indicator (ADI)

Description: //STERROR// controls the position of the vertical needle on the ADI. A positive value moves the pointer to the right when looking at the display. A value of zero centers the needle.

Characteristics of Values

Unit: Degrees

Range: -2.5 to +2.5

Accuracy: + .1

Resolution: .00122

Instruction Sequence: WRITE 229   (Channel 7)
                      Test Carry Bit = 0 for request acknowledged
                      If not, restart

Data Representation: 11-bit two's complement number, bit 0 and bits 3-12
                     scale = 512/1.25 = 409.6
                     offset = 0

```
(   )        (              INDICATED VALUE                   )
___ Not used ___  ___ ___ ___ ___ ___ ___ ___ ___ ___   0   0   0
0    1    2    3    4    5    6    7    8    9   10   11   12   13   14   15
BIT
```

Timing Characteristics: Digital to DC voltage conversion. See Section 1.5.7.

Comments: The pointer hits a mechanical stop at + 2.5 degrees.

Fig. 3. Completed output data item form.

it uses to determine the climb or dive angle the aircraft should use during terrain following. We avoid giving any meaning to an output value that is not a characteristic of the hardware.

Example of an Output Data Item Description

Fig. 3 shows the completed form for a numerical output data item. Notice how the value is described in terms of its effect on a needle in a display, rather than in terms of what the needle is supposed to communicate to the pilot. The value is characterized by a standard set of parameters, such as range and resolution, which are used for all numerical data items. For Data representation, we show how the 16-bit output word is constructed, including which bits must be zero, which bits are ignored by the device, and which bits encode the out-

put value. Since the actual output value is not in any standard units of measurement, we also show how it can be derived from a value in standard units, in this case degrees. The relation between output values and values in standard units is given by the equation

output value = scale $\times$ (standard value + offset)

Since the same equation is used for all numerical data items, we need only provide the scale and offset values for a particular data item. Thus the output value for the data item //STERROR// in Fig. 3 is derived from a value in degrees by the following expression:

output value = 409.6 $\times$ (standard value + 0)

75

The Timing considerations section contains a pointer to another section; since many output data items have the same timing characteristics, we describe them once, and include cross references. The comment shows a physical limit of the device.

VI. Techniques for Describing Software Functions

Organization by Functions

We describe the software as a set of functions associated with output data items: each function determines the values for one or more output data items and each output data item is given values by exactly one function. Thus every function can be described in terms of externally visible effects. For example, the function calculating values for the output data item //STERROR// is described in terms of its effects on a needle in a display. The meaning conveyed to the pilot by the needle is expressed here.

This approach, identifying functions by working backward from output data items, works well because most A-7 outputs are specialized; most output data items are used for only a small set of purposes. The approach breaks down somewhat for a general-purpose device, such as a terminal, where the same data items are used to express many different types of information. We have one general-purpose device, the computer panel, where the same set of thirteen seven-segment displays can display many types of information, including present position, wind speed, and sensor status. We handled this situation by acting as if each type of information had its own panel, each controlled by a separate function. Thus, we have forty-eight panel functions, each described as if it always controlled a panel, and a set of rules to determine which function controls the real panel at any given moment. This approach, creating *virtual panels*, allows us to separate decisions about what the values are from decisions about when they are displayed. It also causes the description to be less dependent on the characteristics of the particular panel device than it otherwise would be.

Software functions are classified as either demand or periodic. A *demand function* must be requested by the occurrence of some event every time it is performed. For example, the computer-failed light is turned on by a demand function when a computer malfunction is detected. A *periodic function* is performed repeatedly without being requested each time. For example, the coordinates of symbols on the head-up display are updated by periodic functions. If a periodic function need not be performed all the time, it is started and stopped by specific events. For example, a symbol may be removed from the head-up display when a certain event occurs.

This distinction is useful because different performance and timing information is required for demand and periodic functions. To describe a demand function one must give the events that cause it to occur; an appropriate timing question is *"What is the maximum delay that can be tolerated between request and action?"* To describe a periodic function, one must give the events that cause it to start and stop and the

conditions that affect how it is performed after it is started; an appropriate timing question is *"What are the minimum and maximum repetition rates for this function?"*

Output Values as Functions of Conditions and Events

Originally we thought we would describe each output as a mathematical function of input values. This turned out to be a naive approach. We found we could seldom describe output values directly in terms of input values; instead we had to define intermediate values that the current program calculated, but that did not correspond to any output values. These in turn had to be described in terms of other intermediate values. By the time we reached input values, we would have described an implementation.

Instead, we expressed requirements by giving output values as functions of aircraft operating conditions. For example, the output data item named //LATGT70// should change value when the aircraft crosses 70° latitude; how the program detects this event is left to the implementation. In order to describe outputs in terms of aircraft operating conditions, we defined a simple language of conditions and events. *Conditions* are predicates that characterize some aspect of the system for a measurable period of time. For example, /IMSMODE/ = $Gndal$ is a condition that is true when the IMS mode switch in the cockpit is set to the GND ALIGN position (see Fig. 2). If a pilot expects a certain display whenever the switch is in this position, the function controlling the display is affected by the value of /IMSMODE/. An *event* occurs when the value of a condition changes from true to false or vice versa. Events therefore specify instants of time, whereas conditions specify intervals of time. Events start and stop periodic functions, and they trigger demand functions. Events provide a convenient way to describe functions where something is done when a button is first pushed, but not if the pilot continues to hold it down. Before we distinguished clearly between events and conditions, situations of this sort were very difficult to describe simply.

Consistent Notation for Aircraft Operating Conditions

Text Macros: To keep the function descriptions concise, we introduced over two hundred terms that serve as text macros. The terms are bracketed in exclamation points and defined in an alphabetical dictionary. A text macro can define a quantity that affects an output value, but that cannot be directly obtained from an input. An example is "!ground track angle!", defined as "the angle measured from the line from the aircraft to true north to !ground track!, measured clockwise looking down." Although the derivation of such values is left to the implementation, text macros provide a consistent, encapsulated means to refer to them while specifying function values.

Text macros also serve as abbreviations for compound conditions that are frequently used or very detailed. For example, !Desig! is a condition that is true when the pilot has performed a sequence of actions that designates a target to the computer. The list of events defining !Desig! appears only in the dictionary; while writing or reading the rest of the document, these events need not be considered. If designation procedures change, only the definition in the dictionary changes. Another example of a text macro for a compound condition is !IMS Reasonable!,[2] which represents the following bulky, specific condition:

!IMS total velocity! ⩽ 1440 fps AND
change of !IMS total velocity! from .2 seconds
ago ⩽ 50 fps

Even though this term is used many times in the function descriptions, only one place in the document need be changed if the reasonableness criteria change for the sensor.

The use of text macros is an application of stepwise refinement: while describing functions, we give names to complicated operating conditions or values, postponing the precise definitions. As the examples above show, we continue introducing new terms in the definitions themselves. This allows us to limit the amount of detail we deal with at one time. Furthermore, like the use of /, //, and $ brackets in the hardware descriptions, the use of ! brackets for text macros indicates to the reader that reference is being made to something that is defined precisely elsewhere. This reduces the risk of ambiguity that usually accompanies prose descriptions (e.g., !Desig! versus designated).

Conditions: We represent these predicates as expressions on input data items, for example, /IMSMODE/=$Gndal$, or expressions on quantities represented by text macros, for example, !ground track angle! = 30°. A condition can also be represented by a text macro, such as !IMS Reasonable!. Compound conditions can be composed by connecting simple conditions with the logical operators AND, OR, and NOT. For example, (!IMS Reasonable! AND /IMSMODE/=$Gndal$) is true only when both the component conditions are true.

Events: We use the notation @T(condition 1) to denote the occurrence of condition 1 becoming *true* and @F(condition 2) to denote the occurrence of condition 2 becoming *false.*

For example, the event @T(!ground track angle! < 30°) occurs when the !ground track angle! value crosses the 30° threshold from a larger value. The event @T(!ground track angle!=30°) occurs when the value reaches the 30° threshold from either direction. The event @T(/IMSMODE/ = $Gndal$) occurs when the pilot moves the switch to the GND ALIGN position. In some cases, an event only occurs if one condition changes when another condition is true, denoted by

@T(condition 3) WHEN (condition 4).

Thus, @T(/ACAIRB/=Yes) WHEN (/IMSMODE/=$Gndal$) refers to the event of the aircraft becoming airborne while the IMS mode switch is in the GND ALIGN position, while @T(/IMSMODE/=$Gndal$) WHEN (/ACAIRB/=Yes) refers to the event of the IMS mode being switched to GND ALIGN while the airplane is airborne.

---

[2] This text macro represents the condition that the values read from the inertial measurement set are reasonable; i.e., the magnitude of the aircraft velocity vector, calculated from inertial measurement set inputs, is less than or equal to 1440 feet per second and has changed less than 50 feet per second from the magnitude 0.2 seconds ago.

Using Modes to Organize and Simplify

Although each function is affected by only a small subset of the total set of conditions, we still need to organize conditions into groups in order to keep the function descriptions simple. To do this, we define *modes* or classes of system states. Because the functions differ more between modes than they do within a single mode, a mode-by-mode description is simpler than a general description. For example, by setting three switches, deselecting guns, and keying a single digit on the panel, the pilot can enter what is called the visual navigation update mode. In this mode, several displays and the radar are dedicated to helping him get a new position estimate by sighting off a local landmark. Thus the mode affects the correct behavior of the functions associated with these displays. The use of modes has an additional advantage: if something goes wrong during a flight, the pilot is much more likely when he makes the trouble report to remember the mode than the values of various conditions.

Each mode is given a short mnemonic name enclosed in asterisks, for example, *DIG* for Doppler-inertial-gyrocompassing navigation mode. The mode name is used in the rest of the document as an abbreviation for the conditions that are true whenever the system is in that mode.

The current mode is defined by the history of events that have occurred in the program. The document shows this by giving the initial mode and the set of events that cause transitions between any pair of modes. For example, the transition list includes the entry

DIG TO *DI*
@T(!latitude! > 70°)
@(/IMSMODE/=$Iner$) WHEN (!Doppler coupled!)

Thus the system will move from *DIG* mode to Doppler-inertial (*DI*) mode either if the aircraft goes above 70° latitude or if the inertial platform mode switch is changed to INERTIAL while the Doppler Radar is in use.

The table in Fig. 4 summarizes conditions that are true whenever the system is in a particular navigation mode. Thus in *DIG* mode the inertial platform mode switch is set to NORM, the aircraft is airborne, the latitude is less than 70°, and both the Doppler Radar and the inertial platform are functioning correctly. "X" table entries mean the value of that condition does not matter in that mode.

The mode condition tables are redundant because the information can be derived from the mode transition lists. However, the mode condition tables present the information in a more convenient form. Since the mode condition tables do not contain all the mode transition information, they do not uniquely define the current mode.

Special Tables for Precision and Completeness

In an early version of the document, function characteristics were described in prose; this was unsatisfactory because it was difficult to find answers to specific questions and because gaps and inconsistencies did not show up. We invented two types of tables that helped us express information precisely and completely.

MODE	/IMSMODE/	/ACAIRB/	!latitude!	Other
DIG	$Norm$	Yes	<70o	!IMS Up! AND !Doppler Up!
DI	$Norm$ OR $Iner$	Yes	<80o	!IMS Up! AND !Doppler Up! AND !Doppler Coupled!
I	$Iner$	X	<80o	!IMS Up!
IMS fail	X	X	X	!IMS Down!

Fig. 4. Section from the navigation mode condition table.

Condition Table: Magnetic heading (//MAGHDGH//) output values

MODES	CONDITIONS	
DIG, *DI*, *I* *Mag sl*,*Grid*	Always	X
IMS fail	(NOT /IMSMODE/=$Offnone$)	/IMSMODE/=$Offnone$
//MAGHDGH// value	angle defined by /MAGHCOS/ and /MAGHSIN/	0 (North)

Fig. 5. Example of a condition table.

Condition tables are used to define some aspect of an output value that is determined by an active mode and a condition that occurs within that mode. Fig. 5 gives an example of a condition table. Each row corresponds to a group of one or more modes in which this function acts alike. The rows are mutually exclusive; only one mode affects the function at a time. In each row are a set of mutually exclusive conditions; exactly one should be true whenever the program is in the modes denoted by the row. At the bottom of the column is the information appropriate for the interval identified by the mode-condition intersection. Thus to find the information appropriate for a given mode and given condition, first find the row corresponding to the mode, find the condition within the row, and follow that column to the bottom of the table. An "X" instead of a condition indicates that information at the bottom of the column is never appropriate for that mode.

In Fig. 5, the magnetic heading value is 0 when the system is in mode *IMS fail* and the condition (/IMSMODE/=$Offnone$) is true. Whenever the system is in *IMS fail* mode, the following condition is true, showing that the row is complete,

(/IMSMODE/=$Offnone$ OR(NOT /IMSMODE/=$Offnone$))

and the following statement is false, showing the row entries are mutually exclusive.

(/IMSMODE/=$Offnone$ AND(NOT/IMSMODE/=$Offnone$))

Condition tables are used in the descriptions of periodic functions. Periodic functions are performed differently in differ-

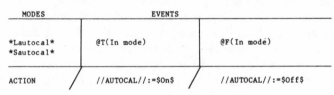

Event table : When AUTOCAL Light Switched on/off

MODES	EVENTS	
Lautocal *Sautocal*	@T(In mode)	@F(In mode)
ACTION	//AUTOCAL//:=On	//AUTOCAL//:=Off

Fig. 6. Example of an event table.

ent time intervals; the appropriate time interval is determined by the prevailing mode and conditions. Each row in the table completely characterizes the intervals within a mode that are meaningful for that function. The conditions must be mutually exclusive, and together they must describe the entire time the program is within the mode. These characteristics ensure that condition tables be complete, that is, all relevant intervals are indicated. They also ensure that condition tables be unambiguous, that is, given the aircraft operating conditions, the correct interval can be determined.

Event tables show when demand functions should be performed or when periodic functions should be started or stopped. Each row in an event table corresponds to a mode or group of modes. Table entries are events that cause an action to be taken when the system is in a mode associated with the row. The action to be taken is given at the bottom of the column.

The event table in Fig. 6 specifies that the autocalibration light controlled by output data item //AUTOCAL// be turned

Modes in which function required:
Lautocal, *Sautocal*, *Landaln*, *SINSaln*, *HUDaln*, *Airaln*

Output data item: //IMSSCAL//

Function Request and Output Description:

Event Table: When the Scale Factor Is Changed

MODES	EVENTS	
Lautocal *Landaln*	@T(In mode) WHEN (//IMSSCAL//=$Coarse$)	X
HUDaln	@T(In mode) WHEN (/IMSMODE/ = $Gndal$ AND //IMSSCAL//=$Coarse$)	@T(In mode) WHEN (NOT (/IMSMODE/=$Gndal$) AND //IMSSCAL//=$Fine$)
Sautocal *SINSaln* *Airaln*	X	@T(In mode) WHEN (//IMSSCAL//=$Fine$)
ACTION	//IMSSCAL//:=$Fine$	//IMSSCAL//:=$Coarse$

Fig. 7. Completed demand function form.

Periodic function name: Update Flight Path Marker coordinates

Modes in which function required:
DIG, *DI*, *I*, *Mag Sl*, *Grid*, *IMS fail*

Output Data Items: //FPMAZ//, //FPMEL//

Initiation and Termination Events:
Start: @T(//HUDVEL// = On)
Stop: @T(//HUDVEL// = Off)

Output description:

The Flight Path Marker (FPM) symbol on the head-up display shows the direction of the aircraft velocity vector. If the aircraft is moving straight ahead from the nose of the aircraft, the FPM is centered on the display. The horizontal displacement from display center shows the lateral velocity component and elevation displacement shows the vertical velocity component.

Although the means for deriving Flight Path Marker position varies as shown in the table below, the position is usually derived from the current !System velocities!. The velocities are first resolved into forward, lateral, and vertical components. Then FPM coordinates are derived in the following manner:

//FPMAZ// shows $\dfrac{\text{Lateral velocity}}{\text{Forward velocity}}$ //FPMEL// shows $\dfrac{\text{Vertical velocity}}{\text{Forward velocity}}$

Condition Table: Coordinates of the Flight Path Marker

MODES	CONDITIONS		
DIG, *DI*	X	Always	X
I	/ACAIRB/ = No	/ACAIRB/ = Yes	X
Mag sl, *Grid*	/ACAIRB/=No	!ADC Up! AND /ACAIRB/=Yes	!ADC Down! AND /ACAIRB/=Yes
IMS fail	/ACAIRB/=No	X	/ACAIRB/=Yes
FPM COORDINATES	//FPMAZ//:= 0 //FPMEL//:= 0	based on !System velocities!	//FPMAZ//:= 0 //FPMEL//:=/AOA/

Fig. 8. Completed periodic function form.

on when the two listed modes are entered and off when they are exited. We use the symbol ":=" to denote assignment. The event @T(In mode) occurs when all the conditions represented by the mode become true, i.e., when the mode is entered. @F(In mode) occurs when any one of the conditions represented by the mode becomes false, i.e., when the system changes to a different mode.

Function Description Examples

Figs. 7 and 8 illustrate the forms we created for demand and periodic functions, respectively. All function descriptions indicate the associated output data items, thereby providing a cross reference to the hardware description. The list of modes gives the reader an overview of when the function is performed; the overview is refined in the rest of the description.

The event table in Fig. 7 shows both the events that request the function and the values output by the function at different times. For example, if the //IMSSCAL// value is $Coarse$ when the *Landaln* mode is entered, the function assigns it the value $Fine$. Notice how the table uses the symbolic names introduced in the hardware section for data items and data item values.

In Fig. 8 the initiation and termination section gives the events that cause this periodic function to start and stop. This function starts when another output data item, //HUDVEL//, is assigned the value On, and stops when //HUDVEL// is assigned the value Off. The function positions a symbol on a display device. The position of the symbol usually represents the direction of the aircraft velocity vector, but under some conditions the output data items are given other values. The output description consists of two parts: a brief prose description of the usual meaning of the symbol and a condition table that shows what will happen under different conditions. Notice that every mode in the mode list is accounted for in the table. The relevant conditions for this function are !ADC Up! or !ADC Down!, (the operating status of the air data computer sensor which provides a measurement of true airspeed) and /ACAIRB/= Yes and /ACAIRB/=No (whether the aircraft is airborne). Thus, if the system is in the inertial mode (*I*) and the aircraft is not airborne (/ACAIRB/=No is true), both coordinates of the symbol are set to zero.

VII. TECHNIQUES FOR SPECIFYING UNDESIRED EVENTS

Lists of Undesired Events

In order to characterize the desired response of the system when undesired events occur, we started with a list of undesired events and interviewed pilots and maintenance programmers to find out both what they would like to have happen and what they considered feasible. The key was the list of possible undesired events. To derive this list, we used the classification scheme shown in Fig. 9 as a guide.

For example, in the class "Resource failure—temporary," we include the malfunctioning of each sensor since the sensors tend to resume correct functioning; in the class "Resource failure—permanent," we include the loss of areas of memory.

VIII. TECHNIQUES FOR CHARACTERIZING TYPES OF CHANGES

In order to characterize types of changes, we looked through a file of change requests and interviewed the maintainers. To define requirements for a new system, we would have looked at change requests for similar systems. We also made a long list of fundamental assumptions that we thought would always be true about the system, no matter what. In a meeting with several maintenance system engineers and programmers, all but four of the fundamental assumptions were rejected; each rejected assumption was moved to the list of possible changes! For example, the following assumption is true about the cur-

```
1 Resource Failure
    1.1 Temporary
    1.2 Permanent
2 Incorrect input data
    2.1 Detected by examining input only
    2.2 Detected by comparison with internal data
    2.3 Detected by user realizing he made a mistake
    2.4 Detected by user from incorrect output
3 Incorrect internal data
    3.1 Detected by internal inconsistency
    3.2 Detected by comparison with input data
    3.3 Detected by user from incorrect output
```

Fig. 9. Undesired event classification derived from Parnas [19].

rent program, but may change in the future: "The computer will perform weapon release calculations for only one target at a time. When a target is designated, the previously designated target is forgotten." By writing two complementary lists—possible changes and fundamental assumptions—we thought about the problem from two directions, and we detected many misunderstandings. Producing a list of fundamental assumptions forced us to voice some implicit assumptions, so that we discovered possible changes we would have omitted otherwise. One reason for the success of this procedure is that it is much easier for a reviewer to recognize an error than an omission.

Listed below are examples of feasible changes.

1) Assignment of devices to channels may be changed.

2) The rate of symbol movement on the display in response to joystick displacement might be changed.

3) New sensors may be added. (This has occurred already in the history of the program.)

4) Future weapons may require computer control after release.

5) Computer self-test might be required in the air (at present it is only required on the ground).

6) It may be necessary to cease certain lower priority functions to free resources for higher priority functions during stress moments. (At present the program halts if it does not have sufficient time to perform all functions, assuming a program error.)

IX. DISCUSSION

We expect the document to be kept up-to-date as the program evolves because it is useful in many ways that are independent of our project. The maintainers of the current program plan to use it to train new maintenance personnel, since it presents the program's purpose in a consistent, systematic way. It is the only complete, up-to-date description of their hardware interfaces. One of the problems they now face when making changes is that they cannot tell easily if there are other places in the code that should be changed to preserve consistency. For example, they changed the code in one place to turn on a display when the target is twenty-two nautical miles away; in another place, the display is still turned on when the target is twenty nautical miles away. The unintended two-nautical-mile difference causes no major problems, but it adds unnecessary complexity for the pilot and the programmer. Inconsistencies such as this show up conspicuously in the function tables in our document. Besides using the document to check the implications of small changes, the maintenance staff want to modify it to document the next version of the program. They expect major benefits as they prepare system tests, since the document provides a description of acceptable program behavior that is independent of the program. In the past, testers have had to infer what the program is supposed to do by looking at the code. Finally they also intend to derive test cases systematically from the tables and mode transition charts.

The usefulness of these ideas is not limited to existing programs. They could be used during the requirements definition phase for a new product in order to record decisions for easy retrieval, to check new decisions for consistency with previously made decisions, and to suggest questions that ought to be considered. However, a requirements document for a new system would not be as specific as our document. We can describe acceptable behavior exactly because all the decisions about the external interfaces have been made. For a new program a requirements document describes a set of possible behaviors, giving the characteristics that distinguish acceptable from unacceptable behavior. The system designer chooses the exact behavior for the new product. The questions are the same for a new system; the answers are less restrictive. For example, where we give a specific number for the accuracy of an input, there might be a range of acceptable accuracy values for a new program.

X. Conclusions

The requirements document for the A-7 program demonstrates that a substantial system can be described in terms of its external stimuli and its externally visible behavior. The techniques discussed in this paper guided us in obtaining information, helped us to control its complexity, and allowed us to avoid dealing with implementation details. The document gives a headstart on the design phase of our project. Many questions are answered precisely that usually would be left to programmers to decide or to discover as they build the code. Since the information is expressed systematically, we can plan for it systematically, instead of working each detail into the program in an ad hoc fashion.

All of the techniques described in this paper are based on three principles: formulate questions before trying to answer them, separate concerns, and use precise notation. From these principles we developed a disciplined approach including the following techniques:

symbolic names for data items and values
special brackets to indicate type of name
templates for value descriptions
standard forms
inputs described as resources
outputs described in terms of effects
demand versus periodic functions
output values given as functions of conditions and events
consistent notation for conditions and events
modes for describing equivalence classes of system states
special tables for consistency and completeness checking

undesired event classification
complementary lists of changes and fundamental assumptions.

This paper is only an introduction to the ideas that are illustrated in the requirements document [5]. The document is a fully worked-out example; no details have been left out to simplify the problem. Developing and applying the techniques required approximately seventeen man-months of effort. The document is available to anyone interested in pursuing the ideas. Most engineering is accomplished by emulating models. We believe that our document is a good model of requirements documentation.

Acknowledgment

The techniques described in this paper were developed by the author together with D. Parnas, J. Shore, and J. Kallander. The author thanks E. Britton, H. S. Elovitz, D. Parnas, J. Shore, and D. Weiss for their careful and constructive reviews of the manuscript.

References

[1] P. Brinch Hansen, *Operating Systems Principles*. Englewood Cliffs, NJ: Prentice-Hall, 1973.
[2] E. W. Dijkstra, "Co-operating sequential processes," in *Programming Languages*, F. Genuys, Ed. New York: Academic, 1968, pp. 43–112.
[3] —, *A Discipline of Programming*. Englewood Cliffs, NJ: Prentice-Hall, 1977.
[4] J. V. Guttag, "Abstract data types and the development of data structures," *Commun. Ass. Comput. Mach.*, vol. 20, pp. 396–404, June 1976.
[5] K. Heninger, J. Kallander, D. L. Parnas, and J. Shore, *Software Requirements for the A-7E Aircraft*, Naval Res. Lab., Washington, DC, Memo Rep. 3876, Nov. 27, 1978.
[6] C. A. R. Hoare, "Monitors: An operating system structuring concept," *Commun. Ass. Comput. Mach.*, vol. 17, pp. 549–557, Oct. 1974.
[7] J. Howard, "Proving monitors," *Commun. Ass. Comput. Mach.*, vol. 19, pp. 273–279, May 1976.
[8] R. Lipton, *On Synchronization Primitive Systems*, Ph.D. dissertation, Carnegie-Mellon Univ., Pittsburgh, PA, 1973.
[9] B. Liskov and S. Zilles, "Specification techniques for data abstractions," *IEEE Trans. Software Eng.*, vol. SE-1, pp. 7–19, Mar. 1975.
[10] B. Liskov and V. Berzins, "An appraisal of program specifications," in *Proc. Conf. on Research Directions in Software Technology*, Oct. 10–12, 1977, pp. 13.1–13.24.
[11] D. L. Parnas, "Information distribution aspects of design methodology," in *Proc. Int. Fed. Inform. Processing Congr.*, Aug. 1971, vol. TA-3.
[12] —, "On the criteria to be used in decomposing systems into modules," *Commun. Ass. Comput. Mach.*, vol. 15, pp. 1053–1058, Dec. 1972.
[13] D. L. Parnas and G. Handzel, *More on Specification Techniques for Software Modules*, Fachbereich Informatik, Technische Hochschule Darmstadt, Darmstadt, W. Germany, 1975.
[14] D. L. Parnas and H. Würges, "Response to undesired events in software systems," in *Proc. 2nd Int. Conf. Software Eng.*, 1976, pp. 437–446.
[15] D. L. Parnas, *Use of Abstract Interfaces in the Development of Software for Embedded Computer Systems*, Naval Res. Lab., Washington, DC, Rep. 8047, 1977.
[16] —, "The use of precise specifications in the development of software," in *Proc. Int. Fed. Inform. Processing Congr.*, 1977.
[17] —, "Designing software for ease of extension and contraction," in *Proc. 3rd Int. Conf. Software Eng.*, May 1978.
[18] D. L. Parnas and K. Heninger, "Implementing processes in HAS," in *Software Engineering Principles*, Naval Res. Lab., Washington, DC, course notes, 1978, Document HAS.9.

[19] D. L. Parnas, "Desired system behavior in undesired situations," in *Software Engineering Principles*, Naval Res. Lab., Washington, DC, course notes, 1978, Document UE.1.

[20] O. Roubine and L. Robinson, *SPECIAL Reference Manual*, Stanford Res. Inst., Menlo Park, CA, SRI Tech. Rep. CSL-45, SRI project 4828, 3rd ed., 1977.

[21] A. C. Shaw, *The Logical Design of Operating Systems*. Englewood Cliffs, NJ: Prentice-Hall, 1974.

[22] D. M. Weiss, *The MUDD Report: A Case Study of Navy Software Development Practices*, Naval Res. Lab., Washington, DC, Rep. 7909, 1975.

Kathryn L. Heninger received the B.A. degree in English from Stanford University, Stanford, CA, in 1972, the M.S.L.S. degree in library science in 1975 and the M.S. degree in computer science in 1977, both from the University of North Carolina, Chapel Hill.

She is presently a Computer Scientist for the Information Systems Staff at the Naval Research Laboratory, Washington, DC. Her research interests include program design methodologies and parallel processing.

Introduction

Parikh, G. "Structured maintenance: the Warnier/Orr way." *Computerworld* (September 21, 1981), IN DEPTH section.

"Warnier/Orr" is a term made from the names of a Frenchman, Jean-Dominique Warnier, and an American, Ken Orr. Of all the modern software engineering technologies, the Warnier/Orr methodology has had the most influence in maintenance. The next two articles, by Parikh and Higgins, respectively, demonstrate and explain the Warnier/Orr methodology in the analysis and modification of existing programs. In Part IV, Warnier himself describes the methodology as applied to the reliability and maintenance of large ongoing systems.

The Warnier/Orr methodology, also known as Data Structured Systems Development (DSSD™), provides a framework for the analysis and synthesis of systems. It is output-oriented; that is, it derives the structure of the system from the structure of its outputs. It primarily uses a single diagramming technique that portrays control flow, data structure, and system function with the same notation.

Preeminence of the Warnier/Orr methodology in the maintenance field is due to several reasons.

- It provides support not only for designing structured systems, but also for disentangling unstructured ones as well.

- Warnier has worked long enough with the methodology to follow his clients into the maintenance phase.

- Warnier recognized in the early 1970's that most of his pupils "work on the modification and correction of existing programs." To help these pupils he wrote the world's first book on software maintenance, *Program modification*, published in French in 1975 and in English in 1978 (Martinus Nijhoff Social Sciences Division, Boston).

- Three leading American-based practitioners in the maintenance field—Orr, Higgins, and Parikh—recommend his methodologies (among others). (Incidentally, Orr's company, Ken Orr & Associates, held the first conference on maintenance in October 1981 in conjunction with the Data Structured Systems Development User's Conference. The Warnier paper in Part IV was delivered at that conference.)

In *A powerful structured tool: the Warnier-Orr diagram* (Shetal Enterprises, 1980), Parikh gives the following account of how he became a believer.

> Not so long ago, I started to design the batch part of a claims system for an insurance company. The requirements, written in narrative English, were voluminous and ambiguous. The required inputs, and the necessary processes, were not clear. Not knowing where and how to begin, I was terribly depressed and about to give up.
>
> Then on Friday I took home the book *Structured systems development* by Kenneth T. Orr (Yourdon Press, 1979). Once I started reading, I couldn't put it down, and read almost the whole night. During the weekend I almost finished it.
>
> On Monday, I returned to work, confident, and knowing exactly where to start. Fortunately, the systems requirements included the detailed descriptions of outputs. I started working from the outputs using the Warnier-Orr diagram. Following the guidelines given in the book, I completed the initial design in a few days.
>
> Later I converted the design documentation to HIPO, the installation standard. The conversion was easy, and in addition, provided an additional check on the design.
>
> The system has been in production for several months and is working well.

After the system became operational, Parikh continued to use the Warnier/Orr diagram for designing major modifications. The diagram proved to be a precise and effective tool for enhancements as well. The modified programs worked on the second or third test.

In the following paper, Parikh outlines the history of the Warnier/Orr methodology, gives the basics of its use, suggests its applicability in the maintenance environment, and includes a case history. Unfortunately, most authors of books on maintenance do not mention Warnier, let alone cover his work. This is like writing a book on physics without mentioning Newton!

STRUCTURED MAINTENANCE

THE WARNIER/ORR WAY

Jean-Dominique Warnier

By Girish Parikh

© Copyright 1981 by Girish Parikh. Portions of this article are excerpted from the report "A Powerful Structured Tool: The Warnier-Orr Diagram" by Girish Parikh. The report is available for $12 (prepaid) from Shetal Enterprises, Dept. CW-IEEE, 1787 B West Touhy, Chicago, Ill. 60626. Material from this article also appears in the author's book, The Guide to Software Maintenance, *to be published by Little, Brown and Company.*

S oftware maintenance consumes two-thirds (67%) of a life cycle; only 33% is development. Most DP organizations spend more than 50% of their budgets on maintenance and most programmers devote 50%, and in some cases 80%, of their time to maintenance. The budgets for maintenance will keep on growing and may reach 60% by 1985 as we continue to add new code to the existing inventory.

Emerging and now rapidly spreading structured methodologies (structured analysis, structured design, structured programming and related productivity techniques) claim to produce more maintainable systems.

However, most work in these methodologies has been done in the front-end area of development. To my knowledge, no one except Warnier (and to some extent Warnier/Orr and Jackson methodologies) has yet provided guidelines for maintaining structured systems.

Some of the structured techniques can also be applied to maintain existing systems. The Warnier/Orr methodology and especially the powerful Warnier/Orr diagram have been used successfully for modifying and documenting existing systems.

The Warnier/Orr methodology, described later, is an offshoot of Warnier's Logical Construction of Programs (LCP) and Logical Construction of Systems (LCS).

Jean-Dominique Warnier of CII Honeywell Bull, France, is one of the original inventors of structured programming ideas. He is especially noted for developing the data-driven program and system design concepts.

In the late 1960s, he completed development of a procedural method of designing programs, the Logical Construction of Programs (LCP). Warnier later developed the method of designing systems, theLogical Construction of Systems (LCS). The concepts of his methods are based largely on set theory and Boolean algebra. He invented the Warnier diagram, the principal designing tool of his methodologies.

Warnier is deeply concerned with change — the modification of programs and systems. In his book

Program Modification he shows exactly how to do modifications of LCP programs. It is intriguing to know there is a way to do modifications correctly without upsetting the original structure of a program. Moreover, the documentation is also updated in the process, reflecting the changes in the program.

Warnier provides steps for converting an unstructured program to an LCP program in his book *Logical Construction of Programs*.

In the following interview, Warnier answers several questions regarding LCP/LCS and program modification:

How effective are the program modification techniques? Do they always work?

The program modification techniques work except when the set of logical sequences is not correctly defined — for example, if empty sets are neglected. Sometimes the modifications are so important that it seems better to build a new program.

[Empty sets included in a design and coded in a pro-

gram make future modifications easier. The concept of empty sets and its value are discussed later.]

Do programmers find modification work interesting or boring?

Programmers find modifications interesting on the conditions that they have to modify good LCP programs and they have learned how to modify a program.

Has much conversion work (existing programs to LCP) has been done?

Many conversion works have been done in many DP centers in many countries and we have no means to measure the result. In 1974, a French company converted 150 programs. The builder of the new computer had planned 450 days on programming and 450 hours on the computer for testing and debugging the programs. When all the programs worked on the new computer, only 150 days for programming and 75 hours on the computer had been used.

What effect does LCS have on modification and maintenance?

The effect of LCS on modification and maintenance is very important because the LCS systems make the technical organization of the data easy to change.

What is the user experience in modifying and maintaining LCP and LCS systems and programs?

The user's experience in modifying LCP and LCS systems and programs is very satisfying, but in many companies staff turnover is too important to ensure the continuity. For that reason, many good systems and programs are built, destroyed and rebuilt. It's more a problem of management and training than a technical one.

Has any automation been done for LCP/LCS procedures? For modification and documentation procedures?

We have a long-range plan

Kenneth T. Orr

to produce in my section software for modification and documentation procedures. The first step concerns the documentation of the DP system. For this first step, the LCS design was completed last February [1980] and half of the programs work.

What is the future? What will be the effect on the Warnier/Orr methodology?

I think our methodology is a powerful one, but the use of a powerful tool could be true or wrong according to the goals sought.

Warnier/Orr Methodology

According to American systems scientist Kenneth T. Orr (of Ken Orr & Associates in Topeka, Kan.), one of the important elements of Warnier's work is the difference between the contents and the container. If the container — the design — is sound,

---

Case Study

Michael E. Coleman of Aetna Bearing Co., Chicago, chose Warnier/Orr diagrams for redevelopment. Here in his words is the logic behind his choice:

All 750 programs of Aetna Bearing Co.'s Data Processing Department must be redeveloped because we are converting from a Singer System 10 to an IBM System 38. The language utilized by the Singer is not compatible with an Ansi-standard language. Also, there are vast architectural differences between the machines that will produce a change in the logic of the program.

Our current system of development is unstructured. Usually, the programmer is given a rough description or a problem and begins coding immediately. Corrective iterations performed while writing the code often result in the omission of items and valuable time is lost. If this method were to continue, redevelopment would be long and tedious.

Theoretically, the method used should rely on available documentation, but in this situation no documentation standards had ever been established. Each program has comments and some narratives are available but not very reliable. File layouts exist for every file. The key factors of cost and learning time must also be considered since the manpower of the department is limited.

Thus, a logical solution would be to utilize current inputs and outputs to produce the new design. Warnier/Orr diagrams, which are data driven, were chosen because they meet many of the department's current requirements as well as those of the new data base-driven computer.

While the system design is being developed, structured code can be introduced at the same time. The three basic control structures are used

and "GOTOs" disappear because they are designed out. (See "A Powerful Structured Tool: The Warnier/Orr Diagram," Girish Parikh, Shetal Enterprises, Chicago, 1980.) The condensability of Warnier/Orr diagrams eliminates mounds of paperwork and lengthy narratives and ensures proper documentation at implementation.

Warnier/Orr diagramming can be cost-effective to implement. It is a straightforward method, that one can learn on his own by practice. Once the technique is learned, it can be applied to activities, functions or file layouts. Equally important, the diagrams can be understood by the users in the departments supported by data processing. Also, information regarding Warnier/Orr diagramming is readily available which, therefore, makes it Aetna's preferred choice.

the contents — the program — can be changed or modified easily. Thus, Warnier has done profound work in data-driven design methodologies and his work on program and system modifications will have a farreaching impact.

Orr and his colleagues added to the LCP notation developed by Warnier. The Warnier/Orr methodology helps design systems, programs, data files and even manual procedures. It usually consumes more time in requirements analysis and design, but the coding and testing time and subsequent maintenance costs and efforts are considerably reduced.

After some practice, Warnier/Orr diagrams, the heart of the methodology, are surprisingly easy to read and use. They clearly show the hierarchy of the system. This improves communication among all involved. The hierarchical and symmetrical nature of the diagram makes the logical errors easy to spot. The Warnier/Orr diagrams will be dealt with in more detail below.

Design Phase

The output-oriented Warnier/Orr methodology starts with output definition. Using the Warnier/Orr diagramming technique, the designer then decomposes the outputs into individual data items. Thus a data control structure is developed from which program control structure is derived. The next steps refine and verify the design.

In the next step, time sequencing is studied. Using the Warnier/Orr diagram, the scheduling of the user-defined outputs is done into the processing cycles, such as annually, quarterly, monthly, weekly and daily. This step ensures that the needed inputs are available at the right time for each processig cycle.

Then comes the "change analysis." The question, "What real-world event could cause this item to change?" should be asked for every input item. If the changes cannot be incorporated into the design, then the design should be done again up to this stage. In addition, changes in the processing cycles should be considered at this time.

Finally, using the data diagrams already developed, the program structure is derived.

More details on the Warnier/Orr methodology may be gleaned from Orr's books *Structured Systems Development* (published by Yourdon, Inc.) and *Structured Requirements Definition* (published by Ken Orr & Associates), as well as from David A. Higgins' *Program Design and Construction* (published by Prentice-Hall).

Warnier/Orr Diagram

The Warnier/Orr diagram is a graphic design and documentation tool that has been called a "little giant" of the structured revolution. It is an extremely powerful tool for designing modifications and also for documenting existing systems. Let us take a closer look at the components of the diagram:

The Warnier/Orr diagram provides a formal method of hierarchic decomposition of entries. The entries may consist of activities, functions or data elements. For a particular decomposition, all the entries must be of the same type.

The Warnier/Orr diagram also includes a sequence of events or flow of control, and the basic structures of structured programming (sequence, alternation and repetition). The conventional hierarchy chart does not show the relationship between various functions.

The Warnier/Orr diagram shows the hierarchical structure as well as the process flow (where, when and how many times an event occurs). How does it show all this?

The events occur in the sequence from left to right and top to bottom for each column (beginning from the left). The symbols in the parentheses below the names of each item in the diagram show the number of times that item occurs. The brackets enclose logically related operations. The hierarchy is also from left to right, which can be observed by turning a Warnier/Orr diagram 90° clockwise.

Following are symbols and their meanings, when listed below a function:

(N): The function is executed N times, where "N" is a variable. A meaningful variable is usually chosen. For example, PRINT POLICIES (P), means execute the "PRINT POLICIES" function (P) times for P number of policies.

Note that "N" could be zero. This notation provides DOWHILE structure.

For a DOWHILE structure, Warnier provides a better structure in his book *Logical Construction of Programs* (published by Van Nostrand Reinhold Co.) making the future modifications easier:

"If a set of data is present A times in a set D and if A can be 0," Warnier states, "the hierarchical organization of the data can then be described as follows:

D $\left\{\begin{array}{l} \text{Group A} \\ \text{(0 or 1 times)} \end{array}\right.$ $\left\{\begin{array}{l} \text{Batch of data} \\ \text{(A times)} \end{array}\right.$

When "N" is not a variable, but a fixed number, for example 12 — representing the months in a year — it can be expressed as "(12)" if iteration is to be done 12 times; otherwise, the notation would be "(0,12)." If a function is executed only once, "(1)" is usually omitted.

(0,1): The function is executed zero to one times, depending on whether the function has not been selected or has been selected at this point. This notation provides the alternation (or selection) structure (in conjunction with the exclusive OR symbol "θ" explained later). The case structure is a "generalized" alternation with more than two cases to consider.

(1,t): The function is to be executed at least once, and possibly (t) times. When t is a fixed number, such as 12 months in a year, "(1,12)" can be used, meaning one to 12 times. This notation provides the DOUNTIL structure.

θ: This symbol appears between the names of two (or more) functions and signifies exclusive choice between two or more functions. It is used in conjunction with "(0,1)" notation, and means one or the other, but not both.

With the above notations, the three basic constructs of structured programming — sequence, alternation and iteration (both DOWHILE and DOUNTIL) — and the additional case structure are added to the hierarchical diagram, providing order and logic and making it comprehensive. In case of iterations, it also tells (using a variable or a constant) how many iterations.

+: Inclusive OR — that is, one or the other or both. (This symbol is also used for concurrency.)

Note that for most applications, exclusive OR and sequential operations are sufficient.

——— : Appears above the name (of a function) and means not. For example, $\overline{\text{EQUAL}}$ means NOT equal.

The following are conventions: Each function comprises the subfunctions "Begin" (initialize, open files and so on), "Process" and "End" (such as close files and print totals). The subsequent functions are decomposed in a similar fashion ("Begin," "Process," "End").

This structure of functions is based on the fact that logically certain events can happen at the beginning of the functions, while others take place in the processing and the remaining occur at the end. (This struc-

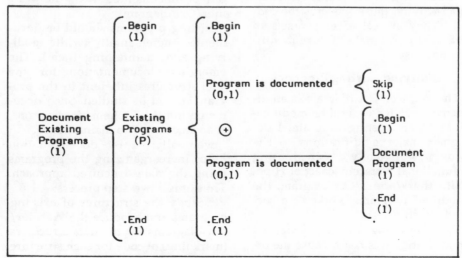

Warnier/Orr Diagram for a Manual Procedure
(Document Existing Programs)

89

ture also makes the future maintenance and modification of the program easy.)

An example of a Warnier/Orr diagram is shown in the accompanying figure, depicting a manual procedure familiar to us!

The Maintenance Problem

There are two aspects of the maintenance problem: One is dealing with the existing, mostly unstructured or semistructured code. The second aspect is maintaining the structure of the structured systems while modifying and maintaining them.

The first aspect, already critical, is likely to become more severe as we keep adding new code (structured, it is to be hoped) to the inventory and do not replace the old code. The acute shortage of resources prevents the early redevelopment of existing code. The old code generally works; however, modifying and maintaining it is usually a problem.

The Warnier/Orr methodology and the diagram can help solve both aspects of the maintenance problem.

The Warnier/Orr methodology is for effective, efficient and economical development, as well as for change and redevelopment — that is, maintenance.

Because of the structure provided by the Warnier/Orr methodology to new programs (and enhancements to existing programs), modifications are easier. The symmetry of programs make missing elements easier to spot. Each bracket of the Warnier/Orr diagram has "Begin" "Process" and "End." Even if nothing is to be done in "Begin" or "End" in a particular activity, those sets must be coded. (They are called empty sets in this case.) This makes future modifications easy.

Modifying Existing Programs

The Warnier/Orr diagram is an effective tool for designing modifications to an existing program. I designed major modifications to the programs originally designed, using a functional hierarchy chart of Hipo. With the Warnier/Orr diagram, the modified programs worked on second effective tests.

The designing for the proposed modification was fast because the diagrams were easy to draw and needed very little writing. Alternate designs were done on paper,

preventing costly alterations during or after coding. The evaluation of alternate designs was easy because they were compact and precise.

After the design decision was made, transferring it to code was a relatively simple process.

Documenting Existing Systems

Orr, in his article "Warnier/Orr Technology and Systems Maintenance" (from "Futures," a quarterly newsletter published by Ken Orr & Associates, Vol. 3, No. 2), gives the following guidelines for documenting existing systems with the Warnier/Orr diagram.

The Warnier/Orr diagram has been used successfully to document existing systems. The "in-out" or "assembly line" version of the diagram is used. Systems are often easier to document at the top. It is simpler to document at the procedure and program level than it is below. Make the first cut at process documentation.

The first cut at data documentation might be to develop Warnier/Orr diagrams of the major data files or data bases within the system. Diagrams should be done strictly from a logical standpoint. By documenting the data files, it is possible to come up with a dictionary/directory describing what data exists and where it is used.

The long-term goal in structured maintenance is to replace the existing system over time, piece by piece from the output back.

Documenting Existing Programs

It has been found that any program can be documented with the Warnier/Orr diagram.

Existing programs should be documented incrementally (while modifying and maintaining them). The emerging documentation for the data structures inherent in the program should be studied. Such documentation, like schematic diagrams, is a valuable aid to maintenance.

Eventually, this documentation helps in reorganizing the programs using the data-structured approach. Thus, it is a two-step process:

1. Study the structures of existing programs and produce the Warnier/Orr diagrams for the data structures (mark lines of code for each structure in the existing program). This diagram is useful in current maintenance and enhancement work.

2. Use the Warnier/Orr diagrams to redesign and rewrite the programs incrementally.

Maintenance Improved?

Jim Hanna of the Office of the Administration for the Courts, State of Washington, studied the program maintenance histories to find out whether structured systems continue to be "better" systems after they become operational. He found too many variables to be able to draw conclusions.

However, one aspect intrigued him. All programs had been developed using structured techniques, yet some required considerably more time to maintain than others.

On further analysis, Hanna found that among the structured programs, the traditional structured programs (programs developed top-down, consisting of modules with limited entry and exit points and using structured code) required highest maintenance.

But the traditional structured programs were better than the unstructured ones. In the former, the amount of coupling between the components was reduced, cutting down maintenance. However, the effect of binding between the program structure and data structure remained unaffected.

The second group of programs used the structured techniques (mentioned earlier), and were data structured according to the Warnier/Orr technique. They required less maintenance than the first group; however, changes to the data structure to meet changes to requirements increased maintenance.

The third group of programs were developed according to the method Ken Orr and Associates calls Structured Systems Development (SSD). In these programs, program coupling and data-structure binding were reduced, because of the Warnier/Orr approach of starting from the real-world output data structure to program structure to input structure. These programs needed the least effort to maintain.

Automating With 'Structure(s)'

Structure(s) is a systems development and documentation package that helps designers, analysts and programmers to document and maintain existing programs and systems. It also supports new development from the beginning. As new pieces of the system take shape, they are consistently integrated into the system and a set of formatted, cross-referenced documents is generated.

The heart of the package is a document handler, which assembles and draws Warnier/Orr diagrams on a line printer. The designer may control the formatting of the diagrams.

The package also includes features to:

• Report and maintain all diagram cross-references.

• Report and flag all undefined cross-references.

• Produce an index of all the elements used in the diagram.

It is a batch-oriented system. The package may be interfaced with any of the popular source library systems. It is written in Cobol and designed for IBM computers, but is easily installed on most other machines. It requires a minimum partition of 210K bytes for IBM systems.

The package is available from Ken Orr & Associates, Inc., 715 E. 8th St., Topeka, Kan. 66607.

The same vendor is currently developing on-line Structure(s), providing capabilities of on-line development and modifications of Warnier/Orr diagrams. A program generator, capable of generating a Cobol program directly from the input to Structure(s) is also being developed.

The enhanced version of Structure(s) (Version 3.0) supports the IBM laser printer and asynchronous terminals. Source code is provided. Improved error handling is included and additional hardware and operating systems are accommodated. This package provides the capacity of Documentation Processing — it makes it simple to use an existing Warnier/Orr diagram to create the next diagram needed, or to use it as a model to create similar systems.

Conclusion

The 1960s and 1970s were spent in developing and propagating the structured technologies. The rapidly emerging software engineering disciplines now comprise management and technical functions and include structured technologies. Software maintenance from all angles, including conversion, redesign and redevelopment is an extremely important part of software engineering.

The 1980s and perhaps 1990s will be spent in refining and further propagating the structured technologies.

Introduction

Higgins, D.A. "Structured maintenance—new tools for old problems." *Computerworld* (June 15, 1981), IN DEPTH section.

The following article is the second of three papers in this Tutorial that describes the Warnier/Orr methodology as it applies to maintenance. The first is Parikh's which precedes this one; the third is Warnier's in Part IV. In the second paper, David Higgins shows the importance of analyzing the different (and sometimes clashing) structures that underlie a real-world system, and he shows the application of this analysis to simplifying and restructuring an existing system.

The cost-effectiveness of maintenance relative to redevelopment lies in its capability to save the functionality of a system while revising its fabric. The functionality of a system—its outputs and their relationship to the users—is its productive core; function is where the major development cost is incurred, and where all of the benefit is recovered. The fabric of a system—code, manuals, hardware—tends to decay through obsolescence and unplanned changes. Is it possible to reconfigure the fabric of a system while preserving its function?

In the following paper, Higgins answers this question with a qualified yes. He reasonably asserts the impossibility of turning "unstructured" code into "structured" code without explicitly considering structure. In fact, following Warnier/Orr methodology, it is necessary to consider several structures—the Logical Output Structure, the Physical Output Structure, and others described in the paper. Higgins advises that one must study the functionality of the system to derive the structures necessary to support it, and then one must rebuild the fabric of the system on those structures.

In conversation with us about this paper, Higgins used the phrase "Maintenance by Requirements," which suggests the goal-oriented singleness of purpose necessary to find the forest rather than being lost in the trees. It also recalls the "Design by Objectives" described in Gilb's article on Maintainability in Part III.

Higgins suggests incremental investigation and redesign (possibly while maintaining those parts) of the program by using a data-structured approach. However, he does not address the process of fitting the pieces together for the entire redevelopment. How can a coherent data structured design of a system/program be obtained from the data structured pieces? This seems to be an area for future research.

The following paper will give the reader a small introduction to Higgins' clear and persuasive style. An interesting companion piece is "Fingerprinting a program," written in collaboration with Karl J. Dakin, in the April 1982 *Datamation*; here the structures of a program are used to identify possible plagiarized versions. Higgins has also authored two books: *Program design and construction* (Prentice-Hall, 1979), and *Designing structured programs* (Prentice-Hall, 1982). He also publishes the semiannual newsletter *Software maintenance techniques*.

Higgins is unusual in being as clear in spoken communication as he is in written communication. His undergraduate majors were mathematics and computer science. He told us:

> I stumbled into computing in college. I had originally intended to become a mathematician until I found out there was no money in it. I was trying to wheedle some free computer time from the director of the university computer center when he suggested that I apply for an analyst/programmer/operator position that was open. Until that point, I had not realised that I could actually get paid for something I considered to be 'tinkering.'

After college, Higgins went to work for Ken Orr's consulting group as an instructor. Now he offers his own five-day Structured Maintenance seminar as part of a complete series on the Warnier/Orr methodology. Readers interested in the books, the periodical, or the seminars should contact Higgins at EduCo Corporation, Arvada, CO, at 303-424-4425.

STRUCTURED MAINTENANCE

New Tools For Old Problems

By David A. Higgins

Reprinted with permission from *Computerworld*, June 15, 1981, IN DEPTH section. Copyright © 1981 by CW Communications, Inc.

Over the last few years we have learned a great deal about the creation of more reliable computer software. Indeed, it seems that today we are on the verge of being able to correctly engineer our programs and systems through the use of structured analysis and design techniques.

But even after such a design technology is well understood, widely accepted and consistently applied, much more work will need to be done. Users will have to deal with the question of what to do with all of the software created prior to the existence of the structured methodologies. There is already a huge body of work in place representing literally millions of hours of effort and billions of dollars of investment.

Must we discard our old programs outright and recreate them using state-of-the-art methods? Or can we find some way to apply our current knowledge of structured design methods to the great mass of so-called "unstructured" software we already have? In order to properly answer this question, we will first need to dispel some popular notions concerning programs and structuring and examine some of the problems we face when trying to define the attributes of a good program.

Structured Programs

Can one structure an unstructured program? Depending on how one defines the buzzwords involved, the answer could be either yes or no. It seems we must first decide what the term "structured" means with respect to a program.

We began talking about structured programs in the late 1960s and in the intervening years have applied the term to nearly every new concept that comes along. At times it seems that one is forced to append the word "structured" to the front of a concept in order for people in DP to think it worthwhile, such as in "structured analysis," "structured design" and "structured walk-throughs."

The problem is, what specifically does someone mean when he uses the term "structured program"? That all depends on who is doing the talking and what time of the day it is.

People unfamiliar with data processing commonly believe the computer programmer's primary task is building new programs. For most programmers today, however, this is not the case. Industry statistics indicate that upward of 75% of all work done by software people is program and system maintenance. The fact of the matter is that resources devoted to maintenance outweigh those devoted to new development by a factor of three to one. Anyone who has been active in DP for any length of time knows that maintenance is a major problem in almost every shop in the world.

The term has been tossed around so freely that it means many different things to many different people.

For most people in data processing, structured programming is synonymous with a peculiar style of coding programs. When pressed for a definition, many will further describe the phrase by giving a list of attributes to be found in a structured program: no GOTO statements; nested IF statements to reflect different levels of logic; one-entry/one-exit modules of code less than a page long; meaningful data and procedure names and so on.

From this kind of definition we should be able to tell if a particular program is structured simply by inspection. If it has all or most of these features, we will pronounce the program structured and it will receive our blessings; otherwise, we will condemn it to Program Hell for being (gasp) unstructured.

There is only one problem, though. Does it follow that such a program would necessarily be a good one? Do we even know enough about what a good program looks like that we could recognize one if it were to walk up to us on the street and introduce itself?

Two Essentials

After sifting through all of the rhetoric and the personal prejudices that get in the way of such an evaluation, it seems that there are two essential attributes a good program would have to possess. First, it would have to produce correct results reliably when used properly. Second, it would have to be easy to enhance when requirements changed.

Put more simply, a good program should work and be maintainable. The importance of the first attribute is obvious and unarguable, but what about the second? Why should we attach such importance to maintainability in a program?

Consider this for a moment: How long does the average program persist in a system? After all, if most of our programs are of the "one-shot" variety — written for one specific purpose and then immediately discarded — then program maintainability is a moot point and need not be considered. In practice, however, such programs are very few and far between, if not entirely nonexistent. Nearly all of the programs we create hang around for far longer than just a single execution. Most last for a very long time indeed.

There are still thousands of programs in production today that were written in the early 1960s for generations of machines now found mostly in museums. Some of these programs have been translated from their original language into Cobol or PL/I, but they were never really discarded and rewritten. So relatively few programs have ever actually expired that it is hard to say for certain how long the average program's lifetime is. It is not uncommon to find programs that are 10, 20 or more years old.

If a program is going to hang around in a system for a couple of decades, we need to consider the ratio of dollars spent modifying that program over its lifetime to the dollars spent creating it initially. Statistics published in 1978 suggest that for conventional programs that ratio is around two to one (Zelkowitz, M.V., "Perspectives on Software Engineering," ACM Computing Surveys, June 1978). At least two-thirds of the dollars invested in a program are invested in its modification; less than a third of a program's cost is in writing it for the very first time.

For future estimates, that ratio is probably low. As we begin to build programs with an eye toward future modification, we may find that our programs last a lot longer than they do now, so that a much bigger percentage of the total investment comes in their enhancement. We may eventually find that upward of 80% or 90% of the total cost of a program comes in adapting it to new requirements.

Building modifiability into programs is crucial to our long-term productivity. As a matter of fact, a lack of modifiability has caused us to label a lot of our existing software as unacceptable. It isn't that our old programs do not work (although it is sometimes hard to tell why they do), but they are difficult if not downright impossible for the average human being to modify. Consequently, we have saddled these programs with the distinction of being unstructured and have made up our minds that we should get rid of them somehow.

Actually, the term "unstructured" is a misnomer. All programs have some structure, although it may not be discernible or may not be the one we want.

Just how does one go about getting rid of a program that cannot be easily maintained, short of pitching it out a window? Is there some method we can use to transform a program that is not currently modifiable into one that is?

One way people have tried to approach this question is by asking what features make for a bad program. We can examine bad programs (there are certainly enough of them available) and identify the different characteristics that seem to make the program hard to change. This would seem at first blush to be a reasonable and logical approach to solving the problem, but it is not. It ultimately will lead us into a subtle trap from which it may be difficult to escape.

Bad Programs

When looking at any given bad program, one is apt to notice many features that apparently hinder the maintenance effort. One of the most obvious hindrances is the presence of nonsense or misleading names in the code (some people have even asserted that using misleading names is an excellent security device for code). An otherwise well-organized and well-designed program is rendered useless by the use of poor names. The conclusion we draw: Programs are made more maintainable by using meaningful data and procedure names.

Another apparent problem with bad code was pointed out by Edsger Dijkstra in a much quoted (and much misunderstood) article about branching in a program ("GOTO Statement Considered Harmful," *Communications of the ACM*, March 1968). It seems that Dijkstra noticed that programs containing a lot of GOTO statements were harder to maintain than those that did not. From this observation, many people drew the conclusion that programs should be created with few or no GOTO statements and that already-existing programs can be made more maintainable if their GOTO statements are removed.

Unfortunately, this conclusion is faulty, and reliance upon it can generate some weird results.

The Nasty GOTO

Does the use of the GOTO statement introduce irreparable damage to the maintainability of a program? Is its use so disastrous that we should try to eliminate it wherever it occurs? Many people have asserted that we should. But before we pass final judgment, let us do some investigation.

Assume for the moment that the GOTO statement is a bad influence and that we don't want any of them hanging around in our programs. One way we could evaluate their effect on program maintainability would be to remove the GOTOs from a program and determine firsthand if any improvement was noted. In doing this exercise, we will find out two things: In practice it is often quite difficult to remove GOTOs from existing code, and even when you do, it doesn't help very much.

Consider the following Cobol Procedure Division:

```
PROCEDURE DIVISION.
OPEN-FILES.
    OPEN INPUT CUSTOMER-FILE, OUTPUT
    PRINT-FILE.
PAGE HEADING.
    MOVE TITLE-LINE TO PRINT-LINE.
    WRITE PRINT-LINE AFTER ADVANCING TOP-
    OF-PAGE.
    MOVE HEADING-LINE-1 TO PRINT-LINE.
    WRITE PRINT-LINE AFTER ADVANCING 2
    LINES.
    MOVE HEADING-LINE-2 TO PRINT-LINE.
    WRITE PRINT-LINE AFTER ADVANCING 1
    LINES.
    MOVE ZERO TO LINE-COUNTER.
MAINLINE.
    READ CUSTOMER-FILE
        AT END GO TO TERMINATE.
    IF CUSTOMER-VOLUME > 1000.0
        THEN GO TO PRINT-A-LINE
    GO TO MAINLINE.
PRINT-A-LINE.
    MOVE SPACES TO PRINT-LINE.
    ADD CUSTOMER-VOLUME TO TOTAL-VOL-
    UME.
    ADD 1 TO CUSTOMER-COUNT.
    MOVE CUSTOMER-NUMBER TO CUSTOMER-
    NUMBER-OUT.
    MOVE CUSTOMER-NAME TO CUSTOMER-
    NAME-OUT.
    MOVE CUSTOMER-VOLUME TO CUSTOMER-
    VOLUME-OUT.
    WRITE PRINT-LINE AFTER ADVANCING 1
    LINES.
    ADD 1 TO LINE-COUNTER.
    IF LINE-COUNTER > 55
        GO TO PAGE-HEADING.
    GO TO MAINLINE.
TERMINATE.
    MOVE TOTAL-VOLUME TO TOTAL-VOLUME-
    OUT
```

```
MOVE  CUSTOMER-COUNT  TO  MAJOR-
COUNT-OUT.
MOVE TOTAL-LINE TO PRINT-LINE.
WRITE  PRINT-LINE  AFTER  ADVANCING  2
LINES.
CLOSE CUSTOMER-FILE, PRINT-FILE.
GOBACK.
```

This is by intent a very simple program that we can understand easily
as it is. Since it is so simple we
should be able to evaluate whether
any real improvement (or degradation) is made by removing the GOTO
statements in it. Now all we have to
do is figure out how to take the GO-
TOs out of an existing program.

Since GOTOs deal with the transfer
of control in a program, the first step
we will take involves the separation
of the control statements in the code
from the detail statements. The control statements include all of the tests
(including the AT END and the IN-
VALID KEY clauses of the READ and
WRITE statements), the branches
(both conditional and unconditional)
and the targets of the branches (the
paragraph and section names). The
detail statements are those that perform some elemental task such as
READ, WRITE, OPEN, CLOSE,
MOVE and the arithmetic expressions and do not participate in program control.

In doing this, it becomes obvious
that the program consists of five separate blocks or sections of detail
code. Each section has only one entrance point, one exit point and contains only sequential processing
within; thus, each detail block fits
the classic definition for the term
"code module." Since the entire
module is executed from top to bottom each time it is invoked, we will
not need to examine the interior of
the modules any further. For our
purposes here, we will consider that
this program consists of five indivis-
ible units held together by the control structure.

Since the five detail blocks can be
treated as single units, we can boil
the program down to a pseudocode
skeleton:

```
Procedure Division.
Open Files.
   BLOCK A
Page-Heading.
   BLOCK B
Mainline.
   BLOCK C
      At End Go To Terminate.
   If Customer-Volume > 1000.0
      Then Go To Print-A-Line.
```

```
      Go To Mainline.
Print-A-Line.
   BLOCK D
   If Line-Counter > 55
      Then Go To Page-Heading.
   Go To Mainline.
Terminate.
   BLOCK E
   Goback.
```

Since the control structure is so easy
to find now, we can begin to translate this program into a more graphic
representation form. It is but a short
step from the skeleton program to a
conventional program flowchart,
such as the one shown in Figure 1.
The flowchart is the classic method
of diagrammatically - representing
program logic.

And, as flowcharts go, this one is
simple enough. Unfortunately we
won't be able to use this kind of diagram to accomplish our immediate
goal. This charting form cannot usually tell us how we can rebuild our
program without any GOTO statements. For that we must employ a
more organized diagramming form
— one that is far more restrictive in
terms of allowable logic constructs.
In this case we will use the Warnier/
Orr diagram.

With a little effort, this flowchart
can be represented as a Warnier/Orr
diagram as shown in Figure 2.

In Figure 2 we have shown that the
first module, BLOCK A, of the program is executed at the beginning of
the program. BLOCK B is executed at
the beginning of the section we have
called Loop One. BLOCK C is executed at the beginning of the section labeled Loop Two. Within this second
loop there is a test to see if the input
file is at end or not. When the end of
the file is encountered, BLOCK E is
executed and the program ends.

When the file is not at end, a test is
made to see if the customer volume
exceeds 1,000. When the volume exceeds 1,000, BLOCK D is executed,
followed by a test to see if the Line
Counter has exceeded 55. When the
counter exceeds 55, the Loop One
section of the diagram is invoked
again. When the counter is not greater than 55 and when the volume is
not greater than 1,000, Loop Two is
invoked again. This completes the
description of the program's logic.

(Just as a side note on this diagram:
the three dashed brackets on the
right side of this chart indicate that
the procedures defined at that point

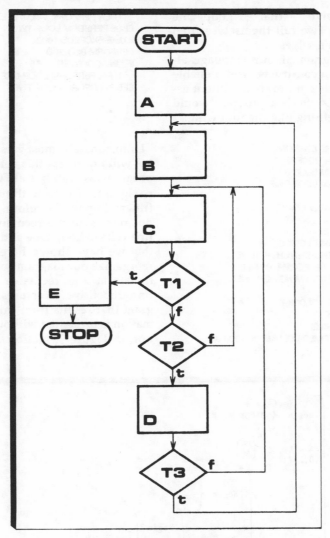

Figure 1. Program Flowchart

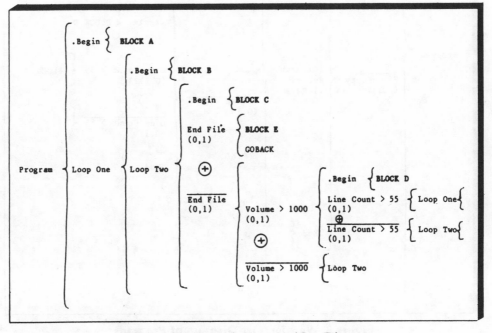

Figure 2. First Draft Warnier/Orr Diagram

are recursive — that is, Loop One and Loop Two call themselves from within themselves.)

This diagram, if our language allowed such constructs, would enable us to recode our program without using GOTOs. Such a program would look something like the following:

```
PROCEDURE DIVISION.
PROGRAM-PROCESS.
    PERFORM BLOCK-A.
    PERFORM LOOP-ONE.
LOOP ONE.
    PERFORM BLOCK-B.
    PERFORM LOOP-TWO.
LOOP TWO.
    PERFORM BLOCK-C.
    IF FILE-END-SWITCH = TRUE
        THEN PERFORM-END-FILE
    ELSE PERFORM NOT-END-FILE.
END-FILE.
    PERFORM BLOCK-E.
    GOBACK.
NOT-END-FILE.
    IF CUSTOMER-VOLUME > 1000.0
```

```
    THEN PERFORM VOLUME-EXCEEDS-1000
    ELSE PERFORM LOOP-TWO.
VOLUME-EXCEEDS-1000.
    PERFORM BLOCK-D.
    IF LINE-COUNTER > 55
        THEN PERFORM LOOP-ONE
    ELSE PERFORM LOOP-TWO.
            •
            •
            •
```

Unfortunately, most versions of Cobol will not accept this version of the program as valid; PERFORMing a paragraph from within itself is frowned upon. Therefore, Cobol will not recognize the recursive subroutine calls to Loop One and Loop Two that we have shown here. We must reorganize our diagram somewhat to transform the recursive structures into repetitive structures. The diagram that results from this transformation is presented without explanation in Figure 3. Notice that we set

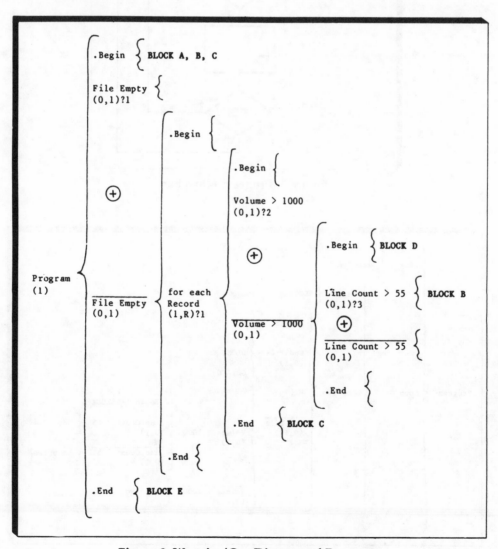

Figure 3. Warnier/Orr Diagram of Program

100

up an "end of file" switch to facilitate correct termination of the loops.

This diagram can be coded into most versions of Cobol without any difficulty. We simply make each bracket on the diagram into a separate paragraph of code and then use the PERFORM ..., the PERFORM ... UNTIL ... and the IF ... THEN ... ELSE ... constructs to implement the logical structures of hierarchy, repetition and alternation, respectively.

The resulting code is operationally equivalent to the program code we began with, only in this incarnation it has no GOTO statements in its logic. Most everyone you might ask would tell you that the new version is indeed a structured program.

But is it a better program? Is it a more modifiable piece of code? Probably not, but not for the reasons one might immediately suspect.

In evaluating this new program, one is greatly tempted to find fault with all of the "extras" the program has acquired in the transition. It appears that this version has taken on a whole cartful of excess baggage where there was none before. First, the new version is physically much larger than the original: more than a third larger in terms of number of lines of code present. Second, an end-of-file switch has been added to control the loops where there was none before.

Third, the use of the PERFORM statement to invoke subroutines is objectionable to many. The PERFORM has a long and distinguished history of persecution for high program overhead, even though today such fears are groundless. However, many people would still argue that it is silly to PERFORM a paragraph when an in-line module would work just as well.

Perhaps worst of all, though, the new version seems to have become badly fragmented in the transition. With all of the PERFORMing going on, it would appear that it is harder for someone to pick up and read than the original. For a program of any size, we would be constantly flipping back and forth, trying to find and keep track of things.

But even if we do not accept the aforementioned complaints as valid and in fact believe the new version of the code to be improved, we still have some serious philosophical problems to contend with. The language constructs we used to implement the Warnier/Orr diagram are specific to Cobol and a handful of other high-level languages like PL/I and Pascal and are features not even available in many versions of Fortran, Basic, Assembler and RPG.

Does this mean that structured programming is a concept that applies only to a few high-level languages? If so, it would naturally follow that those unfortunate enough to be stuck with some other unstructured language are condemned to repeat the mistakes of the past and can never even hope to build quality software.

But wait one minute. Something about that last conclusion seems contrary to normal experience. Many people have built and continue to build quality software in all kinds of languages, even the so-called unstructured ones. How did we end up reaching a conclusion that is contrary to established fact?

False Assumption

We wandered off on the wrong track because the assumption with which we began — that programs without GOTOs are better — is not correct. One passage of code cannot be said to be any better than another simply because it is written in a different style. That is akin to asserting that Steinbeck's novels are inherently better than Hemingway's: an assertion impossible to support with objective facts. The truth of the matter is that code without GOTOs is not automatically better than code with them.

How does one get drawn into a discussion of the relative merits of the GOTO statement in the first place? Well, it was all innocent enough to begin with. In his article, Dijkstra observed that natively good programs have fewer GOTOs than natively bad ones — this is true. But the conclusion that GOTOs are a problem is not valid: excessive GOTOs are a symptom — a sympton of poor program design. It is no wonder that removing the GOTOs doesn't help. Even though we have removed the obvious symptoms, we have not done a thing to improve the underlying design of the bad program.

However, having represented this

program in a well-organized diagramming form, we now have more information about the underlying structure of both the old and new versions of the code. If the Warnier/Orr diagram is easy to understand and to modify, then either version of the code could be more easily enhanced. The diagram that one creates from an old program, though, often has its own problems. Will this diagram tell us anything significant about the nature of the old program, or will it tell us much of anything at all?

For very poorly written and poorly documented programs, this kind of Warnier/Orr diagram is quite often useful for understanding the location and nature of code functions. For most normal applications, however, it is usually less than completely helpful. The fault lies not with the diagramming form, but with the kind of structure that is typically discerned.

Curious Findings

All programs can be represented using the Warnier/Orr diagramming form; likewise, all data sets. It turns out that some curious results begin to emerge when one investigates the relationship between data structures and program structures. Such an investigation was done independently by Jean-Dominique Warnier in France and Michael Jackson in England during the late 1960s and early 1970s. Warnier and Jackson used different graphic forms of representing data and process, but both came to the same conclusion: They found that the structures of the "good" programs, the ones that were the easiest to understand and modify, closely resembled the structures of the data sets on which they operated.

Consequently, Warnier and Jackson began to recommend that people create data-structured programs, as opposed to plain old vanilla structured programs, to improve program quality. Indeed, the code created in this fashion was better. It was easier to get running and to modify when requirements changed. Many programmers even found that they could write programs that would run correctly on the very first try.

It was not, though, a different coding style that enabled them to achieve that success. Two things

were responsible: 1) the techniques imposed a consistent program design strategy and 2) people had to create a good, data-structured design before they could create code.

This realization is all well and good for the creation of new software, but it presents some drawbacks when one begins to consider existing software. Programs, unfortunately, do not just have one data structure to contend with. Every program has four data structures buried somewhere in the logic of the code.

The first and most obvious data structure one finds comes not from the program, but from the output it produces, shown here in Figure 4A. It is called the logical output file (LOF) by Warnier, or the logical output structure (LOS) by Kenneth T. Orr, the American researcher primarily responsible for importing and refining the data-structured design methods. This structure is referred to as being "logical" because it is a hardware- and language-independent view of the output requirements.

The LOS for the program we have been considering is given in Figure 4B. It indicates that this output for the company will contain a report title and column headings at its beginning, followed by from zero to many major customer information sets, followed by a report footing, a major customer count and a total volume at its end. For each major customer found on the output, we will find a customer number, a customer name and a customer volume.

Physical Output Structure

In addition to this logical view of the output, there is a physical output structure as well, which tends to be much the same for most printed outputs. It is shown in Figure 4C and simply indicates that the physical output is known as a report, which is composed of pages composed of lines.

Aside from the output structures, there is the structure of the physical input file to be considered. It is given in Figure 4D. This physical input structure indicates that the input file for this application contains a number of customer records, each one of which either is or is not a record for a major customer.

The last structure to consider is one

that can be characterized as the physical algorithm structure. In this example, as in most normal applications, the structure is very similar to the LOS found earlier. It is shown in Figure 4E. For some applications, however, this structure can become the most complex of the four. Consider, for instance, the structure of the algorithm for the calculation of the net pay field on the average paycheck.

Data Structures and Old Programs

The realization that every program must contain all four of these data structures embedded in its logic is a significant one. But, as was mentioned earlier, applying this knowledge is at least an order of magnitude more difficult when dealing with existing programs than it is with new ones.

When creating new software, one can easily devise coding mechanisms that isolate these four structures from one another, thus limiting the impact of change when it occurs. This can be done either by creating separate job steps or by creating a series of partitioned coroutines.

Using the first method, one creates a three-step procedure. First the major customers are selected from the customer file. Second, the selected file of major customers is read in and processed to produce an internal file of detail print lines. Third, the internal file of print lines is processed and formatted into pages and lines on a printer.

The advantage to this method is its simplicity: The different structures are isolated from one another in the program and each step is quite small. The disadvantage, of course, is time. This kind of program must make three passes at essentially the same data, thus increasing the execution time and the I/O overhead by a factor of around three.

The second method of implementation is the one generally preferred. In this approach, the LOS is the dominant structure in the program, and the structures of the physical input and physical output are reflected in input and output coroutines (which are usually coded as subroutines or subprograms). These routines allow the main program to ignore the fact that the real input and output files

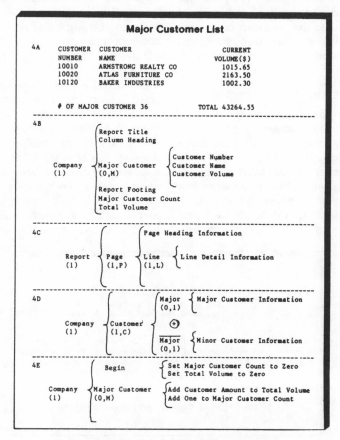

Figure 4. Program Data Structures

are less than ideal. This kind of program is derived from the LOS and the calculation structure and is shown in Figure 5. It is called a logical process structure (LPS).

This diagram can be easily augmented with code-level details specific to the particular physical environment in which it will operate. With this approach, the Get and the Print instructions indicated are not simple reads and writes. They are entire subroutines that do as much physical I/O as is necessary to respond to the physical input and output environment.

Thus, the main program believes it is reading from a file that contains only and all the records it needs in precisely the order in which it expects them and is printing on an infinitely long sheet of paper. Again, this method of implementation allows us to maintain the program easily. If the input file structures change, the only modification required is one to the input coroutine and so on.

The program that would be created from such a design has some odd features: It has no GOTOs or nested IFs and is modular, loosely coupled and highly cohesive. In fact, it has all of the attributes that are normally associated with a structured program. Code created from such designs always will.

Structured Maintenance

The aforementioned design method works well for creating good programs, but we must still find some way to apply it to old code. We have already observed that taking the GOTOs out of an old program does not significantly improve its maintainability and will not result in a program such as the one just described.

Having discussed data-structured design and structured coding techniques, we are ready to make two rather radical statements concerning software maintenance:

• Programs cannot be made more maintainable by simply changing their code.

This assertion must be accompanied by an equally strange-sounding one.

• No program is maintainable unless it is accompanied by a data-structured design.

We in data processing have known something fundamental about the relationship between good programs and sound designs for a long time. Many of us, though, have tried to ignore the problem with the hope that it would go away if we could just get better languages or better debugging tools. Code, by itself, can never be adequately maintained, only changed. Only designs created with a reliable and consistent strategy can be reliably enhanced to meet the new requirements.

Two Choices

Thus we are left with only two alternatives for old programs: We must either try to resurrect the design for an existing program, or we must create a good design and reorganize the code around it.

It has become obvious through analyzing many different programs in many different languages that a magical "structure analyzer," which would take old code and generate from it a new structured program and a set of comprehensive documentation, cannot exist as such. Such a Rosetta Stone has been sought for years, and only recently have we come to realize that even if you can mechanically generate the structure of a bad program, all you get is a pic-

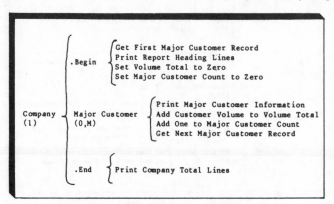

Figure 5. Logical Process Structure

ture of the mess that is there. You do not get a picture of the design that is *supposed* to be there. Such diagrams are relatively uninteresting and typically not very useful for maintenance.

On the other hand, if one invests the time to detail the four data structures that we mentioned — the structures of the logical output, physical output, physical input and physical calculations — one can learn a great deal about what an old program is supposed to be doing. Understanding a program then becomes a matter of going into the existing code to find out where and how it does the things you know it has to, and modification is then a matter of redesign. Of course, for large programs or for programs with multiple outputs, this procedure may well be incremental, with only small sections of the code being investigated at any one sitting.

Managing Maintenance

Unfortunately, any bifurcated system that separates design from code has some inherent difficulties. In the day-to-day press of trying to get things done, many programmers understate the importance of maintaining the design before the code.

This attitude is often reinforced by management and users. When constantly barraged with speeches concerning the shortage of resources and the enormous backlog of work to be done, programmers and analysts get the idea that their primary concern should be program code and not some silly design documents that don't do anything. In some places this practice is mandated by shop standard. Programmers are told they must develop code first and design documents later. This management attitude has been characterized as the Wisc (Why Isn't Sammy Coding?) syndrome.

Stressing the maintenance of code before design is confusing motion with progress. It is an extremely short-sighted approach that has already proved to be disastrous in the long run. It is also an attitude that must be overcome somehow if we are ever to make any progress toward controlling the maintenance problem.

When you think about it, it seems somehow odd that such an attitude ever developed. After all, computer hardware is designed before it is constructed, and the design is of different stuff than the construction. Schematic diagrams and logic diagrams are used to describe the electronics design and are checked and rechecked for correctness before the first components are wired together. Separating design from construction is a technique found in every other engineering profession, and it is based on one fundamental observation: Paper changes are cheap.

A similar attitude must be fostered in the minds of software people as well. Until technicians, managers and DP users realize that the languages and the coding styles are not the real problem, we are not going to make any headway toward the goal of improving the maintenance problem.

Maintenance will not go away. As long as the real world is dynamic, our software systems must continue to respond to changing user requirements. It is by definition impossible to build software systems that anticipate and automatically provide for requirements changes. Such systems would consume infinite resources. The best we can do is build systems that are easy to enhance when change occurs and to make a long-term commitment to having a data-structured design for every piece of software we keep. This obviously will not happen overnight, nor will it be cheap. And, I'm sorry to say, there are no panaceas.

It has taken many years for some of our software to degrade to the extent that it has, and we should not be too surprised to find that it takes us almost as long to correct the problem. Just as losing weight is not an overnight prospect, making software that isn't maintainable into software that is will take some time and require adjusting some old habits. The alternative, however, is to keep doing maintenance the same old way, effectively digging ourselves deeper into the hole in which we are already standing.

Introduction

Brooks, R. "Using a behavioral theory of program comprehension in software engineering." IEEE Computer Society, *3rd International Conference on Software Engineering*, 1978, 196-201.

Ruven Brooks is a young computer scientist who began as a psychologist and whose major research interest for at least six years has been to develop a behavioral theory or model of the comprehension of computer programs by experienced programmers. The paper reprinted here is an exceptionally clear and convincing statement of Brooks' theory. Brooks argues that when a programmer understands a program,

> what he knows can be described as a succession of knowledge domains that bridge between the problem being solved and the program in execution.

In Brooks' example, a program may deal with a cargo-routing problem, in which the important objects are weights and costs and distances. This problem is expressed with numbers, so that at the next level down the important objects are numbers. These numbers may be manipulated according to linear algebra, so that at this level the important concepts are algebraic. And, at the bottom level, the algebra may be expressed in FORTRAN, so that at this level computer language and code are the important concepts.

Understanding, as we paraphrased Brooks in the introduction to this part of the Tutorial, is knowing the right levels, knowing how each level functions, and knowing how they fit together. This model corresponds rather closely to recent Artifical Intelligence inquiries by Erman, Hayes-Roth, Lesser, and Reddy into how to understand spoken English ("The Hearsay-II Speech-Understanding System: integrating knowledge to resolve uncertainty," *ACM Computing Surveys*, 12, 2, (June 1980), 213-253). Hearers use knowledge about words, phrases, grammar, and the actual topic being discussed to build an interpretation of what they hear. Similarly, programmers use knowledge about code, control, data, modularization, and the task performed by the program to build an interpretation of what they are programming.

Brooks' theory has important implications for the direction of software engineering. Purity of structure is insufficient to guarantee understandability of a program, just as purity of diction does not guarantee the understandability of a speaker. Very recent work by two distinguished computer scientists, Basili and Mills, who derived the function of a program from its code by strict software engineering methods ("Understanding and documenting programs," *IEEE Trans. on Software Engineering*, SE-8, 3 (May 1982), 270-283), bears out Brooks' argument that other techniques beside clarifying the program flow enter into disentangling meaning.

Brooks is continuing his research into program understanding. Since 1982 he has been working on an integrated design environment at International Telephone and Telegraph Corporation. He told us that the essence of the following paper is simple:

> There is a clearly describable process that takes place when a programmer attempts to read and understand a computer program, and software engineering tools and methods must be constructed to fit this process.

Using A Behavioral Theory of Program Comprehension
in Software Engineering

Ruven Brooks

Department of Information and Computer Science
University of California at Irvine
Irvine, CA

Abstract

A theory is presented of how a programmer goes about understanding a program. The theory is based on a representation of knowledge about programs as a succession of knowledge domains which bridge between the problem domain and the executing program. A hypothesis and verify process is used by programmers to reconstruct these domains when they seek to understand a program.

The theory is useful in several ways in software engineering: It makes accurate predictions about the effectiveness of documentation; it can be used to systematically evaluate and critique other claims about documentation, and it may even be a useful guideline to a programmer in actually constructing documentation.

The past decade has seen a major shift in viewpoint on the use of a computer program. Rather than seeing it solely as an object for machine consumption - one which is only compiled or executed - the program is increasingly viewed as an object for programmer consumption as well; programmers read it, understand it, and modify it. Given this shift in emphasis, the value of a program is in part based on how easy it is to understand, and a partial goal of many of the newer methods of software construction is to yield programs that are more comprehensible.

The construction of understandable programs requires knowledge about the particular factors that make a program hard or easy to understand. A useful and powerful source of such knowledge is a model, or theory, of how a programmer understand a program. Such a theory would specify the kinds of information needed to understand a program and the processes used by a programmer to acquire this information. In this paper, we intend to present such a theory and to demonstrate its value for software engineering in three ways: First, the theory can be used to make accurate predictions about the value of different kinds of documentation. Second, it can be used to evaluate proposed programming styles and, third, it can be used to generate new documentation techniques.

What does it mean to understand a program?

The starting point for this theory is an analysis of the organization of the knowledge acquired by a programmer when he has understood a program. In this analysis, a program as understood by a programmer effectively consists of a considerably larger body of information than that which is used during its machine interpretation or compilation and execution. This information is described in terms of the psychological concept of knowledge domains. A knowledge domain consists of a closed set of primitive objects, properties of the objects, relations among objects, and operators which manipulate these properties or relations.

When a programmer completely understands a program, what he knows can be described as a succession of knowledge domains that bridge between the problem being solved and the program in execution. As an example, consider a cargo routing problem. In the application or problem domain, the objects are cargoes that have destinations which must be reached within time and cost constraints, and there are means of transportation that carry these cargoes with various time and cost parameters. Before a program can be written to solve the problem, numbers must be first assigned to the cost and time elements, and identifiers, which also may be numbers, are assigned to cargoes and destinations. This results in a new knowledge domain, one in which the objects have become numbers.

In order to use the numbers in the program, an algorithm must be selected. This results in the creation of still another domain, one in which mathematical

Reprinted from *The Third International Conference on Software Engineering Proceedings*, 1978, pages 196-201. Copyright © 1978 by The Institute of Electrical and Electronics Engineers, Inc.

objects, such as trees or matrices, are operated upon, and in which operators such as "invert a matrix" are used. Translation of the algorithm into a programming language creates yet another domain, with data structure implementations and the primitive operations of the programming language. Finally, execution of the program produces a domain in which the objects are the contents of the memory locations and the operations are those of the hardware.

While this example has mentioned five modeling domains, these same five would not necessarily be present in every task or for all parts of a task. If the task is to implement a particular algorithm for a general purpose algorithm, say, a matrix inversion routine, there will be no domain corresponding to the original domain of cargoes and routes in the example. On the other hand, use of a primitive operation of searching a tree at one level might require use of an intermediate domain, containing methods of tree traversal, before the knowledge could be represented at the programming language level.

In this analysis, complete understanding of a program involves two types of information. First, within each domain, there is information about the basic set of objects, including their properties and relationships, the set of operations that can be performed on these objects, and the order in which these operations take place. Second, there will be information about the relationship between objects and operators in one domain and those in a nearby domain. These relationships will generally not be one to one, and new operations in one domain may be built up out of both objects or operands in a previous one. As an example, the operation of traversing a tree in an algorithm domain may map unto a sequence of statements and a set of variables in the programming language domain.

Using this idea of knowledge domains, the task of understanding a program for a programmer becomes one of constructing, or reconstructing, enough information about the modeling domains that bridge between problem and executing program to perform the requested tasks. The amount of knowledge necessary will be a function of the particular task and may change as the task progresses. Thus, in the example, the programmer debugging the program may, initially, not concern himself with the peculiarities of cargo rate tables, but later finds that the problem is that air freight rates are per pound while those for ships are per 100 pounds and that this is causing problems in the program.

In performing this reconstruction

process, the programmer makes use of a variety of different sources of information which may be roughly catagorized into those which are present in the program text or listing and those which are external to it; Table 1 lists some examples from both groups.

Table 1

Cues to Understanding a Program

Internal to the Program Text.

1. Prologue comments, including data and variable dictionaries.

2. Variable, structure, procedure and label names.
3. Declarations or Data Divisions.
4. Interline Comments.
5. Indentation or pretty-printing.
6. Subroutine or module structure.
7. I/O formats, headers, and device or channel assignments.

8. Action of statements, including organization.

External.

1. User's manuals.
2. Program logic manuals.
3. Flowcharts.
4. Cross reference listings.
5. Published descriptions of algorithms or techniques.

The process of using this information to reconstruct the knowledge domain is based on the successive refinement of hypotheses about the program's operation. These hypotheses are initially generated from the programmer's knowledge of the task domain and of programming. In the example given previously, the programmer may use his knowledge of transportation problems to guess that the program is based on a dynamic programming algorithm. The role that the sources of information listed earlier play is to aid the programmer in refining and elaborating his hypotheses by confirming or refuting parts of them and suggesting alternatives. In the example, the programmer may use variable names together with the indentation structure to decide which dynamic programming algorithm is being used. The refinement process is concluded when the programmer feels he knows enough about the knowledge domains to begin his task.

Summarizing the theory, a programmer's knowledge about a program is viewed as a succession of knowledge domains which bridge between the problem domain and the executing program. To understand a program, the programmer uses internal and external sources of information to successively refine hypotheses about the program's operation.

Application to the Theory

In addition to its general scientific value, this theory is useful to software engineering in three ways:
Making predictions.

The theory can be used to make predictions about the effectiveness of different kinds of documentation. An example of the kind of predictions that can be made on the basis of the theory is one concerning the commenting of data structures. Consider a data type such as a FORTRAN array. Some uses of an array, which might be called the native uses, require that few, if any, additional constraints must be applied to the operations on the data structure. An example of such a native use would be sorting an ordered sequence of numbers in the elements of the array. Other uses add more constraints and might be called derived uses; use of a FORTRAN array to hold a tree is an example.

The use made of a datatype is interpreted relative to other knowledge domains than that of the programming language. The knowledge that an array is used to hold an algebraic expression in tree form draws on the domain of algebraic knowledge and on the domain of knowledge about tree traversal algorithms. To understand the use made of a variable which is of a complex type, the programmer must be able to not only interpret the variable in terms of objects in other domains but he must also be able to interpret operations on the variable in terms of their counterparts in other domains. If the use made of the variable is a native one, then the interpretation should be quite easy to make; each statement in the programming language will usually correspond to one operation in another domain. If the use is a highly derived one, however, it will frequently be the case that several operations in the programming language domain are required to carry out an operation in another domain. For example, finding the left descendent of a node in a tree requires several FORTRAN statements if the tree is represented in a FORTRAN array. If several statements are required, then the programmer is faced with the task of deciding which statements form an operation, so that program comprehension is more difficult. Under these circumstances, the theory predicts that comments which precede a group of statements, and which describe them in terms of operations in another domain, will be particularly helpful.

A second example of a prediction derived from the theory is one on the effectiveness of flowcharts. In an earlier study, Shneiderman, Mayer, McKay and Heller (1977) found results which suggested that macro flowcharts are of little help in understanding, debugging, or modifying programs. Since a wide range of intersubject differences in several of their studies may have obscured the effects of the flowcharts, their research cannot be interpreted as clear-cut evidence against flowcharts; however, it does show that the effects of flowcharts, if any, are weak. How does this result compare with predictions derived from the theory?

According to the theory, documentation operates by aiding the programmer in reconstructing the knowledge domains that bridge between the problem domain and the program in execution. Each domain consists of objects and their properties and operations on these objects. Flowcharts provide information on the bridge between the domain of algorithms and that of code, but only in regard to the sequence of operations, not in regard to the objects being operated on. Knowledge of the objects in a program usually means knowledge of the variables in a program and what they stand for. Hence, flowcharts are likely to be helpful in the (relatively rare) situation in which the programmer is already aware of the variables and data structures in a program, but in which he has difficulty figuring out the sequence of operations to be performed on the objects.

A circumstance which may result in a programmer's learning about the variables without simultaneously learning about control flow is if the program listing begins with a variable dictionary, a set of comments which explain the uses of the variables in the program. Knowledge about variables or data structures can be used before the control flow is known, but the reverse is not true; knowing the sequence of operations isn't much use unless the nature of the operations themselves is known. Therefore, the theory leads to the prediction that whereas the use of a variable dictionary alone will make a program easier to understand, flowcharts will be useful only as an addition to the variable dictionary in cases where the control flow is particularly complicated.

An experimental test was made of this prediction. For the test, a set of four FORTRAN programs, ranging in length from 109 to 231 lines, was constructed. For each program, three versions of documentation were constructed. The first consisted of just a macro flowchart, the second of just a variable dictionary, while the third contained both. Subjects, who were FORTRAN programmers with at least two years professional experience, were asked to answer a set of questions about the control and data structures in the programs. The total time taken to answer the questions correctly was used as the measure of the effectiveness of the documentation.

The results of this experiment strongly supported the prediction about the superiority as sole documentation of variable dictionaries over macro flowcharts. The prediction about the combined effect of flowcharts and variable dictionaries was not supported, probably because the programs used did not have complex enough control structures.

Evaluating Proposed Programming Styles

Kernighan and Plauger (1974) make the following statement at the beginning of their chapter on documentation:

The best documentation for a computer program is a clean structure. It also helps if the code is well formatted, with good mnemonic identifiers, labels, and a smattering of enlightening comments. Flowcharts and program descriptions are of secondary importance; the only reliable documentation of a computer program is the code itself. The reason is simple - whenever there are multiple representations of a program, the chance for discrepancy exists. If the code is in error, artistic flowcharts and detailed comments are to no avail.

According to the theory described here, this whole statement is of doubtful validity. As a starting point, their statement is based on the explicit assumption that the code is the ultimate statement of the function a program performs. In this theory, in contrast, a complete description of the function performed by a program must include the representation of the program in all the intervening domains. Since this information is not present in the code alone, the code itself cannot be a complete or accurate description of what the program does.

Two arguments can be made in favor of this position. The first is that a program's function is partially defined by the interpretation given to the input or output. To make this point in an extreme form, in some cases it might be possible to use exactly the same code as either a payroll program or as an inventory update program. The function the program performs will depend on whether the input is a payroll file or a parts file and on whether the output is interpreted as a list of wages to be paid or as the current value of parts on hand. Note that this interpretation issue is independent of any constraints about the value of the input and that no kind of checks on the input can be used to resolve it.

A second argument in favor of the primacy of materials outside of the program text as documentation is based on the uses made of documentation. Documentation is never of concern if the program is performing the task the user desires to perform; only when the program is to be modified in some way does documentation become important. In making modifications, issues other than what the code is currently doing may be of paramount importance. For example, assumptions about statistical characteristics of the data may have lead to the choice of a certain algorithm - bubble sort, if the data are only slightly out of order - and the reason for making the modification is because these assumptions no longer hold. A statement of what the assumptions were may be considerably more useful and important than any statement, regardless of how accurate of what the code is doing currently. Indeed, in this situation, it may not even matter if the documentation about what the current code is doing is wrong in places, if these are the places where the code will be changed anyway! For this kind of information that is necessary for many types of modification, the code itself is neither a reliable nor an ultimate source of documentation.

Given that the code is always an incomplete source of information about a program, then it can hardly be argued that the best documentation for a computer program is a clean structure. Indeed, for most programs, a clean structure will be of secondary or tertiary importance in understanding what a program does.

This statement is based on the following argument. According to the theory, a programmer understands a program by successively refining guesses about how the program operates. These guesses are made on the basis of knowledge of the problem domain or of intervening domains. The actual code is used primarily to confirm or deny these hypotheses. The major benefit of a clean structure should be to make this confirmation process easier and faster, but this benefit should only be visible if the programmer is able to rapidly find the correct hypothesis. If he must try many hypotheses before hitting a correct one, then it may take him as much or more time to understand a cleanly structured program as for a poorly structured one for which he quickly hits upon a correct hypothesis.

This line of argument suggests that any kind of documentation which helps the programmer to initially select the correct hypothesis will usually lead to a greater improvement in understandability than will improvements in structure. Consider as an example one of the newer, automata theory based string matching algorithms. Suppose that a programmer who is not familiar with these algorithms is given a program which uses one of them and told to modify it. To make the modification, he must, of course, first understand how the algorithm works. The availability of prose explanations of the algorithm will have a much larger influence on the speed with which the programmer understands the program than variations in the structure of the program; indeed, the algorithms are sufficiently counterintuitive that, without the prose explanation, the programmer may never be able to understand the program at all! Thus, in situations like this, the prose documentation will clearly have the primary effect on program understandability, a statement which should also hold for other programs of equivalent difficulty. (A possible exception to this statement is in situations in which the programmer is almost invariably correct in his guesses about the program as, for example, in the case of a simple payroll program.)

As this discussion of the Kernighan and Plauger statement indicates, the theory can, indeed, be used to evaluate claims about program comprehensibility. While being used in this way, the theory, of course, generates counterclaims of its own. The question must then be raised of why these counterclaims should be considered superior to the original statements. The answer is that, while the theoretical claims must each be individually experimentally tested, claims generated from the theory gain support from other studies which also support the theory as a whole. To the extent that the experiment discussed previously supports the theory, it also lends credence to the counterclaims that disagree with the Kernighan and Plauger statement.

Providing New Documentation Techniques.

Writers on programming practice (Kernighan and Plauger, 1974; Ledgard, 1975) are in agreement that comments should be accurate and useful, but they offer little in the way of advice on how to actually go about constructing the comments. While the theory does not yet provide a computable algorithm for generating comments, it can be used to suggest what kinds of comments will be most helpful.

According to the theory, the role of comments is to bridge between knowledge domains. Consider this piece of code and comment in a FORTRAN program:

```
C   THIS SHIFTS B LEFT 4 BITS
    A = B*2**4
```

While the comment comes close to violating Kernighan and Plauger's prohibition against echoing the code, it does provide useful information to the programmer; it alerts him to the fact that an operation in the programming language domain - multiplication - is to be mapped into an operation - shifting - in the domain of program execution. In writing comments, then, the programmer should be aware of possible knowledge domains and should strive to make each comment provide information about the mapping from the programming language domain into another domain.

The weakness in this advice is that a selection must be made about which mappings to comment, since commenting all of them would be a monumental task. This, of course, depends on the programmer's perception of the audience for his comments. Guidelines, such as "comment derived uses of data structures" may prove helpful in guiding these perceptions. Even with this drawback, using the concept of bridges between knowledge domains could still be a useful principle in comment construction.

Summary

The theory that has been presented here is intended as a descriptive theory of programmer behavior; it describes how programmers actually behave under current conditions, not how they ought to behave under ideal conditions. Further, the theory is unconcerned with personality characteristics of programmers, with the effects of varying motivational conditions or with social interaction in programming groups. Within these constraints, and noting that the theory is still in the process of being verified, the theory is still a useful tool in software engineering. It makes accurate predictions about the effectiveness of documentation; it can be used to systematically evaluate and critique other claims about documentation, and it may even be a useful guideline to a programmer in actually constructing documentation.

Bibliography

Kernighan, B.W. & Plauger, P.J. The Elements of Programming Style. New York: McGraw-Hill Book Company, 1974.

Ledgard, H. Programming Proverbs. Rochelle Park, N.J.:Hayden Book Company, Inc., 1975.

Shneiderman, B., Mayer, R., McKay, D. & Heller, P. Experimental investigation of the utility of detailed flowcharts in programming. Communications of the A. C. M., 1977, 20(6), 373-381.

Part III: The modification of software

In the Introduction to this Tutorial, we defined software maintenance as: *Work done on a software system after it becomes operational.* Therefore, the modification of software—the actual process of changing a system—is central to maintenance. This is what maintainers are primarily paid to do.

One would expect, then, that the literature on maintenance would be rich with descriptions of the process of change, with breakdowns of the phases and activities of change, and with lists of the tools, techniques, and records appropriate to each part of the change process. This is not so. The process of software change is little understood and little studied. In reviewing material for this part, we found more on issues that arise in software modification than on modification itself. Nevertheless, the topics discussed in this part of the Tutorial are at the center of a proper understanding of maintenance.

Hetzel sketches the context of maintenance in an applications organization; the users demand continuous change, since continuous change is what they themselves must cope with in the real world. Basili and Turner describe a software development project in which expectations for continuous change were factored into the development methodology. Parnas discusses how to construct a system so that it can be assembled into larger or smaller versions. Moriconi describes a prototype software tool that embodies some of the decision processes that a maintainer uses in making a change. Gilb gives a yardstick with which the changeability of a system can be measured. Finally, Belady, one of the pioneers of maintenance research, suggests good engineering principles by which the process of software change might be regulated.

One reason why the process of change has not been popular in the software literature is that change is often a brutish activity in which the software engineer's ideals of elegance and economy are sacrificed to a compromise between need and resources. Changes are initiated by an external agent—the user—who is neither concerned nor familiar with the structure or dynamics of the existing system. Some changes originate as justified complaints about malfunction. Changes are requested at unpredictable times. By an application of Murphy's Law, a change is often exactly what was *not* envisioned in the original design. The resources for making the change are usually limited to what the user regards as reasonable; the only criterion for reasonableness is an assessment of how much the change appears to modify the external capabilities of the system; the user makes no allowance for redesign. All in all, the process of change is usually the application of limited resources to a limited goal in a context of limited understanding.

Nevertheless, the process of making a change has a characteristic structure that can be analyzed and taught. In the paper "What life? What cycle?" (*AFIPS Conference Proceedings*, 51, 1982), Zvegintzov presents a model that analyzes the change process into six activities:

1 Understand the request.
2 Transform the request to a change.
3 Specify the change; choose cut-line and patch.
4 Develop the patch.
5 Test the change.
6 Install the change.

1. *Understand the request.* The request is a statement by the user in the user's language of something the user wants relative to the operational system. Understanding the user's request involves knowing the user's language and the user's system well enough to construct an external description of the new system that the user is requesting.

2. *Transform the request to a change.* The maintainer has a description of the existing system as well as one of the desired system. Transforming the request to a change entails finding the differences between the two systems; the activity of change is to reduce these differences.

3. *Specify the change; choose cut-line and patch.* The maintainer now specifies the modifications to be made to the existing system. These modifications consist of the *cut-line*, which is existing code, data, or procedures to be modified, and the *patch*, which is new code, data, or procedures to be developed. Specifying the cut-line is the major challenge of the change process; if the change is performed by a team, choosing the cut-line is the responsibility of the most skilled member. The cut-line must be chosen to minimize interaction between the existing system and the patch; this minimizes the danger of unintentionally damaging existing functions of the system and provides for orderly development of the patch.

4. *Develop the patch.* The patch is developed by the use of any standard development methodology. The goals and requirements of the patch development are that the patch should perform the desired new function. The specifications of the patch development are that the patch must fit with the cut-line.

115

The design, code, and unit test phases of the patch development are performed as a classic development project, which should be managed with modern structured methods.

5. *Test the change.* The patch is tested in its development environment. The cut-line is tested for appropriate switching between existing functions and the functions of the patch. The patch is installed at the cut-line, and the new system is probed for unanticipated ripple effects. The system undergoes regression testing by executing tests saved from previous change cycles.

6. *Install the change.* The maintainer announces to the users a cut-over date, disseminates updated documentation, and monitors the new system for post-implementation problems.

The six activities are intended to summarize the stages of change just as the more familiar milestones of the development life cycle summarize the stages of development. Like the development model, this model is intended to provide a checklist for instructing novices, a guideline for dividing roles within a team, and a framework for managing a change project. Only by evolving and validating such models can the researcher contribute to the core activity of software maintenance, i.e. the modification of software.

Introduction

Hetzel, B. "A perspective on software development." IEEE Computer Society, *3rd International Conference on Software Engineering*, 1978, 260-263.

Many of the authors included in this Tutorial use the word "evolution" to denote the changes a system undergoes in the context of the changing requirements of its users; in fact, Part IV is titled "The evolution of software." In the following paper, Hetzel uses the word more personally, to describe the "evolution" of his own view of the software development process as he gains a perspective on the nature of the user's relationship to the system.

Hetzel has had an interesting variety of experiences to give him such a perspective. Throughout his career, he has blended research and practical management. After a stint in the U.S. Navy, he ran the academic computer center at the University of North Carolina. Here, among a faculty that included Frederick P. Brooks, Jr., author of *The Mythical Man-Month* (Addison-Wesley Publishing Company, 1975), he completed Ph.D. research on program testing. Hetzel also edited the collection *Program test methods* (Prentice-Hall, 1973).

Hetzel then moved to Blue Cross and Blue Shield, where he advanced through data processing management to be Senior Vice-President of Administration. In 1979 he left Blue Cross to found the Information Management Institute. In his consulting work, Hetzel now specializes in various aspects of software testing and the management of the testing and quality assurance functions.

The paper reprinted below is based on an answer that Hetzel gave in a panel discussion to a question posed by the development expert Michael Jackson: "What is wrong with software system development?" In answering the question, Hetzel recapitulated the evolution of his attitudes to development and thereby condensed the evolution of these attitudes in the management community at large.

This evolution has had three phases. In the first phase, managers transformed the software project from an exercise of intuition and improvisation into one of orderly processes and appropriate tools. In the second phase, having tamed the process, they turned their attention to the orderly capture of the user's requirements, since the user's requirements are the motivation for the software process. In the third phase, having learned to capture the user's requirements, managers became aware that these requirements are not static but are themselves in continual evolution.

The challenge of software maintenance—or "software evolution" as many authors prefer to call it—is to find tools and techniques for guiding and modifying a system that currently satisfies requirements so that it may continue to do so. The double capability of a system—first, to satisfy today's requirements and, second, to be modifiable to tomorrow's—is what Hetzel terms "manageability."

A PERSPECTIVE ON SOFTWARE DEVELOPMENT

Bill Hetzel, Ph.D.

Blue Cross and Blue Shield of Indiana

Abstract

This paper retraces an evolution of thought
on the key problems in producing software. The
author's perspective is traced through an early
emphasis on development tools and methodology to
an emphasis on specifications and requirements to
a broader emphasis on overall manageability. The
evolving thought process is projected ahead and
illustrated by some current efforts and activities.
The paper concludes with a discussion of the
approaches to further enhancing the development
process and the author's view on which areas
should be given the main attention.

The Problem - In Reflection

It is generally taken for granted that there
is something wrong with the way we produce software. The question of just what the problem is
has been in front of all of us for many years, but
we have avoided careful definition and plunged
ahead with all sorts of purported solutions. Many
cures have been promoted and pursued with little
serious examination of the problem they address
and whether that problem really lies at the heart
of our difficulties. Reflecting back, I realize
my own thinking about what the main problem is
has changed sharply during the past several years
and want to share that evolution.

When I was first involved as a development
manager, I was convinced that the key problem was
the development methodology we were using. The
absence of formalism and structure and the inadequate tools with which to work seemed to me to
be at the heart of the difficulties encountered.
I was convinced that a disciplined process built
around new tools was needed and based on that conviction, I spent a number of years working on software development tools. I became involved in
several research projects aimed at creating tools
to assist in program testing and validation. We
built a tool to monitor software modules and feed
back information about the instructions that were
executed and the states and conditions of the
variables. We also built a tool to generate test
data and generally assist in the testing process.
The motivation for the tools was to automate some
parts of the development process and provide
better information about the software being produced.

We felt that the existence of good tools would
give a basis for structuring the largely unstructured activities that were a part of the
development process. In retrospect, we encountered
some early signals that were troubling. In
building the tools we found it convenient and
necessary to restrict their scope so as to ignore
many practical problems. Gradually we came to
recognize that all of the validation tools were
only as good as the program specifications permitted them to be, and as we learned more about
the difficulties of producing good specifications,
our troubles increased. Yet, we plunged ahead in
the blind belief that the practical difficulties
could be erased in time.

My own focus changed somewhat when I became
responsible for a data processing shop with a
larger size development group of about fifty
people. My first initiatives were to put in the
kind of disciplined methodology I believed in --
standards, structured design, programmer teams,
inspections and reviews, rigorous documentation
control and as many other tools and aids as we
could find. This helped, some might even say it
helped tremendously, however, our problems did
not go away as we did not create the kind of
peaceful bliss so sought after. The clients we
served were impressed with our professional
approach and structured process, but were seldom
happy with the products. We began to realize how
difficult it was to communicate needs and desires
well and gradually my feelings about what was
wrong with software development began to change.
I came to believe that the key problem was in
getting the software requirements right, expressed clearly and without ambiguity and that
this was more fundamental than the particular
tools or methodology employed.

The problems in a larger shop of communicating from the client area manager with an idea,
to the individual designated by that manager,
to the analyst, to the system designer, to the
program designer and finally to the programmer
are enormous. We tried all kinds of techniques
for getting good requirements and increased
client involvement. We had clients run projects;
we had client requirement walkthrus and formal
validation and signoff. We tried typewriter simulations in which the client was given the simulated outputs of the proposed system to walk

Reprinted from *The Third International Conference on Software
Engineering Proceedings*, 1978, pages 260-263. Copyright © 1978
by The Institute of Electrical and Electronics Engineers, Inc.

through their own operations. Finally, we emphasized systems education and involvement so our clients could understand the process better. None of this really seemed to make a big difference. We began to realize that even if the requirements were clearly set, they quickly changed with time and the constant turnover of people and ideas. The requirements began to look more and more like a way for us to protect ourselves. When the client complained about something that was wrong, we could say -- "What did you expect? You didn't specify that in the requirements, so naturally it was not a part of the system." But that did not make the client with a real need anything but more frustrated. He still did not come away feeling that we were really responsive to his need or that the quality of our products was good.

My focus changed again when I came to Indiana Blue Cross Blue Shield with a systems group of almost two hundred analysts and programmers. Like most large shops, structure and discipline in the development process are central to our efforts to produce quality systems effectively. We have a formal requirements specification process through which each new system passes, and we spend a great deal of time and money developing and documenting the functional requirements and ensuring their completeness. While far from perfect, our process represents an effort that is substantial and that is well developed. Overall, we feel that the tools we are using, the development process itself and the attention we pay to getting good requirements are considerably above industry norms.

However, our troubles are certainly still with us. Again, new problems are emerging and changing our thinking. We are being forced to give more emphasis to a systems approach to the total business activity being addressed. We seem to need to look at the interaction of information and people in the broadest sense. Instead of being concerned about a software system, we are thinking about a business solution as a mix of customs, policies, procedures, client notions and staff ideas and philosophy. All of this mixes together to address a particular problem with the role of automation seen as just another part in the ever changing blend. What we seem to be doing is shifting our attention from the software requirements to a higher level set of business requirements and reaching the conclusion that we need to develop a more mature perspective on the entire development process -- even to the point of what can be expected.

Perhaps a better view to give to clients goes something like this. First, let's sit down and work out broad success criteria that can be meaningfully measured. What do we really want to achieve? How can we measure a successful effort in the broadest sense? What do we not want to happen? This would be similar to the goal setting corporate planning process used at the start of any project activity and would result in criteria to define project success and client expectation. Included would be the major functional characteristics to be provided, cost ranges to build and

operate, operating productivity and performance measures and other high level metrics that might be applicable. The system would then be developed and measured against those criteria.

Clients would be urged to view that process as inherently iterative. The emphasis on defining everything about a new system in advance seems unwarranted and unwise. It is not the customary business approach for solving problems; and considering that we expect as much as five times the effort to be spent in later maintenance and at least ten times the cost in operation, our time would be better spent trying to ensure flexibility and simplicity than to ensure completeness. The notion is to establish a different perspective on what we are trying to achieve and how we define its success so that clients perceive us more as partners in addressing a business problem than technically mysterious builders of complex automated systems.

The Problem - In Projection

With the changes that I have traced in my own thinking about what our real problem in building software is or has been, I guess I should be wary of thinking what I feel today has any real permanence. My evolution of thought has come from an early concern with the development methodology, to an emphasis on requirements and specifications, to a broader emphasis on the total activity view and higher level requirements. What does this tell us about where our problem really lies and what it is likely to be in the future?

It seems clear that significant improvements in our ability to develop software can come about only by eliminating part of the work; or streamlining and simplifying the parts we do perform; or managing and controlling the whole process better. The attention during the past decade has been on the first two approaches. We have tried to automate and eliminate various steps in the process and have steadily enhanced the power of our languages. We have added a host of techniques to structure and streamline the process. We have emphasized tools, methodology and requirements specification. All the cures we have tended to promote have probably been overstated and have passed over the deeper problem of effective manageability. Clearly though, they are important elements. Much more can still be done in some of the areas -- particularly to improve productivity. Further efforts to reuse standardized pieces of programs is a notable example. However, for the most part, this author is convinced that the major limiting factor in most projects is basic management and improvements that concentrate on allowing us to effectively measure and control our efforts are the most fruitful efforts we can make.

I am convinced that we are at least very close to the point where factors other than methodology are pacing. Numerous studies have been made to determine why software projects (or for that matter, projects of any type) have turned out unsuccessfully, and they almost always identify improper planning and lack of control as the key factors. The methodology

employed may affect productivity and cost significantly, but it seems to bear little consistent
relationship to other aspects of project success.
Other related factors have also been suggested as
limiting. Motivation of the client and data processing personnel along with top management support
are examples. All of these notions relate to the
management aspects of a project and lead me to
conclude that the problem in projection is really
manageability -- that is, our ability to meaningfully oversee and control the projects we undertake. In retrospect this is a natural extension
of my evolution in thought. Much of the focus
behind the early tool work was to establish some
controls over the development process; the focus
on requirements was to stress the planning phase
of a project and better organize the solution
and the focus on a total system view was to provide
a high level goal setting and control mechanism.
All of these contained an element that was trying
to address project manageability. What I believe
we really have been looking for is an effective
means of managing our software efforts and demon-
strating that manageability to the clients we
serve.

An Example - Our Proposed Test System

Recognizing manageability as the principal
problem brings about a very different approach
toward improving the development process. As
an example, the test system now under development
at Indiana Blue Cross and Blue Shield is described. The installation serves about 200 people,
submitting approximately 8,000 test jobs a month.
An IBM 370/158 is virtually dedicated to testing
and provides interactive services to 40 TSO
terminals, supported by a background source
management system. Like many installations, ours
has had continuing difficulty in effectively
managing the testing process for our projects. I
believe our problems are fairly typical -- widely
varying and unpredictable resource and time needs,
staff and supervisor complaints and end products
that are poorly tested and buggy. As a result,
we made a commitment to review the entire testing
process with manageability uppermost in our minds.
This effort was quite unlike the typical testing
study. We did not look at tools and compare ROSCOE
vrs. TSO or anything even similar. Instead, we
concentrated on defining the testing behavior that
we wanted and how we could manage that behavior.
The emphasis was on management concerns. Technical
staff supported a fact base that was collected to
give management meaningful data on the way testing
was actually being performed but played only a
minor role in the conclusions. Data was obtained
from questionnaires, interviews, system monitoring,
workflow studies and behavior observations. A few
points noted were the following:

. The vast majority (nearly 70%) of the jobs have
     nothing to do with actually testing a problem,
     but are support activities leading up to the
     creation of a test situation.
. Print usage for test jobs is amazingly high;
     averaging between 400,000 and 500,000 lines of
     print per month per individual.

. The vast majority of the test system users
    (nearly 90%) use only a few of the features
    available to them through TSO.
. The delay in test turnaround is primarily from
    completion of the job until the test output
    is returned.
. Only a selected few individuals truly understand
    all of the testing facilities available to
    them and how they interact.
. Terminal users lose as much as two hours per
    test through distraction, wait time, difficul-
    ties and failures. Rarely do they lose less
    than thirty minutes.

After the data was gathered, we decided on the
results that management should see if the right
test system existed. The idea was to define the
behavior management wanted as precisely as we
could, and then to build in from the beginning a
manageable set of controls to monitor and realize
that behavior. Inherent in this was the belief
that an effective control system was the heart
of the matter and the most important part of our
new test process. The results statements that
were agreed upon are shown below. (In these statements, the term TESTOR is used to refer to the
programmer using the test system.)

. Unit testing of new programs should be a
    short intensive period of continuous
    activity.
. The TESTOR should feel an obligation
    (or pressure) to complete a testing
    situation within a specified number
    of test sessions or a specified cost.
. The TESTOR should rarely have to leave his
    desk to submit tests or receive results.
. The TESTOR establishes test conditions only
    on unit testing a new program. For any
    exception test, test data is created for
    him.
. Successful test results should be defined
    prior to initiation of the test.
. Programs placed into production should
    fail only 5% of the time due to pro-
    gramming error within the first four
    production uses.
. The total cost of testing should not
    exceed 40% of the personnel budget and
    25% of the equipment use.
. The TESTOR and his management should
    receive feedback on his use and
    efficiency interacting with the test
    system.
. The test system procedure should be
    simple enough to be expressed on one
    normal piece of typing paper or committed
    to memory.
. No more than 1 of 100 jobs submitted by
    all TESTORS should require any computer
    operator intervention.
. The access to production files should be
    limited to a small number of people.

- Test resources belong to the test system and its manager. Use of the test system (establishing priorities, scheduling, etc.) should be performed with the resources allocated to the test system rather than each test priority competing with all production jobs.
- Each time a new system, job or program is delivered to production, the new test conditions which are used to create it follow to update the test system.
- The TESTOR need only learn one set of test procedures which are the same 24 hours per day seven days per week.
- From submission of a test until receipt of output on exception testing should not exceed three hours.
- The TESTOR should not have to work abnormal hours to do his testing.
- The TESTOR should be rewarded for efficient and effective testing.
- The TESTOR should be isolated from any support activity required to set up a test.
- "Unusual" testing activity should be isolated and performed outside the test system.
- The TESTOR should do no unnecessary coding and concentrate strictly on the application logic.
- A TESTOR should seek assistance when he has a difficult testing problem he cannot resolve.
- Testing should be managed; there should be clear management accountability for its management.

We felt that any test system that delivered these results was an excellent one and have placed our development emphasis on the controls needed to tell management what is actually happening. We are stressing how management can encourage the desired behavior and know what behavior is really taking place. The basic strategy that we are proposing is to set up a paraprofessional test unit that will take over the functions of test setup, compiler error correction and test execution. However, the particular approach is less important than the motivation for it and the fact that the technical aspects have very little significance in our minds.

Although we are still in the planning stage for our new test system, we are convinced that we can greatly improve the testing process and shorten the time required to develop new programs or make changes to existing ones. We feel that the desired behavior and management control approach to that effort is the best direction we can pursue to realize enhanced productivity consistently.

Conclusion

We have traced an evolution of thought about what, if anything, is wrong with the way we develop software. While I agree that the state of the art is not conspicuously satisfactory, I am convinced that more of that is due to ineffective management than to a serious illness. My conclusion is that the process for producing software does not need radical surgery. My answer to the "main" problem is that there is no one main problem. Good tools, good specifications and a total systems view are all important, and a useful perspective is gained by thinking of those problems in the light of the broad goal of good software management. I see our failures as chiefly due to management factors rather than technical ones and feel that even the technical issues require serious management attention.

David King, President of Infotech, recently remarked that the "state of software is not yet at the point that one can start prescribing cures for whatever ails it and that doing so would be like trying to play the role of doctor at a time when medicine is almost totally undeveloped." Perhaps that is a correct assessment. However, I would argue that the case is unconvincing that there is anything really seriously wrong other than our continuing failure to pay enough attention to how we manage our projects. The importance of personal accountability and objective yardsticks that management can relate to cannot be underestimated. I am certain that they are far more critical to project success than the methodologies we continue to pursue so intensively. Directing our attentions toward better manageability is overdue, and in the eyes of this author is the area we will increasingly focus upon.

I have ended with a perspective that places a premium on effective software management. A better understanding of how management measures a project and what is expected is an important and essential element in achieving maturity. Tom Gilb has suggested that a fundamental error we make is trying to achieve control by indirect technical methods and suggests instead the use of various metrics as a safer and more flexible means of achieving the control desired. I feel he is right, and that software metrics is one important example of the shifting attention to manageability. While past efforts have tended to ignore or de-emphasize manageability, we now see it becoming the central issue in successful software production and welcome that shift with anticipation.

Introduction

Basili, V.R., Turner, A.J. "Iterative enhancement: a practical technique for software development." *IEEE Trans. Software Engineering*, SE-1, 4, (1975), 390-396.

One of the pleasures of editing this Tutorial is to find that we have selected papers for which the demand for copies is steady or rising. This is true for the following paper, which appeared in the first volume, now out of print except in microfiche form, of a relatively new journal—the *IEEE Transactions on Software Engineering*. Victor Basili and Albert Turner, the authors of the following paper, report a constant stream of requests for copies of it.

The strength of the paper is that it reports a development project of substantial size (a language compiler), carried out in the research environment of a major university and managed from its inception with a philosophy of incremental change. The developers delivered at each release a usable subset of the "ideal" system. They kept a "project control list"—essentially a binder or file—of pending enhancements, which measured the "distance" between the current release and the ideal system. These enhancements included announced but unimplemented features, new features requested by the users, and design changes generated by the developers themselves. As Basili told us, the developers put themselves into the maintenance phase early in the project.

The greatest strength of their approach was to take an activist rather than a defensive approach to maintenance. One of their guidelines was

> Modifications should become easier to make as the iterations progress. If not, then there is a basic problem such as a design flaw or a proliferation of 'patches.'

Therefore, Basili and Turner were quick to rewrite code, and to reorganize module and data structures in order to limit the complexity of the growing system. They told us that three or four times as much code must have been written than that which appeared in the final system, but the code rewriting, as well as the modifications themselves, became easier as the system grew. Their statistics, quoted in the second half of the paper, show the system becoming more tightly structured as it evolved.

In retrospect they regard the project as an instance of the positive side of Lehman and Belady's "Law of Increasing Complexity." This law is quoted by Lehman in his paper reprinted in Part IV of this Tutorial:

> As an evolving program is continually changed, its complexity, reflecting deteriorating structure, increases *unless work is done to maintain or reduce it.* [Emphasis added.]

This "law of increasing complexity" is usually cited in its negative aspect to indicate that a software system must decay into unmodifiable complexity. Basili and Turner feel that their project shows that the positive aspect of the law is just as important. This aspect must be disseminated into the maintenance community as a whole if the full benefit of the enormous investment in existing software is to be achieved.

Both authors are leaders in the field of software engineering. In 1982 Basili was one of two Program Chairpersons for the 6th International Conference on Software Engineering in Tokyo. In 1982 he also became chairman of the Department of Computer Science at the University of Maryland.

Turner completed his Ph.D. in 1976 and moved to the Department of Mathematical Sciences at Clemson University. In 1978 he helped form the Department of Computer Science there, and in 1979 he became its Head.

The term "iterative enhancement," as initiated by these authors, has somewhat penetrated the often conservative corpus of academic computer science. Theirs is the only term relating to maintenance used anywhere in the Association for Computing Machinery's recommended curriculum for an undergraduate program in computer science! (Austing, R.H., et al. "Curriculum '78—Recommendations for the undergraduate program in computer science." *Comm. ACM*, 22, 3 (1979), 147-166)

Iterative Enhancement: A Practical Technique for Software Development

VICTOR R. BASILI AND ALBERT J. TURNER

Abstract—This paper recommends the "iterative enhancement" technique as a practical means of using a top-down, stepwise refinement approach to software development. This technique begins with a simple initial implementation of a properly chosen (skeletal) subproject which is followed by the gradual enhancement of successive implementations in order to build the full implementation. The development and quantitative analysis of a production compiler for the language SIMPL-T is used to demonstrate that the application of iterative enhancement to software development is practical and efficient, encourages the generation of an easily modifiable product, and facilitates reliability.

Index Terms—Iterative enhancement, SIMPL, software analysis, software development, software evaluation measures, top-down design.

INTRODUCTION

SEVERAL techniques have been suggested as aids for producing reliable software that can be easily updated to meet changing needs [1]–[4]. These include the use of a top-down modular design, a careful design before coding, modular well-structured components, and a minimal number of implementors. Although it is generally agreed that the basic guideline is the use of a top-down modular approach using "stepwise refinement" [5], this technique is often not easy to apply in practice when the project is of reasonable size. Building a system using a well-modularized, top-down approach requires that the problem and its solution be well understood. Even if the implementors have previously undertaken a similar project, it is still difficult to achieve a good design for a new system on the first try. Furthermore, design flaws often do not show up until the implementation is well underway so that correcting the problems can require major effort.

One practical approach to this problem is to start with a simple initial implementation of a subset of the problem and iteratively enhance existing versions until the full system is implemented. At each step of the process, not only extensions but also design modifications can be made. In fact, each step can make use of stepwise refinement in a more effective way as the system becomes better

understood through the iterative process. As these iterations converge to the full solution, fewer and fewer modifications need be made. "Iterative enhancement" represents a practical means of applying stepwise refinement.

This paper discusses the heuristic iterative enhancement algorithm and its application to the implementation of a fully instrumented production compiler for the programming language SIMPL-T [6]. The SIMPL-T project represents a successful practical experience in using the approach in conjunction with several of the standard informal techniques to develop a highly reliable and easily modifiable product in a relatively short amount of time.

The next section of this paper contains a discussion of the basic iterative enhancement method, independent of a specific application. The following section discusses the application of the method as used in the development of the compiler for SIMPL-T, and includes some initial results from a quantitative analysis of the SIMPL-T project.

OVERVIEW OF THE METHOD

The first step in the application of the iterative enhancement technique to a software development project consists of a simple initial implementation of a skeletal subproblem of the project. This skeletal implementation acts as an initial guess in the process of developing a final implementation which meets the complete set of project specifications. A *project control list* is created that contains all the tasks that need to be performed in order to achieve the desired final implementation. At any given point in the process, the project control list acts as a measure of the "distance" between the current and final implementations.

In the remaining steps of the technique the current implementation is iteratively enhanced until the final implementation is achieved. Each iterative step consists of selecting and removing the next task from the list, designing the implementation for the selected task (the *design phase*), coding and debugging the implementation of the task (the *implementation phase*), performing an analysis of the existing partial implementation developed at this step of the iteration (the *analysis phase*), and updating the project control list as a result of this analysis. The process is iterated until the project control list is empty, i.e., until a final implementation is developed that meets the project specifications.

Although the details of the algorithm vary with the particular problem class and implementation environment,

Manuscript received August 5, 1975. This work was supported in part by the Office of Naval Research under Grant N00014-67-A-0239-0021 (NR-044-431) to the Computer Science Center of the University of Maryland, and in part by the Computer Science Center of the University of Maryland.

V. R. Basili is with the Department of Computer Science, University of Maryland, College Park, Md. 20742.
A. J. Turner is with the Department of Mathematical Sciences, Clemson University, Clemson, S. C.

125

a set of guidelines can be given to further specify the various steps in the process. The development of the first step, the skeletal initial implementation, may be achieved by defining the implementation of a skeletal subset of the problem. A skeletal subset is one that contains a good sampling of the key aspects of the problem, that is simple enough to understand and implement easily, and whose implementation would make a usable and useful product available to the user. This subset should be devoid of special case analysis and should impose whatever restrictions might be necessary to facilitate its implementation without seriously affecting its usability. The implementation itself should be simple and straightforward in overall design and straightforward and modular at lower levels of design and coding so that it can be modified easily in the iterations leading to the final implementation.

The project control list guides the iterative process by keeping track of all the work that needs to be done in order to achieve the final implementation. The tasks on the list include the redesign or recoding of components in which flaws have been discovered, the design and implementation of features and facilities that are missing from the current implementation, and the solution of unsolved problems. The sequence of lists corresponding to the sequence of partial implementations is a valuable component of the historical documentation of the project.

Each entry in the project control list is a task to be performed in one step of the iterative process. It is important that each task be conceptually simple enough to be completely understood in order to minimize the chance of error in the design and implementation phases of the process.

A major component of the iterative process is the analysis phase that is performed on each successive implementation. The project control list is constantly being revised as a result of this analysis. This is how redesign and recoding work their way into the control list. Specific topics for analysis include such items as the structure, modularity, modifiability, usability, reliability and efficiency of the current implementation as well as an assessment of the achievement of the goals of the project. One approach to a careful analysis is the use of an appropriate set of guidelines as follows.

1) Any difficulty in design, coding, or debugging a modification should signal the need for redesign or recoding of existing components.
2) Modifications should fit easily into isolated and easy-to-find modules. If not, then some redesign is needed.
3) Modifications to tables should be especially easy to make. If any table modification is not quickly and easily done, then a redesign is indicated.
4) Modifications should become easier to make as the iterations progress. If not, then there is a basic problem such as a design flaw or a proliferation of "patches."
5) "Patches" should normally be allowed to exist for only one or two iterations. Patches should be allowed, however, in order to avoid redesigning during an implementation phase.
6) The existing implementation should be analyzed frequently to determine how well it measures up to the project goals.
7) Program analysis facilities should be used whenever available to aid in the analysis of the partial implementations.
8) User reaction should always be solicited and analyzed for indications of deficiencies in the existing implementation.

Certain aspects of the iteration process are dependent on the local environment in which the work is being performed, rather than on the specific project. Although the techniques used in the design and implementation phases of each iteration step should basically be top-down stepwise refinement techniques, the specifics can vary depending on such factors as installation standards and the number of people involved. Much has been written elsewhere about such techniques, and they will not be discussed further here. The procedures used in the analysis phase for each partial implementation are dependent upon such local factors as the program analysis facilities available, the programming languages used, and the availability of user feedback. Thus, to some extent the efficient use of the iterative enhancement technique must be tailored to the implementation environment.

In summary, iterative enhancement is a heuristic algorithm that begins with the implementation of a subproblem and proceeds with the iterative modification of existing implementations based on a set of informal guidelines in order to achieve the desired full implementation. Variants of this technique have undoubtedly been used in many applications. However, iterative enhancement is different from the iterative techniques often discussed in the literature, in which the entire problem is initially implemented and the existing implementations are iteratively refined or reorganized [2] to achieve a good final design and implementation.

APPLICATION OF THE METHOD TO COMPILER DEVELOPMENT

Compiler development falls into a class of problems that can be called *input directed*. Such problems have well-defined inputs that determine the processing to be performed. The application of the iterative enhancement method to compiler development will be discussed in this section. In order to be more specific, it is assumed that the syntax of the language L to be compiled is defined by a context free grammar G.

Since a compiler is input directed, the skeletal compiler to be initially implemented can be specified by choosing a skeletal language, L_0, for L. The language L_0 may be slightly modified sublanguage of L with a grammar G_0 that is essentially a subgrammar of G.

In choosing L_0, a small number of features of L are

chosen as a basis. For example, this basis might include one data type, three or four statement types, one parameter mechanism, a few operators, and other features needed to give L_0 the overall general flavor of L. The language derived from this basis can then be modified for ease of implementation and improved usability to obtain L_0.

The remainder of this section describes the use of iterative enhancement in an actual compiler implementation.

A Case Study: the SIMPL-T Project

The iterative enhancement method was used at the University of Maryland in the implementation of a compiler for the procedure-oriented algorithmic language SIMPL-T [6] on a Univac 1108. The SIMPL-T project is discussed in this section, beginning with a brief illustration of the scope of the project.

Overview: SIMPL-T is designed to be the base language for a family of programming languages [7]. Some of its features are as follows.

1) A program consists of a set of separately compiled modules.
2) Each module consists of a set of global variables and a set of procedures and functions.
3) The statement types are assignment, if-then-else, while, case, call, exit, and return.
4) The data types are integer, character, and character string.
5) There are extensive sets of operators and intrinsics for data manipulation.
6) There is a one-dimensional array of any data type.
7) Procedures and functions may optionally be recursive.
8) Scalar arguments may be passed by reference or by value; arrays are passed by reference.
9) Procedures and functions may not have internal procedures or functions; neither procedures nor functions may be passed as parameters.
10) There is no block structure (but there are compound statements).
11) Procedures, functions, and data may be shared by separately compiled modules.

Characterizing the overall design of the language, its syntax and semantics are relatively conservative, consistent and uncluttered. There are a minimal number of language constructs, and they are all rather basic. A stack is adequate for the runtime environment. These design features contributed to a reasonably well-defined language design which permitted the development of a reasonably well-understood compiler design.

The following are characteristics and facilities of the SIMPL-T compiler:

1) It is programmed in SIMPL-T and is designed to be transportable by rewriting the code generation modules [8].
2) It generates very good object code on the 1108. (In

the only extensive test [9], the code produced was better than that generated by the Univac optimizing Fortran compiler.)
3) Good diagnostics are provided at both compile and runtimes.
4) An attribute and cross-reference listing is available.
5) There are traces available for line numbers, calls and returns, and variable values.
6) Subscript and case range checking are available.
7) There are facilities for obtaining statistics both at compile time and after a program execution.
8) Execution timing for procedures, functions, and separately compiled modules is available.

In summary, the compiler is a production compiler that generates efficient object code, provides good diagnostics, and has a variety of testing, debugging, and program analysis facilities. The compiler itself consists of about 6400 SIMPL-T statements, and the library consists of about 3500 (assembly language) instructions. (The statement count does not include declarations, comments, or spacing. The compiler consists of 17 000 lines of code.)

The Initial Implementation: The skeletal language implemented initially in the SIMPL-T project was essentially the language SIMPL-X [10]. Some of the restrictions (with respect to SIMPL-T) imposed for the initial implementation were:

1) There was only one data type (integer).
2) Only call by value was allowed for scalar parameters.
3) All procedures and functions were recursive.
4) Only the first 12 characters of an identifier name were used.
5) Case numbers were restricted to the range 0–99.
6) Both operands of a logical operator (·AND·, ·OR·) were always evaluated.

Since the compiler was to be self-compiling, some character handling facility was needed. This was provided by an extension that allowed character data to be packed in an integer variable just as in Fortran.

Restrictions were also made on compiler facilities for the initial implementation. Only a source listing and reasonable diagnostics were provided, leaving the debugging and analysis facilities for later enhancements.

The design of the initial skeletal implementation was a rather straightforward attempt to provide a basis for future enhancements. This allowed the initial implementation to be completed rather quickly so that the enhancement process could get underway. It is instructive to note that while most of the higher level design of the compiler proved to be valid throughout the implementation, most of the lower level design and code was redone during the enhancement process. This illustrates the difficulty in doing a good complete project design initially, especially in light of the fact that the initial implementation was an honest attempt to achieve a good basis upon which to build later extensions.

The importance of using a simple approach in the initial

implementation was illustrated by the experience with the initial SIMPL-X code generation module. Although it was not intended to generate really good code, far too much effort was expended in an attempt to generate moderately good code. As a result, most of the initial debugging effort was spent on the code generator (which was later almost completely rewritten anyhow). A simple straightforward approach would have allowed the project to get underway much faster and with much less effort.

A final comment on the skeletal implementation is that it is clear in retrospect that had the compiler not been self-compiling it would have been better to use an even more restricted subset of SIMPL-T. This was not considered at the time because programming the compiler in the initial subset would have been more difficult.

The design and implementation phases of each iteration were performed using a basic top-down approach. Every attempt was made to ensure a high level of clarity and logical construction.

It is worth noting that the SIMPL-T language itself was also being iteratively enhanced in parallel with the compiler development. As experience was gained by using the language to program the compiler, new features were added and old features were modified on the basis of this experience. Thus user experience played a major role not only in the implementation of the software project (i.e., the compiler) but also in the specification of the project (i.e., the language design).

The Analysis Phase: The analysis performed at the end of each iterative step was basically centered around the guidelines given above in the overview of the method. Some of the specific techniques used are briefly discussed below.

Since the intermediate compilers were mostly self-compiling, a large amount of user experience was available from the project itself. This user experience together with the valuable test case provided by the compiler for itself represent two of the advantages of self-compilers.

A second source of user experience in the SIMPL-T project was derived from student use in the classroom. Since classroom projects are not generally ongoing, there was normally no inconvenience to students in releasing the intermediate versions of the compiler as they were completed. These two sources of user experience are examples of how the details of applying iterative enhancement can be tailored to the resources available in the implementation environment.

Testing the intermediate compilers was done by the usual method of using test data. Again the self-compiling feature of the compiler was valuable since the compiler was often its own best test program. The bug farm and bug contest techniques [11] were also used and some of the results are given below.

Timing analyses of the compiler were first done using the University of Maryland Program Instrumentation Package (PIP). PIP provides timing information based on a partition of core and is thus more suitable for assem-

bly language programs than for programs written in higher level languages. However the information obtained from PIP was of some value in locating bottlenecks, especially in the library routines.

When the timing and statistics facilities for object programs were added to the compiler, new tools for analysis of the compiler itself became available. The timing facility has been used to improve the execution speed through the elimination of bottlenecks, and the statistics facilities have been used to obtain information such as the frequency of hashing collisions. Future plans call for further use of the timing information to help improve compiler performance. The statistical facilities were also used to obtain the quantitative analysis discussed at the end of this section.

Project Summary: The SIMPL-T project was completed during a 16 calendar month period. Since other activities took place in parallel with the implementation effort, it is difficult to accurately estimate the total effort, but a fairly accurate effort for the language and compiler design, implementation, and maintenance (excluding the bootstrap and library implementations) is 10 man-months. Counting only the code in the final compiler, this time requirement represents an average output of almost 30 statements (75 lines) of debugged code per man-day. It is felt that the use of iterative enhancement was a major contributing factor in this achievement.

Experience has thus far indicated that the compiler is reasonably easy to modify. Two fairly large modifications have been made by people not previously participating in the compiler implementation. One of these efforts involved the addition of a macro facility and in the other, single and double precision reals were added [9]. Both efforts were accomplished relatively easily even though there was little documentation other than the compiler source listing.

Finally, the reliability of the compiler has been quite satisfactory. During the two and one-half month duration of the bug contest a total of 18 bugs were found, many of which were quite minor. (All bugs regardless of severity were counted.) Of course, several additional bugs had been found before the contest and some have been found since, but overall their number has been small. As could be predicted, most of the bugs occurred in the least well understood components: error recovery and code generation.

Project Analysis: In an attempt to justify that the heuristic iterative enhancement algorithm gives quantitative results, an extensive analysis of four of the intermediate compilers plus the final compiler was performed. As of this writing (June 1975) the analysis is only in the early stages, but some of the preliminary statistics computed are given in Table I. The interpretation of some of these statistics has not been completed, but they have been included as a matter of interest.

The compilers referenced in Table I are

1) One of the early SIMPL-X compilers (SIMPL-X 2.0).

2) The SIMPL-X compiler after a major revision to correct some structural defects (SIMPL-X 3.1).
3) The first SIMPL-T compiler, written in SIMPL-X (SIMPL-X 4.0).
4) Compiler (3), rewritten in SIMPL-T (SIMPL-T 1.0).
5) The current SIMPL-T compiler at the time of the analysis (SIMPL-T 1.6).

The statistics were computed by using the existing statistical facilities of the SIMPL-T compiler, and by adding some new facilities.

An explanation of the statistics given is as follows.

1) Statements are counted as defined by the syntax. A compound statement such as a WHILE statement counts as one statement plus one for each statement in its statement list.
2) A separately compiled module is a collection of globals, procedures, and functions that is compiled independently of other separately compiled modules and combined with the other modules for execution.
3) A token is a syntactic entity such as a keyword, identifier, or operator.
4) Globals were only counted if they were ever modified. That is, named constants and constant tables were not counted.
5) A data binding occurs when a procedure or function P modifies a global X and procedure or function Q accesses (uses the value of) X. This causes a binding (P,X,Q). It is also possible to have the (different) binding (Q,X,P); however (P,X,P) is not counted. The counting procedure was modified so that if P and Q execute only in separate passes and the execution of P precedes that of Q, then (P,X,Q) is counted but (Q,X,P) is not counted.

The reasons for choosing these statistics were based on intuition and a desire to investigate quantitatively the data and control structure characteristics of the sequence of compilers.

It is interesting to note that the statistics indicate a trend towards improvement in the compiler with respect to many generally accepted theories of good programming principles, even though the redesign and recoding efforts that caused this trend were done only on the basis of the informal guidelines of the iterative enhancement algorithm. As the project progressed, the trend was toward more procedures and functions with fewer statements, more independently compiled segments, less nesting of statements, and a decrease in the use of global variables. These improvements occurred even though the changes were being made primarily to correct difficulties that were encountered in incorporating modifications during the iterative enhancement process.

The meaning of many of the trends indicated in Table I is clear. For example, due to the difficulties encountered in working with larger units of code, the number of procedures and functions and the number of separately compiled modules increased much more than did the number of statements. Similarly, the decrease in nesting level corresponds to the increase in the number of procedures and functions.

One of the harder to explain sequences of statistics is the average number of tokens per statement. The probable cause for the large jump between compilers 1) and 2) is the relaxation of several Fortran-like restrictions imposed for the initial bootstrap. The more interesting jump between compilers 3), written in SIMPL-X, and 4), written in SIMPL-T, seems to suggest that writing in a more powerful language (SIMPL-T) may also affect the writing style used by a programmer. That is, with more powerful operators more operators are used per statement.

The statistics for globals, locals, and parameters indicate a clear trend away from the use of globals and toward increased usage of locals and parameters. The large drop in the number of globals accessible to the average procedure or function between compilers 3) and 4) and compilers 4) and 5) corresponds to the increase in the number of separately compiled modules for 4) and 5). Splitting one separately compiled module into several modules decreases the number of accessible globals because the globals are also divided among the modules and are usually not made accessible between modules.

The notion of data binding is more complex than the notions considered above and the data binding statistics require more effort to interpret. Note, for example, that if the number of procedures and functions doubles, then the data binding count would most likely more than double due to the interactions between the new and old procedures and functions. Similarly, splitting a separately compiled module into several modules would tend to decrease the number of possible bindings due to the decrease in the number of accessible globals.

In light of these considerations, the data binding counts in Table I seem reasonable except for the decrease in actual bindings from compiler 4) to compiler 5). A more detailed investigation of this decrease revealed that it was primarily due to the elimination of the improper usage of a set of global variables in the code generation component of the compiler. The sharing of these variables by two logically independent sets of procedure had caused several problems in modifying the code generator, and the data accessing was restructured in an attempt to eliminate these problems.

Finally, the percentage of possible data bindings that actually occurred can be interpreted as an indication of how much variables that are declared globally are really used as globals. (If every procedure and function both modified and accessed all its accessible globals, then the percentage would be 100.) As with the other measures, ideal values (in an absolute sense) are not clear, but the trend toward higher values that is shown in Table I is the desired result.

CONCLUSION

Two major goals for the development of a software product are that it be reasonably modifiable and reliable.

TABLE I
MEASURES MADE ON FIVE DIFFERENT COMPILERS IN THE SIMPL-T PROJECT

	(1)	(2)	(3)	(4)	(5)
Number of Statements	3404	4217	5181	5847	6350
Number of Procedures and Functions	89	189	213	240	289
Number of Separately Compiled Modules	4	4	7	15	37
Average Number of Statements per Proc/Func	38.2	22.3	24.3	24.4	22.0
Average Nesting Level	3.4	2.9	2.9	2.9	2.8
Average Number of Tokens per Statement	5.7	6.3	6.6	7.2	7.3
Number of Data Variables:					
Globals	155	132	151	180	193
Locals	112	381	496	550	621
Parameters	35	184	215	257	388
Average Number of Data Variables per Proc/Func:					
Globals	1.7	0.7	0.7	0.8	0.7
Locals	1.3	2.0	2.3	2.3	2.1
Parameters	0.4	1.0	1.0	1.1	1.3
Percentage of:					
Globals	51.3	18.9	17.5	18.2	16.1
Locals	37.1	54.7	57.5	55.7	51.7
Parameters	11.6	26.4	24.9	26.0	32.3
Average Number of Globals Accessible by a Proc/Func	52.0	52.2	57.4	33.9	22.3
Number of Actual Data Bindings	2610	6662	8759	12006	10442
Number of Possible Data Bindings	243780	814950	1337692	497339	342727
Percentage of Possible Bindings that Occurred	1.1	0.8	0.7	2.4	3.0

This paper recommends the iterative enhancement technique as a methodology for software development that for many projects facilitates the achievement of these goals and provides a practical means of using a top-down stepwise refinement approach.

The technique involves the development of a software product through a sequence of successive design and implementation steps, beginning with an initial "guess" design and implementation of a skeletal subproblem. Each step of the iterative process consists of either a simple, well-understood extension, or a design or implementation modification motivated by a better understanding of the problem obtained through the development process.

It is difficult to make a nonsubjective qualitative judgment about the success of a software technique. However the preliminary statistics from an analysis of the SIMPL-T project do indicate some desirable quantitative results. These statistics suggest that the informal guidelines of the heuristic iterative enhancement algorithm encourage the development of a software product that satisfies a number of generally accepted evaluation criteria.

The measure of accomplishment for the SIMPL-T project was based upon relative improvement with respect to a set of measures. A question remains as to what are absolute measures that indicate acceptable algorithm termination criteria. More work on several different projects and studies of the implications of these measures are needed to help determine some quantitative characteristics of good software.

A need also exists for developing a formal basis for software evaluation measures. An analytical basis for evaluation would not only increase the understanding of the meaning of the measures but should also shed some light on appropriate absolute values that indicate the achievement of good characteristics.

The implementation and analysis of the SIMPL-T system have demonstrated that not only is the iterative enhancement technique an effective means of applying a modular, top-down approach to software implementation, but it is also a practical and efficient approach as witnessed by the time and effort figures for the project. The development of a final product which is easily modified is a by-product of the iterative way in which the product is developed. This can be partially substantiated by the ease with which present extensions and modifications can be made to the system. A reliable product is facilitated since understanding of the overall system and its components is aided by the iterative process in which the design and code are examined and reevaluated as enhancements are made.

REFERENCES

[1] H. D. Mills, "On the development of large, reliable programs," Rec. 1973 IEEE Symp. Comp. Software Reliability, Apr. 1973, pp. 155–159.

[2] ——, "Techniques for the specification and design of complex programs," in *Proc. 3rd Texas Conf. Computing Systems*, Univ. Texas, Austin, Nov. 1974, pp. 8.1.1–8.1.4.

[3] O. J. Dahl, E. W. Dijkstra, and C. A. R. Hoare, *Structured Programming*. London: Academic, 1972.

[4] D. L. Parnas, "On the criteria to be used in decomposing systems into modules," *Commun. Ass. Comput. Mach.*, vol. 15, pp. 1053–1062, Dec. 1972.

[5] N. Wirth, "Program development by stepwise refinement," *Commun. Ass. Comput. Mach.*, vol. 14, pp. 221–227, Apr. 1971.

[6] V. R. Basili and A. J. Turner, "SIMPL-T: a structured programming language," Univ. of Maryland, Comp. Sci. Ctr., CN-14, Jan. 1974.

[7] V. R. Basili, "The SIMPL family of programming languages and compilers," Univ. of Maryland, Comp. Sci. Ctr., TR-305, June 1974.

[8] V. R. Basili and A. J. Turner, "A transportable extendable compiler," in *Software—Practice and Experience*, vol. 5, 1975, pp. 269–278.

[9] J. McHugh and V. R. Basili, "SIMPL-R and its application to large, sparse matrix problems," Univ. of Maryland, Comp. Sci. Ctr., TR-310, July 1974.

[10] V. R. Basili, "SIMPL-X, a language for writing structured programs," Univ. Maryland, Comp. Sci. Ctr., TR-223, Jan. 1973.

[11] M. Rain, "Two unusual methods for debugging system software," in *Software—Practice and Experience*, vol. 3, pp. 61–63, 1973.

Victor R. Basili was born in New York, N.Y., on April 13, 1940. He recieved the B.S. degree in mathematics from Fordham College, New York, N.Y., the M.S. degree in mathematics from Syracuse University, Syracuse, N.Y., and the Ph.D. degree in computer science from the University of Texas, Austin, in 1961, 1963, and 1970, respectively.

From 1963 to 1967 he was with the Department of Mathematics and Computer Science, Providence College, as an Instructor, and for the latter two years, as Assistant Professor. From 1970 to 1975 he was Assistant Professor, and is currently Associate Professor, in the Department of Computer Science, University of Maryland, College Park. He is a consultant with the Institute for Computer Applications in Science and Engineering, NASA Langley Research Center, Hampton, Va., the Naval Research Laboratory, Washington, D.C., and the Naval Surface Weapons Center, Dahlgren Laboratory, Dahlgren, Va. He has been involved in the design and development of the graph algorithmic language, GRAAL, the SIMPL family of programming languages and compilers, and the SL/1 language for the CDC Star computer. His special fields of interest include design, implementation, modeling, and analysis of programming languages and software methodology.

Dr. Basili is a member of the Association for Computing Machinery, the IEEE Computer Society, and the American Association of University Professors.

Albert J. Turner received the B.S. and M.S. degrees in mathematics from the Georgia Institute of Technology, Atlanta, and is currently a candidate for the Ph.D. degree in computer science from the University of Maryland, College Park.

Software development efforts in which he has had a major role include the implementation of an administrative data processing system at West Georgia College, and the development of the SIMPL family of programming languages and compilers at the University of Maryland. He is currently a faculty member in the Department of Mathematical Sciences, Clemson University, Clemson, S.C. His major interests are the design, modeling, and implementation of programming languages, and the design and implementation of computer software.

Introduction

Parnas, D.L. "Designing software for ease of extension and contraction." *IEEE Trans. Software Engineering*, SE-5, 2 (1979), 128-138.

David Parnas, the author of the next paper, was in the audience when Zvegintzov, one of the editors of this Tutorial, gave a talk at the University of Maryland in 1981. Zvegintzov's general theme was to explore why academic computer science has had a hard time grappling with the question of maintenance. (Or, as Parnas remembers it "You had spent 45 minutes of a 50 minute talk telling us that maintenance was important and that we should teach more about it.") In any case, Parnas stood up and said: "You have five minutes to tell me something that we should be teaching that we are not already teaching."

This disconcerting comment was an instance of the notoriously quick tongue which expresses Parnas's fierce dedication to clarity and impatience with conventional ideas. Naturally, Zvegintzov is looking for just the right opportunity to be in the audience of one of Parnas's talks.

Parnas is a leading theorist in computer science who has not lost touch with the realities of computing practice. He admits that after nearly ten years of education and then teaching in computer science, a year spent at the Philips-Electrologica factory observing the real-life problems of programmers changed his view of the priorities of computing research. He was also principal investigator on the project reported by Heninger in Part II of this Tutorial in which the specifications of a complex software system were recovered from its code and its users. Since the fall of 1982 Parnas has been Lansdowne Professor in the Department of Computer Science at the University of Victoria in British Columbia, Canada.

The paper reprinted below can be thought of as one of a sequence of Parnas' papers which explores in a characteristically iconoclastic way the $64,000 question of software engineering: "What can we *really* do to write better systems?" Other papers in the sequence, both referenced in the paper reprinted here, were "On the criteria to be used in decomposing systems into modules," which introduced the idea that every module should "hide a design decision," and "On the design and development of program families," which applied that principle to the design of multi-version programs.

In the paper reprinted below, Parnas continues to discuss the prerequisites for designing a set of related but not identical systems—the classic multiversion problem handled by any software group that distributes a widely used system. Parnas first notes that this problem is not faced by academic computer scientists, who write of "the" task to be performed by "the" system. In real life, each group of users has a somewhat different system implementing somewhat different tasks on a somewhat different configuration. Next, he distinguishes the real-world requirement for flexibility from the mathematician's solution to the problem of multiple versions—finding the most general system of which the multiple versions are special cases. Even though software systems are mathematical objects, they are also working objects; the users will not pay for overrefinement in generality.

How then should one construct a system so that it can be released in multiple working versions? The key is to give criteria for when one program should "use" another, where "use" is carefully defined:

We say of two programs A and B that A *uses* B if correct execution of B may be necessary for A to complete the task described in its specification.

No two programs should "use" each other (otherwise they must both be present if one is present). In addition, A may "use" B if:

- A is essentially simpler because it "uses" B.
- B is not substantially more complex because it is not allowed to "use" A.
- There is a useful subset containing B and not A.
- There is no conceivably useful subset containing A but not B.

With these criteria, Parnas provides operational guidelines for simplicity in the design of multiversion systems. This paper received the Association for Computing Machinery's 1979 Programming Systems and Languages Paper Award.

Designing Software for Ease of Extension
and Contraction

DAVID L. PARNAS

Abstract—Designing software to be extensible and easily contracted is discussed as a special case of design for change. A number of ways that extension and contraction problems manifest themselves in current software are explained. Four steps in the design of software that is more flexible are then discussed. The most critical step is the design of a software structure called the "uses" relation. Some criteria for design decisions are given and illustrated using a small example. It is shown that the identification of *minimal* subsets and *minimal* extensions can lead to software that can be tailored to the needs of a broad variety of users.

Index Terms—Contractibility, extensibility, modularity, software engineering, subsets, supersets.

Manuscript received June 7, 1978; revised October 26, 1978. The earliest work in this paper was supported by NV Phillips Computer Industrie, Apeldoorn, The Netherlands. This work was also supported by the National Science Foundation and the German Federal Ministry for Research and Technology (BMFT). This paper was presented at the Third International Conference on Software Engineering, Atlanta, GA, May 1978.

The author is with the Department of Computer Science, University of North Carolina, Chapel Hill, NC 27514. He is also with the Information Systems Staff, Communications Sciences Division, Naval Research Laboratory, Washington, DC.

I. INTRODUCTION

THIS paper is being written because the following complaints about software systems are so common.

1) "We were behind schedule and wanted to deliver an early release with only a <proper subset of intended capabilities>, but found that that subset would not work until everything worked."

2) "We wanted to add <simple capability>, but to do so would have meant rewriting all or most of the current code."

3) "We wanted to simplify and speed up the system by removing the <unneeded capability>, but to take advantage of this simplification we would have had to rewrite major sections of the code."

4) "Our SYSGEN was intended to allow us to tailor a system to our customers' needs but it was not flexible enough to suit us."

After studying a number of such systems, I have identified some simple concepts that can help programmers to design software so that subsets and extensions are more easily obtained. These concepts are simple if you think about software in the way suggested by this paper. Programmers do not commonly do so.

Reprinted from *IEEE Transactions on Software Engineering*, Volume SE-5, Number 2, March 1979, pages 128-138. Copyright © 1979 by The Institute of Electrical and Electronics Engineers, Inc.

II. Software As a Family of Programs

When we were first taught how to program, we were given a specific problem and told to write one program to do that job. Later we compared our program to others, considering such issues as space and time utilization, but still assuming that we were producing a single product. Even the most recent literature on programming methodology is written on that basis. Dijkstra's *A Discipline of Programming* [1] uses predicate transformers to specify *the* task to be performed by *the* program to be written. The use of the definite article implies that there is a unique problem to be solved and but one program to write.

Today, the software designer should be aware that he is not designing a single program but a family of programs. As discussed in an earlier paper [2], we consider a set of programs to be a program family if they have so much in common that it pays to study their common aspects before looking at the aspects that differentiate them. This rather pragmatic definition does not tell us what pays, but it does explain the motivation for designing program families. We want to exploit the commonalities, share code, and reduce maintenance costs.

Some of the ways that the members of a program family may differ are listed below.

1) They may run on different hardware configurations.

2) They may perform the same functions but differ in the format of the input and output data.

3) They may differ in certain data structures or algorithms because of differences in the available resources.

4) They may differ in some data structures or algorithms because of differences in the size of the input data sets or the relative frequency of certain events.

5) Some users may require only a subset of the services or features that other users need. These "less demanding" users may demand that they not be forced to pay for the resources consumed by the unneeded features.

Engineers are taught that they must try to anticipate the changes that may be made, and are shown how to achieve designs that can easily be altered when these anticipated changes occur. For example, an electrical engineer will be advised that the world has not standardized the 60-cycle 110-V current. Television designers are fully aware of the differing transmission conventions that exist in the world. It is standard practice to design products that are easily changed in those aspects. Unfortunately, there is no magic technique for handling unanticipated changes. The makers of conventional watches have no difficulty altering a watch that shows the day so that it displays "MER" instead of "WED," but I would except a long delay for redesign were the world to switch to a ten day week.

Software engineers have not been trained to design for change. The usual programming courses neither mention the need to anticipate changes nor do they offer techniques for designing programs in which changes are easy. Because programs are abstract mathematical objects, the software engineers' techniques for responding to anticipated changes are more subtle and more difficult to grasp than the techniques used by designers of physical objects. Further, we have been led astray by the other designers of abstract objects—mathematicians who state

and prove theorems. When a mathematician becomes aware of the need for a set of closely related theorems, he responds by proving a more general theorem. For mathematicians, a more general result is always superior to a more specialized product. The engineering analogy to the mathematician's approach would be to design television sets containing variable transformers and tuners that are capable of detecting several types of signals. Except for the U.S. armed forces stationed overseas, there is little market for such a product. Few of us consider relocations so likely that we are willing to pay to have the generality present in the product. My guess is that the market for calendar watches for a variable length week is even smaller than the market for the television sets just described.

In [2] I have treated the subject of the design of program families rather generally and in terms of text in a programming language. In this paper I focus on the fifth situation described above; families of programs in which some members are subsets of other family members or several family members share a common subset. I discuss an earlier stage of design, the stage when one identifies the major components of the system and defines relations between those components. We focus on this early stage because the problems described in the introduction result from failure to consider early design decisions carefully.

III. How Does the Lack of Subsets and Extensions Manifest Itself?

Although we often speak of programs that are "not subsetable" or "not extensible," we must recognize that phrase as inaccurate. It is always possible to remove code from a program and have a runable result. Any software system can be extended (TSO proves that). The problem is that the subsets and extensions are not the programs that we would have designed if we had set out to design just that product. Further, the amount of work needed to obtain the product seems all out of proportion to the nature of the change. The obstacles commonly encountered in trying to extend or shrink systems fall into four classes.

A. Excessive Information Distribution

A system may be hard to extend or contract if too many programs were written assuming that a given feature is present or not present. This was illustrated by an operating system in which an early design decision was that the system would support three conversational languages. There were many sections of the system where knowledge of this decision was used. For example, error message tables had room for exactly three entries. An extension to allow four languages would have required that a great deal of code be rewritten. More surprisingly, it would have been difficult to reduce the system to one that efficiently supported only two of the languages. One could remove the third language, but to regain the table space, one would have had to rewrite the same sections of code that would be rewritten to add a language.

B. A Chain of Data Transforming Components

Many programs are structured as a chain of components, each receiving data from the previous component, processing it (and changing the format), before sending the data to the next program in the chain. If one component in this chain is not needed, that code is often hard to remove because the output of its predecessor is not compatible with the input requirements of its successor. A program that does nothing but change the format must be substituted. One illustration would be a payroll program that assumed unsorted input. One of the components of the system accepts the unsorted input and produces output that is sorted by some key. If the firm adopts an office procedure that results in sorted input, this phase of the processing is unnecessary. To eliminate that program, one may have to add a program that transfers data from a file in the input format to a file in the format appropriate for the next phase. It may be almost as efficient to allow the original SORT component to sort the sorted input.

C. Components That Perform More Than One Function

Another common error is to combine two simple functions into one component because the functions seem too simple to separate. For example, one might be tempted to combine synchronization with message sending and acknowledgment in building an operating system. The two functions seem closely related; one might expect that for the sake of reliability one should insist on a "handshake" with each exchange of synchronization signals. If one later encounters an application in which synchronization is needed very frequently, one may find that there is no simple way to strip the message sending out of the synchronization routines. Another example is the inclusion of run-time type-checking in the basic subroutine call mechanism. In applications where compile-time checking or verification eliminates the need for the run-time type-check, another subroutine call mechanism will be needed. The irony of these situations is that the "more powerful" mechanism could have been built separately from, but *using*, simpler mechanisms. Separation would result in a system in which the simpler mechanism was available for use where it sufficed.

D. Loops in the "Uses" Relation

In many software design projects, the decisions about what other component programs to use are left to individual systems programmers. If a programmer knows of a program in another module, and feels that it would be useful in his program, he includes a call on that program in his text. Programmers are encouraged to use the work of other programmers as much as possible because, when each programmer writes his own routines to perform common functions, we end up with a system that is much larger than it need be.

Unfortunately, there are two sides to the question of program usage. Unless some restraint is exercised, one may end up with a system in which nothing works until everything works. For example, while it may seem wise to have an operating system scheduler use the file system to store its data (rather than use its own disk routines), the result will be that the file system must be present and working before any task scheduling is possible. There are users for whom an operating system subset without a file system would be useful. Even if one has no such users, the subset would be useful during development and testing.

IV. Steps Towards a Better Structure

This section discusses four parts of a methodology that I believe will help the software engineer to build systems that do not evidence the problems discussed above.

A. Requirements Definition: Identifying the Subsets First

One of the clearest morals in the earlier discussion about "design for change" as it is taught in other areas of engineering is that one must anticipate changes before one begins the design. At a past conference [3] many of the papers exhorted the audience to spend more time identifying the actual requirements before starting on a design. I do not want to repeat such exhortations, but I do want to point out that the identification of the possible subsets is part of identifying the requirements. Treating the easy availability of certain subsets as an operational requirement is especially important to government officials who purchase software. Many officials despair of placing strict controls on the production methods used by their contractors because they are forbidden by law to tell the contractor how to perform his job. They may tell him what they require, but not how to build it. Fortunately, the availability of subsets may be construed as an operational property of the software.

On the other hand, the identification of the required subsets is not a simple matter of asking potential users what they could do without. First, users tend to overstate their requirements. Second, the answer will not characterize the set of subsets that might be wanted in the future. In my experience, identification of the potentially desirable subsets is a demanding intellectual exercise in which one first searches for the *minimal* subset that might conceivably perform a useful service and then searches for a set of *minimal* increments to the system. Each increment is small—sometimes so small that it seems trivial. The emphasis on minimality stems from our desire to avoid components that perform more than one function (as discussed in Section III-C). Identifying the minimal subset is difficult because the minimal system is not usually a program that anyone would ask for. If we are going to build the software family, the minimal subset is useful; it is not usually worth building by itself. Similarly, the maximum flexibility is obtained by looking for the smallest possible increments in capability: often these are smaller increments than a user would think of. Whether or not he would think of them before system development, he is likely to want that flexibility later.

The search for a minimal subset and minimal extensions can best be shown by an example. One example of a minimal subset is given in [4]. Another example will be given later in this paper.

B. Information Hiding: Interface and Module Definition

In an earlier section we touched upon the difference between the mathematician's concept of generality and an engineer's approach to design flexibility. Where the mathematician wants his product, a theorem or method of proof, to be as general as possible, i.e., applicable, without change, in as many situations as possible, an engineer often must tailor his product to the situation actually at hand. Lack of generality is necessary to make the program as efficient or inexpensive as possible. If he must develop a family of products, he tries to isolate the changeable parts in modules and to develop an interface between the module and the rest of the product that remains valid for all versions. The crucial steps are as follows.

1) Identification of the items that are likely to change. These items are termed "secrets."

2) Location of the specialized components in separate modules.

3) Designing intermodule interfaces that are insensitive to the anticipated changes. The changeable aspects or "secrets" of the modules are not revealed by the interface.

It is exactly this that the concept of information hiding [5], encapsulation, or abstraction [6] is intended to do for software. Because software is an abstract or mathematical product, the modules may not have any easily recognized physical identity. They are not necessarily separately compilable or coincident with memory overlay units. The interface must be general but the contents should not be. Specialization is necessary for economy and efficiency.

The concept of information hiding is very general and is applicable in many software change situations—not just the issue of subsets and extensions that we address in this paper. The ideas have also been extensively discussed in the literature [5]-[9]. The special implications for our problem are simply that, as far as possible, even the presence or absence of a component should be hidden from other components. If one program uses another directly, the presence of the second program cannot be fully hidden from its user. However, there is never any reason for a component to "know" how many other programs use it. All data structures that reveal the presence or number of certain components should be included in separate information hiding modules with abstract interfaces [10]. Space and other considerations make it impossible to discuss this concept further in this paper; it will be illustrated in the example. Readers for whom this concept is new are advised to read some of the articles mentioned above.

C. The Virtual Machine (VM) Concept

To avoid the problems that we have described as "a chain of data transforming components," it is necessary to stop thinking of systems in terms of components that correspond to steps in the processing. This way of thinking dies hard. It is almost certain that your first introduction to programming was in terms of a series of statements intended to be executed in the order that they were explained to you. We are goal oriented; we know what we start with and what we want to produce. It is natural to think in terms of steps progressing towards that goal. It is the fact that we are designing a family of systems that makes this "natural" approach the wrong one.

The viewpoint that seems most appropriate to designing software families is often termed the virtual machine approach. Rather than write programs that perform the transformation from input data to output data, we design software machine extensions that will be useful in writing many such programs. Where our hardware machine provides us with a set of instructions that operate on a small set of data types, the extended or virtual machine will have additional data types as well as "software instructions" that operate on those data types. These added features will be tailored to the class of programs that we are building. While the VM instructions are designed to be generally useful, they can be left out of a final product if the user's programs do not use them. The programmer writing programs for the virtual machine should not need to distinguish between instructions that are implemented in software and those that are hardware implemented. To achieve a true virtual machine, the hardware resources that are used in implementing the extended instruction set must be unavailable to the user of the virtual machine. The designer has traded these resources for the new data elements and instructions. Any attempt to use those resources again will invalidate the concept of virtual machine and lead to complications. Failure to provide for isolation of resources is one of the reasons for the failure of some attempts to use macros to provide a virtual machine. The macro user must be careful not to use the resources used in the code generated by the macros.

There is no reason to accomplish the transformation from the hardware machine to a virtual machine with all of the desired features in a single leap. Instead we will use the machine at hand to implement a few new instructions. At each step we take advantage of the newly introduced features. Such a step-by-step approach turns a large problem into a set of small ones and, as we will see later, eases the problem of finding the appropriate subsets. Each element in this series of virtual machines is a useful subset of the system.

D. Designing the "Uses" Structure

The concept of an abstract machine is an intuitive way of thinking about design. A precise description of the concept comes through a discussion of the relation "uses" [11], [12].

1) The relation "uses": We consider a system to be divided into a set of programs that can be invoked either by the normal flow of control mechanisms, by an interrupt, or by an exception handling mechanism. Each of these programs is assumed to have a specification that defines exactly the effect that an invocation of the program should have.

We say of two programs A and B that A *uses* B if correct execution of B may be necessary for A to complete the task described in its specification. That is, A *uses* B if there exist situations in which the correct functioning of A depends upon the availability of a correct implementation of B. Note that to decide whether A *uses* B or not, one must examine both the implementation *and* the specification of A.

The "*uses*" relation and "invokes" very often coincide, but *uses* differs from *invokes* in two ways:

a) Certain invocations may not be instances of "*uses*." If A's specification requires only that A *invoke* B when certain conditions occur, then A has fulfilled its specification when it has generated a correct call to B. A is correct even if B is incorrect or absent. A proof of correctness of A need only make assumptions about the way to invoke B.

b) A program A may use B even though it never invokes it. The best illustration of this is interrupt handling. Most programs in a computer system are only correct on the assumption that the interrupt handling routine will correctly handle the interrupts (leave the processor in an acceptable state). Such programs use the interrupt handling routines even though they never call them. *"Uses"* can also be formulated as *"requires the presence of a correct version of."*

Systems that have achieved a certain "elegance" (e.g., T.H.E. [5], Venus [6]) have done so by having parts of the system *"use"* other parts in such a way that the "user" programs were simplified. For example, the transput stream mechanism in T.H.E. *uses* the segmenting mechanism to great advantage. In contrast, many large and complex operating systems achieve their size and complexity by having "independent" parts. For example, there are many systems in which "spooling," virtual memory management, and the file system all perform their own backup store operations. Code to perform these functions is present in each of the components. Whenever such components must share a single device, complex interfaces exist.

The disadvantage of unrestrained "usage" of each others facilities is that the system parts become highly interdependent. Often there are no subsets of the system that can be used before the whole system is complete. In practice, some duplication of effort seems preferable to a system in which nothing runs unless everything runs.

2) The uses hierarchy: By restricting the relation *"uses"* so that its graph is loop free we can retain the primary advantages of having system parts *"use"* each other while eliminating the problems. In that case it is possible to assign the programs to the levels of a hierarchy by the following rules:

a) level 0 is the set of all programs that *use* no other program;

b) level i (i ⩾ 1) is the set of all programs that *use* at least one program on level i - 1 and no program at a level higher than i - 1.

If such a hierarchical ordering exists, then each level offers a testable and usable subset of the system. In fact, one can get additional subsets by including only parts of a level. The easy availability of these subsets is very valuable for the construction of any software systems and is vital for developing a *broad* family of systems.

The design of the "uses" hierarchy should be one of the major milestones in a design effort. The division of the system into independently callable subprograms has to go on in parallel with the decisions about *uses*, because they influence each other.

3) The criteria to be used in allowing one program to use another: We propose to allow A *"uses"* B when all of the following conditions hold:

a) A is essentially simpler because it uses B;

b) B is not substantially more complex because it is not allowed to use A;

c) there is a useful subset containing B and not A;

d) there is no conceivably useful subset containing A but not B.

During the process of designing the "uses" relation, we often find ourselves in a situation where two programs could obviously benefit from using each other and the conditions above cannot be satisfied. In such situations, we resolve the apparent conflicts by a technique that we call "sandwiching." One of the programs is "sliced" into two parts in a way that allows the programs to "use" each other and still satisfy the above conditions. If we find ourselves in a position where A would benefit from using B, but B can also benefit from using A, we may split B into two programs: B1 and B2. We then allow A to use B2 and B1 to use A. The result would appear to be a sandwich with B as the bread and A as the filling. Often, we then go on to split A. We start with a few levels and end up with many.

An earlier report [11] introduced many of the ideas that are in this paper and illustrated them by proposing a "uses" relation for a family of operating systems. It contains several examples of situations where "sandwiching" led us from a "T.H.E.-like structure" [14] to a structure with more than twice as many levels. For example, the virtual memory mechanism was split into address translation and dynamic allocation of memory areas to segments.

The most frequent instances of splitting and sandwiching came because initially we were assuming that a "level" would be a "module" in the sense of Section IV-B. We will discuss this in the final part of this paper.

4) Use of the word "convenience": It will trouble some readers that it is usual to use the word "convenience" to describe a reason for introducing a certain facility at a given level of the hierarchy. A more substantial basis would seem more scientific.

As discussed in [11] and [13], we must assume that the hardware itself is capable of performing all necessary functions. As one goes higher in the levels, one can lose capabilities (as resources are consumed)—not gain them. On the other hand, at the higher levels the new functions can be implemented with simpler programs because of the additional programs that can be used. We speak of "convenience" to make it clear that one could implement any functions on a lower level, but the availability of the additional programs at the higher level is useful. For each function we give the lowest level at which the features that are useful for implementing that function (with the stated restrictions) are available. In each case, we see no functions available at the next higher level that would be useful for implementing the functions as described. If we implemented the program one level lower we would have to duplicate programs that become available at that level.

V. Example: An Address Processing Subsystem

As an example of designing for extensibility and subsets, we consider a set of programs to read in, store, and write out lists of addresses. This example has also been used, to illustrate a different point, in [10] and has been used in several classroom experiments to demonstrate module interchangeability. This

```
The following items of information will
be found in the addresses to be processed
and constitute the only items of relevance
to the application programs:

  • Last name
  • Given names (first name and possible
      middle names)
  • Organization (Command or Activity)
  • Internal identifier (Branch or Code)
  • Street address or P.O. box
  • City or mail unit identifier
  • State
  • Zip code
  • Title
  • Branch of service if military
  • GS grade if civil service
Each of the above will be strings of
characters in the standard ANSI alphabet,
and each of the above may be empty or blank.
```

Fig. 1.

example is intended as an integral part of this paper; several statements in the final summation are supported only in this section.

A. *Our Basic Assumptions*

1) The information items discussed in Fig. 1 will be the items to be processed by all application programs.

2) The input formats of the addresses are subject to change.

3) The output formats of the addresses are subject to change.

4) Some systems will use a single fixed format for input and output. Other systems will need the ability to choose from several input or output formats at run-time. Some systems will be required in which the user can specify the format using a format definition language.

5) The representation of addresses in main storage will vary from system to system.

6) In most systems, only a subset of the total set of addresses stored in the system need be in main storage at any one time. The number of addresses needed may vary from system to system, and in some systems the number of addresses to be kept in main memory may vary at run-time.

B. *We Propose the Following Design Decisions*

1) The input and output programs will be table driven: the table will specify the format to be used for input and output. The contents and organization of these format tables will be the "secrets" of the input and output modules.

2) The representation of addresses in core will be the "secret" of an address storage module (ASM). The implementation chosen for this module will be such that the operations of changing a portion of an address will be relatively inexpensive, compared to making the address table larger or smaller.

3) When the number of addresses to be stored exceeds the capacity of an ASM, programs will use an address file module (AFM). An AFM can be made upward compatible with an ASM; programs that were written to use ASM's could operate using an AFM in the same way. The AFM provides additional commands to allow more efficient usage by programs that do not assume the random access properties of an ASM. These programs are described below.

4) Our implementation of an AFM would use an ASM as a submodule as well as another submodule that we will call block file module (BFM). The BFM stores blocks of data that are sufficiently large to represent an address, but the BFM is not specialized to the handling of addresses. An ASM that is used within an AFM may be said to have two interfaces. In the "normal interface" that an ASM presents to an outside user, an address is a set of fields and the access functions hide or abstract from the representation. Fig. 2 is a list of the access programs that comprise this interface. In the second interface, the ASM deals with blocks of contiguous storage and abstract from the contents. There are commands for the ASM to input and output "addresses" but the operands are storage blocks whose interpretation as addresses is known only within the ASM. The AFM makes assumptions about the association between blocks and addresses but not about the way that an address's components are represented as blocks. The BFM is completely independent of the fact that the blocks contain address information. The BFM might, in fact, be a manufacturer supplied access method.

C. *Component Programs*

1) Module: Address Input

INAD: Reads in an address that is assumed to be in a format specified by a format table and calls ASM or AFM functions to store it.

INFSL: Selects a format from an existing set of format tables. The selected format is the one that will be used by INAD. There is always a format selected.

INFCR: Adds a new format to the tables used by INFSL. The format is specified in a "format language." Selection is *not* changed (i.e., INAD still uses the same format table).

INTABEXT: Adds a blank table to the set of input format tables.

INTABCHG: Rewrites a table in the input format tables using a description in a format language. Selection is not changed.

INFDEL: Deletes a table from the set of format tables. The selected format cannot be deleted.

INADSEL: Reads in an address using one of a set of formats. Choice is specified by an integer parameter.

INADFO: Reads in an address in a format specified as one of its parameters (a string in the format definition language). The format is selected and added to the tables and subsequent addresses could be read in using INAD.

2) Module: Address Output

OUTAD: Prints an address in a format specified by a format table. The information to be printed

MODULE: ASM NAME OF ACCESS PROGRAM*	INPUT PARAMETERS						OUTPUT	
*ADDTIT:	asm	X	integer	X	string	→	asm	•
ADDGN:	asm	X	integer	X	string	→	asm	•
ADDLN:	asm	X	integer	X	string	→	asm	•
ADDSERV:	asm	X	integer	X	string	→	asm	•
ADDBORC:	asm	X	integer	X	string	→	asm	•
ADDCORA:	asm	X	integer	X	string	→	asm	•
ADDSORP:	asm	X	integer	X	string	→	asm	•
ADDCITY:	asm	X	integer	X	string	→	asm	•
ADDSTATE:	asm	X	integer	X	string	→	asm	•
ADDZIP:	asm	X	integer	X	string	→	asm	•
ADDGSL:	asm	X	integer	X	string	→	asm	•
SETNUM:	asm	X	integer	→	asm •			
FETTIT:	asm	X	integer	→	string			
FETGN:	asm	X	integer	→	string			
FETGN:	asm	X	integer	→	string			
FETLN:	asm	X	integer	→	string			
FETSERV:	asm	X	integer	→	string			
FETBORC:	asm	X	integer	→	string			
FETCORA:	asm	X	integer	→	string			
FETSORP:	asm	X	integer	→	string			
FETCITY:	asm	X	integer	→	string			
FETSTATE:	asm	X	integer	→	string			
FETZIP:	asm	X	integer	→	string			
FETGSL:	asm	X	integer	→	string			
FETNUM:	asm	→	integer					

*These are abbreviations: ADDTIT = ADD TITLE; ADDGN = ADD GIVEN NAME, etc.

Fig. 2. Syntax of ASM functions.

is assumed to be in an ASM and identified by its position in an ASM.

OUTFSL: Selects a format table from an existing set of output format tables. The selected format is the one that will be used by OUTAD.

OUTTABEXT: Adds a "blank" table to the set of output format tables.

OUTTABCHG: Rewrites the contents of a format table using information in a format language.

OUTFCR: Adds a new format to the set of formats that can be selected by OUTFSL in a format description language.

OUTFDEL: Deletes a table from the set of format tables that can be selected by OUTFSL.

OUTADSEL: Prints out an address using one of a set of formats.

OUTADFO: Prints out an address in a format specified in a format definition language string, which is one of the actual parameters. The format is added to the tables and selected.

3) Module: Address Storage (ASM)

FET: (Component Name): This is a set of functions used to read information from an address store. Returns a string as a value. See Fig. 2.

ADD: (Component Name): This is a set of functions used to write information in an address store. Each takes a string and an integer as parameters. The integer specifies an address within the ASM. See Fig. 2.

0BLOCK: Takes an integer parameter, returns a storage block as a value.

1BLOCK: Accepts a storage block and integer as parameters. Its effect is to change the contents of an address store—which is reflected by a change in the values of the FET programs.

ASMEXT: Extends an address store by appending a new address with empty components at the end of the address store.

ASMSHR: "Shrinks" the address store.

ASMCR: Creates a new address store. The parameter specifies the number of components. All components are initially empty.

ASMDEL: Deletes an existing address store.

4) Module: Block File Module

BLFET: Accepts an integer as a parameter and returns a "block."

141

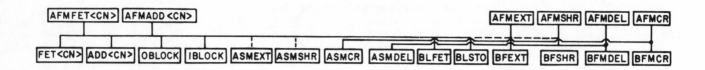

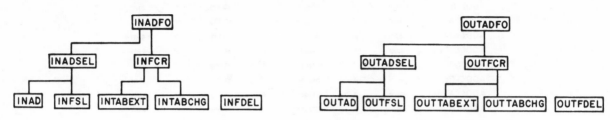

Fig. 3.

BLSTO: Accepts a block and an integer and stores the block.

BFEXT: Extends BFM by adding additional blocks to its capacity.

BFSHR: Reduces the size of the BFM by removing some blocks.

BFMCR: Creates a file of blocks.

BFMDEL: Deletes an existing file of blocks.

5) Module: Address File Module

This module includes implementations of all of the ASM functions except OBLOCK and IBLOCK. To avoid confusion in the diagram showing the uses hierarchy we have changed the names to:

AFMADD (Component Name) defined as in Fig. 2
AFMFET (Component Name) defined as in Fig. 1
AFMEXT defined as in BFM above
AMFSHR defined as in BFM above
AFMCR defined as in BFM above
AFMDEL defined as in BFM above.

D. Uses Relation

Fig. 3 shows the *uses* relation between the component programs. It is important to note that we are now discussing the implementation of those programs, not just their specifications. The *uses* relation is characterized by the fact that there are a large number of relatively simple, *single-purpose* programs on the lowest level. The upper level programs are implemented by means of these lower level programs so that they too are quite simple. This *uses* relation diagram characterizes the set of possible subsets.

E. Discussion

To pick a subset, one identifies the set of upper level programs that the user needs and includes only those programs that those programs use (directly or indirectly). For example, a user who uses addresses in a single format does not need the component programs that interpret format description lan-

guages. Systems that work with a small set of addresses can be built without any BFM components. A program that works as a query system and never prints out a complete address would not need any Address Output components.

The system is also easily extended. For example, one could add a capability to read in addresses with self-defining files. If the first record on a file was a description of the format in something equivalent to the format description language, one could write a program that would be able to read in that record, use INTABCHG to build a new format table, and then read in the addresses. Programs that do things with addresses (such as print out "personalized" form letters) can also be added using these programs and selecting only those capabilities that they actually need.

One other observation that can be made is that the upper level programs can be used to "generate" lower level versions. For example, the format description languages can be used to generate the tables used for the fixed format versions. There is no need for a separate SYSGEN program.

We will elaborate on this observation in the conclusion.

VI. SOME REMARKS ON OPERATING SYSTEMS: WHY GENERALS ARE SUPERIOR TO COLONELS

An earlier report [11] discusses the design of a "uses" hierarchy for operating systems. Although there have been some refinements to the proposals of that report, its basic contents are consistent with the present proposals. This section compares the approach outlined in this paper and the "kernel" approach or "nucleus" approach to OS design [18]-[20]. It is tempting to say that the suggestions in this paper do not conflict with the "kernel" approach. These proposals can be viewed as a refinement of the nucleus approach. The first few levels of our system could be labeled "kernel," and one could conclude that we are just discussing a fine structure within the kernel.

To yield to that temptation would be to ignore an essential difference between the approaches suggested in this paper and the kernel approach. The system kernels known to me are

142

such that some desirable subsets cannot be obtained without major surgery. It was assumed that the nucleus must be in every system family member. In the RC4000 system the inability to separate synchronization from message passing has led some users to bypass the kernel to perform teletype handling functions. In Hydra as originally proposed [19], "type checking" was so intrinsic to the call mechanism that it appeared impossible to disable it when it was not needed or affordable.[1]

Drawing a line between "kernel" and the rest of the system, and putting "essential" services of "critical programs" in the nucleus yields a system in which kernel features cannot be removed and certain extensions are impractical. Looking for a *minimal* subset and a set of *minimal* independent incremental function leads to a system in which one can trim away unneeded features. I know of no feature that is always needed. When we say that two functions are *almost* always used together, we should remember that "almost" is a euphemism for "not."

VII. Summation

This paper describes an approach to software intended to result in systems that can be tailored to fit the needs of a broad variety of users. The points most worthy of emphasis are as follows.

1) The Requirements Include Subsets and Extensions: It is essential to recognize the identification of useable subsets as part of the preliminaries to software design. Flexibility cannot be an afterthought. Subsetability is needed, not just to meet a variety of customers' needs, but to provide a fail-safe way of handling schedule slippage.

2) Advantages of the Virtual Machine Approach: Designing software as a set of virtual machines has definite advantages over the conventional (flowchart) approach to system design. The virtual machine "instructions" provide facilities that are useful for purposes beyond those originally conceived. These instructions can easily be omitted from a system if they are not needed. Remove a major box from a flowchart and there is often a need to "fill the hole" with conversion programs.

3) On the Difference Between Software Generality and Software Flexibility: Software can be considered "general" if it can be used, *without change*, in a variety of situations. Software can be considered flexible, if it is *easily changed* to be used in a variety of situations. It appears unavoidable that there is a run-time cost to be paid for generality. Clever designers can achieve flexibility without significant run-time cost, but there is a design-time cost. One should incur the design-time cost only if one expects to recover it when changes are made.

Some organizations may choose to pay the run-time cost for generality. They build general software rather than flexible software because of the maintenance problems associated with maintaining several different versions. Factors influencing this decision include a) the availability of extra computer resources,

b) the facilities for program change and maintenance available at each installation, and c) the extent to which design techniques ease the task of applying the same change to many versions of a program.

No one can tell a designer how much flexibility and generality should be built into a product, but the decision should be a conscious one. Often, it just happens.

4) On the Distinction Between Modules, Subprograms, and Levels: Several systems and at least one dissertation [14]–[17] have, in my opinion, blurred the distinction between modules, subprograms, and levels. Conventional programming techniques consider a subroutine or other callable program to be a module. If one wants the modules to include all programs that must be designed together and changed together, then, as our example illustrates, one will usually include many small subprograms in a single module. If does not matter what word we use; the point is that the unit of change is not a single callable subprogram.

In several systems, modules and levels have coincided [14], [15]. This had led to the phrase "level of abstraction." Each of the modules in the example abstract from some detail that is assumed likely to change. In our approach there is no correspondence between modules and levels. Further, I have not found a relation, "more abstract than," that would allow me to define an abstraction hierarchy [12]. Although I am myself guilty of using it, in most cases the phrase "levels of abstraction" is an abuse of language.

Janson has suggested that a design such as this one (or the one discussed in [11]) contain "soft modules" that can represent a breach of security principles. Obviously an error in any program in one of our modules can violate the integrity of that module. All module programs that will be included in a given subset must be considered in proving the correctness of that module. However, I see no way that allowing the component programs to be on different levels of a "uses" hierarchy makes this process more difficult or makes the system less secure. The boundaries of our modules are quite firm and clearly identified.

The essential difference between this paper and other discussions of hierarchically structured designs is the emphasis on subsets and extensions. My search for a criterion to be used in designing the *uses* hierarchy has convinced me that if one does not care about the existence of subsets, it does not really matter what hierarchy one uses. Any design can be bent until it works. It is only in the ease of change that they differ.

5) On Avoiding Duplication: Some earlier work [21] has suggested that one needs to have duplicate or near duplicate modules in a hierarchically structured system. For example, they suggest that one needs one implementation of processes to give a fixed number of processes at a low level and another to provide for a varying number of processes at a user's level. Similar ideas have appeared elsewhere. Were such duplication to be necessary, it would be a sound argument against the use of "structured" approaches. One can avoid such duplication if one allows the programs that vary the size of a data structure to be on a higher level than the other programs that operate on that data structure. For example, in an operating system, the programs to create and delete processes need not be on the

---

[1] Accurate reports on the current status and performance of that system are not available to me.

same level as the more frequently used scheduling operations. In designing software, I regard the need to code similar functions in two separate programs as an indication of a fundamental error in my thinking.

6) Designing for Subsets and Extensions Can Reduce the Need for Support Software: We have already mentioned that this design approach can eliminate the need for separate SYSGEN programs. We can also eliminate the need for *special*-purpose compilers. The price of the convenience features offered by such languages is often a compiler and run-time package distinctly larger than the system being built. In our approach, each level provides a "language extention" available to the programmer of the next level. We never build a compiler; we just build our system, but we get convenience features anyway.

7) Extension at Run-Time Versus Extension During SYSGEN: At a later stage in the design we will have to choose data structures and take the difference between run-time extension and SYSGEN extension into consideration. Certain data structures are more easily accessed but harder to extend while the program is running; others are easily extended but at the expense of a higher access cost. These differences do not affect our early design decisions because they are hidden in modules.

8) On the Value of a Model: My work on this example and similar ones has gone much faster because I have learned to exploit a pattern that I first noticed in the design discussed in [11]. Low level operations assume the existence of a fixed data structure of some type. The operations on the next level allow the swapping of a data element with others from a fixed set of similar elements. The high level programs allow the creation and deletion of such data elements. This pattern appears several times in both designs. Although I have not designed your system for you, I believe that you can take advantage of a similar pattern. If so, this paper has served its purpose.

ACKNOWLEDGMENT

The ideas presented in this paper have been developed over a lengthy period and with the cooperation and help of many collaborators. I am grateful to numerous Philips employees for thought provoking comments and questions. Price's collaboration was invaluable at Carnegie-Mellon University. The help of W. Bartussek, G. Handzel, and H. Wuerges at the Technische Hochschule Darmstadt led to substantial improvements. Heninger, Weiss, and J. Shore at the Naval Research Laboratory helped me to understand the application of the concepts in areas other than operating systems. B. Trombka and J. Guttag both helped in the design of pilots of the address process system. Discussions with P. J. Courtois have helped me to better understand the relation between software structure and run-time characteristics of computer systems. Dr. E. Britton, H. Rettenmaier, L. Belady, Dr. D. Stanat, G. Fran, and Dr. W. Wright made many helpful suggestions about an earlier draft of this paper. If you find portions of this paper helpful, these people deserve your thanks.

REFERENCES

[1] E. W. Dijkstra, *A Discipline of Programming*. Englewood Cliffs, NJ: Prentice-Hall, 1976.

[2] D. L. Parnas, "On the design and development of program families," *IEEE Trans. Software Eng.*, vol. SE-2, pp. 1–9, Mar. 1976.

[3] 2nd Int. Conf. Software Engineering, Oct. 13–15, 1976; also, *IEEE Trans. Software Eng.*, (Special Issue), vol. SE-2, Dec. 1976.

[4] D. L. Parnas, G. Handzel, and H. Würges, "Design and specification of the minimal subset of an operating system family," presented at the 2nd Int. Conf. Software Engineering, Oct. 13–15, 1976; also, *IEEE Trans. Software Eng.*, (Special Issue), vol. SE-2, pp. 301–307, Dec. 1976.

[5] D. L. Parnas, "On the criteria to be used in decomposing systems into modules," *Commun. Ass. Comput. Mach.*, Dec. 1972.

[6] T. A. Linden, "The use of abstract data types to simplify program modifications," in *Proc. Conf. Data: Abstraction, Definition and Structure*, Mar. 22–24, 1976; also, *ACM SIGPLAN Notices* (Special Issue), vol. II, 1976.

[7] D. L. Parnas, "A technique for software module specification with examples," *Commun. Ass. Comput. Mach.*, May 1972.

[8] ——, "Information distribution aspects of design methodology," in *1971 Proc. IFIP Congr.* Amsterdam, The Netherlands: North-Holland, 1971.

[9] ——, "The use of precise specifications in the development of software," in *1977 Proc. IFIP Congr.* Amsterdam, The Netherlands: North-Holland, 1977.

[10] ——, "Use of abstract interfaces in the development of software for embedded computer systems," Naval Res. Lab., Washington, DC, NRL Rep. 8047, June 1977.

[11] ——, "Some hypotheses about the 'uses' hierarchy for operating systems," Technische Hochschule Darmstadt, Darmstadt, West Germany, Tech. Rep., Mar. 1976.

[12] ——, "On a 'buzzword': Hierarchical structure," in *1974 Proc. IFIP Congr.* Amsterdam, The Netherlands: North-Holland, 1974.

[13] D. L. Parnas and D. L. Siewiorek, "Use of the concept of transparency in the design of hierarchically structured systems," *Commun. Ass. Comput. Mach.*, vol. 18, July 1975.

[14] E. W. Dijkstra, "The structure of the "THE"-multiprogramming system," *Commun. Ass. Comput. Mach.*, vol. 11, pp. 341–346, May 1968.

[15] B. Liskov, "The design of the Venus operating system," *Commun. Ass. Comput. Mach.*, vol. 15, pp. 144–149, Mar. 1972.

[16] P. A. Janson, "Using type extension to organize virtual memory mechanisms," Lab. for Comput. Sci., M.I.T., Cambridge, MA, MIT-LCS-TR167, Sept. 1976.

[17] ——, "Using type-extension to organize virtual memory mechanisms," IBM Zurich Res. Lab., Switzerland, Res. Rep. RZ 858 (#28909), August 31, 1977.

[18] P. Brinch Hansen, "The nucleus of the multiprogramming system," *Commun. Ass. Comput. Mach.*, vol. 13, pp. 238–241, 250, Apr. 1970.

[19] W. Wulf, E. Cohen, A. Jones, R. Lewin, C. Pierson, and F. Pollack, "HYDRA: The kernel of a multiprocessor operating system," *Commun. Ass. Comput. Mach.*, vol. 17, pp. 337–345, June 1974.

[20] G. J. Popek and C. S. Kline, "The design of a verified protection system," in *Proc. Int. Workshop Prot. In Oper. Syst.*, IRIA, pp. 183–196.

[21] A. R. Saxena and T. H. Bredt, "A structured specification of a hierarchical operating system," in *Proc. 1975 Int. Conf. Reliable Software*.

David L. Parnas received the B.S., M.S., and Ph.D. degrees in electrical engineering–systems and communications sciences from the Carnegie Institute of Technology, Pittsburgh, PA.

He held the position of Assistant Professor of Computer Science at the University of Maryland and at Carnegie-Mellon University. During the period 1969–1970 he was employed by Philips-Electrologica, Apeldoorn, The Netherlands, and at the MBLE Research Laboratory, Brussels, Belgium. He then returned to Carnegie-Mellon

University where he held the rank of Associate Professor until 1973. In June of 1973 he was appointed Professor and Head of the Research Group on Operating Systems I at the Technical University of Darmstadt, Germany, where he remained through August 1976. He is presently Professor in the Department of Computer Science, University of North Carolina, Chapel Hill. He is also with the Information Systems Staff, Communications Sciences Division, at the Naval Research Laboratory, Washington, DC. He has published papers in the areas of computer design languages and simulation techniques. His current interests are in the field of software engineering methods, computer system design, abstract specification for programs, verification that a program meets its specifications, and cooperating sequential processes.

Introduction

Moriconi, M.S. "A designer/verifier's assistant." *IEEE Trans. Software Engineering*, SE-5, 4 (1979), 387-401.

A software system can be described at many levels: the level of what it does, the level of how it does it, and the level of the code that does the work. The maintainer who modifies a system continually shifts between levels:

- What change does the user want in what the system does?
- How does the system do what it does, and how can I modify it?
- What will the system do if I change this code?

This constant shift between What, How, and Why is the reason that we discussed the problems of understanding systems in Part II of this Tutorial. Now, in Part III, we introduce a major research project by Mark Moriconi that implements a maintainer's "assistant" that works with these questions.

In Moriconi's system, the programmer writes both source code which implements a function (for instance, to sort an array of numbers) and specifications which state the properties of the desired function (for instance, "Upon exit from this procedure the numbers in the parameter array are in ascending order"). The system produces a set of logical formulas called "verification conditions." If all the verification conditions are true, the code is guaranteed to satisfy its specifications. Failure to prove a verification condition indicates that the code, its specifications, or both, could be "wrong," or at least incomplete, and therefore in need of change.

When the programmer modifies the system—by changing the code or the specifications—the system reports the effect of the modification. Typical reports are

- This new code is consistent with the specifications of module A and does not affect module B. (Informally: "This code makes A do what you say it does, and therefore makes B work too.")
- This new code is inconsistent with the specification of module A... ("This code introduces a bug...")

The programmer can even ask the system for a suggestion on what to do next!

Moriconi's paper is not easy reading, but it reports research on the frontier of computer science as it relates to the concerns of maintainers. Moriconi told us that his current research—on graphical imagery to represent the properties of software—is also relevant to maintenance.

The idea is to take advantage of the clarity and compactness of graphics as a communications medium, while retaining the rigor and precision of a linear logical language. The user will be able to draw hierarchies of pictures on the display terminal, with the system understanding their meaning and relationship to the source code. The system will provide several forms of programming support. For instance, it will be able to recognize graphical representations of certain 'design clichés' and suggest source code implementations. It will be able to advise maintainers whether a planned change will make the pictured design inconsistent with the source code.

We look forward to the fruits of this new research.

IEEE TRANSACTIONS ON SOFTWARE ENGINEERING, VOL. SE-5, NO. 4, JULY 1979

A Designer/Verifier's Assistant

MARK S. MORICONI, MEMBER, IEEE

Abstract—Since developing and maintaining formally verified programs is an incremental activity, one is not only faced with the problem of constructing specifications, programs, and proofs, but also with the complex problem of determining what previous work remains valid following incremental changes. A system that reasons about changes must build a detailed model of each development and be able to apply its knowledge, the same kind of knowledge an expert would have, to integrate new or changed information into an existing model.

This paper describes a working computer program called the designer/verifier's assistant, which is the initial prototype of such a system. The assistant embodies a unified theory of how to reason about changes to a design or verification. This theory also serves as the basis for answering questions about the effects of hypothesized changes and for making proposals on how to proceed with the development in an orderly fashion. Excerpts from a sample session are used to illustrate the key ideas.

Index Terms—Automated program verifier, automated programmer assistance, design of incremental systems, effects of incremental changes, incremental program design and verification, maintenance, program design, program specifications, program verification, proofs of programs, question answering.

I. INTRODUCTION

DEVELOPING and maintaining formally verified programs, especially large ones, is an incremental activity. Specifications, programs, and proofs are gradually built up and frequently revised. Consequently, one is faced not only with the problem of constructing this data, but also with the complex problem of determining the effects of incremental changes to it.

Consider the task of developing a formally verified operating system. A good strategy is first to decompose the system into its functional parts, then to design and verify each part separately. The file system, for example, can be broken down into files and directories, each of whose design and verification involves developing a large, highly interrelated collection of specifications, programs, verification conditions, and proofs. Certainly, numerous revisions—e.g., to correct an error in a program or to augment or reformulate a specification—would

be made in getting this myriad of detailed information to fit together properly. Each revision can raise a variety of complex issues. If, for example, some specifications and programs dealing with files are changed to allow blocks of file storage to be scattered throughout memory, instead of allocated sequentially as originally planned, some of the key issues are: Do any previous proofs about files remain valid? Does any code for directories need to be recompiled? Do all established properties of the file system still hold? Is the rest of the operating system affected? If so, how? These are just some of the questions that must be answered to avoid excessive redoing of still-valid work.

The same problems arise when maintaining verified software, whether it be recoding programs to increase efficiency, extending specifications, or changing design decisions. However, it may be even more difficult to determine the effects of these "after-the-fact" changes because of the time that may have elapsed since the original development.

Much research has focused on the problem of constructing specifications, programs, and proofs. Several programming and specification languages and structuring and proof techniques, as well as tools to support them, have been developed to aid in the construction process. For example, there are several program verification systems (including [2], [3], [5], [7], [10], [11], and [17]) capable of parsing programs and specifications and of generating and proving verification conditions.[1] They support a variety of languages (such as subsets of Algol, Jovial, Lisp, and Pascal) and proof methods (such as inductive assertions and structural induction).

The next step is to develop a highly incremental system—one that 1) parses programs and specifications and generates and proves verification conditions (like previous systems) and 2) has an *understanding* of the kinds of structures that can be changed and added, and the ways they can interact. This new system must be able to build a detailed *model* of each development. The model must contain information about key parts of a program's design and verification and their relationships. The system must be able to apply its *knowledge*—the same kind of knowledge an expert would have—to integrate new

Manuscript received November 6, 1978; revised March 5, 1979. This research was supported in part by the Defense Advanced Research Projects Agency under Contract DAHC 15-72-C-0308 (at the University of Southern California Information Sciences Institute), by the National Science Foundation under Grant MCS74-12866 (at the University of Texas at Austin), and by the Rome Air Development Center under Contract F30602-78-C-0031 (at SRI International).

The author is with the Computer Science Laboratory, SRI International, Menlo Park, CA 94025.

[1] The question of whether a program is consistent with its specifications can be reduced to proving a set of logical formulas called *verification conditions*. These formulas are derived directly from the program and its specifications. This paper presumes only a general familiarity with the area of formal program verification. Detailed knowledge, such as how to derive verification conditions, is not required.

or changed information into an existing model in a way that keeps intact previous work that remains valid. For example, if the specification of a function is changed, the system should be able to deduce what parts of the verification are unaffected.

A working system that has this kind of understanding is the *designer/verifier's assistant*. The assistant actively assists and cooperates with the user throughout a design and verification by accepting and reasoning about new or changed information, by proposing actions, and by answering questions. Programs and specifications can be constructed using a top-down, bottom-up, or mixed strategy, verified in parallel or any desired order, and revised at any time. The assistant is useful not only during a design and verification, but also afterwards for maintenance purposes.

The assistant has been implemented in a version of Lisp (developed at the University of California at Irvine) and runs on a PDP-10 computer under TOPS-10 at The University of Texas at Austin. All transcripts presented in this paper were actually produced by this running program. In order to test the validity of the ideas to be described, it was necessary to integrate the assistant into a program verification system, which is described in [12]. Like the assistant, this verification system reflects an incremental philosophy and has several capabilities that complement those of the assistant. It supports the combined programming and specification language Gypsy [1], which is Pascal based and includes features for data abstraction, error handling, and limited forms of concurrency. Another version of the assistant is currently being developed, again in the context of a verification system, at SRI International. It is being implemented in a release of Interlisp that runs on a PDP-10 computer under TOPS-20. This version of the assistant will handle programs written in any of several programming languages (namely, significant subsets of Jovial, Modula, and Pascal) and formally specified in a revised version of the specification language SPECIAL [16].

The work described here relates two areas of research: automated verification and automated programmer assistance. The first topic to be considered is how the designer/verifier's assistant represents a contribution to the area of automated verification. Traditional program verification systems (e.g., [2], [3], [5], [7], [10], [11], and [17]) can be viewed as consisting of a translator, a verification condition generator, and a theorem prover. As mentioned above, the assistant has been integrated into such a verification system [12]. In this augmented verification system, the human designer/verifier communicates with the assistant, which in turn calls the traditional verification system only as needed. When a program or specification is changed, the assistant determines what parts of the overall design and verification could possibly be affected, then uses the verification system to reverify only those parts. The assistant, in effect, decides how to use the verification system efficiently. This is extremely important due to the high cost of formally verifying programs of even moderate size and complexity.

The other important aspect of the assistant is its ability to provide useful assistance throughout the evolution of a consistent set of specifications, programs, and proofs. Specifically,

the assistant can provide the human designer/verifier with an explanation of the effects of possible revisions (before they are actually made) and with guidance on how to proceed with the development in an orderly fashion. Early work on facilities for assisting in the development of programs was done by Teitelman [19]. From this work evolved a set of useful tools (e.g., an editor, a cross-reference facility, a spelling corrector, and a specialized error corrector) that are part of the Interlisp system [18]. Two other extensively used systems that assist in program development are the ECL programming system [20] and the Programmer's Workbench [9], and a system that reasons about certain incremental changes to proofs is described by Doyle [4]. An imagined scenario illustrating several ways in which the computer might assist during the design and the verification of a program is found in [6]. A proposal for how one might construct a similar elaborate programming system has been made by Hewitt and Smith [8], and more recently a similar proposal, which stops short of formal verification, has been made by Rich and Shrobe [14].

The next section presents a brief excerpt from a session to illustrate the kinds of things the assistant does to facilitate incremental design and verification, and subsequent sections describe how the assistant works. Section III explains how the assistant can guide the user through an entire development, and Section IV describes how it answers "what" and "why" questions about the effects of hypothesized changes. These sections will show that both of these capabilities are relatively straightforward to provide once a theory for reasoning about incremental changes has been elaborated. This underlying theory is presented in Section V, which discusses important design issues, the model of a program's design and verification, and the knowledge used to analyze changes to any specific model. This material is then used to explain the reasoning done by the assistant throughout the scenario of Section II. Section VI concludes with a brief recounting of our experience in using the assistant and an outline of future plans.

II. BRIEF SCENARIO

The scenario described in this section, taken from the middle of an actual session, is a very simple illustration of some of the ways the assistant helps the user in incrementally designing and verifying programs. This includes allowing both the assistant and user to take the initiative in directing the development, using the assistant to preview the effects of intended changes, adding various kinds of new and changed information to an existing model, and automatically retaining still-valid work following changes.

The scenario starts in the middle of a session in which a sorting program is being incrementally designed and verified. Taken from the session is a sequence of three events that typically occur for each set of revisions. Before actually making any revisions, the user first engages in a conversation with the assistant to gain an understanding of the effects of the changes he might make. Guided by this interchange, the user makes the desired changes. The assistant then fits these changes into the current model, keeping intact previous work that remains valid. It should be reemphasized that the pur-

(1) Suggest fully defining ExchangeSort ──→<u>Explain</u>

(2) ←──<u>What are the effects of fully defining ExchangeSort?</u>
ExchangeSort may have additional VCs.

(3) ←──<u>What are the effects of changing the exit assertion of ValueOfMax?</u>
No effects on ValueOfMax. The verification of other programs is not affected.

(4) ←──<u>Why?</u>
No effects on ValueOfMax because it is for specifications only and does not
have VCs. No external effects because properties from ValueOfMax have not been
used in proving any VCs.

(5) ←──<u>What are the effects of changing the exit of IsPerm?</u>
No effects on IsPerm. The verification of other programs is not affected if the formula
Changed exit specification $\Rightarrow$ all Z : IntArray, IsPerm(Z, Z)
is true. If not, the change invalidates the verification of ExchangeSort.

(6) ←──<u>Why?</u>
No effects on IsPerm because it is for specifications only and does not have
VCs. Invalid verification because a property from IsPerm has been used in proving
ExchangeSort#1.

(7) ←──<u>Done</u>

(8) Suggest fully defining ExchangeSort ──→<u>Edit</u>

Fig. 1. An actual dialog with the assistant.

pose of the scenario is to illustrate what the assistant does and how it is used; specific details of the sorting program are unimportant.

Fig. 1 joins the session just after the program ExchangeSort has been partially defined and proved. ExchangeSort is currently of the form

    function ExchangeSort ... = begin ... pending ... end;

The completed part of ExchangeSort has already been verified; the keyword "pending" identifies the part of ExchangeSort that has not yet been defined. In all figures, the parenthesized numbers are for reference in the text and underlining designates lines typed by the user to distinguish them from the computer's response. Throughout the scenario, the assistant and user intermittently exchange initiative in directing the course of the development. To eliminate the risk of impeding progress, the assistant assumes the dominating position only when the user intentionally relinquishes it, and retains it until it is unlikely that its guidance will be helpful. At line (1), the assistant has the initiative. The user can either accept the suggestion by typing "$", or he can issue a command. Rather than going ahead and completing the definition of ExchangeSort as suggested, the user decides to use the assistant to preview the effects of some intended changes. Typing the command "Explain" in line (1) initiates a conversation with the *explanation facility*, whose prompting symbol for input is "←──" in line (2).

The following dialog provides a sample of the kinds of in-

teraction possible.[2] ValueOfMax in (3) and IsPerm in (5) are functions introduced only for specifying ExchangeSort and are not intended to be implemented. Thus, any change to their exit assertions[3] cannot affect their (nonexistent) verification. The dialogue also illustrates some useful characteristics of the explanation facility. It shows how remembering the immediately preceding "what" questions makes it easy to state questions such as the ones at (4) and (6). It shows how answers not only tell the user about the potential effects of different kinds of changes, but also give hints about how to make the changes. For example, the response to (5) describes the exact formula that must hold for revisions to the exit specification of IsPerm not to have effects. (The current exit specification of IsPerm is "all Z:IntArray, IsPerm(Z,Z).") Of course, different formulas and combinations of formulas are described in different situations. No relationships are described when revisions cannot have effects, as in the answer to (3). This is also illustrated when the assistant says "No effects on IsPerm" in the first part of the answer to (5). The dialog also shows how answers are given at two levels of detail. Answers to "why" questions refine answers to "what" questions. The potential effects of the change indicated at (5) are narrowed down from ExchangeSort in the response to (5) to the single

---

[2] In transcripts, the term "verification conditions" is abbreviated as "VCs."

[3] An *exit assertion* is a specification that is intended to hold if the associated program terminates.

151

verification condition called ExchangeSort#1 in the response to (6).

Knowing the potential effects of intended changes, the user types "Done" in line (7) to indicate a readiness to continue working with the assistant toward a problem solution. Upon leaving the explanation facility, the suggestion initially given at (1) is reproposed at (8) since it still makes sense. Typing "Edit" in (8) invokes a standard text editor.

Fig. 2 rejoins the session immediately after the editing is finished. At line (9) the assistant is directed to read the just-edited file into the system. The file contains Gypsy programs and specifications[4] that are echoed as they are parsed and type checked. All type checking is done in the existing context. For example, the previously defined type IntArray is used in type checking the exit specification of IsPerm. Notice that the changes explored in Fig. 1 have all been made, and also that several new programs have been introduced. The assistant figures out how to fit all this information into the existing model, while keeping intact previous work that remains valid. This requires, for example, assembling and proving the formula described in the response to the question at (5). After all the necessary reasoning has been done, the assistant [by printing "Exec⟶" at line (10)] asks for user direction, instead of offering a suggestion. The assistant observes that there are many reasonable courses of action following all these revisions. It therefore wants the user to at least initiate a line of attack by giving the appropriate command. (Had the user accepted the suggestion at (8), the assistant would have offered a suggestion about ExchangeSort.)

Fig. 3 completes the scenario by showing how the replacement of the "pending" in ExchangeSort by two new statements had the effects described in the response to the question at line (2). After the suggestion at (11) is accepted, the changed path through the loop of ExchangeSort is traced and some new verification conditions are generated. Three previously generated verification conditions (which came from the unchanged paths) were unaffected by the change. Proving the first new verification condition is suggested at (12), and the rest of the development proceeds from there.

III. SUGGESTING WHAT TO DO NEXT

Throughout a development, one is continually faced with the problem of recalling what tasks remain to be done and then choosing which one to do next. Initially, the number of choices is very limited. But, as a program's design and verification is evolved, the choices increase in number and become more varied. This is due not only to the gradual in-

---

[4] Notice that Gypsy specifications are included directly in Gypsy programs. The keywords "entry," "exit," and "assert" all designate specifications to be proved about the associated program. A proof shows that the entry assertion always implies the exit assertion if the program terminates. The assert statements supply the intermediate assertions for a proof by inductive assertions, and each loop in a program must contain at least one assert statement. Also notice that some functions are implemented as programs (e.g., ExchangeSort), while others are solely for specification purposes (e.g., ValueOfMax). The latter have "null" bodies. These general observations provide all the needed background on Gypsy. Its syntax is important here only insofar as it defines the overall structure of a program.

(9)   Suggest fully defining ExchangeSort ⟶ Read FileOfChanges.Sort

```
function ExchangeSort(A:IntArray):IntArray =
begin
    entry N ge 1;
    exit (all I:int,
            I in [1..N] ⟹ ExchangeSort(A)[I]
                        = ValueOfMax(ExchangeSort(A),1,I)
        and IsPerm(A, ExchangeSort(A));
    var B:IntArray := A;
    var K:int := N;
    keep K in [1..N];
    loop
        assert (all I:int, I in [K + 1..N] ⟹ ValueOfMax(B,1,I))
            and K in [1..N] and IsPerm(A,B);
        if K = 1 then leave end;
      ⌈ B := Exchange(B,LocationOfMax(B,1,K),K);
      ⌊ K := K-1;
    end;
    result := B;
end;

function ValueOfMax(A:IntArray; I,J:int):int =
begin
  ⌈ exit (all k:int, k in [1..J] and I in [1..N] and J in [1..N]
  ⌊     ⟹ A[k] le ValueOfMax(A,I,J)) and ... ;
end;

function IsPerm(X,Y:IntArray) : boolean =
begin
    exit (all Z:IntArray, IsPerm(Z,Z))
      ⌈ and (all Z:IntArray,
      ⌊     IsPerm(X,Z) and IsPerm(Z,Y) ⟹ IsPerm(X,Y));
end;

⌈ function LocationOfMax(A:IntArray; I,J:int):int =
  begin
      entry I in [1..N] and J in [1..N] and I le J;
      exit LocationOfMax(A,I,J) in [I..J]
          and A[LocationOfMax(A,I,J)] = ValueOfMax(A,I,J);
      pending
  end;

  function Exchange(A:IntArray; I,J:int):IntArray = ... ;

⌊ function IsExchanged(A,B:IntArray;I,J:int):boolean = ... ;
```

(10)   Exec ⟶ Suggest

Fig. 2. The assistant incorporates several changes, some of which were discussed in Fig. 1, into the existing model. These changes are indicated by brackets.

crease in size (i.e., the building up of more and more programs, specifications, verification conditions, etc.), but also to the impact of revisions. Changing a specification, for example, can invalidate several parts of the verification, all of which must eventually be redone. To help in remembering these kinds of things, the assistant displays, on request, a detailed

(11) **Suggest generating new VCs for ExchangeSort $\longrightarrow$ \$**

        Tracing new path in loop
        Assume loop assertion
             (all I#1 : INT, I#1 in [K + 1..N]
                    $\Rightarrow$ B[I#1] = ValueOfMax(B, 1, I#1))
             and K in [1..N]
             and IsPerm(A, B)
        . . .
        Generating new verification condition ExchangeSort#4
        . . .
        End of path

        Unaffected VCs: ExchangeSort#1, ExchangeSort#2, ExchangeSort#3

(12) **Suggest proving VC called ExchangeSort#4 $\longrightarrow$**

Fig. 3. Impact of changes in Fig. 2 on ExchangeSort. Some new verification conditions are generated, while three existing ones (along with their proofs) have been kept intact by the assistant.

summary of what has been done and what remains to be done. However, status summaries are lists of alternatives; the user must figure out which alternative to pursue. Consequently, a mechanism was developed that actively assists the user in making such decisions by always having available a reasonable suggestion for the next step in a design and verification.

Although this mechanism can be very helpful, it may at times "get in the way." If the scenario being suggested is different from what the user wants, a suggestion mechanism can hinder, rather than enhance, progress. Therefore, the assistant embodies a dual-mode philosophy, giving the user the option of directing the system by giving commands, or being guided through the system by accepting suggestions, or a combination of both. Suggestions are based on the current state of development. The remainder of this section describes the suggestion mechanism and how it works.

The suggestion mechanism maintains an *agenda* of tasks that need to be done, each one having an assigned priority based on its relation to a particular development strategy. The *scheduling policy* is to find the highest priority task on the agenda, and then suggest it to the user. Agenda entries that have the same priority are handled on a first-come first-serve basis. If the user accepts a suggestion, the corresponding task is removed from the agenda and executed. Its execution may cause new tasks to be merged into the agenda, or existing ones to be deleted.

Each entry on the agenda is of the form (operation object priority). An example is (GENERATE-VCS ExchangeSort 5) which gets translated into the suggestion "Suggest generating VCs for ExchangeSort." The main problem, of course, is determining what should be on the agenda and how agenda entries should be ordered. This is done by applying heuristics that revise the agenda when built-in operations (such as parsing or generating verification conditions) are executed and when revisions are made to the design or verification. Each heuristic is represented as a *production rule* consisting of a condition/action pair. The condition on the left side of a rule tests whether

the rule is applicable; if it is, the action on its right side is a list of things to do.

At the beginning of the scenario in Fig. 1, the only entry on the agenda is (FULLY-DEFINE ExchangeSort 4), causing the scheduler to make the suggestion "Suggest fully defining ExchangeSort." A heuristic rule is applied to determine the impact on the agenda of each new or revised *program unit*, defined to be a program and its specifications, in Fig. 2. The rule is

if program unit X was successfully parsed
then delete all entries about X
    and if X has type errors **then** add (CORRECT-TYPE-ERRORS X 5)
        elseif X has a pending body **then** add (FULLY-DEFINE X 3)
        elseif X is new and has a body **then** add (GENERATE-VCS X 5)
    and for every change C that was made to X and that has effects,
        execute the rule associated with C

Starting with ExchangeSort, this rule removes (FULLY-DEFINE ExchangeSort 4) from the agenda, then its last conjunct handles the change to the body of ExchangeSort. The theory described in Section V is used to determine that this change has effects, causing the rule

if the body of program unit X has changed
then if X already has one or more verification conditions
    then add (GENERATE-NEW-VCS X 5)
    else add (GENERATE-VCS X 5)

to be selected and executed. Since ExchangeSort already has some verification conditions, (GENERATE-NEW-VCS ExchangeSort 5) is added to the agenda. Next, ValueOfMax and IsPerm are determined not to affect the agenda. Both have "null" bodies, instead of "pending" ones, indicating that the user intends to use them solely for specification purposes and not implement them. Therefore, entries of the form (FULLY-DEFINE · · ·) are inappropriate. Also, the changes to their specifications do not cause the agenda to be changed, since no existing verification work is invalidated. An entry for

LocationOfMax is then added to the agenda, which now looks like

```
((GENERATE-NEW-VCS ExchangeSort 5)
 (FULLY-DEFINE LocationOfMax 3) ...)
```

The first entry is removed when the user accepts the first suggestion "Suggest generating new VCs for ExchangeSort" in Fig. 3. Next, the rule

if verification conditions were generated for program unit X
then for each new verification condition V, add (PROVE V 5)
    and for each unaffected verification condition V,
        re-add every just-deleted entry about V
    and **if** X has a pending path **then** add (FULLY-DEFINE X 4)

determines how generating verification conditions affects the agenda. Executing this rule makes (PROVE ExchangeSort#4 5) the highest priority item on the agenda, as evidenced by the last suggestion in Fig. 3.

It should be emphasized that the implemented rules work best for a top-down development strategy, such as the one illustrated in the scenario. The top-level program unit Exchange-Sort was completely designed and verified before lower-level ones, such as LocationOfMax, were completed. Attention was properly kept on ExchangeSort even after LocationOfMax was partially defined and specified. LocationOfMax was introduced solely to allow ExchangeSort's external reference to it to be resolved and to allow its specifications to be used in the proof of ExchangeSort. But what if the user wanted to work on LocationOfMax, instead of going back to ExchangeSort? He could simply have ignored the suggestion and issued the appropriate commands. Suppose, for example, that the user chose to define LocationOfMax and to prove some of its verification conditions. Rather than adapting to this diversion and making suggestions about LocationOfMax's remaining verification conditions, the suggestion mechanism would retain ExchangeSort as the highest priority item. It assumes that diversions are not intended to alter the basic top-down strategy. The suggestion mechanism can be modified to take the alternate view of adapting to certain diversions by handling agenda entries on a last-in-first-out basis. The fundamental top-down strategy modeled by the rules can be changed to a bottom up or mixed strategy by adjusting the priority ratings.

IV. PREVIEWING THE EFFECTS OF CHANGES

One of the most difficult problems in designing and verifying programs is trying to understand the effects of a change. Before changing the type of an argument in the parameter list of a function, for example, it helps to know what programs or specifications could have type conflicts, what part of the verification could be invalidated, why it could be invalidated, etc. The purpose of the explanation facility is to make this kind of information available in order to give the user a general understanding of the potential effects of revisions before they are actually made.

All "what" and "why" questions answered by the explanation facility are variants of a few basic kinds of questions. A sample of each is given below:

> What are the effects of fully defining X?
> What are the effects of changing its exit assertion?
> What are the effects of changing the header of X?
> What are the effects of changing X's body?
> What is affected if lemma X is modified?
> What does altering type definition X affect?
> Why is X affected?
> Why?

Questions like the second one can be asked about any Gypsy specification, not just exit assertions. Answers to these questions vary in form and content according to context.

A user's question is processed in three stages:

1) **Understanding the question.** A simple pattern-matching scheme that looks for keywords works well for the limited domain of discourse. Context is used only in resolving pronoun references. These patterns of keywords are translated into calls to functions responsible for answering the question. If a question is not understood, the user is informed of the options for the missing or incorrect sentence fragments.

2) **Getting the answer.** This involves two interleaved processes—deducing what could be affected if the indicated change were made and formatting the answer for English output. The formatted, English answer is generated by dynamically assembling and filling in language templates (which represent part of the answer) with actual, problem-specific data, such as the name ExchangeSort. The theory described in the next section is used at each step to guide the choice of templates and to supply actual data for filling them in.

3) **Reporting the answer.** A set of routines for formatted printing of templates is used for typing the English answer on the terminal.

It is worth noting that the explanation facility could have been implemented to answer questions about specific changes, instead of "classes" of changes. The intention, however, was to avoid involved language-understanding issues and to have a smooth interface with the techniques in the next section, while still providing an effective question-answering facility. The current design seems to meet these criteria.

V. REASONING ABOUT CHANGES

This section explains how the assistant reasons about incremental changes to a program's design or verification, then shows how this theory was applied in the scenario of Section II.

A. Overview of the Approach

1) A General Strategy

It is important to distinguish the user's conception of *what* an incremental system does from *how* the system does it. From the user's viewpoint, an incremental system responds to changes by keeping intact previous work that remains valid, *without* any unnecessary reprocessing. But, a system can convey this impression even though it does a certain amount of reprocessing. In fact, there is a spectrum of strategies a system could employ. At one end of the spectrum is the most straightforward strategy—reprocess everything completely, then bring to the user's attention any information that is not currently correct. This is the way traditional compilers work. If a source file is changed, the entire file is recompiled, and the user is informed of any errors that are detected. The approach at the other end of the spectrum is to isolate the exact impact of changes, thereby avoiding all unnecessary reprocessing. A compiler based on this approach would never recompile unaffected parts of a changed file.

As a general strategy, both of these approaches to reasoning about incremental changes can be highly inefficient. Complete reprocessing, although generally acceptable in compilers, is too costly in program verifiers, mostly because of the expense involved in redoing proofs. Determining the exact effects of changes is too costly since it can take as much effort (or more) to figure out how to keep from redoing still-valid work as it would take to redo it.

An efficient general strategy lies somewhere between these endpoints. The idea is to *localize the effects of changes to a small amount of information, redo everything in that locality, then bring to the user's attention only that which is actually affected.* If applied properly, this strategy can minimize the amount of effort spent determining the effects of incremental changes. The main problem, of course, is in achieving the right balance between the amount of effort invested in approximating the effects of a change and the amount of unnecessary reprocessing. The discussion below will show how the assistant attempts to achieve this balance.

2) The Theory Embodied in the Assistant

The assistant expends much more effort trying to avoid unnecessary reprocessing of the verification than the design. In fact, the costly activity of reproving still-valid theorems is nearly always avoided, while a limited amount of retranslation (which, unlike proving theorems, is entirely automated) is accepted. The scenario for determining the effects of changes is as follows. If a program is changed, the assistant first approximates the affected part of the design and verification. Then, it retranslates the *potentially* affected part of the design and logically analyzes the *potentially* affected verification conditions to determine the *actual* effects of the change. This two-stage approach seems to be considerably more efficient than directly analyzing changes to programs on a case-by-case basis. In contrast, changes to specifications are analyzed without a preliminary approximation of their effects. The assistant performs certain logical analyses on the changed specification, often establishing that the change has no, or only limited, effects on the verification.

Let us now consider some of the key ideas used by the assistant in determining the effects of changes to programs. The main problem is that of quickly making a good initial approximation of what is affected, whereas the subsequent reprocessing needed to isolate the actual effects of the change is relatively straightforward. The assistant divides a program unit into an *external part* that defines its interface with its external environment and an *internal part* that gives details not visible to its callers. As an illustration, consider the definition of ExchangeSort:

```
        function ExchangeSort(...):IntArray =
        begin
            entry ... ;
            exit ... ;
(1)         ... Exchange(...) ... ;
        end;
```

Its internal part is its body at line (1), and its external part is everything else. This distinction was brought about by the observation that only a change to the external part of a program unit can have global effects; or conversely, a change to an internal part can have only local effects.

The assistant can use this fact to significantly limit the amount of information that is reprocessed following a change to a program. As a simple illustration, consider the following definitions:

```
        function Exchange(...):IntArray =
        begin
(2)         exit ... IsExchanged(...);
        ...
        end;

(3)     function IsExchanged(...):boolean = ... ;
```

Now suppose that the parameter list of IsExchanged, in line (3), is revised. Since this is a change to an external part of IsExchanged, it may affect Exchange. Specifically, the exit specification of Exchange, line (2), may contain a *design inconsistency*, defined to be a syntactic or type error in a program or specification. Exchange may also have a *verification inconsistency*, a situation in which a verification condition does not correspond to a *design-consistent* part of the *current* design. (Note that this definition singles out verification conditions that 1) contain design-inconsistent information or 2)·reflect a previous, instead of the current, version of the design.) ExchangeSort, on the other hand, can only be verification inconsistent. Since the design-inconsistent specification at line (2) is in an external part of Exchange, it appears in Exchange-Sort's verification condition across the call at line (1). Since this call is from an internal part of ExchangeSort, the effects of the original change *cannot* propagate any further. Thus, any design changes needed to correct the exit specification of Exchange at line (2) must be balanced by changes to the verification of only Exchange and ExchangeSort.

Notice that the specific change in line (3) was not mentioned. The strategy is to determine whether an internal or external part of IsExchanged has been changed, and then approximate what *might* be affected accordingly. Once the effects of a change are approximated, the assistant next must determine its actual effects. Rather than reprocessing the potentially inconsistent parts of the development immediately, the assistant *delays reprocessing until necessary*. Immediate reprocessing is often fruitless, since a sequence of changes to the design is often made, the last of which resolves all intermediate inconsistencies. When the reprocessing is finally done, the assistant isolates the actual design inconsistencies and any verification conditions causing a verification inconsistency. These verification conditions are identified by generating new verification conditions and then logically comparing them with the old verification conditions. The logical technique employed is similar to the one described next for analyzing changes to specifications.

Changes to specifications often can be shown not to have effects with just one simple proof. When a specification is changed, the assistant figures out what logical relationship must hold between the changed specification and its preceding version in order for the change not to have effects. This is illustrated by the following interchange:

<table>
<tr><td>←What are the effects of changing the exit specification of LocationOfMax?</td></tr>
</table>

This change does not affect LocationOfMax if the formula

LocationOfMax(A, I, J) in [I . .J] . . . $\Rightarrow$ *Changed exit specification*

is true . . . . The verification of other programs is not affected if the formula

Changed exit specification $\Rightarrow$ LocationOfMax(A, I, J) in [I . .J] . . .

is true . . . .

If the exit specification of LocationOfMax is actually modified, the assistant forms the designated implications and invokes the proof system to attempt an automatic proof. If the attempted proof fails, the formula is assumed to be false and, guided by internal/external calling relationships, the assistant identifies those program units that are verification inconsistent.

The remaining problem is that of resolving confirmed inconsistencies. When can inconsistencies in the development be resolved? And how do they get resolved? The answer to the first question is that inconsistencies can be resolved in any intermediate stage in the development. This significantly enhances incremental development. The user, for example, can define programs that call as yet undefined programs, then define the callees whenever convenient. In short, the assistant's ability to retain and reason about temporarily inconsistent information gives the user the freedom to evolve a development according to any strategy that is convenient. In answer to the second question, the user and the assistant share the responsibility for removing inconsistencies. The assistant detects design inconsistencies which the user must correct (since the assistant does not embody a theory of automatic debugging), while the assistant removes verification inconsistencies by replacing irrelevant verification conditions with the appropriate new ones.

A final remark is in order concerning the use of the assistant. Despite its ability to reason about incremental changes, if misused, the assistant can suffer from the same kind of inefficiency as traditional verifiers suffer from—namely, excessive and unnecessary redoing of still-valid previous work. The problem for the assistant, however, is on a much smaller scale (since only a small portion of the development is usually reprocessed) and can easily be circumvented. The source of the problem is the iterative nature of the process of making revisions. Traditional verifiers can provide little, if any, assistance in helping the user avoid costly iterations. The assistant, on the other hand, can effectively assist the user via its explanation facility. The user can ask about the effects of an intended change, then ask about the effects of changing the affected information, etc., until an understanding of the total impact of the original change is gleaned. With this knowledge, all needed changes can be made at once.

The next two sections give the specifics of the ideas just presented. A model for describing a program's design and verification is given, followed by a discussion of the knowledge used in approximating, isolating, and resolving inconsistencies that result from a change to any specific model. The discussion assumes that programs and their specifications can be type checked at compile time and that programs do not have side effects except through call-by-reference parameters.

B. Model of a Program's Design and Verification

In general, a model will contain information about individual parts of a design and verification and information about how they interrelate. This information is represented as a network of nodes and relations. Suppose there is a program A that calls another program B, as in Fig. 4. Programs A and B are represented by the nodes labeled A and B, and the fact that A has a call to B is carried by the labeled pointer between the nodes. Individually, A and B can have properties like the one indicated by the HAS-STATUS-OF pointers in the second part of Fig. 4.

Let us now look at a sample model that the model-building programs would construct. A model of a program's development is really a collection of models—one model for each major task performed by the overall design and verification system. Recall that the major tasks performed by the overall system are translation (specifically, parsing and type checking), verification condition generation, and theorem proving. So there are three models, each of which can initially be viewed as an independent entity.

The parser/type-checker model is shown in the first part of Fig. 5. (From now on, all nodes labeled with individual letters represent program units.) Notice that calls in external parts of a program (i.e., those parts that are visible to its callers) are distinguished from calls in internal parts of programs (i.e., those parts that are not visible to its callers). Further observe that calling relationships are described with inverse pointers such as HAS-CALL-IN-INTERNAL-PART-TO and HAS-CALL-FROM-INTERNAL-PART-OF. The second part of Fig. 5 shows a model of the verification condition generation process. Naturally, the information contained in this model is different from the information contained in the parser/type-checker model. The focus is on the program paths traced by the verification condition generator and the verification conditions associated with each path. The proof system model, which describes certain proof dependencies, is in the third part of Fig. 5.

While it is easier to think of these models as independent

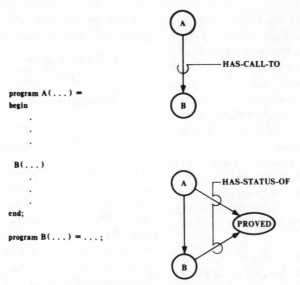

```
program A(...) =
begin
    .
    .
    .

    B(...)
    .
    .
    .
end;

program B(...) = ...;
```

Fig. 4. The first network shows that program A has a call to program B; the second shows that both have been proved.

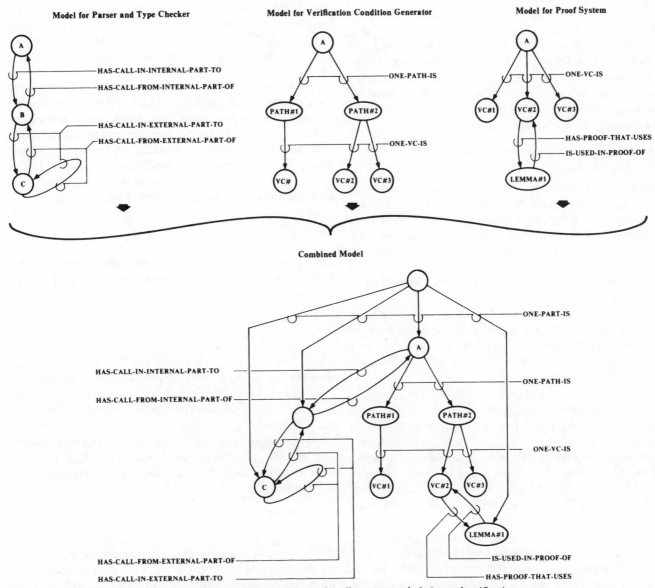

Fig. 5. Different models combine to describe a program's design and verification.

entities, there are, in fact, important ties among them that must be made apparent in order to handle incremental changes. For example, a change to a program in the parser/type-checker model may need to be reflected in the program's verification conditions in the verification condition generator model. There are several ways to represent model connections. The assistant does it by integrating all models into a single, unified model as shown in Fig. 5. The algorithms given in the next section reason about changes to this combined model.

Consider now the generation of a development's description. The starting point is a file containing programs and their specifications, and the end result is a network relating and describing various objects with pointers such as HAS-CALL-IN-EXTERNAL-PART-TO, ONE-PATH-IS, HAS-STATUS-OF, and HAS-PROOF-THAT-USES.

The first step in processing a file is to parse and type check all programs and specifications on the file, using the context supplied by the existing model to resolve external references. Processed entities that either have no errors or have only type errors are incorporated into the model by the algorithms described in the next section, whereas entities containing syntax errors are not. Typically, a single file contains only a small part of an entire design. As the design is evolved and refined, and as verification conditions are generated and proved, the model is gradually filled in. The final model describes a completed design and verification with all effects of incremental changes compensated for. Any subsequent changes made for maintenance purposes cause the model to be adjusted just as if the changes were made during the development.

C. Knowledge for Reasoning About Changes to Any Specific Model

This section further explains the main procedures introduced earlier in the overview. It elaborates on 1) how the assistant approximates the effects of a change and 2) how, by refining this approximation, the actual inconsistencies are eventually isolated. The algorithms described use the logical techniques described below.

1) Determining Whether Changes to Specifications Affect the Verification

To show that changes to specifications do not have effects, it suffices to establish certain logical relationships between the changed specification and its previous version. What these relationships are depends on how the specification in question has been used in proofs.

Specifications are used in well-defined ways, as prescribed by the program proof techniques employed. The assistant is given a set of templates that describe, for each kind of specification, which formula to prove in order to show that a change has no effects. There are two classes of relationship templates—those for showing that a change does not have global effects and those for showing that a change does not have local effects. Changes to external specifications (e.g., traditional entry and exit assertions) can have global and local effects, while changes to internal specifications (e.g., inductive assertions) can have only local effects.

Consider what the relationship templates would be for entry and exit specifications. The relationships for deciding

if a change does not have local effects are obtained by observing that Hoare's rule of consequence

$$\frac{P \Rightarrow Q, Q \{S\} R, R \Rightarrow T}{P \{S\} T}$$

can be instantiated as

$$\frac{entry' \Rightarrow entry, entry \{program\text{-}body\}exit, exit \Rightarrow exit'}{entry'\{program\text{-}body\}exit'}$$

The notational convention of designating changed information with a prime symbol is adopted throughout. For example, the revised version of the specification called exit is $exit'$. The notation $entry\{program\text{-}body\}exit$ means that if entry holds before executing the program, and if execution terminates, then exit will hold afterwards. The rule says that if it can be shown that $entry' \Rightarrow entry$, $entry\{program\text{-}body\}exit$, and $exit \Rightarrow exit'$, then the consequent $entry'\{program\text{-}body\}exit'$ can be inferred. We are interested here in the question of what happens when entry and exit are revised after $entry\{program\text{-}body\}exit$ has been proved. If $entry' \Rightarrow entry$ and $exit \Rightarrow exit'$ can be proved, then $entry'\{program\text{-}body\}exit'$ can be inferred, meaning that neither change invalidates any part of the verification of the associated program. The case when only entry or only exit is changed is handled in the obvious way.

Globally, entry and exit specifications of a program can arise in verification conditions of its callers in several ways. Suppose the program proof techniques handle subprogram calls 1) by proving that entry specifications hold at all calling sites and 2) by adding formulas of the form $entry \Rightarrow exit$ from callees to verification conditions of callers. Just as Hoare's rule of consequence was used in the derivation of local relationship templates, the *derived inference rule*

$$\frac{P \Rightarrow Q, Q \wedge R \Rightarrow S}{P \wedge R \Rightarrow S}$$

can be used in the derivation of global relationship templates. P, Q, R, and S are arbitrary logical formulas that are instantiated to give

$$\frac{P \Rightarrow entry, entry \Rightarrow entry'}{P \Rightarrow entry'}$$

where true has been substituted for R. This instantiation shows what to do if a verification condition of the form $P \Rightarrow entry$ has been proved, and subsequently entry is changed to $entry'$. If $entry \Rightarrow entry'$ can be established, then $P \Rightarrow entry'$ follows.

For the second case, let us start out by assuming that just exit, instead of $entry \Rightarrow exit$, is added to verification conditions at calling sites. Consider the following instantiation of the derived rule:

$$\frac{exit' \Rightarrow exit, exit \wedge R \Rightarrow S}{exit' \wedge R \Rightarrow S}$$

If $exit' \Rightarrow exit$ can be established, then proofs of verification conditions of the form $exit \wedge R \Rightarrow S$ also hold for those of the form $exit' \wedge R \Rightarrow S$. Similarly, if $((entry' \Rightarrow exit') \Rightarrow (en\text{-}$

try $\Rightarrow$ exit)) can be established, then proofs of verification conditions of the form (entry $\Rightarrow$ exit)$\wedge$R $\Rightarrow$ S also hold for those of the form (entry$'$ $\Rightarrow$ exit$'$)$\wedge$R $\Rightarrow$ S.

Even if verification conditions are always of the last form, the assistant can often take the shortcut of attempting to prove only exit$'$ $\Rightarrow$ exit, as is described by the following rule:

if entry = entry$'$ then exit$'$ $\Rightarrow$ exit
else (entry$'$ $\Rightarrow$ exit$'$) $\Rightarrow$ (entry $\Rightarrow$ exit)

This kind of rule allows the assistant to take advantage of its knowledge about what has changed. If the entry has not changed and the exit has, the test is true and a proof of the simpler formula on the then-branch is attempted. This simplification surfaces to the user level during explanations, as is evident in the following interchange:

$\longleftarrow$**What are the effects of changing the exit specification of LocationOfMax?**

... The verification of other programs is not affected if the formula

Changed exit specification $\Rightarrow$ **LocationOfMax(A, I, J) in [I . .J] ...**

is true ...

The answer refers only to the exit specification of LocationOfMax because the user did not hypothesize changing its entry specification too.

The scenario for applying the relationship templates is as follows. When a specification is changed, the assistant selects and instantiates the appropriate templates. It then invokes a fully automatic portion of the proof system in an effort to prove the desired formula without involving the user. In practice, the formula can often be established automatically with propositional inferences. For example, it is commonplace in top-down development to conjoin additional exit assertions onto a program before it has been implemented or verified. This was illustrated in the sample scenario when the proof of Exchange-Sort required adding a new conjunct to the exit specification of the lower-level program IsPerm. The formula exit$\wedge$"new conjunct" $\Rightarrow$ exit was easily proved. But what if it could not be proved automatically? If the attempted proof fails, the unproved formula is brought to the attention of the user, who can choose to invoke the more powerful capabilities of the interactive theorem prover or indicate that the formula should be treated as if it were false. How to identify what is affected when such attempted proofs fail and the conditions under which such proofs cannot even be attempted will be explained later.

Changes to verification conditions can be analyzed in much

which can be made automatically, is used to make this determination—two verification conditions must be the same syntactically within a uniform change of variables and they must be the same semantically symbol for symbol. Uniform variable renaming is considered as a special case so that the common source code change of uniformly renaming an identifier will not necessitate any reverifying. When checking the semantic criteria for equivalence, the types of free variables are found in the appropriate symbol tables.

This section has presented *sufficient* conditions for showing that a change to an entry or exit specification or to a verification condition has no effects. Any scheme for doing this is subject to certain theoretical limitations. Since the formula to be proved is typically a statement in number theory, Godel's Incompleteness Theorem says that there will be some true theorems that cannot be proved, meaning that the *exact* effects of changes cannot always be determined. Thus, no matter how clever a scheme is employed, some previous work may need to be redone unnecessarily.

2) Isolating and Resolving Inconsistencies

The assistant combines the process of isolating inconsistencies (i.e., refining its initial approximation of the effects of a change) and the process of resolving verification inconsistencies (i.e., discarding verification conditions that no longer apply). The choice of when and on what part of the design and verification to initiate these processes centers around what might be thought of as an *invariant* at a particular point in a development.

This invariant, which is often (and perhaps incorrectly) assumed to hold, describes an important relationship between a particular part of the design and a particular program's verification conditions. The invariant states a condition under which newly generated verification conditions will be "well formed"—namely, when design inconsistencies are not contained in the program of interest, its specifications, or specifications that would be imported from other program units. This invariant guides the assistant's search for *relevant* design errors and *irrelevant* verification conditions. For example, suppose that the user issues a command to verify the function ExchangeSort. If the invariant does not hold for ExchangeSort, the assistant rejects the command:

Exec$\longrightarrow$**VCs ExchangeSort**

****Verification conditions cannot be generated for ExchangeSort,
because there is a type mismatch in the exit specification of IsExchanged.

---

the same way as changes to specifications. If a verification condition for a particular program is changed, the assistant loops through all the program's at least partially proved verification conditions to see if any of their proofs hold for the new verification condition. A simple "equivalence" test,

For now, observe only that the assistant detected a relevant design inconsistency, which must be corrected before verification conditions can be generated for ExchangeSort. (The reasons for this rejection are explained later in this section.) Suppose, on the other hand, that the invariant had been satisfied. In this case, the assistant would generate well-formed verification conditions for ExchangeSort and perform the logical equivalence test described in the preceding section to keep intact previous proofs that still apply. As was illustrated in Fig. 3, all this detailed reasoning is hidden from the user.

Let us now consider the issue of how the assistant tests the invariant. Before considering the algorithm, the model will be augmented to associate special variables with every program unit for recording whether it has inconsistencies. CHECK-DESIGN-FLAG is a boolean variable that is True if the associated program unit is thought to have a design error. Similarly, a variable called CHECK-VERIFICATION-FLAG is used to record verification inconsistencies. The algorithms described in the next section assign truth values to these flags so that the model properly reflects the development.

A nice property of the model is that the invariant is guaranteed to hold for a particular program if both of its flags are False. If either flag is True, the assistant must examine certain calling relationships to make its determination. A slightly more detailed view of the programs referred to earlier will be used to illustrate the general procedure:

```
      function ExchangeSort(. . .):IntArray =
      begin
          entry . . . ;
          exit . . . ;
(1)       . . . Exchange(. . .) . . . ;
      end;
      function Exchange(. . .):IntArray =
      begin
(2)       exit . . . IsExchanged(. . .);
          . . .
      end;
(3)   function IsExchanged(A,B:IntArray;I,J:int):boolean =
      begin
(4)       exit (IsExchanged(A,B,i) iff . . . A[I] = B[J] and A[J] = B[I]);
      end;
```

The calling relationships among these programs are reflected by internal/external calling pointers in the model (as illustrated by the parser/type checker model of Fig. 5 with the substitutions of ExchangeSort for A, Exchange for B, and IsExchanged for C), CHECK-DESIGN-FLAG is True for IsExchanged, and CHECK-VERIFICATION-FLAG is True for all three functions. Recall that "HAS-CALL-FROM" pointers were traced in propagating the effects of changes. In contrast, "HAS-CALL-TO" pointers are traced in testing the invariant. The general procedure is illustrated by following the assistant as it determines whether the invariant holds for ExchangeSort. The assistant first observes that, since the CHECK-DESIGN-FLAG of ExchangeSort is False, ExchangeSort does not contain any design inconsistencies. The next step is to determine whether there is an inconsistency in some other part of the design that would appear in ExchangeSort's verification conditions. For generality, assume that hierarchies of specifications are fully expanded in verification conditions.

Then, the search for a relevant design error traces sequences of pointers $p_1, p_2, \cdots, p_n$, where p_1 is any "HAS-CALL-TO" pointer and $p_2, \cdots, p_n$ are HAS-CALL-IN-EXTERNAL-PART-TO pointers. (The tracing algorithm must, of course, handle cycles properly.) Only program units encountered in tracing these sequences can contain relevant design inconsistencies. In the example being considered, the calls at lines (1) and (2) indicate that Exchange and IsExchanged must be considered. The assistant immediately knows that Exchange does not contain a design inconsistency because its CHECK-DESIGN-FLAG is False, but it must reanalyze IsExchanged because its CHECK-DESIGN-FLAG is True. IsExchanged is, in fact, found to have a design inconsistency, because the recursive call in line (4) has only three arguments [instead of four as required by line (3)]. Consequently, verification conditions cannot be generated for ExchangeSort until this error is corrected.

3) Approximating the Effects of Changes

The process of approximating the effects of a change to a program or its specifications culminates in certain truth value assignments to the special variables. CHECK-DESIGN-FLAG and CHECK-VERIFICATION-FLAG. No further background is needed to understand how the assistant makes these assignments. The algorithm is roughly as follows.

1) If the header of program unit X has changed, then assign the value True to both flags of all callers of X and to the CHECK-VERIFICATION-FLAG of all programs whose verifications use a specification that calls X.

2) If there is a change to an externally visible specification of X that has global effects, then assign the value True to the CHECK-VERIFICATION-FLAG of all programs that have used the preceding version of the changed specification in their verification.

3) If X contains design inconsistencies, then assign the value True to both of its flags. Otherwise, assign its CHECK-VERIFICATION-FLAG the value True if a) its body has changed, b) there is a change in one of its specifications that has local effects, or c) the invariant described in the immediately preceding section does not hold for X.

The first two steps approximate the global effects of a change, while the last step focuses on local effects. One additional point is that the logical reasoning needed to show that a change to a specification does not have effects cannot be done unless the changed specification and its preceding version are free of design inconsistencies and cannot depend on other design inconsistent specifications. If either condition is violated, the change is simply assumed to have effects.

The one kind of change left to consider is that of adding entirely new program units to the model. The local truth value assignments are very similar to those in step 3) above. Both flags are assigned the value True if the new program unit contains design inconsistencies; if it does not, its CHECK-VERIFICATION-FLAG is assigned the value True if the invariant does not hold. However, no global truth value assignments are ever required. To illustrate why, suppose the program units ExchangeSort and IsExchanged are defined before Exchange. When Exchange is defined, both of ExchangeSort's flags would already be True, and IsExchanged could not possibly be affected because the effects of defining Exchange propagate through "HAS-CALL-FROM" pointers.

For expository purposes, this discussion has not considered data type definitions or certain logical properties that are not part of a program unit's specifications. An example of such a property is rewrite rules that are used in proofs. The implementation handles both kinds of constructs, using straightforward extensions of the ideas already discussed. Appendix A gives a tabular summary of the key relations in the complete model.

D. The Scenario Revisited

As implemented, the assistant does not adopt the "worst case" view of completely expanding verification conditions during their generation because imported specifications, especially lower-level ones in a specification hierarchy, are not always needed in proofs. Only references to specifications of called programs, instead of the specifications themselves, are added to verification conditions during their generation. Then, complete specifications, or parts of specifications, are expanded as needed during proofs. A record of these expansions is then used to identify what proofs must be redone following changes to specifications or changes that affect specifications.

Let us now return to the scenario of Section II and see how the assistant reasons about the hypothesized and actual changes. In the dialog in Fig. 1, the explanation facility answers questions by querying the model directly or by invoking one of the assistant's main algorithms. The answer to the question "What are the effects of fully defining ExchangeSort?" requires only an interpretation of the status of ExchangeSort. The value of its HAS-STATUS-OF pointer is "waiting for body to be fully defined." So the assistant immediately concludes that "ExchangeSort may have additional VCs." (The word "may" allows for the possibility of replacing the "pending" in the body of ExchangeSort with the "null statement," which would not cause any new verification conditions to be generated.) More complex reasoning is done, for example, in answering the question "What are the effects of changing the exit of IsPerm?" The assistant selects and instantiates a relationship template that describes the logical implication that must hold. Pointers from IsPerm tell the assistant that the verification of ExchangeSort, specifically the proof of ExchangeSort#1, will be invalidated if the displayed implication cannot be proved.

Next, the revisions in Fig. 2 are reflected in the model by executing the appropriate reasoning programs. The assistant, observing that some new verification conditions need to be generated for ExchangeSort, assigns its CHECK-VERIFICATION-FLAG the value True. It also deduces that the changed exit specifications of ValueOfMax and IsPerm do not invalidate previous verification work, and incorporates new programs (such as LocationOfMax) into the existing model.

Finally, Fig. 3 shows the generation of the new verification conditions for ExchangeSort, with the assistant working in the background to formally establish that the change to Exchange-Sort did not affect previous proofs. Appendix B shows the resulting model.

VI. CONCLUSION

This paper has explained how to build a computer program that provides several useful kinds of assistance to the human designer/verifier and that also interfaces with traditional program verifiers to significantly increase their performance in working situations. A theory for determining the effects of incremental changes to a design or verification has been presented, and it has been shown how this theory can serve as the basis for answering questions about the effects of hypothesized changes and for making proposals for how to proceed with the design and verification in an orderly fashion. Since attention has been primarily on how the assistant works, only a glimpse of how it is used in a real working situation has been seen. A transcript illustrating the role of the assistant at each stage in the development of a message switching network (which allows secure, asynchronous message transfer among a fixed number of users) is presented in [13].

Experience in using the designer/verifier's assistant is very encouraging. As expected, its utility grows proportionately with the size and complexity of the program being developed. This is particularly evident when the assistant is used to obtain explanations of the effects of hypothesized changes. In all but the simplest cases, it is totally impractical to carry out the requisite calculations reliably by hand. This is true not only during a development, but even more so afterwards when confronted with the problem of "maintaining" formally verified software. A common problem is that of determining how to change specifications and programs to reflect new design constraints. If the human designer/verifier has forgotten relevant details about the development, the assistant is used to regain the necessary understanding—namely, to get explanations of the potential effects of any intended revisions and to get hints about how to make them. Similarly, as the tasks that remain to be done increase in number and variety, the importance of the assistant's ability to suggest a next logical step in the development also becomes more and more evident.

The amount of computional efficiency gained by using the assistant also grows proportionately with the size and complexity of the program being developed. When incremental changes are made, the assistant typically limits the scope of their effects to a relatively small fraction of the overall development, thereby generally avoiding unnecessary reapplication of the program verifier to unaffected parts of the development. As a result, the total savings in processing increases rapidly as the development evolves. This overall improvement in efficiency emanates from the cumulative impact of several design decisions. The fundamental ones of allowing a certain amount of unnecessary reprocessing in specific instances and of expending more effort trying to avoid unnecessary reverification than retranslation appear to have been very sound. The way in which these desiderata were reflected in the theory for reasoning about changes has resulted in the general avoidance of the costly activity of reproving still-valid theorems

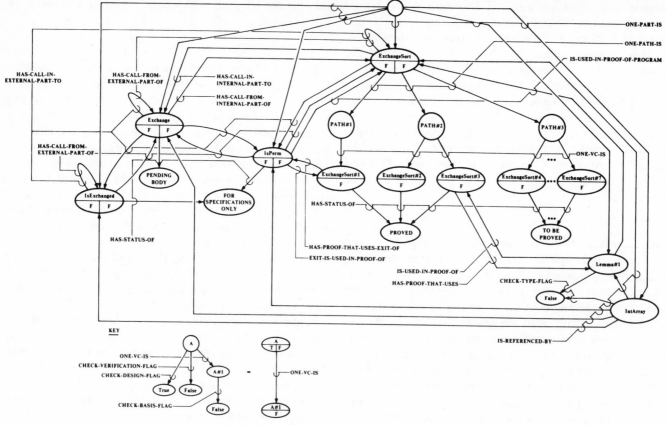

Fig. 6. Fairly detailed view of an actual model.

and in only a limited amount of the much cheaper activity of retranslation. The balance achieved between the amount of effort invested in approximating the effects of a change and the amount of unnecessary reprocessing generally appears to be appropriate for interfacing with traditional program verifiers. Another impact of the fundamental design decisions has been the simplifications they have allowed in both the model for representing a design and verification and the codified knowledge used for reasoning about changes to any specific model.

The assistant represents a beginning step towards the construction of an incremental system for use in developing and maintaining formally verified programs. Experimentation with the current version of the assistant suggests that, although it generally seems to reason at the appropriate level of detail, there are times when it would be better to analyze design changes individually, rather than by category as it does now. It also suggests a need for more structuring in explanations, specifically for the assistant to make available a hierarchy of explanations, ranging from very high level to very detailed. These issues are, in fact, closely related and are being actively explored. Further research is also being carried out to broaden the scope of the assistant to handle multiple version systems, additional programming languages, a hierarchical development methodology [15], and to eventually support a complete environment which includes editors, interpreters, etc. Another complementary line of investigation being conducted is the exploration of the principles which underlie any kind of incremental system. The goal is to evolve a general mathematical framework that explains how to build and extend incremental systems, such as the assistant.

APPENDIX A

RELATIONS IN A MODEL

The tables below summarize the key relations used in modeling a program's design and verification. The term *basis property* refers to logical properties, which are not part of a program's specifications, that are assumed in proofs (e.g., rewrite rules).

TABLE I
KEY RELATIONSHIPS BETWEEN NODES

Relationship Pointer	Meaning
CALLS	Points from a basis property to a function it calls
HAS-CALL-FROM	Inverse of CALLS
HAS-CALL-FROM-EXTERNAL-PART-OF	Inverse of HAS-CALL-IN-EXTERNAL-PART-TO
HAS-CALL-FROM-INTERNAL-PART-OF	Inverse of HAS-CALL-IN-INTERNAL-PART-TO
HAS-CALL-IN-INTERNAL-PART-TO	Points from program A to program B if B is called from a part of A that is not visible to callers of A
HAS-CALL-IN-EXTERNAL-PART-TO	Points from program A to program B if B is called from a part of A that is visible to callers of A
HAS-PROOF-THAT-USES	Points from a verification condition to a basis property used in its proof
IS-REFERENCED-BY	Points from type definition A to program B if B uses A
IS-USED-IN-PROOF-OF	Inverse of HAS-PROOF-THAT-USES
IS-USED-IN-PROOF-OF-PROGRAM	Points from basis property B to program A if B IS-USED-IN-PROOF-OF at least one verification condition of A
ONE-PATH-IS	Associates paths with programs
ONE-PART-IS	Ties together the "main" parts of a program's design and verification
ONE-VC-IS	Associates verification conditions with paths
REFERENCES	Inverse of IS-REFERENCED-BY

TABLE II
KEY PROPERTIES OF NODES

Property Pointer	Meaning
CHECK-DESIGN-FLAG	Set to True if a program or basis property may be design inconsistent and to False otherwise
CHECK-VERIFICATION-FLAG	Set to True if a program may be verification inconsistent and to False otherwise
HAS-STATUS-OF	Associated with all programs and logical formulas to describe their state of development
CHECK-BASIS-FLAG	Set to True if the proof of a logical formula depends on a potentially incorrect basis property and to False otherwise

APPENDIX B
A SAMPLE MODEL

Fig. 6 shows the model resulting from the scenario of Section II. It is given in a fair amount of detail to convey a feeling for the complexity dealt with even at an early stage in a development. The primary simplification in this rendition of the model is the omission of all information about Location-OfMax and ValueOfMax.

There is one new relation, along with its inverse, shown in the model. HAS-PROOF-THAT-USES-EXIT-OF, along with EXIT-IS-USED-IN-PROOF-OF, were added because the assistant does not always expand specifications from called programs into verification conditions. These additional relations keep track of those proofs in which the associated exit specification has actually been used.

ACKNOWLEDGMENT

This research was initiated as my Ph.D. dissertation at The University of Texas at Austin and partially carried out at the University of Southern California Information Sciences Institute. I would like to thank my advisors and committee members: W. W. Bledsoe, D. Good, R. London, and R. Yeh. In addition, I would like to thank D. Wile for his helpful suggestions on how to reason about incremental changes. This presentation has been improved by valuable comments from L. Flon, S. Katz, K. Levitt, L. Robinson, and one of the referees.

REFERENCES

[1] A. L. Ambler, D. I. Good, J. C. Browne, W. F. Burger, R. M. Cohen, C. G. Hoch, and R. E. Wells, "Gypsy: A language for specification and implementation of verifiable programs," in *Proc. ACM Conf. Language Design for Reliable Software, SIGPLAN Notices*, vol. 12, Mar. 1977, pp. 1-10.

[2] R. S. Boyer and J S. Moore, "A lemma driven automatic theorem prover for recursive function theory," in *Proc. 5th Int. Conf. Artificial Intelligence*, vol. 1, Aug. 1977, pp. 511-519.

[3] L. P. Deutsch, "An interactive program verifier," Ph.D. dissertation, Univ. California, Berkeley, 1973; also, Xerox Palo Alto Res. Center Rep. CSL-73-1, May 1973.

[4] J. Doyle, "Truth maintenance systems for problem solving," M.S. thesis, MIT Artificial Intelligence Laboratory Rep. AI-TR-419, Jan. 1978.

[5] B. Elspas, R. E. Shostak, and J. M. Spitzen, "A verification system for Jocit/J3 programs (Rugged Programming Environment-RPE/2)," SRI International Comput. Sci. Lab. Rep., Apr. 1977.

[6] R. W. Floyd, "Toward interactive design of correct programs," in *Proc. IFIP Congr. 71*. Amsterdam, The Netherlands: North-Holland, 1972, pp. 7-10.

[7] D. I. Good, R. L. London, and W. W. Bledsoe, "An interactive program verification system," *IEEE Trans. Software Eng.*, vol. SE-1, pp. 59-67, Mar. 1975.

[8] C. E. Hewitt and B. Smith, "Towards a programming apprentice," *IEEE Trans. Software Eng.*, vol. SE-1, pp. 26-45, Mar. 1975.

[9] E. L. Ivie, "The programmer's workbench—A machine for software development," *Commun. Ass. Comput. Mach.*, vol. 20, pp. 746-753, Oct. 1977.

[10] J. C. King, "A program verifier," Ph.D. dissertation, Carnegie-Mellon Univ., 1969.

[11] D. C. Luckham, "Program verification and verification-oriented programming," in *Proc. IFIP Cong. 77*. Amsterdam, The Netherlands: North-Holland, 1977, pp. 783-793.

[12] M. S. Moriconi, "A system for incrementally designing and verifying programs," Ph.D. dissertation, The University of Texas at Austin, Dec. 1977; also, SRI International Comput. Sci. Lab. Rep. CSL-73 and CSL-74.

[13] —, "Interactive design and verification: A message switching network example," SRI International Comput. Sci. Lab. Rep. CSL-90, May 1979; also, to appear in *Lecture Notes in Computer Science* (Springer-Verlag).

[14] C. Rich and H. E. Shrobe, "Initial report on a Lisp programmer's apprentice," *IEEE Trans. Software Eng.*, vol. SE-4, pp. 456-467, Nov. 1978.

[15] L. Robinson and K. N. Levitt, "Proof techniques for hierarchically structured programs," *Commun. Ass. Comput. Mach.*, vol. 20, pp. 271-283, Apr. 1977.

[16] O. Roubine and L. Robinson, *Special Reference Manual*, SRI International Comput. Sci. Lab. Rep. CSL-45, Jan. 1977.

[17] N. Suzuki, "Verifying programs by algebraic and logical reduction," in *Proc. Int. Conf. Reliable Software*, pp. 473-481, Apr. 1975, pp. 473-481.

[18] W. Teitelman, *Interlisp Reference Manual*, Xerox Palo Alto Res. Center, Oct. 1978.

[19] —, "Toward a programming laboratory," in *Proc. Int. Joint Conf. Artificial Intelligence*, May 1969, pp. 1-8.

[20] B. Wegbreit, "The ECL programming system," in *AFIPS Conf. Proc.*, vol. 39, Nov. 1971, pp. 253-262.

Mark S. Moriconi (S'74-M'76) was born in Pittsburg, KS, on May 7, 1948. He received the B.S. degree with honors in mathematics from Wichita State University, Wichita, KS, in 1970, and the Ph.D. degree in computer science from The University of Texas, Austin, in 1977.

He has been a Research Staff Member in the Computer Science Laboratory at SRI International (formerly Stanford Research Institute), Menlo Park, CA, since 1978. Prior to this appointment he conducted his doctoral research as a Research Assistant at The University of Texas, Austin, from 1974-1977 and at the University of Southern California Information Sciences Institute, Marina del Rey, CA, from 1975-1977. His current research interests are in the theory and development of incremental systems and in program verification, particularly in computer systems which assist in developing verified programs and programming methodologies which reduce the difficulties of verification.

Dr. Moriconi is a member of the Association for Computing Machinery and Sigma Xi.

Introduction

Gilb, T. "Design by Objectives: maintainability." First published in this Tutorial.

Tom Gilb is a globe-trotting EDP consultant who resides in Kolbotn, near Oslo in Norway. Design by Objectives is his technique for specifying a system in operational terms and then carrying the specifications through to an operationally equivalent implementation. Gilb's book on the technique, also titled *Design by Objectives*, will be published by North-Holland Publishing Company in 1983. In the following paper, Gilb describes Design by Objectives and applies it to the specification of a system's maintainability.

The strength of this paper is that it makes maintainability a measurable attribute. (Not coincidentally, Gilb authored the first book on yardsticks of software quality, published as *Software Metrics* by Winthrop Publishers, Inc., in 1977.) Maintainability is often a buzzword and a fuzzword in research reports and advertising copy. Every new design technique and every fourth generation language will make your system maintainable just as every mouthwash will make your lover faithful. This is not at all the way Gilb treats maintainability.

In his paper, *maintainability* is the measurable attribute of reducing the cost of *maintenance*. Gilb analyzes maintenance as a sequence of eleven activities, assigns a yardstick to each one (time to complete the activity), and defines maintainability in terms of the expected cost of maintenance, measured according to the yardstick. You may not agree with his analysis of activities or with his assigned costs, but if you sign off on his definition you will be able to measure whether the delivered system does or does not reach the agreed level of maintainability. This is what it means to say that Design by Objectives specifies a system in operational terms and carries the specifications through to an operationally equivalent implementation.

This is not the first time that Gilb has brought his unconventional scrutiny to bear on problems of maintenance. His short pieces "Structured program coding: does it really increase program maintainability?", "'Maintainability' is more than structured coding," "Guaranteeing program maintainability," "Spare parts maintenance strategy for programs," and "Should we specialize in hiring and training of application program maintenance technicians?" all appeared in Parikh's *Techniques of program and system maintenance* (Little, Brown and Company, 1982). They originally appeared in the British *Computer Weekly* in the column "Gilb's Mythodology," where their down-to-earth style masked a deadly attack on conventional and sloppy thinking.

Gilb is a man who enjoys upsetting plausible but mythical conclusions. His Norwegian domicile, Nordic name, bearded Viking look, melodious speech, and faintly formal syntax suggest a Norwegian who has learned to make his way in the English-speaking world. In fact he is a Californian who went to Norway at the age of 17, married a Norwegian, and has lived there ever since. Along with his friend and collaborator Gerald Weinberg (represented in Parts IV and V of this Tutorial), he is the source of much of the most original thinking on the maintenance problem.

DESIGN BY OBJECTIVES: MAINTAINABILITY

Tom Gilb
Iver Holtersvei 2
N-1410 Kolbotn
Norway
tel: (47 2) 80 16 97

Design by Objectives is a methodology for specifying the architecture of an information system. In the world of buildings, an architect explores with a customer the functions that a building must perform and the attributes that it must satisfy. He then selects from the available stock of building materials and techniques to compose a structure and a plan for building it. In the world of information systems, the information systems architect, or "infotect", explores the functions and attributes of the desired information system, and selects from the materials of software engineering and management to compose a system and a plan for building it. Design by Objectives is a toolkit for the infotect.

The three basic steps of Design by Objectives are:

1. Specify objectives in terms of functions (the desired capabilities of the system) and attributes (the characteristics such as cost constraints, ease of use, maintainability, etc., with which the functions are to be carried out). Objectives must be expressible and measurable in units that the customer understands.

2. Search for and specify techniques that satisfy the attributes. Make trade-off's between attributes. Iterate until an acceptable level on all attributes is attained.

3. Plan a schedule of evolutionary delivery which interleaves planning, detailed design, user experience, and learning.

Design by Objectives is a set of techniques and tools to help the infotect carry out these steps. The components of Design by Objectives are taken from the experience and research of many groups. They were assembled by this writer in the course of his consulting work in order to help clients specify information systems in ways that can be measured and controlled.

The purpose of this paper is to describe some of the techniques of Design by Objectives, and to illustrate them with an example. The content of the example is the objective of maintainability. This attribute was chosen as a sample of the kind of elusive objective which is often the downfall of other methodologies. In this paper we shall show how Design by Objectives can make maintainability a measurable and attainable objective.

FUNCTIONS AND ATTRIBUTES

In Design by Objectives, we divide the customer's objectives into functions and attributes.

A function is a non-negotiable requirement of the customer; it is something that the delivered system must do or offer or have if it is to be the desired system at all. An example of a system function is:

> PROJECT TRACKING: The system enables management to track the cost and schedule of projects.

The functional description of a system is the most fundamental way of defining it. The infotect must define the functions of the system before working on its attributes. For this reason, there are already many established methods for analyzing and specifying the functions of a system. This is, for instance, the province of Structured Analysis as defined by DeMarco (1978) or by Ross (Ross and Schoman, 1977), or of the specification techniques of Heninger and Parnas (Heninger, 1980).

A function is, in a sense, binary; if the delivered system fulfills the function, it is an implementation of the desired system; otherwise, it is not. An attribute, on the other hand, is a negotiable, measurable quality of the system. Examples of attributes are cost, delivery schedule, and (the attribute that we consider here) maintainability. Attributes are measured on a scale more complex than binary; this is where the customer and the infotect can negotiate levels of one attribute against another to arrive at a system that has acceptable levels on all attributes.

The functions of a system are decided by the customer with the aid of the tools and techniques of the systems analyst. Attributes, on the other hand, require far more attention by systems designers. The creativity of design is in choosing or devising techniques that will give the system the desired attributes. This is the major province of the tools of Design by Objectives.

In this paper, we shall deal with the functions of the system only at the most general level. We shall assume that we are developing a computerized project tracking system to replace a current manual system. We shall explode the functions of the example system down only to its first level of components:

PROJECT TRACKING
1. HARDWARE
2. SOFTWARE
3. PEOPLEWARE
4. PAPERWARE

This hierarchical explosion of the system function should be interpreted as follows. "The system enables management to TRACK the cost and schedule of PROJECTS. It uses processors, communication lines, and terminals (HARDWARE), programs and procedure manuals (SOFTWARE), staff time (PEOPLEWARE), and forms and reports (PAPERWARE)."

In a real project, the infotect would analyze the functions of the system in far more detail -- for example, who will enter data, how it will be processed, who will get the reports, and so on. However, the first level breakdown is sufficient here to illustrate how the techniques of Design by Objectives help in attaining maintainability, which is an attribute.

THE MAINTAINABILITY ATTRIBUTE

Any objective that is not measurable and controllable will not be deliverable either, and many systems have failed because the desired attributes were not attained: a system is just as dead if it is too costly or not reliable enough or not maintainable enough as if it did not perform at all.

The following guidelines must be followed in specifying an attribute:

1. The attribute must be measurable in practice.

2. It must be expressed in language that both the customer and the infotect understand.

Maintainability is the capacity of the user to perform maintenance, therefore the first prerequisite is to break down maintenance -- the making of a change in a system -- into its life cycle or phases. This is done in Table 1, in which the activity of maintenance is broken down into seven phases.

TABLE 1

PHASES OF MAINTENANCE

Problem recognition: Something needs to be changed, but it takes some time before a person knows it.

Administrative delay: Time passes until someone is assigned to do the maintenance.

Tool and documentation collection: The maintainer assembles materials for the change.

Problem analysis: The maintainer investigates what needs to be changed to reach the desired state of the program or system.

Change specification: The maintainer specifies new and changed code or procedures to be installed.

Active correction: The change is made as specified.

Test: The new function is tested and its side effects probed, and the change is independently reviewed and approved.

Having specified the components of maintenance, it is necessary to attach a cost measurement to them. Table 2 shows a System Attribute Specification Table for expressing such measurements.

The rows are the exploded levels of the attribute -- in this case, the seven phases of maintenance. The UNIT column indicates a measuring unit for each row. Since the costs of maintenance are related to the elapsed time in which the system remains in an unsatisfactory state and the consumed time of user maintenance staff, the appropriate units are time.

The next four columns indicate a WORST LEVEL, BEST LEVEL, PLANNED LEVEL, and NOW LEVEL for each attribute. These levels are measured in the unit specified in the UNIT column. If the attribute falls below the WORST LEVEL, the system will be rated as unacceptable.

The PLANNED LEVEL is the level at which the customer and infotect are aiming. The BEST LEVEL gives the customer an idea of the state of the art for this attribute. The NOW LEVEL indicates the performance of the current system. (Remember that most "new" information systems are new in techniques, not in function; they replace something that is already working.)

The cells in the LEVEL columns must be filled, but there is allowance here for "?"s, ranges, and relative figures. The cells in the NOW LEVEL column of Table 2 refer to a current manual system. Its reports are issued monthly, so the elapsed time to detect a problem, fix it, and test it is at least a month for each activity. The customer would like an on-line system with daily update and immediate query. The customer plans to recognize problems within an hour of receiving the system's reports, and have them fixed within two working days. The infotect estimates that the state of the art with such a system would be to fix a problem by the end of half a day.

The infotect also points out that some changes are easy to specify and easy to code and others are hard to specify and hard to code. Therefore the estimates for attribute A6 (active correction time) are expressed as a multiple of attribute A4 (problem analysis time).

The MORE IMPORTANT THAN column allows for attributes to be ranked against each other. This gives the infotect a guideline when one attribute has to be traded off against another. In this case, the customer regards speed in recognition (A1) and in problem analysis (A4) as more important than speed in active correction (A6).

The REF column provides for references to supporting documents.

THE TECHNIQUE / ATTRIBUTE TABLE

Having fully specified the functions and attributes of the desired system, the infotect now proceeds to select a set of techniques that will enable a

TABLE 2

SYSTEM ATTRIBUTE SPECIFICATION TABLE: MAINTAINABILITY

SPECI-FICATION / ATTRIB-UTES	UNIT	WORST LEVEL	BEST LEVEL	PLANNED LEVEL	NOW LEVEL	MORE IMPORTANT THAN	REF
A1 PROBLEM RECOG-NITION	TIME	24 HRS	1 MIN	60 MIN	1 MONTH	A6	
A2 ADMINIS-TRATIVE DELAY	TIME	1 WEEK	5 MIN	1 DAY	1 WEEK		
A3 TOOL,DOC COLLECT-ION	TIME	1 HOUR	2 MIN	10 MIN	10 MIN		
A4 PROBLEM ANALYSIS	TIME	50 MIN	30 SEC	10 MIN	10 MIN	A6	
A5 CHANGE SPECIFIC-ATION	TIME	1 HOUR?	30 SEC	5 MIN?	1 HOUR		
A6 ACTIVE CORREC-TION	TIME	3 X A4	30 SEC	2 X A4	1 MONTH		
A7 TEST	TIME	2 WEEKS	1/2 DAY	1 DAY	1 MONTH		

system to be built within acceptable values of the attributes. Where do technique ideas come from?

* From our own heads - memory, training, experiences.

* From publications - books, professional technical journals.

* From colleagues - perhaps a project team or design team.

Other design professionals -- engineers, chemists, physicists -- have access to systematic handbooks of information. These handbooks list techniques and the attributes that they support, or formulas for calculating the contribution of techniques to attributes. These handbooks are a necessary way of organizing a large and complex body of technical knowledge. They are also a way of keeping the professionals up to date in a changing profession. When the handbooks are updated, so is the professional. Professionals are taught the languages and principles for understanding the handbooks: they do not have to be taught all the details in them.

The software and computer systems design profession is not yet well organized along these lines. Until a Software Engineering Handbook appears, you can use the basic idea to organize your technique knowledge -- by beginning to compile Technique / Attribute Tables. These tables will become the basis of your own Software Engineering Handbook.

A Technique / Attribute Table summarizes the applicability of techniques to the attainment of attributes. Techniques are the rows of the table, attributes are the columns, and the cells indicate the contribution of a technique to attaining an attribute.

Before forming such a table, we need a list of techniques. A sample list of techniques in the maintainability area is given as Table 3. Each technique has a shorthand code (e.g. M.TEL indicates "Maintainability - telephone numbers"), a description, and possibly a reference to a source or a fuller discussion. You can add to your list of techniques as you learn them from the literature, classes, experience, or your colleagues.

TABLE 3

MAINTAINABILITY TECHNIQUES

M.TEL
Shift operators shall have home telephone numbers and duty rosters for the qualified maintenance programmers, and rules for when to call.

M.MPG
Maintenance programmers shall be considered qualified only when they can pass an artificial bug finding exam at 90% in five minutes.

M.DBA
Full database audit programs shall be built to test all stored data.
Ref: Gilb, 1977, p. 124.

M.LIB
All programs and text documentation shall be available on a central machine library.

M.TXT
Program text shall be logically grouped by indentation; comments shall be made for at least 30% on average of lines.
Ref: Gilb, 1977, p. 121.

M.LST
Program logic structure shall be forward flow only -- no backward GOTO's; maximum module size shall be 50 statements excluding comments.

M.INS
Formal inspection of all proposed changes shall be carried out before approval.
Refs: Fagan, 1976. Gilb, 1977, p. 229.

The Technique / Attribute Table relates techniques to attributes by giving a quantified expectation for each combination: how much does this technique contribute to that attribute? Table 4 is an example of such a table, relating the techniques of Table 3 to the maintainability attributes of Tables 1 and 2.

The relationship between techniques and attributes can take any of several

TABLE 4

TECHNIQUE / ATTRIBUTE TABLE: MAINTAINABILITY

NOTE: 10% = some contribution   25% = important   100% = essential

ATTRIB-UTES / TECHNIQUES	PROBLEM RECOG-NITION	ADMINIS-TRATIVE DELAY	TOOL,DOC COLLECT-ION	PROBLEM ANALYSIS	CHANGE SPECIFIC-ATION	ACTIVE CORREC-TION	TEST
T1 M.TEL (TELEPH. ROSTER)	SAVE 1/2 DAY	–	–	SAVE 1/2 DAY	–	–	SAVE 2 DAYS
T2 M.MPG (PROGRAM-MER EXAM)	10%	–	10%	100%	10%	10%	10%
T3 M.DBA (DATABASE AUDIT)	25%	–	10%	10%	–	–	25%
T4 M.LIB (CENTRAL LIBRARY)	–	–	100%	25%	–10%	–10%	–10%
T5 M.TXT (PROGRAM TEXT)	–	–	–	25%	–10%	–10%	10%
T6 M.LST (PROGRAM STRUC-TURE)	–	–	–	25%	–10%	–10%	25%
T7 M.INS (INSPEC-TION)	10%	–10%	–	25%	–	–	100%

forms, such as likely ranges, data from experience, formulas for calculation of the attribute value, or simply advice ("try it on a pilot version"). Little work has been published on these relationships to date, but one model might be Phister's books on data processing technology and economics (1976, 1980). The following paragraphs explain the notations used in Table 4, but these are not intended to be an exhaustive sample of all the notations that might be useful.

Dashes (-) indicate that the technique has no effect on the attribute.

Technique M.TEL ("Shift operators should have home telephone numbers and duty rosters for the qualified maintenance programmers, and rules for when to call") indicates the use of an absolute measure of effectiveness. We have entered "SAVE 1/2 DAY" under PROBLEM RECOGNITION and PROBLEM ANALYSIS, and "SAVE 1 DAY" under TEST. The telephone roster can save time in each activity by giving the programmer quick feedback of unexpected behavior during operation.

Measures for the other techniques are expressed as percentages, indicating the contribution of a technique to an attribute. Some percentages are negative, indicating that the technique actually degrades the attribute; the fact that each technique helps some attributes and hinders others provides for trade-offs and compromises, and offers one of the main challenges of design. Since our assessment of the contribution of techniques to attributes is quite rough, the percentages are limited to 10% ("some contribution"), 25% ("important"), and 100% ("essential").

An illustration of a technique with both positive and negative impacts, and of the three percentage levels, is the technique M.INS ("Formal inspection of all proposed changes shall be carried out before approval"):

PROBLEM RECOGNITION: 10% Inspection will tend to maintain a level of system awareness among maintenance personnel, and therefore has some effect on speed of recognition.

ADMINISTRATIVE DELAY: -10% Management steps to ensure that inspection takes place will make some addition to administrative delay.

PROBLEM ANALYSIS: 25% The practice of inspections will make an important contribution to speed in problem analysis.

TEST: 100% Formal inspection is an essential component of an effective test strategy (Fagan, 1976).

Absolute measurements or percentages in a column can be roughly summed to give an indication of whether the techniques could possibly satisfy it. A column whose contributions sum to 100% or more is an attribute that can be satisfied by the set of techniques -- or even over-satisfied, with a margin of safety or an opportunity for reducing the resources put into one or other technique.

Not all cells need to be filled, but a blank row indicates a technique that has no application, and a blank column indicates an attribute that is not affected by any technique. In Table 4, the percentage sum for ADMINISTRATIVE DELAY is -10%, indicating that all the techniques selected so far have only worsened this element of maintainability. This illustrates several points:

* Design by Objectives reminds the infotect of objectives that have not yet been met.

* Technical solutions often fail if they are not accompanied by management solutions.

* Design by Objectives is not limited to technical solutions.

THE

ATTRIBUTE / FUNCTION / TECHNIQUE TABLE

It is now time to put functions (system capability objectives), attributes (system characteristic objectives), and techniques (methods) together into the Attribute / Function / Technique Table (Table 5).

The rows are the attributes from Tables 1 and 2. The columns are the system functions. The entry in a cell is a technique, indicating that this technique contributes to the attainment of the row attribute as it applies to the column function. The table is created from the Technique / Attribute Table of Table 4 by accumulating the positive techniques from each column and attributing them to each applicable system function.

This is the first table to feature the functions of the system -- its non-negotiable capabilities. The importance of the two-dimensional presentation of attributes and functions is to remind the infotect that attainment of an attribute depends on attaining it with respect to each function. The desired maximum on (say) problem recognition time (Attribute 1) must be attained with respect to hardware and software and peopleware and paperware. Blank or scantily filled areas are warnings that some objective of the system may not be sufficiently covered.

The aim is to fill all cells, or to understand why certain cells cannot be filled. A 0 entry is used to indicate that a certain attribute is not applicable to a certain function, but it should be used sparingly. In Table 5, for instance, there are no 0 entries; it is not far-fetched to argue that each of the stages of maintenance applies to each of the functions. When correcting a PEOPLEWARE problem, one still has to recognize the problem, handle administrative delay, collect tools and documents (job descriptions, for example), analyze the problem, correct it, and test the new procedure.

A blank cell is a warning signal that no technique has been included that attains the row attribute with respect to the column function. This may indicate an undeliverable objective. A blank row, such as ADMINISTRATIVE DELAY, indicates an attribute for which no techniques have been selected. A blank or scantily filled column indicates a function for which few techniques have been selected.

Table 5 makes it clear that the techniques of Table 3 are oriented toward software, especially the PROBLEM ANALYSIS and TEST attributes. The techniques of Table 3 aid the maintainability of hardware to the extent that reliable software aids the detection and repair of hardware errors, but the large gaps in the HARDWARE column alert the infotect to the need for further techniques for this function -- vendor maintenance contracts, for instance. A function that is even less well served is PAPERWARE, which highlights the fact that the techniques of Table 3 ignore the clerical function.

The idea of the Attribute / Function / Technique Table was derived from the Requirements / Properties matrix presented by Barry Boehm et al. in Characteristics of software quality (1978). The technique seems to have been used in cost / value analysis engineering technology even earlier.

The value of such tables is in controlling the use of resources and techniques to achieve specific objectives, such as maintainability. Thayer et al. reported in Software reliability - a study of large project reality (1978) that the use of such a table was a major corrective tool in countering the effects of wasted programming effort due to incomplete and incorrect design, which accounted for about 62% of the maintenance changes to operational systems. Thus the Attribute / Function / Technique Table can be viewed not merely as a means of building maintainability into a program or system, but also of reducing significantly the need to perform maintenance changes that are the result of poor design.

TABLE 5

ATTRIBUTE / FUNCTION / TECHNIQUE TABLE: MAINTAINABILITY

FUNCTIONS \\ ATTRIBUTES	HARDWARE	SOFTWARE	PEOPLE-WARE	PAPER-WARE
A1 PROBLEM RECOG-NITION	M.TEL M.DBA M.INS	M.TEL M.DBA M.INS	M.TEL M.MPG	
A2 ADMINIS-TRATIVE DELAY				
A3 TOOL,DOC COLLECT-ION	M.LIB	M.MPG M.DBA M.LIB	M.LIB	M.LIB
A4 PROBLEM ANALYSIS		M.TEL M.MPG,DBA M.LIB,TXT M.LST,INS	M.MPG	
A5 CHANGE SPECIFIC-ATION		M.MPG	M.MPG	
A6 ACTIVE CORREC-TION		M.MPG		
A7 TEST	M.TEL M.INS M.DBA	M.TEL,MPG M.DBA,TXT M.LST,INS	M.INS	

THE QUOTA CONTROL TABLE

Up to now we have been dealing with intentions. We documented the customer's objectives, we specified a system to perform the desired functions, and we chose techniques that, according to our experience or our Software Engineering Handbook, should achieve the desired level of the customer's attributes. Now it is time to estimate the success of our intentions. This is the function of the Quota Control Table (Table 6).

The Quota Control Table provides a tool for estimating the contribution of each technique to the planned level of each attribute and for estimating the side effects of techniques. The rows are the attributes from Tables 1 and 2. The columns are the techniques from Table 3. The cells show the percentage contribution to each attribute of each technique. The final column is a row total made by summing the percentages. A figure greater than or equal to 100% indicates an attribute attained, possibly with a margin of safety. A figure less than 100% is a warning signal, indicating an attribute not yet attained in the design.

The Quota Control Table deals with achievements, not intentions. Its aim is to show the actual contribution of the chosen techniques to the actual attributes within the actual design. It should be used throughout the development process to summarize the distance between the contribution of the techniques as presently specified and the planned level of the attributes.

Quota Control Tables help to keep all development participants interested and motivated in designing all critical qualities into the system from the very beginning of the project. This is always a cheaper and more reliable way of getting what the customer and the infotect have agreed on. If you simply stated goals on the System Attribute Specification Table at the start of the project, and then measured whether or not you got them at the end -- six months or five years later, for example -- then you would usually be disappointed. Several of your planned levels of critical attributes would not be reached. The cost of "patching up" a design after it has been implemented is quite high.

The alternative is to fill out Quota Control Tables at every stage of the development process, and use them as a continuous guide to the adequacy of the evolving system. The assessments guide the infotect in altering the mix of techniques in the evolving system, and the evolving design refines and corrects the assessments.

The infotect fills out the Quota Control Tables on the basis of experience, simulations, prototypes, partial systems delivered under an evolutionary delivery schedule, and even intuition. (A quantified assessment based on intuition is better than no assessment at all.) The basic unit is percentage (percentage of the attribute satisfied by the technique), but ranges (50%±20%), question marks, and comments may also be used to carry the message.

The Quota Control Table in Table 6 reflects the strengths and weaknesses detected in earlier analyses. The techniques selected so far favor the SOFTWARE function over any other. They also favor the attributes of PROBLEM RECOGNITION, TOOL AND DOCUMENTATION COLLECTION, and PROBLEM ANALYSIS. ADMINISTRATIVE DELAY, CHANGE SPECIFICATION, and ACTIVE CORRECTION have not been addressed at all.

CONCLUSIONS

The above example has only used a subset of the tools and techniques of Design by Objectives, but, hopefully, it has demonstrated that this methodology is effective in making concrete an objective such as "maintainability", and in carrying it through the complex design process to whatever level of detail is necessary. Figure 1 gives an outline of the whole process. A complete exposition will be found in the book Design by Objectives (Gilb, forthcoming).

TABLE 6

QUOTA CONTROL TABLE: MAINTAINABILITY

NOTE: All cells are the percentage of the attribute satisfied by the technique.

TECHNIQUES / ATTRIBUTES (PLANNED LEVEL)	M.TEL (TELEPH ROSTER)	M.MPG (PROGR EXAM)	M.DBA (DB AUDIT)	M.LIB (CENTR LIB)	M.TXT (PROG TEXT)	M.LST (PROG STRUC)	M.INS (INSPEC TION)	TOTAL
A1 PROBLEM RECOGNITION (60 MIN)	50%	10%	25%	–	–	–	10%	95%
A2 ADMINIS-TRATIVE DELAY (1 DAY)	–	–	–	–	–	–	–	NOT HANDLED
A3 TOOL, DOC COLLECTION (10 MIN)	–	10%	10%	100%	–	–	–	120%
A4 PROBLEM ANALYSIS (10 MIN)	25%	100%	10%	25%	25%	25%	25%	235% SOFTWR ONLY
A5 CHANGE SPECIFICATION (5 MIN?)	–	10%	–	–10%	–10%	–10%	–	NOT HANDLED
A6 ACTIVE CORRECTION (20 MIN)	–	10%	–	–10%	–10%	–10%	–	NOT HANDLED
A7 TEST (1 DAY)	50%	10%	25%	–10%	10%	25%	100%	210% SOFTWR ONLY

FIGURE 1

DESIGN BY OBJECTIVES: MAINTAINABILITY

OVERVIEW

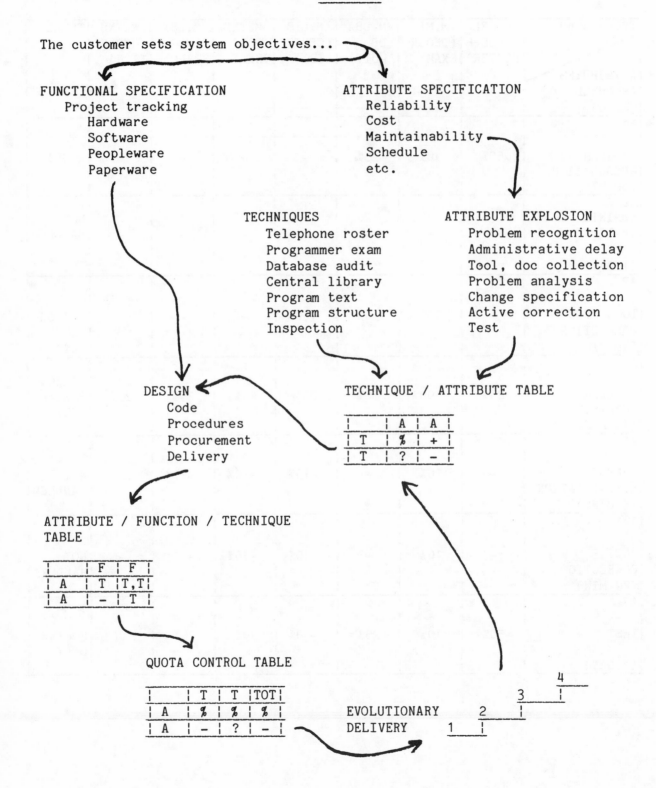

The customer sets system objectives...

FUNCTIONAL SPECIFICATION
    Project tracking
        Hardware
        Software
        Peopleware
        Paperware

ATTRIBUTE SPECIFICATION
    Reliability
    Cost
    Maintainability
    Schedule
    etc.

TECHNIQUES
    Telephone roster
    Programmer exam
    Database audit
    Central library
    Program text
    Program structure
    Inspection

ATTRIBUTE EXPLOSION
    Problem recognition
    Administrative delay
    Tool, doc collection
    Problem analysis
    Change specification
    Active correction
    Test

DESIGN
    Code
    Procedures
    Procurement
    Delivery

TECHNIQUE / ATTRIBUTE TABLE

	A	A
T	%	+
T	?	-

ATTRIBUTE / FUNCTION / TECHNIQUE
TABLE

	F	F
A	T	T,T
A	-	T

QUOTA CONTROL TABLE

	T	T	TOT
A	%	%	%
A	-	?	-

EVOLUTIONARY
DELIVERY

```
                         4
                    3    |
               2    |
          1    |
```

The Tables of Design by Objectives are like a chess-board. A few exceptional players can play chess blindfold, using just a list of the moves to visualize the game position. But the aim in systems design is not to show one's ability to operate blindfold -- for few of us can boast such ability -- but to give us every help in "winning" the "game" of systems design.

This game is far more complicated than chess, because:

* There are more squares on the board.

* There are more pieces.

* The rules are several orders of magnitude more complex.

* All parts of the game are clouded in fuzzy uncertainty.

In systems design we need all the help we can get -- and that is why we offer Design by Objectives.

ACKNOWLEDGEMENTS

The author thanks William L. Anderson, Ned Chapin, and Nicholas Zvegintzov for their contributions to re-shaping this paper. A version was delivered orally at the 1979 National Computer Conference, and again at a Professional Development Seminar in conjunction with the 1980 National Computer Conference. An expanded version will appear in the book Design by Objectives (Gilb, forthcoming).

REFERENCES

Boehm, B.W., Brown, J.R., Kaspar, H., Lipow, M., MacLeod, G.J. Characteristics of software quality. Amsterdam: North-Holland Publishing Co., 1978.

DeMarco, T. Structured analysis and system specification. New York, NY: Yourdon, Inc., 1978.

Fagan, M.E. Design and code inspections to reduce errors in program development. IBM Systems J., 15, 3 (1976), 182-211. IBM Reprint Order No. G321-5033.

Gilb, T. Software metrics. Cambridge, MA: Winthrop Publishers, Inc., 1977 (out of print). Lund, Sweden: Studentlitteratur AB, 1977 (in print, in English).

Gilb, T. Design by Objectives. Amsterdam: North-Holland Publishing Co., forthcoming.

Heninger, K.L. Specifying software requirements for complex systems: new techniques and their application. IEEE Trans. Software Engineering, SE-6, 1 (1980), 2-13.

Phister, M., Jr. Data processing technology and economics. Santa Monica, CA: Santa Monica Publishing Co., Inc., 1976. Maynard, MA: Digital Press.

Phister, M., Jr. Data processing technology and economics, 1975-78 supplement. Santa Monica, CA: Santa Monica Publishing Co., Inc., 1980.

Ross, D.T., Schoman, K.E., Jr. Structured analysis for requirements definition. IEEE Trans. Software Engineering, SE-3, 1 (1977), 6-15.

Thayer, T.A., Lipow, M., Nelson, E.C. Software reliability - a study of large project reality. New York, NY: Elsevier North-Holland Publishing Co., TRW Series on Software Technology, 2, 1978.

Introduction

Belady, L.A. "Evolved software for the 80's." *IEEE Computer,* 12, 2 (1979), 79-82.

Laszlo Belady describes himself as a man who has had at least four careers. He was trained in aeronautical engineering in his native Hungary and practiced it there and, after 1956, in France. During the 1960's, having moved to the United States, he investigated what he calls the "execution dynamics" of software (its behavior during execution), and was a leading theorist of virtual memory strategies ("A study of replacement algorithms for a virtual storage computer," *IBM Systems Journal,* 5, 2 (June 1966), 78-101). During the 1970's he investigated what he calls, by contrast, the "evolution dynamics" of software (its behavior during maintenance), becoming Senior Manager for Software Engineering at IBM's Thomas J. Watson Research Center. In the 1980's, he told us ruefully, he thinks of himself as a bureaucrat, spending his time in meetings, giving talks, and on the road. In 1980 he was appointed Editor of the *IEEE Transactions on Software Engineering,* and in 1981 became program manager for software technology at IBM Corporate Headquarters.

Belady, along with Lehman whose work is included in Part IV of this Tutorial, founded the serious study of software maintenance. Like penicillin, which first appeared as an unwanted mold on a biologist's culture, the study of maintenance came to its originators as a by-product of other work. In 1969, Lehman was writing an IBM internal Research Report titled *The programming process,* which discussed what came later to be known as the "Improved Programming Technologies." Lehman wanted to highlight the growth of the software problem, and hit on the idea of using publicly available statistics on the growth and change of the OS/360 operating system, then some four years old. The Improved Program-

ming Technologies passed into the bloodstream of software engineering, and the idea of measuring the growth characteristics of a software system became the foundation of Belady and Lehman's work on maintenance. This work, embodying the first version of their "Laws of program evolution dynamics," was published as "A model of large program development," in *IBM Systems Journal,* 15, 3 (1976), 225-252.

In the following paper, Belady envisions the evolution (another use of that versatile word) of a true engineering discipline in the software field. The software engineer, like the aeronautical engineer, should be able to create software solutions from a stock of tested components with known characteristics. This stock of components must be refined from the inventory of existing software, which forms a repository of ingenious solutions to systems and applications problems. The work of this refinement calls for a revival of the "experimental element" in software engineering — the painstaking analysis of working software to cut through its surface roughness and real world compromises to find the structures that make it work.

This emphasis on the challenge and opportunity represented by real world software makes this paper a suitable finale to Part III, which deals with software modification. It also shows that Belady is not just a pioneer but a continuing explorer in software maintenance.

It is hard for us to write impersonally about Belady. When we came as newcomers to the field of maintenance, he welcomed us with a warm generosity that went beyond the courtesies of scholarly interaction. In the memorable first sentence of the following paper, he describes himself as having been "a happy man" as a young aeronautical engineer. We wish him the same happiness as the dean of the maintenance field.

To reach a better balance between free innovation and disciplined construction, we must bring an experimental element to software engineering, creating a modifiable and configurable software inventory composed of reusable and verified program parts.

SPECIAL FEATURE

Evolved Software for the 80's

L. A. Belady
IBM Thomas J. Watson Research Center

Many years ago I was a happy man, a young aeronautical engineer helping to build airplanes. Although these machines were complex creations, my job appeared pleasantly simple. Having learned my trade reasonably well, I could safely apply novel ideas in my assigned range of responsibility, which was clearly localized, my place with respect to other engineers being well specified. Information about state-of-the-art solutions, as well as novel but tested ideas, was easily available.

I also knew how to sketch my ideas in a form that allowed colleagues to understand and criticize them. My manager, I recall, always helped me to keep innovation just at the right level: nothing esoteric, nothing obsolete. And what made me most comfortable was the carefully devised process my creations had to go through before they became tangible objects that other people could depend on. Well before delivery, the design would be looked at and, if acceptable, built, then experimented with both in isolation and in configuration with other parts. Parts often came back to me for modifications that were suggested by test or field experiments. Eventually, however, my designs became products and formed a basis, perhaps a standard, for future developments. My work integrated experience and innovation, and the reward was a great feeling of accomplishment.

Engineering vs. software engineering

The young engineer is no more. For the last two decades or so I have been in software: a different world. Yet by now I have become so used to it that I don't even mind being called a software engineer. This new profession involves developing and maintaining complex but intangible systems. However, serious problems retard progress and are likely to remain with us for the next decade. How would a young aeronautical engineer find this field today? How would he or she compare it to the "classical" profession? Let us assess the state of large software systems and the current knowhow of building and manipulating them as such an engineer might.

The most striking aspect of contemporary software development is the virtually unlimited freedom of action for everybody involved. Working with programs is fun. Once you learn how the computer responds to a set of coded instructions, you are allowed to join in and build ever larger and more complex systems for many applications: process control, banking, satellite tracking, management information—the list is endless.

It is, for example, entirely possible to design software components using textbook examples, friends' recommendations, or your own imagination, for that matter. You alone must decide, and chances are that no one will ever question your choice, as long as the resulting program more or less resembles the specification prose, and a few test samples will easily "verify" this. Your module becomes delightfully unique, since you did not have to search for existing solutions or standard componentry, which, give and take a few parameters, could be fit into place. No, it's easier to start fresh, from scratch. Sure, there are a few rules, such as structured programming, but as long as you adhere to them, the new module will be just fine.

Reprinted from *Computer*, Volume 12, Number 2, February 1979, pages 79-82. Copyright © 1979 by The Institute of Electrical and Electronics Engineers, Inc.

Joy and complexity

The entire team enjoys the same freedom. Everybody is an individual craftsman, constructing large or small components in a so-called hierarchical arrangement. The man on top is the architect who issues the original specifications to start the construction of the components and later, when they are declared complete, collects them into a system. The architect rarely bothers to examine the parts; they are at too low a level for him. Besides, he probably can't read the code anyway—the language he learned is not used anymore.

Existing programs—even old ones—contain an invaluable inventory of functional solutions based on years of experience.

Since there are no experiments during development, it is worth pointing out that there are no lengthy delays of waiting for experimental evidence. This safely accommodates an unconstrained flow of innovation, all the way to the end product. But what if there are no new ideas? Obviously one can always use the solutions that were used the last time. The point is to avoid the tedium of reading about other people's ideas in journals and assorted documents. The time thus freed can be used more creatively to keep increasing the gorgeous variety of components and the resulting complexity of the software system.

Of course, error reports are constantly coming in from the users. Since all that is wanted is the resumption of operation as soon as possible, a simple fix, fortunately, suffices—no need for cumbersome and time-wasting redesign activities, coupled with update of documentation and other bureaucratic procedures. To find the easiest patch that kicks off operation quickly is the real challenge.

Ahoy, the future!

The software scientist, too, is blessed with liberty. His pursuit of truth is independent of systems already in operation, so he may focus on the future. Since his results—algorithms, techniques, and the like—are never tested in the context of today's systems, the turnaround time of research is phenomenal. Once an idea is outlined, attention can immediately be turned to the next one, and the next, and the next.... It is no wonder that such an enormous wealth of ideas has already been collected! True, some critics complain that the ideas remain essentially untested, but what they don't realize is that actual systems are under the control of the equally independently minded developers who can afford to convert the software to a testbed; for the luxury of pure experimentation.

Growth is also unconstrained. For example, with operating systems, as the hardware people dream up new devices and gadgets, the production of corresponding software support is soon under way; an army of workers will crank out the few hundred thousand extra lines of code necessary to do the job. And the entire block of old code also remains; removing or reducing it is not a worthy effort.

Sometimes trouble develops. Adding new code is more difficult than anticipated. Managers puzzle about the slippage of schedules and complain about unpredictability. Some propose long-term solutions to make the software more extensible, only to find that there is no money for this. The accelerating stream of new functions must be accommodated first; this makes the required skills unavailable for redesign. Yet the majority of the software people are busy modifying and repairing existing programs. With a very large software system, many changes are performed concurrently on several components. Since freedom prevails again, modifications are performed independently; the interactions and dependencies among local changes will be discovered later in operation anyway. Something like a concurrent modification discipline based on solid research could be useful, but no one works on this problem. Rather, the concurrency of machine processes and their synchronization occupy the researchers' minds.

The future in fact

In this new world of software, where freedom and independence prevail, beginners are somewhat disadvantaged. They populate maintenance organizations. But this is actually not too bad. It frees the creativity of the more experienced and allows the young to learn the many beautiful solutions used in the software made by their elders, and to perpetuate this beauty. The best programmers are quickly moved from maintenance to design so as to keep the quality of maintenance at the right level. After all, only the operation of the machines depends on this quality.

So our friend from aeronautics concludes that there is too much freedom in softwareland. He believes that the 80's must find us busy searching for a *better balance between free innovation and disciplined evolution.* Briefly stated, the challenge of the 80's in engineering large-scale software systems will be this:

How do we evolve, out of the current inventory of large programs, an inventory of easily modifiable and reconfigurable software components?

What follows is a particular combination of proposals that, in my opinion, must be adopted.*

---

*See, for example, *On Classification of Application Independent Modules* by Edwards and Lamb, IBM Research Report RC 6717, September 1977.

Evolved software

A significant portion of our current large software investment will be with us for a long time. These systems, which span a broad spectrum of commercial and military applications, were built and refined over many years—a decade or more. Although they have been expanded, repaired, and patched over a long period, and perhaps in a haphazard fashion, they cannot and should not simply be declared obsolete or not worth studying.

First, consider operating systems. The investment in operator and user skills, in associated application programs, and in a variety of interfaces is so large, and the interfaces themselves so rich, that outright switchover to new systems, even though they are cleaner and more efficient, is not possible.

Secondly, view the old programs as manifestations of a large number of interconnected functions—procedures and their data structures. Then take just the specifications of these functions, forgetting for a moment the actual—perhaps outdated and inelegant—design and code that embody the functions. This collection of functions is an important asset. Even with blurred interfaces, it is the list of basic building blocks for our entire software repertoire, summarizing many years of experience—former guesses forged into proven necessities. This wealth of experience is too valuable to discard. Rather, it must be the basis of critical analysis, out of which the most likely and broadly usable components of future systems can be predicted.

Certainly, the review will be tedious and critical. For example, it is difficult to recognize hidden similarities and then decide which similar functional components should be made identical. Do we know, for instance, how many generic classes of algorithms exist in a commercial, general-purpose data-base management system or in an operating system? How many almost identical functions are repeated, many times, in a large software system because its developers did not make the code interchangeable? Even with given requirements, do we know the size in its "canonical" form of an operating system—measured, for instance, in number of statements? What is, at least roughly, the minimum size of a banking system with fixed requirements? Approximate answers to all these questions could be extracted from the billions of dollars worth of programs we already have at hand.

With careful analysis, we can identify software components that occur frequently within a given application area, or across applications. Even more importantly, programs embodying these components are the best candidates for further scrutiny; they will be the future parametric program components worth formal verification. Gradually, these program components must become the building blocks of all future software, replacing the ones that have been arbitrarily constructed earlier. The basic collection of functional components is unlikely to change rapidly, although it may change somewhat faster than machine instruction sets have over the past decade.

The new software engineers

The software engineer then will have to work with sealed components, practicing "programming in the large." His working knowledge must be strongly related to the particular application the program is constructed for, with a correspondingly decreased mastery of programming in the "small." For example, operating-system designers will be experts in computer systems behavior, while supermarket automation experts will construct the software for their specific application. However, both professional groups may pick from the same pool of software componentry, which will be designed and continuously refined by programming experts as we know them today.

With careful analysis, we can identify software components that can be widely reused.

The problems of retraining and educating for so many new trades will be enormous, since computer science and engineering education is currently geared only to programming in the small. This provides expertise to build the best possible software components to use in large numbers of instances, but only superficial knowledge of the particular field.

How large will these reusable software components be? What is the unit of a sharable, generic function? On one hand, we would like to see large components, such as an entire compiler. A system built of large pieces is obviously less complex, especially if the pieces are guaranteed to be correct to specification. But the larger the component, the less the probability of its being widely usable. It is either too closely shaped to a specific application or it is so general that waste due to unused capabilities becomes intolerable. On the other hand, tiny pieces do not help much, either: the lower bound is one instruction per component, and this is what we do today. The best choices for size must then emerge from experience and experimentation.

Future engineered systems

Equally experimental will be the ordinary, evolutionary development of future distributed systems. An abrupt replacement of current centralized installations by widely spread out but interconnected subsystems is highly unlikely. Instead, most existing functions must be gradually remapped onto the set of distributed hardware. Because of the great complexity, the tradeoffs of global economy cannot be predicted by speculation or calculation, nor even by simulation. This leads, again, to experimentation, where the best alternative allocation of function is found by the smooth relocation of functional software components along the network.

Increasing component efficiency. The same approach of constructing systems out of standard componentry will also permit easy reconfiguration to match particular requirements of individual installations within a single application area, or convenience in changing the system to follow the developing needs of a single installation. The best configuration can then be approached rapidly thanks to inherent flexibility, which today is a luxury. While the goal is to keep the fraction of shared components across installations high, a few parts could be customized, or even locally manufactured for a maximum match between requirements and system implementation.

Maintenance will also be facilitated, in two major categories. The first consists of addition, repair, update, and general modernization of components. Such changes may enhance function, respond to new equipment technology, install better compilers, or increase component efficiency. The other type of maintenance lies closer to the application discipline. Beyond the obvious need to repair discovered errors of programming in the large, modifications in this category will be induced by new customer requirements and by the desire to improve overall performance with the same components via better configuration.

Component alternatives. It can be expected that for every generic functional component there will be alternative implementations, offering a repertoire of choices for software designers. But on what basis will the designer choose? How can the designer identify the best alternative against a given environment? Again, the only sensible basis is experimentation. In the future, increasingly more empirical evidence must be collected about the system-level behavior of a great variety of generic components, just as there is a large body of knowledge available today about a wide selection of sorting algorithms. Organized information based on experiments—or analysis if it is sufficient—will then help make intelligent design choices.

By now it must be obvious that the revival of the experimental element in software engineering is envisioned here. A possible form of this could be a "component factory" where the last phase of the production process consists of full-scale testing and careful documentation of test results, which then accompany the delivered product to aid system design wherever the associated component is being used. And this completes the cycle: software becomes engineered by combining parts selected from among tested alternatives.

Conclusion: problems and benefits

And now the problems. The first is the great difficulty of finding the hidden commonality of functions across many applications. The only way to do this is by tediously studying complex and often structurally obsolete software—not considered a pleasant or even respectable activity today. The other great problem is the apparent lack of compact,

unambiguous, standard representation of the components and their associated relevant properties, including experimental results. Without something similar to blueprints representing tangible objects, the software design process will be difficult, the search for the proper component will be cumbersome, and the danger of falling back to the current mode of operation will be great. The missing methodology is not how to describe the way a component works—which is the role of programming languages—but what the component does in response to stimuli from its environment, the system. I think this is a particularly difficult area of research but one of tremendous potential payoff.

The final major difficulty is education. By now, we know how to train programmers or programming experts for all levels of sophistication, including computer scientists. The latter will develop the methods and tools for, and perhaps even construct, the high-quality and formally proven components for a wide spectrum of potential applications, richly documented as to proper use and behavioral characteristics. These components are mathematical objects. And with the added element of experimentation, computer science will be less dominated by strong opinion and more by organized observation.

But out of the beautiful objects—the correct components—useful software systems must be built to support a dazzling variety of applications. Where will the people come from to do this task? Since they must be more system than programming oriented, and backed up with expertise in a particular application area, we may have to rethink the relevant part of our higher educational system. It appears entirely possible that many university departments will have to offer education in software engineering as applied to individual specialties. The trouble is that even this must evolve through experimentation. ∎

Laszlo A. Belady has been a member of the research staff at IBM's Thomas J. Watson Research Center since 1961, with sabbaticals to the University of California, Berkeley, in 1971-72 and to Imperial College, London, in 1974. He has managed a group conducting research in methods of developing and maintaining large software. With M. M. Lehman, he is the codeveloper of program-evolution dynamics. In the sixties he worked and published in the areas of memory management, program behavior, and computer graphics, and was a member of the team conceiving, designing and building the M44/44X, IBM's first experimental virtual system. He has also been an aerodynamicist and design engineer in France, Germany, and Hungary.

Belady graduated in aeronautical engineering at the Technical University of Budapest. He is a member of the ACM, IEEE, and the International Design Group. He was program chairman of the Third International Conference on Software Engineering in Atlanta.

Part IV: The evolution of software

Parts II and III of this Tutorial dealt with maintenance in the short term—how to understand a system in the short term and how to change a system in the short term. Often maintainers feel condemned to an eternity of short terms. There is, however, a longer term view of maintenance, and this is where we look in the second half of this Tutorial.

The most popular model of the growth, renewal, and survival of a software system in the maintenance phase is that of evolution. The words "evolution" and "evolve" occur repeatedly in the literature to describe the process whereby a software system changes. The meanings of "evolution," according to Funk & Wagnalls *Standard Dictionary* (New American Library, 1980), are

1. The process of unfolding, growing, or developing, usu. by slow stages. 2. *Biol. a* The theory that all forms of life originated by descent from earlier forms. *b* The series of changes, as by natural selection, mutation, etc., through which a given type of organism has acquired its present characteristics.

Many characteristics of software change fit this definition. Definition 1 covers the process. Software systems unfold, grow, and develop. They change "usually by slow stages," particularly as seen by the impatient user. Definition 2b, taken from biology, expresses the mechanism of the process—the series of changes. The "etc." in this definition allows for the fact that software systems change, not only through natural selection and mutations, but also through the active intervention of maintainers.

The connotations, or emotional overtones, of the term "evolution" also make the term attractive as a description of software change. The "upward" tone of the word, as in the evolution from single-celled creatures to "higher" mammals, contrasts with the static or defensive tone of "maintenance;" the same upward tone is heard in "adaptive" and "perfective"—two of the three terms used by Swanson to categorize maintenance ("The dimensions of maintenance," IEEE Computer Society, *2nd International Conference on Software Engineering*, 1976, 492-497). On the other hand the gradualness of evolution is also attractive; the cautious manager can be lured by the promise of "evolutionary" rather than "revolutionary" change.

The verb "evolve" has, like "change" and "develop," both a passive and an active form. The system evolves, but the maintainer also evolves the system. In the latter sense, the process of change is once more made active, as the manager guides the system through a series of changes. We have arranged the papers in this Part in a rough continuum from the passive or descriptive treatment of system evolution to the active or prescriptive so that the later papers form a bridge to the management questions treated in Part VI.

The first two papers in this Part are by pioneers in the study of system evolution. Independently, Weinberg and Lehman initiated, respectively, the theoretical and the practical study of software evolution.

In the first paper, written in the early 1960's, Weinberg shows that computer systems are subject to the laws of natural selection, the term used by Charles Darwin to describe the process of biological evolution. In fact Weinberg shows the interesting result that the hardware, the software, and the users of a computer system can each be regarded as a population that adapts to the other two: hardware adapts to the software and users, software adapts to the hardware and users, and users adapt to the hardware and software. As Weinberg points out, any element of the system can find itself remarkably ill-adapted when transferred to another environment.

The second paper is a major statement of the methods, laws, and implications of the evolutionary change of software systems as seen in 1980, by Lehman, who first documented such evolutionary change in 1969. Besides analyzing evolutionary change, Lehman describes how it can be measured and used as a guideline for the prudent manager.

This activist approach is made more specific in the next three papers. Van Horn redefines system development in evolutionary terms and presents the "system evolver" as a skilled professional who determines whether a system improves or decays. Miller succinctly presents the retrofit activity that the system evolver must undertake if the system is not to retrogress. Finally, Warnier explains with case studies how his methodology, Logical Construction of Systems, is used continuously throughout the life of a system to guide its evolution.

In this introduction we have indicated why the term "evolution" seems to fit the change process of software systems. The following papers give persuasive examples. Our aim is not to prove to the reader that software systems follow the pattern of biological evolution. No doubt, software evolution has patterns of its own, many of which are little understood. Our aim is to introduce you to the challenge of seeking these patterns. Only by understanding them can you guide software evolution in productive pathways.

EHO201-4/83/0000/0187$01.00 © 1983 IEEE

Introduction

Weinberg, G.M. "Natural selection as applied to computers and programs." *General Systems*, 15 (1970), 145-150.

Gerald M. Weinberg, author of the following paper as well as another paper in Part V, is the Tom Paine of the software engineering revolution. Like the irrepressible author of *Common sense* and *The rights of man*, Weinberg nudges his readers awake just when they have found a comfortable preconception on which to rest.

Large, energetic, redbearded, and sage-like, he operates from the central but not well-traveled plains of Lincoln, Nebraska. In harmony with his frontier location, he restlessly pioneers the unsettled areas of computing which intimidate less rugged thinkers. His 1971 book *The psychology of computer programming* (Van Nostrand Reinhold Company) upset its early readers (who regarded themselves as program writers) by starting out with a chapter on "Reading programs;" his book also upset the then current ideas of computer science by treating programming as a human rather than as a formal or an engineering activity. His 1977 book with Tom Gilb, *Humanized input—techniques for reliable keyed input* (Winthrop Publishers, Inc.), dealt with data entry as a crucial human-machine interface when other writers regarded it as a trivial chore. His Technical Leadership Workshops played out all the politics and intricacies of project management in the arena of a child's construction set.

He is also a key member of a loose confederacy of individualistic consultants (including, in this Tutorial, the editors ourselves, Gilb, Hetzel, Higgins, Miller, and Overton) who have given maintenance studies much of their current form. In 1979, having unsuccessfully recommended Parikh's book *Techniques of program and system maintenance* to major publishers, he had the company that he founded, Ethnotech, Inc., publish the first edition, in March 1980.

In the following paper, originally presented at a Columbia University faculty seminar in 1965, Weinberg explains how Darwin's theories of Natural Selection apply to computer systems and their users. The paper is based on Weinberg's experience in the early 1960's as head of the operating system design group for the Project Mercury space tracking system. He worried about the reliability of the system, since human lives depended on the result. He observed that as the system became bigger, it resembled more and more a natural system and less an artificial one.

He also recognized the maintenance problems of software, which at that time were treated as an incidental nuisance. The philosophy for software was the same as that for hardware: "Once it was installed, it was done!" Software was minimal at that time, COBOL was yet to come, and most data processors did not want to ponder the problems of the software they were creating. Weinberg recalls raising the question of software maintenance at an IBM internal conference in Bald Peak, New Hampshire, in 1961 and being shouted down. (The conference was, however, a turning point, for it marked the emergence of software as a major concern.)

When the System/360 was being introduced, Weinberg attempted again to raise the question of maintainability, but he failed. He feels that hardware vendors were afraid that people would not buy computers if they were reminded about the problems of software maintenance. He wrote the following paper out of his frustration at that time. It did not have the influence it should have had, perhaps because Weinberg published it in the journal *General Systems* as a contribution to the understanding of systems rather than in a journal read by computer people. Nevertheless, we feel that it deserves to become a classic in the software maintenance field, and we hope that this reprinting will help to make it so.

Weinberg worked at IBM from 1956 to 1969. Others in IBM went on to recognize the importance of software and of maintenance, as will be recounted in the introduction to the paper that follows this one.

NATURAL SELECTION AS APPLIED TO COMPUTERS AND PROGRAMS[*]

Gerald Weinberg

INTRODUCTION

From time to time, a programmer decides to rerun an old job and finds it will no longer run. Computing centers sometimes discover that the older its computer gets, the more difficult it is to get new jobs to run properly. One person tries to run another's programs and finds that they just do not work in a different installation. All of these well-known difficulties, and many lesser known ones, spring from a single source—Natural Selection taking its unswerving and irresistible course, just as it does in the kingdom of living things. In this paper, I propose to show how Natural Selection produces these undesirable effects and to suggest what can be done to diminish some of them.

1. Conditions for Natural Selection

In 1859 Charles Darwin started a scientific earthquake whose aftertremors are still being felt today. In On the Origin of Species, he set forth the conditions under which living systems undergo changes which adapt them to an extraordinary diversity of environments. To quote his own words,[1]

> Owing to this struggle for life, any variation, however slight and from whatever cause preceeding, if it be in any degree profitable to an individual of any species, in its infinitely complex relations to other organic beings and to external nature, will tend to the preservation of that individual, and will generally be inherited by its offspring. The offspring, also, will thus have a better chance of surviving, for, of the many individuals of any species which are periodically born, but a small number can survive. I have called this principle, by which each slight variation, if useful, is preserved, by the term of Natural Selection, in order to mark its relation to man's power of selection (p. 61; emphasis added).

In the tumultuous development of Darwin's ideas in the following century, Natural Selection has been revealed as a phenomena not confined to "living" systems, but explainable in purely abstract terms. All that is necessary is that a population exists under the following three conditions:

(1) Its individuals are capable of making reasonably exact copies of themselves.

(2) A certain amount of inexactitude is present in the copying process.

(3) An environment exists which selectively favors certain variations.

Requirement (1) is called "reproduction"; (2) is called "variation"; (3), "selection." All three must be present for Natural Selection to take place; and when all three are present, Natural Selection must take place. The population must increase in "fitness"—and at a rate which can be determined mathematically if the parameters are known. That variation is a "chance" process has nothing to do with the inevitability of Natural Selection. As R. A. Fisher[2] so ably put it:

> The income derived from a Casino by its proprietor may, in one sense, be said to depend upon a succession of favorable chances, although the phrase contains a suggestion of improbability more appropriate to the hopes of the patrons of his establishment. It is easy without any profound logical analysis to perceive the difference between a succession of favorable deviations from the laws of chance, and on the other hand, the continuous and cumulative action of these laws. It is on the latter that the principle of Natural Selection relies (p. 40).

We must note, however, that increase of fitness of a population is not always a "good" thing for Man. The rat population is constantly increasing its fitness with respect to a largely human environment, and the progressive adaptation of certain bacteria to penicillin and other drugs is an unending source of potential disaster to Man. Thus, although Man participates in Natural Selection of rats and bacteria, he does not, in a certain sense, "direct" the process. In order to distinguish this process from the process directed by Man for his own benefit (Selective Breeding or Artificial Selection), Darwin coined the term "Natural" Selection. About the relative power of the two methods, Darwin went on to say:

> But Natural Selection, as we shall hereafter see, is a power incessantly ready for action, and is as immeasurably superior to man's feeble efforts, as the works of Nature are to those of Art (Darwin, p. 61).

We can abstract from the literature on Natural Selection two laws which we can use in their qualitative form to predict certain consequences of the ways we use our computers. The first of

[*]This article was submitted for publication in 1967, was lost, and rediscovered two years later. The author has stated that he was able to resist the temptation to modify what he said a few years ago.—The Editors.
1. Charles Darwin, On the Origin of the Species. Cambridge, Mass.: Harvard Univ. Press, 1964, facimilie of the 1st ed.
2. Ronald A. Fisher, The Genetical Theory of Natural Selection. New York: Dover, 1958, 2nd. rev. ed.

these laws is the existence theorem of Natural Selection:

> Given the conditions of Natural Selection, the fitness of the population will increase with time.

The second law comes under various names, but we shall refer to it as the Law of Evolutionary Potential. Because a population must show variation in order to undergo Natural Selection while at the same time it must reduce variation in order to be well adapted to particular environment, the second law results:

> The more adapted a population becomes to a particular environment, the less adaptable it is when faced with other environments.

2. The Computer as the Adaptive Population

For our first case, the population undergoing Natural Selection will be the population of components in a single computer. "Components" can be taken to mean the lowest level units which are subject to replacement. In some cases, these might be individual relays, vacuum tubes, resistors, capacitors, or transistors; while in other cases they may be coordinated sets of such parts, as are found in circuit cards and integrated circuits generally.

The first difficulty we face in applying the theory of Natural Selection to this "population" is that it does not "reproduce" in the ordinary biological sense of that word. We overcome this difficulty in the following way.

1. We pick an arbitrary time interval, T, which will be thought of as the generation time of the population.

2. At the end of each interval, T, each element of the population is imagined to "reproduce." If T is short, virtually all of the "offspring" will be identical with their "parents"—for, indeed, they will be the same component.

3. The other way, in which an offspring may differ from its parent, is by "spontaneous" change in the performance of a component. This change may be entirely undetectable from outside the computer, but we know that such changes are always taking place.

4. Selection takes place because not all changes in the components (point 3) are equally detectable by the engineers who are trying to "maintain" the machine. When a component passes into a state ("produces an offspring") which is both detectable and undesirable, it is replaced ("dies"). Thus, the engineers and their diagnostic programs provide a selective environment which is constantly at work to remove certain types of individuals from the population. The environment is, indeed, selective, because all changes in states of components are not equally detectable by the diagnostic procedures of the engineers.

Viewed in this way, the evolution of the population of components in a computer is truly governed by Natural Selection—"Natural" because the engineer is not trying to favor the errors his diagnostic programs do not detect any more than the doctors are trying to favor certain bacterial varieties over others through the use of penicillin.

Once modelled in this way, the qualititive behavior of the system is entirely predictable by our first law:

> "Fitness of the population will increase with time."

In this case, however, fitness of the population is measured by the ability to escape the probings of the diagnostic procedures. From one point of view, this result says that the computer will remain fit—insofar as fitness of the whole is related to the fitness of the parts—to perform the diagnostic programs correctly. Our second law of Natural Selection, however, says that the computer will become increasingly adapted to just that environment, through the accumulation of undiscovered states which will not affect the current set of programs but which might affect some other set.

Some specific instances will be useful here. The first case of this type with which I ever became involved is typical of many situations reported to me by my students. A certain petroleum company had been using a computer for approximately four years on one rather complex application—oil royalty accounting. At that time, a group of chemical engineers in their laboratory became interested in using the computer for matrix calculations. After studying the manuals, they wrote their programs, punched their cards, and wired their control panels (as was necessary on this machine). Nobody was too surprised when their programs did not work immediately, for even in those days it was known that programs could have bugs. Eventually, however, the engineers were able to demonstrate that the reason their programs were not working was that certain relays in the computer were not performing according to the specifications in the manual. They were proved correct when, after the customer engineers spent two days bringing the machine up to specifications, their programs ran correctly.

Another example of this type of trouble was the case of an installation (A) which was endeavoring to use a system supplied by another installation (B). As commonly happens in such cases, the new system would not run successfully in the new installation (A). In most cases like this, a modest amount of effort is made to find the trouble, after which the whole project is dropped with some mumbling about "bugs in the program." In this case, however, one programmer was determined to find out explicitly where the trouble was, and by much diligent effort eventually discovered a number of machine errors which had accumulated in the computer over the years.

It may help clarify matters if two of these errors are examined in detail. The first involved the magnetic tape error routines At installation B, the common procedure in the case of tape reading errors was to make 20 retrials, while in installation A only 3 retrials were ordinarily made. Over the years, the tape units in A had not been subject to as stringent a diagnostic environment as had B's. Consequently they behaved in unpredictable ways when B's system attempted to backspace and reread them 20 times instead of the accustomed 3. A more careful adjustment of the tape units might have solved this problem, though it was actually done by modifying B's error routines.

Errors in tape units, like errors in relays, are essentially "mechanical" errors. It might be tempting to imagine that the electronic components of computers are not subject to Natural Selection in the same way, because they are intrinsically more reliable. Unfortunately, Natural Selection is a universal law, and applies whenever the three conditions are met. To be sure, the rate of Natural Selection may be altered—as in this case when the rate of variation is reduced—but the process inevitably takes place. Indeed, even though the variation in individual components may be less with electronic components, the situation in general could well be worse since there are many more components. This increase in the number of components not only increases the total amount of variation, but it increases the number of components which are not effectively tested by the diagnostic programs.

The second error found by this enterprising programmer will illustrate that electronic components are equally subject to Natural Selection. In this case, the error involved the failure of the circuit driving one bit of all the words in a particular portion of memory. In all of the programs of Installation A—including the diagnostic programs—this segment of memory was never occupied by anything for which this failure made a noticeable difference. In most instructions, this bit was always zero anyway, and, in fixed point numbers, it was a high order non-significant zero. The new system, however, happened to have one number for which this bit could be significant and which lay in the erroneous segment of memory. Consequently, whenever that bit of the critical number was supposed to be a one—which was fairly rare—an error resulted.

We are usually not as aware of Natural Selection in computers as we might be, for the troubles it gets us into are often so difficult that we never trace them down. In this last case, for instance, installation A had been experiencing, as most installations do, unexplained difficulties when modifying certain large programs. We can see

that an error such as the one bit memory failure could cause inexplicable problems if an instruction in a completely different section of memory were added or deleted, thereby bringing a critical instruction or number into the damaged region. In all likelihood, such an error would not be found directly, but rather eliminated by an equally accidental compensating modification in the course of trying to find it. Such an error remains in the machine but not in the programs.

Through the lifetime of a particular computer, such errors continue to accumulate. As long as no new programs are tried, things may function well. Eventually, however, even slight modifications to existing programs become increasingly difficult to make. Furthermore, newly introduced errors, because there are now so many residual errors to combine with, become increasingly difficult for the engineers to find. Finally, the costs and irritations of using the machine grow to the point where it is simpler to replace with a fresh, unadapted machine—thereby pushing the problems of Natural Selection a few more years into the future.

3. The Program as the Adaptive Population and the Computer as Environment

Whenever two different populations are in interaction so that each forms a part of the environment of the other, they participate in a form of mutual Natural Selection. Bats, for example, develop their hearing best at the frequencies most commonly emitted by the species of moths on which they feed; while the moths develop receptors which are sensitive to the echolocation frequencies of the bats which feed upon them. Nor is it necessary for the relationship to be one of predator and prey; symbiotic and parasitic relationship show precisely the same type of mutual adaptation. Formally, it is easy to see that this must be so, for in such cases, it is entirely a matter of arbitrary choice as to which population is system and which is environment.

With computers, it is probably more conventional to think of the machine as the environment in which the program is run, rather than considering the programs as the environment in which the machine evolves, as we did in the last section. Considering the machine as the environment of the programs, in the conventional way, we get some additional insights.

In this case, we may consider each program as a population of instructions—or of microinstructions.

Here, reproduction is taken care of by the successive versions of the programs, and variation is introduced either by intentional or unintentional program modifications. As we have just seen, the computer itself provides as environment in which the programs are developed and which tends to select against program variants which encounter some of the more subtle machine errors present. If the program does not work, we make some changes. If the trouble then goes away, we may not question further; thus, the program gets even better adapted to the machine on which it is run.

It might seem that no harm can come from this type of Natural Selection because the programs will always be able to run on a machine which does not have an accumulation of errors. An interesting contradiction to this argument is provided by our earlier example of the petroleum company. After the computer was brought up to specifications, the matrix calculations worked perfectly, but the oil royalty programs no longer worked at all! Furthermore, all the king's programmers and all the king's engineers never did succeed in getting that Humpty Dumpty set of programs working again! The eventual result was the replacement of the machine by a new model.

Such extreme cases are not as rare as one might imagine. The most typical situation, reported by many of my students, occurs when some new piece of peripheral equipment is installed on an existing computer. The ensuing difficulties are inevitably attributed to the new equipment, but in those cases where the actual cause is tracked down, it is equally likely to be some error residing in the machine which previous programs had avoided.

4. The Program as the Adaptive Population and the Data as Environment

Programs adapt not only to the computers on which they are run, but to the data which is given to them. I do not mean, of course, the Artificial Selection caused when modifications are made to take care of new data cases which arise, but the Natural Selection which takes place because of the data cases which do not arise.

Although program-to-data adaptation takes place in ordinary data processing programs, the most interesting—and most troublesome—cases occur in programs which use other programs as data. Such programs—compilers, for instance—ordinarily encounter a data environment which is potentially several orders of magnitude more complex than that of ordinary programs. Thus, there are many more unexplored data cases—cases which have never been tried by the program, and many more complex cases—cases which are circumvented rather than analyzed and eliminated.

Let us look at some examples. All programmers have had the experience of trying to run a program that once ran and now does not because of a new bug in the operating system. I recall one occasion in which the interval was six months, and where an error had been introduced into one of the three binary card loading routines available in the system. By the time I encountered the trouble, nobody in the installation could recall that this change had been made. Furthermore, when I had narrowed down the trouble to this particular routine, I was repeatedly advised not to try to find anything wrong with the routine but rather to switch to one of the other two routines. Unfortunately (or fortunately) I could not use the other routines because my data cards were not in acceptable formats; thus, I had to investigate the loading routine itself.

What I found was quite simple. Since the three routines shared some common parts, certain switches were set upon entry to discriminate among them. For the option I was using, one of the switches was never set, and the program thus made a wild transfer of control whenever that entry was used. The existence of such a bug in the system could only mean one of two things: either nobody else had used this routine in six months (this installation claimed to have 3000 users) or those who had used it had been successfully steered away from it by helpful advice.

How many other such bugs were accumulating in this system I have no way to estimate. Programmers who have worked with large systems, however, will recognize the experience of tracing through the wild execution path of one bug and finding one or more other bugs that had never been made manifest before. This kind of experience tends to verify the force of the Natural Selection processes on programs, and long ago led me to formulate the law governing the number of errors, n, remaining in a large program at time t:

$$\text{"For all } t, n = 1\text{"}$$

or, informally, n equals "one more."

Compilers, of course, are particularly susceptible to the accumulation of special cases which they cannot handle correctly. I especially recall one assembly language system we were using for writing a large real-time system. Every week we would collect a list of the things that did not seem to be assembling properly and send it to the maintenance crew. Every week we would get back a reply which said in effect that nobody else seemed to be having this particular trouble so it was not worth investigating. They were always helpful, however, in suggesting ways of avoiding difficulty—generally by not using the available language in its full power. Eventually, the accumulation of such cases to be avoided became unbearable, and we undertook the maintenance of the system ourselves. The straw that broke our backs, I recall, was a modification which unwittingly placed a limit on the number of characters of comments at 6×2^{15}. Since we had already far surpassed that number, our system would no longer compile, though "nobody else seemed to be having that trouble." We quickly learned that by keeping the size of the system down we could avoid trouble, but it took two months to discover the source of difficulty so that we could really proceed with our work. If we had not persevered, it might have been years before somebody else encountered the trouble; and at that time they would no longer have had the slightest clue about where to look.

5. Speciation

Although Darwin's great work was entitled On the Origin of Species, Mayr[3] has pointed out that

> It is a familiar and often-told story how Darwin succeeded in convincing the world of the occurrence of evolution and how—in natural selection—he found the mechanism that is responsible for evolutionary change and development. It is not nearly so widely recognized that Darwin failed to solve the problem indicated by the title of his work (p. 12).

This is not the place to present the modern view of the origin of species, but it is interesting to us to note that the weight of evidence now points to the splitting of one species into two or more non-breeding parts (usually by geographic accident) as the inital event in speciation. The parts then proceed to evolve in their own (somewhat different) environments until they are sufficiently differentiated that they will no longer interbreed even if they are brought together again.

Since we have no process analogous to sexual reproduction in our evolutionary models of computers and their programs, we cannot extend the modern species concept directly. We may, however, utilize the idea of isolating mechanisms, leading to progressively more differentiated populations. Thus, we may predict that different versions of the same system—a FORTRAN operating system, for instance—used in different installations not exchanging programs with one another will become more and more widely separated as time passes. The separation will be both explicit (through the addition of new features and the deletion of old) and implicit (through the evolutionary mechanisms we have discussed). Thus, the chances that one system will run on the other's computer, or that both systems will compile the same program to do the same things, diminish with time. Rather than moving toward standardization, then, we are moving toward the state where every computer installation will be an isolated species—unless, that is, some intelligent efforts are expended.

6. Retarding the Rate of Natural Selection

The foregoing arguments and examples have shown how the force of Natural Selection can work against the successful operation of a computer installation. (We do not concern ourselves with advantageous applications.) We cannot eliminate Natural Selection entirely in any of these cases, because we cannot eliminate the necessary conditions which inevitably bring it about. We can, however, do a number of things to slow the rate at which Natural Selection destroys the usefulness of a computer or system of program.

Some of the things we can do are quite obvious. In the case of machine errors, we can reduce the rate of variation by reducing the failure or degradation rate of the components. We can only go so far in this, however, for, as we have seen, this variation is constantly being reintroduced by increasing the number of components in our machines. Furthermore, with more reliable components we get a change in the "environment," for the maintenance engineers have more difficulty getting experience in finding particular bugs, and diagnostic programs have to be much more complicated just to keep up. Consequently, it becomes more and more tempting to modify the programs so that they will avoid the bugs rather than eliminate them. This amounts to buying present convenience for future disaster—a sort of anti-insurance policy.

Another policy which can be adopted to retard the rate of undesired Natural Selection is to refer to external standards. For instance, rather than using tapes written in the installation to test the tape reading mechanism, tapes from a standard outside source should be used. If this is not done, the installation is in danger of having its tape readers adapt to its tape writers—drifting further and further away from compatibility with any other installation.

The external standards, of course, are not limited to mechanical ones. For compilers, for instance, there should be a large set of standard programs which they must compile and execute to produce standard results. The mere existence of such standard programs is not enough, however, for as long as they are not the installation's own programs, errors they reveal are not likely to be treated with the proper respect. Getting the day's work done always takes precedence over keeping the "equipment" in good working order. Only by determined inculcation of certain values can programmers come to the state where they view errors in test programs with the same panic they now use for errors which halt daily production.

Another way in which the progress of Natural Selection may be retarded is by making the diagnostic programming a continuing process, not merely a one-shot job to be done before a machine is first delivered. A continuing stream of new diagnostics will have the effect of constantly shifting the environment in which the components have been evolving, ensuring on a dynamic basis that each machine remains rather close to the "standard" machine in the diagnostic programming shop. Again, however, the maintenance engineers

3. Ernst Mayr, Animal Species and Evolution. Cambridge, Mass.: Harvard Univ. Press, 1963.

are likely to revert to the old diagnostics if the new ones cannot be made to run without undue difficulty.

The avoidance of diagnostics may be prevented, in some situations, by pushing the diagnostic programming to a microprogrammed level, which cannot be reached by the ordinary problem programs at an installation. In this way, error states of the system with respect to the diagnostic programs are automatically more numerous than error states with respect to the problem programs. Thus many errors may be detected before they reach the problem program level. Such errors may be removed before they become part of the environment to which the problem programs adapt. For instance, if the storage devices of the machine have built-in error-correcting codes, the engineers become aware of component failures before they can affect the programs of the installation. Under such a system, an undetected bit failure in some small section of memory could never be retained.

One modern trend in computer use should have a beneficial effect on reducing the rate of accumulation of deleterious states in both software and hardware, namely, the trend to multiprogramming and multiprocessing. For instance, in a multiprogramming environment using dynamic relocation, a problem program would not always occupy the same locations in memory. Thus a portion of memory would not be likely to become partly inoperative for a long time without detection by some program or other. The same argument would apply to the use of peripheral components, which would be dynamically assigned by the supervisory program and thus subject to a wider variety of environments in a given period of time.

These observations lead us to one final suggestion for slowing down the rate of Natural Selection. This suggestion has a paradoxical aspect which is familiar enough to biologists but which might give computer specialists a hard time. Natural Selection causes most difficulty in computer installations because the computer and its programs become adapted to a narrow environment. Thus, when some new thing is finally introduced, the installation is unlikely to be adequately prepared. Indeed, it has most likely been accumulating debilities which will suddenly all become manifest at once—perhaps to the destruction of the installation. The lesson here is the lesson of the Law of Evolutionary Potential.

But the Law of Evolutionary Potential gives us another way of delaying the very death it predicts. By keeping up the variation in the system's environment, we make it less likely that it will get locked onto too narrow an environment. This observation leads us to expect that in those installations supporting the most diverse uses of the computer (not just those with the most users, who may all be doing the same type of thing) the build-up of Natural Selection difficulties will be less severe than in those which support only a few relatively stable applications. Furthermore, it even suggests that those frolicksome programmers who sneak in and try insane things with the computer at night are really doing the installation a great service. Perhaps they should be encouraged—if encouragement will not discourage them. Perhaps with computers—as with people—the way to stay young is through play.

Introduction

Lehman, M.M. "Programs, life cycles, and laws of software evolution." *Proc. IEEE*, 68, 9 (1980), 1060-1076.

Meir M. Lehman, the author of the following paper, has been the Professor of Computing Science since 1972 and Head of the Department of Computing at the Imperial College of Science and Technology in London since 1979. Lehman was educated in England and completed his Ph.D. in mathematics at Imperial College. From 1964 to 1972 he worked for IBM's Thomas J. Watson Research Laboratory in Yorktown Heights, NY.

The introduction to the preceding paper recounted Weinberg's frustrating battle with the problems of software and software maintenance through the early days of IBM's System/360. Lehman's concern with system evolution dovetails neatly, but quite independently, with Weinberg's. In the late 1960's, after the release of the System/360 architecture, IBM was privately worried about the problems of software. In 1969 Lehman wrote a paper for IBM, "The programming process," on potential improvements in the programming process. Although this paper was confidential for many years, it is now available as RC 2722 (#12799).

Lehman saw the problems of software as strongly related to, if not the consequence of, the problems of growth:

> Any view of the IBM or of the U.S. programming scene today leaves an overwhelming impression of growth. Thus, for example, in the last decade SDD annual expenditure for programming development has increased more than an order of magnitude.

To make the concept of growth concrete, Lehman abstracted publicly available statistics on the growth of an actual software system—namely, the OS/360 operating system:

> OS/360 represents an example of increasing size and complexity... Release 1 of March 1966, consisted of 14 components, divided into 1152 modules and 400,359 source statements. Release 16 of September 1968 consisted of 40 components, 3819 modules and some 1,740,364 source statements. Notice that a less than three-fold growth in the number of modules [sic], has required a more than four-fold growth in the number of source statements... The clearest indicator of the rapid growth in the complexity of OS/360, however, is the number of modules that have required some change between successive releases.

This observation, which was originally intended as no more than an example, became the nucleus of the study that Lehman and his colleague Belady (represented in Part III of this Tutorial) soon termed "evolution dynamics." The study was fueled by the observation that, though the costs and other associated statistics of a system under development must be predicted by baroque and unreliable formulae, the corresponding statistics for a system under maintenance are remarkably regular. These regularities are codified in five "Laws of Program Evolution."

The following paper is a succinct but comprehensive review of the state of the art in software engineering, with particular reference to the evolutionary nature of programs. It originally appeared in the *Proceedings of the IEEE* as part of a special issue to bring software engineering to the attention of electrical and electronics engineers. The IEEE, as readers of this Tutorial presumably know, is The Institute of Electrical and Electronics Engineers, Inc., whose 250,000 members are by no means all interested in computers, nor do all of them regard software as a branch of engineering. In 1980 the editor of the *Proceedings of the IEEE*, which is sent to all members, took the initiative of sponsoring a whole issue devoted to "Software Engineering" and asked Belady, Lehman's old friend and collaborator, to edit it. Belady in turn commissioned this paper.

This is a paper full of content, and the reader may find it helpful (as we did) to approach it in outline form:

I. Background: Lehman discusses the cost of software, the nature of programming, and the problem of program maintenance.

II. Programs as Models: Lehman classifies programs into S-programs (those that must satisfy formal specifications), P-programs (those that must satisfy real world needs), and E-programs (programs so pervasive that they modify the human environment in which they operate). P-programs and E-programs together form the class of applications programs in which the problems of validation and modification are most acute.

III. The Life Cycle: The phases through which a system passes in its development and operation must be closely managed because the success of each phase depends closely on the success of the others.

IV. Laws of Program Evolution: Lehman outlines the observations and laws of evolution dynamics.

V. Applied Dynamics: Lehman applies the laws to a real life case: choosing the date and content of the next releases of a major operating system.

VI. Conclusion: "This paper rationalizes the widely held view ... that there is an urgent need for a discipline of software engineering. This should facilitate the cost-effective planning, design, construction, and maintenance of effective programs that provide, and then continue to provide, valid solutions to stated (possibly changing) problems, or satisfactory implementations of (possibly changing) computer applications."

PROCEEDINGS OF THE IEEE, VOL. 68, NO. 9, SEPTEMBER 1980

Programs, Life Cycles, and Laws of Software Evolution

MEIR M. LEHMAN, SENIOR MEMBER, IEEE

Abstract—By classifying programs according to their relationship to the environment in which they are executed, the paper identifies the sources of evolutionary pressure on computer applications and programs and shows why this results in a process of never ending maintenance activity. The resultant life cycle processes are then briefly discussed. The paper then introduces laws of Program Evolution that have been formulated following quantitative studies of the evolution of a number of different systems. Finally an example is provided of the application of Evolution Dynamics models to program release planning.

I. BACKGROUND

A. The Nature of the Problem

THE TOTAL U.S. expenditure on programming in 1977 is estimated to have exceeded $50 billion, and may have been as high as $100 billion. This figure, which represents more than 3 percent of the U.S. GNP for that year, is already an awesome figure. It has increased ever since in real terms and will continue to do so as the microprocessor finds ever wider application. Programming effectiveness is clearly a significant component of national economic health. Even small percentage improvements in productivity can make significant financial impact. The potential for saving is large.

Economic considerations are, however, not necessarily the main cause of widespread concern. As computers play an ever larger role in society and the life of the individual, it becomes more and more critical to be able to create and maintain effective, cost-effective, and timely software. For more than two decades, however, the programming fraternity, and through them the computer-user community, has faced serious problems in achieving this [1]. As the application of microprocessors extends ever deeper into the fabric of society the problems will be compounded unless very basic solutions are found and developed.

B. Programming

The early 1950's had been a pioneering period in programming. The sheer ecstasy of instructing a machine step by step to achieve automatic computation at speeds previously undreamed of, completely hid the intellectually unsatisfying aspects of programming; the lack of a *guiding theory* and *discipline*; the largely *hit* or *miss* nature of the process through which an acceptable program was finally achieved; the ever present uncertainty about the *accuracy*, even the *validity*, of the final result.

More immediately, the gradual penetration of the computer into the academic, industrial, and commercial worlds led to serious problems in the provision and upkeep of satisfactory programs. It also yielded new insights. Programming as then practiced required the breakdown of the problem to be solved into steps far more detailed than those in terms of which people thought about it and its solution. The manual generation of programs at this low level was tedious and error prone for those whose primary concern was the result; for whom programming was a means to an end and not an end in itself. This could not be the basis for widespread computer application.

Thus there was born the concept of *high-level*, problem-oriented, *languages* created to simplify the development of computer applications. These languages did not just raise the level of detail to which programmers had to develop their view of the automated problem-solving process. They also removed at least some of the burdens of procedural organization, resource allocation and scheduling, burdens which were further reduced through the development of operating systems and their associated job-control languages. Above all, however, the high-level language trend permitted a fundamental shift in attitude. To the discerning, at least, it became clear that it was not the programmer's main responsibility to instruct a machine by defining a step-by-step computational process. His task was to state an algorithm that correctly and unambiguously defines a mechanical procedure for obtaining a solution to a given problem [2], [3]. The transformation of this into executable and efficient code sequences could be more safely entrusted to automatic mechanisms. The objective of language design was to facilitate that task.

Languages had become a major tool in the hands of the programmer. Like all tools, they sought to reduce the manual effort of the worker and at the same time improve the quality of his work. They permitted and encouraged concentration on the intellectual tasks which are the real province of the human mind and skill. Thus, ever since, the search for better languages and for improving methodologies for their use, has continued [4].

There are those who believe that the development of *programming methodology*, high-level languages and associated concepts, is by far the most important step for successful computer usage. That may well be, but it is by no means sufficient. There exists a clear need for additional methodologies and tools, a need that arises primarily from program maintenance.

C. Program Maintenance

The sheer level of programming and programming-related activity makes its disciplining important. But a second statistic carries an equally significant message. Of the total U.S. expenditure for 1977, some 70 percent was spent on program *maintenance* and only about 30 percent on program *develop-*

Manuscript received February 27, 1980; revised May 22, 1980.
The author is with the Department of Computing, Imperial College of Science and Technology, 180 Queen's Gate, London SW7 2BZ, England.

199

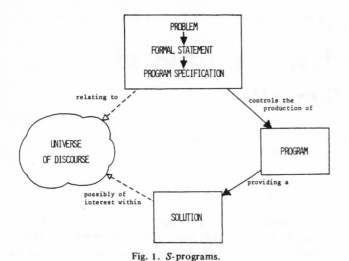

Fig. 1. *S*-programs.

ment. This ratio is generally accepted by the software community as characteristic of the state of the art.

Some clarification is, however, necessary. For software the term *maintenance* is generally used to describe *all* changes made to a program after its first installation. It therefore differs significantly from the more general concept that describes the *restoration* of a system or system component to its *former* state. Deterioration that has occurred as a result of usage or the passage of time, is corrected by repair or replacement. But software does not deteriorate spontaneously or by interaction with its operational environment. Programs do *not* suffer from wear, tear, corrosion, or pollution. They do not change unless and until *people* change them, and this is done whenever the current behavior of a program in execution is found to be wrong, inappropriate, or too restricted. *Repair* actually involves changes *away* from the previous implementation. Faults being corrected during maintenance can originate in any phase of the program *life cycle* (Section III).

Moreover, in hardware systems, major changes to a product are achieved by *redesign*, retooling, and the construction of a new model. With programs *improvements* and *adaptations* to a changing environment are achieved by alterations, deletions, and extensions to existing code. New capability, often not recognized during the earlier life of the system, is superimposed on an existing structure without redesign of the system as a whole.

Since the term software maintenance covers such a wide range of activities, the very high ratio of maintenance to development cost does not necessarily have to be deprecated. We shall, in fact, argue that the need for continuing change is *intrinsic* to the nature of computer usage. Thus the question raised by the high cost of maintenance is not exclusively how to control and reduce that cost by avoiding errors or by detecting them earlier in the development and usage cycle. The *unit cost of change* must initially be made as low as possible and its growth, as the system ages, minimized. Programs must be made more *alterable*, and the alterability *maintained* throughout their lifetime. The change process itself must be *planned* and *controlled*. Assessments of the economic viability of a program must include *total lifetime costs* and their life cycle *distribution*, and not be based exclusively on the initial development costs. We must be concerned with the cost and effectiveness of the life-cycle process itself and not just that of its product.

The opening paragraph highlighted the high cost of software and software maintenance. The economic benefit and potential of the application of computers is, however, so high that present expenditure levels may well be acceptable, at least for certain classes of programs. But we must be concerned with the fact that *performance, capability, quality in general*, cannot at present be designed and built into a program *ab initio*. Rather they are gradually achieved by evolutionary change and refinement. Moreover, when desirable changes are identified and authorized they can usually not be implemented on a time scale fixed by external need. *Responsiveness* is poor. And as mankind relies more and more on the software that controls the computers that in turn guide society, it becomes crucial that people control absolutely the programs and the processes by which they are produced, throughout the useful life of the program. To achieve this requires *insight, theory, models, methodologies, techniques, tools*: a *discipline*. That is what software engineering is all about [5]–[8].

II. PROGRAMS AS MODELS

A. Programs

Program evolution dynamics [9 and its bibliography] and the laws [2], [3], [10], [11] discussed in the next section, have always been associated with a concept of *largeness*, implying a classification into large and nonlarge programs. Great difficulty has, however, been experienced in defining these classes. Recent discussions [12] have produced a more satisfying classification. This is based on a recognition of the fact that, at the very least, any program is *a model of a model within a theory of a model of an abstraction of some portion of the world or of some universe of discourse*. The classification categorizes programs into three classes, *S, P,* and *E*. Since programs considered large by our previous definition will generally be of class *P* or *E*, the new classification represents a broadening and firming of the previous viewpoint.

B. S-Programs

S-programs are programs whose function is formally defined by and derivable from a *specification*. It is the programming form from which most advanced programming methodology and related techniques derive, and to which they directly relate. We shall suggest that as programming methodology evolves still further, all large programs (software systems) will be constructed as structures of *S*-programs.

A specific problem is stated: lowest common multiple of two integers; function evaluation in a specified domain; eight queens; dining philosophers; generation of a rectangle of a size within given limits on a specific type of visual display unit (VDU). Each such problem relates to its universe of discourse. It may also relate directly and primarily to the external world, but be completely defined, e.g., the *classical* travelling salesman problem.

As suggested by Fig. 1 the specification, as a formal definition of the problem, directs and controls the programmer in his creation of the program that defines the desired solution. Correct solution of the problem as *stated*, in terms of the programming language being used, becomes the programmer's sole concern. At most, questions of elegance or efficiency may also creep in.

The problem statement, the program and the solution when obtained may relate to an external world. But it is a casual, noncausal relationship. Even, when it exists we are free to change our interest by redefining the problem. But then it has a *new program* for its solution. It may be possible and time-saving to derive the new program from the old. But it is a *different* program that defines a solution to a *different* problem.

When this view can be legitimately taken the resultant program is conceptually static. One may change it to improve its clarity or its elegance, to decrease resource usage when the program is executed, even to increase confidence in its correctness. But any such changes must not effect the mapping between input and output that the program defines and that it achieves in execution. Whenever program text has been changed or transformed [13], [14] it must be shown that either the input–output relationship remains unchanged, or that the new program satisfies a new specification defining a solution to a new problem. We return to the problem of correctness proving in Section II-E.

C. P-Programs

Consider a program to play chess. The program is completely specified by the rules of chess plus procedure rules. The latter must indicate how the program is to analyze the state of the game and determine possible moves. It must also provide a decision rule to select a next move. The procedure might, for example, be to form the tree of all games that may develop from any current state and adopt a minimax evaluation strategy to select the next move. Such a definition, while complete, is naive, since it is not implementable as an executing program. The tree structure at any given stage is simply too large, by many orders of magnitude, to be developed or to be scanned in feasible time. Thus the chess program must introduce approximation to achieve practicality, judged as it begins to be used, by its performance in actual games.

A further example of a problem that can be precisely formulated but whose solution must inevitably reflect an approximation of the real world is found in weather prediction. In theory, global weather can be modeled as accurately as desired by a set of hydrodynamic equations. In the actual world of weather prediction, approximate solutions of modified equations are compared with the weather patterns that occur. The results of such comparisons are interpreted and used to improve the technology of prediction, to yield ever more usable programs, whose outputs, however, always retain some degree of uncertainty.

Finally consider the travelling salesman problem as it arises in practice, for example from a desire to optimize continuously in some vaguely defined fashion, the travel schedule of salesmen picking up goods from warehouses and visiting clients. The required solution can be based on known approaches and solutions to the classical problem. But it must also involve considerations of cost, time, work schedules, timetables, value judgments, and even salesmens' idiosyncracies.

The problem statement can now, in general, no longer be precise. It is a model of an abstraction of a real-world situation, containing uncertainties, unknowns, arbitrary criteria, continuous variables. To some extent it must reflect the personal viewpoint of the analyst. Both the problem statement and its solution approximate the real-world situation.

Programs such as these are termed *P*-programs (real world *problem* solution). The process of creating such programs is modeled by Fig. 2 which shows the intrinsic feedback loop that is present in the *P*-situation. Despite the fact that the problem to be solved can be precisely defined, the acceptability of a solution is determined by the environment in which it is

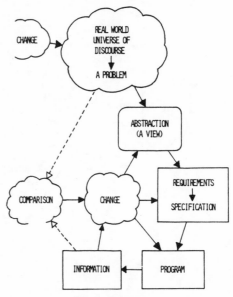

Fig. 2. *P*-programs.

embedded. The solution obtained will be evaluated by comparison with the real environment. That is, the critical difference between *S* and *P*-programs is expressed by the comparison cloud in Fig. 2. In *S*-programs, judgments about the correctness, and therefore the value, of the programs relate by definition *only to its specification*, the problem statement that the latter reflects. In *P*-programs, the concern is not centered on the problem statement but on the *value* and *validity* of the solution obtained *in its real-world context*. Differences between data derived from observation and from computation may cause changes in the world view, the problem perception, its formulation, the model, the program specification and/or the program implementation. Whatever the source of the difference, ultimately it causes the program, its documentation or both to be changed. And the effect or impact of such change cannot be eliminated by declaring the problem a *new* problem, for the real problem has always been as now perceived. It is the perception of users, analysts and/or programmers that has changed.

There is also another fact of life that needs to be considered. Dissatisfaction will arise not only because information received from the program is incomplete or incorrect, or because the original model was less than perfect. These are imperfections that can be overcome given time and care. But *the world too changes* and such changes result in additional pressure for change. Thus *P*-programs are very likely to undergo never-ending change or to become steadily less and less effective and cost effective.

D. E-Programs

The third class, *E*-programs, are inherently even more change prone. They are programs that mechanize a human or societal activity.

Consider again the travelling salesman problem but in a situation where *several* persons are continuously en route, carrying products that change rapidly in value as a function of both time and location, and with the pattern of demand also changing continuously. One will inevitably be tempted to see this situation as an application in which the system is to act as a continuous dispatcher, dynamically controlling the journeys and calls of each individual. The objective will be to maximize

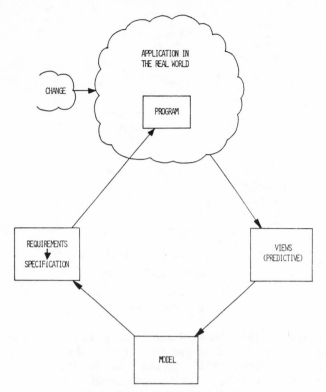

Fig. 3. *E*-programs-The basic cycle.

Fig. 4. *E*-programs.

profit, minimize loss, expedite deliveries, maintain customer satisfaction or achieve some optimum combination of the factors that are accepted as the criteria for success. How does this situation differ from that discussed in the previous sections?

The installation of the program together with its associated system—radio links to the salesmen, for example—change the very nature of the problem to be solved. *The program has become a part of the world it models*, it is *embedded* in it. Conceptually at least the program as a model contains elements that model itself, the consequences of its execution.

The situation is depicted in Figs. 3 and 4. Even without considering program execution and evaluation of its output in the operational environment, the *E*-situation contains an intrinsic feedback loop as in Fig. 3. Analysis of the application to determine requirements, specification, design, implementation now all involve extrapolation and prediction of the consequences of system introduction and the resultant potential for application and system evolution. This prediction must inevitably involve opinion and judgment. In general, several views of the situation will be combined to yield the model, the system specification and, ultimately, *a* program. Once the program is completed and begins to be used, questions of correctness, appropriateness and satisfaction arise as in Fig. 4 and inevitably lead to additional pressure for change.

Examples of *E*-programs abound: computer operating systems, air-traffic control, stock control. In all cases, the behavior of the application system, the demands on the user, and the support required will depend on program characteristics as experienced by the users. As they become familiar with a system whose design and attributes depend at least in part on user attitudes and practice before system installation, users will modify their behavior to minimize effort or maximize effectiveness. Inevitably this leads to pressure for system change. In addition, system exogenous pressures will also cause changes in the application environment within which the system oper-

ates and the program executes. New hardware will be introduced, traffic patterns and demand change, technology advance and society itself evolve. Moreover the nature and rate of this evolution will be markedly influenced by program characteristics, with a new release at intervals ranging from one month to two years, say. Unlike other artificial systems [15] where, relative to the life cycle of process participants, change is occasional, here it appears continually. The pressure for change is built in. It is intrinsic to the nature of computing systems and the way they are developed and used. *P* and *E* programs are clearly closely related. They differ from *S*-programs in that they represent a computer *application* in the real world. We shall refer to members of the union of the *P* and *E* classes as *A*-type programs.

E. Program Correctness

The first consequence of the SPE program classification is a clarification of the concepts of program correctness and program proving. The meaning, reality, and significance of these concepts have recently been examined at great length [16], [17]. Many of the viewpoints and differences expressed by the participants in that discussion become reconcilable or irrelevant under an adequate program classification scheme.

For the SPE scheme, the concept of verification takes on significantly different meanings for the *S* and the *A* classes. If a completely specified problem is computable, its specification may be taken as the starting point for the creation of an *S*-program. In principle a logically connected sequence of statements can always be found, that demonstrates the validity of the program as a solution of the specified problem. Detailed inspection of and reasoning about the code may itself produce the conviction that the program satisfies the specification completely. A true proof must satisfy the accepted standards of mathematics. Even when the correctness argument is expressed in mathematical terms, a lengthy or complex chain of reasoning may be difficult to understand, the proof sequence may even contain an error. But this does not invalidate the concept of program correctness proving, merely this instance of its application.

We cannot discuss here the range of S-programs for which proving is a practical or a valuable technique, the range of applicability of constructive methods for simultaneous construction of a program and its proof [18], [19]; whether confidence in the validity of an S-program can always be increased by a proof. We simply note that since, by definition, the sole criterion of correctness of an S-program is the satisfaction of its specification, (correct) S-programs are always *provably* correct.

This is not purely a philosophical observation. Many important components of a large program, mathematical procedures for example, in conjunction with specified interface rules (calling and output), are certainly S-type. It becomes part of the design process to recognize such potential constituents during the partitioning process and to specify and implement them accordingly. In fact it will be postulated in the next section that an A-program may always be partitioned and structured so that *all* its elements are S-programs. If this is indeed true, no *individual* programmer should *ever* be permitted to begin programming until his task has been defined and delimited by a complete specification against which his completed program can be validated.

For an E-program as an entity on the other hand, validity depends on human assessment of its effectiveness in the intended application. Correctness and proof of correctness of the program as a whole are, in general, irrelevant in that a program may be formally correct but useless, or incorrect in that it does not satisfy some stated specification, yet quite usable, even satisfactory. Formal techniques of representation and proof have a place in the universe of A-programs but their role changes. It is the detailed *behavior* of the program *under operational conditions* that is of concern.

Parts of the program that can be completely specified should be demonstrably correct. But the environment cannot be completely described without abstraction and, therefore, approximation. Hence absolute correctness of the program as a whole is not the real issue. It is the *usability* of the program and the *relevance* of its output in a changing world that must be the main concern.

F. Program Structures and Structural Elements

The classification created above relates to program entities. Any such program will, in general, consist of many parts variously referred to as subsystems, components, modules, procedures, routines. The terms are, of course, not used synonymously but carry imputations of functional identity, level, size, and so on.

The literature discusses criteria [20] and techniques [21]-[23] for partitioning systems into such elements. Related design methodologies and techniques seek to achieve optimum assignment, in some sense, of element content and overall system structure. In the present context we consider only one aspect of partitioning using the term module for convenience. The discussion completes the presentation of the SPE classification and provides a link to other current methodological thinking [24].

Consider the end result of the design process for an A-program to be constructed of primitive elements we term modules.

The analysis and partitioning process will identify some functional elements that can be fully specified and therefore developed as S-program modules. Any specification may of course be less than fully satisfactory. It may even prove to be wrong in relation to what the system purpose demands, in itself or in relation to the remainder of the design. For example the specification may not mention input validity checks, the specified output accuracy may be insufficient or the specified range of an input variable may be wrong. But each of these represents an omission from or an error in the *specification*. Thus it is rectified by first correcting the *specification* and then creating, by one means or another, a new program that satisfies the new specification.

The remainder of the system is required to implement functions that are at least partly heuristic or behavioral in nature and therefore define A-elements. Nevertheless, we suggest that it is *always* possible to continue the system partitioning process until *all* modules are implementable as S-programs. That is, any imprecision or uncertainty emanating from model reflections of incomplete world views will be implicit or, if recognized when the specification is formulated, explicit in the specification statement. The final modules will all be derived from and associated with precise specifications, which *for the moment*, may be treated as complete and correct.

The design may now be viewed and constructed as a data-flow structure with the inputs of one module being the outputs of others (unless emanating from outside the system). Each module will be defined as an abstract data type [25]-[27] defining, in turn, one or more input-to-output transformations. Module specifications include those of the individual interfaces, but for the system as a whole, the latter should, in some sense be standardized [28]. Moreover, given appropriate system and interface architecture and module design, each module could be implemented as a program running on its own microprocessor and the system implemented as a distributed system [9], [24], [28], [92]. The potential advantages for both execution (parallelism) and maintainability (localization of change) cannot be discussed here.

Many problems in connection with the design and construction of such systems need still to be solved. Adequate solutions will represent a major advance in the development of a process methodology (Section III-C). We observe, however, that the concepts presented follow directly from our brief analysis and classification of program types. Interestingly, the conclusions are completely compatible with those of the programming methodologists [24], [29], [30].

III. THE LIFE CYCLE

A. The General Case

The dynamic evolutionary nature of computer applications, of the software that implements them and of the process that produces both, has in recent years given rise to a concept of a program *life cycle* and to techniques for *life-cycle management*. The need for such management has, in fact, been recognized in far wider spheres, particularly by national defense agencies and other organizations concerned with the management of complex artificial systems. In pursuing their responsibilities, these must ensure continuing effectiveness of systems whose elements may involve many different and fast developing technologies. Often they must guarantee utterly reliable operation under harsh, hostile, and unforgiving conditions. The outcome is an ever increasing financial commitment. Only lifetime-orientated management techniques applied from project

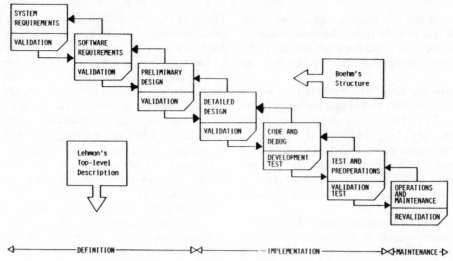

Fig. 5. The software life cycle according to Boehm.

initiation can permit the attainment of lifetime effectiveness and cost effectiveness.

The problems in the more general situation are essentially those we have already explored, except that the time interval between generations is perhaps an order of magnitude greater than in the case of pure software systems. In briefly examining the nature of the life cycle and its management in this section, we use the terminology of programming and software engineering. The reader will be able to generalize and to interpret the remarks in his own area of interest.

B. Software Life Cycles

In studying program evolution, repetitive phenomena that define a life cycle can be observed on different time scales representing various levels of abstraction. The highest level concerns *successive generations* of system sequences. Each generation is represented by a sequence of system releases. This level corresponds most closely to that found in the more general systems situation, with each generation having a life span of from, say, five to twenty years. Because of the relatively slow rate of change it is difficult for any individual to observe this evolution phenomenon, measure its dynamics and model it as a life-cycle process since in the relevant portion of his professional career he will not observe more than two or three generations. It might therefore be argued that this level should not be treated as an instance of the life-cycle phenomenon. The present author has, however, had at least one opportunity to examine program evolution at this level and to make meaningful and significant observations [31]. These indicated that much could be gained in cost effectiveness in the software industry if more attention were paid to the earlier creation of replacement generations, something that can be achieved effectively only if the appropriate predictive models are available.

The second level is concerned with a *sequence* of *releases*. The latter term is also appropriate when a concept of continuous release is followed, that is when each change is made, validated, and immediately installed in user instances of the system.

Fig. 5 shows one view [6] of the *sequence* of *activities* or life-cycle phases that constitute the lowest level, the development of an individual release, if it is assumed that "maintenance" in the seventh box refers to on-site *fixes* and repairs implemented as the system is used. If maintenance is taken to refer to permanent changes, effected through new releases by the system originator, then the structure becomes *recursive* with each maintenance phase comprised of all seven indicated phases. With this interpretation the single recursive model reflects the composite life-cycle structure of all the above levels.

The remainder of this paper is chiefly concerned with the intermediate level, the life cycle of a generation as represented by a sequence of releases. It is at this level that analysis in terms of the S and A classification is particularly relevant and enlightening.

C. Assembly Line Processes

An assembly line manufacturing process is possible when a system can be partitioned into subsystems that are simply coupled and without invisible links. Moreover, the process must be divisible into separate phases without significant feedback control over phases and with relatively little opportunity for tradeoff between them.

Unfortunately, present day programming is not like that. It is constituted of tightly coupled activities that interact in many ways. For example, at least some aspects of the specification and design processes are left over, usually implicitly, to the implementation (coding) phase. Fault detection through inspection [90] is not yet universal practice and by default is often delayed till a system integration or system testing phase. One of the main concerns of life-cycle process methodology research must be to develop techniques, tools, new system architectures (Section II-F) and programming support environments [32]–[34] that permit partitioning of the program development and maintenance process into separated activities.

D. The Significance of the Life-Cycle Concept

For assembly line processes the life-cycle concept is not, generally, of prime importance. For software and other highly complex systems it becomes critical if effectiveness, cost effectiveness, and long life are to be achieved. At each moment in time, a manager's concern concentrates on the successful completion of his current assignment. His success will be assessed by immediately observable product attributes, quality, cost, timeliness, and so on. It is his success in areas such as these that determine the furtherance of his career. Managerial strategy will inevitably be dominated by a desire to achieve maximum local payoff with visible short-term benefit. It will not often take into account long-term penalties, that cannot be precisely predicted and whose cost cannot be assessed. Top-level managerial pressure to apply life-cycle evaluation is therefore essential if a development and maintenance process is to be attained that continuously achieves, say, desired overall balance between the short- and long-term objectives of the organization. Neglect will inevitably result in a lifetime expenditure on the system that exceeds many times the assessed development cost on the basis of which the system or project was initially authorized.

To overcome long time lags and the high cost of software, one may also seek to extend the useful lifetime of a system. The decision to replace a system is taken when maintenance has become too expensive, reliability too low, change responsiveness too sluggish, performance unacceptable, functionality too limiting; in short, when it is economically more satisfactory to replace the system than to maintain it. But its expected life time to that point is determined primarily in its conception, design and initial implementation stages. Hence management planning and control during the formative period of system life, based on lifetime projections and assessment, can be critical in achieving long life software and lifetime cost effectiveness [1].

E. Life-Cycle Phases

1) The Major Activity Classes: At its grossest level a life cycle consists of three phases: definition, implementation and maintenance. As indicated in Fig. 5, these three phases correspond approximately to the activities described in the first three, the second three and the seventh box respectively of Boehm's model. In practice, however, many of these activities are overlapped, interwoven, and repeated iteratively.

2) System Definition: For *E*-class systems in particular, the development process begins with a pragmatic analysis leading into a systematic *systems analysis* to determine total system and program *requirements* [35]-[38]. The analysis must first establish the *real* need and objectives and may examine the manual techniques whereby the same purpose is currently achieved. Where appropriate, it may be based on mathematical or other formal analysis. Whatever the approach, it has now been recognized that the analysis must be *disciplined* and *structured* [29], [30], the term *structured analysis* now being widely used [9], [41], [42].

By their very nature initial requirements, being an expression of the user's view of his needs, are likely to include incompatibilities or even contradictions. Thus the analysis and the negotiation process by and between analysts and potential users that produces the final *requirements specification*, must identify a balanced set that, in some sense, provides the optimum compromise between conflicting desires.

The requirements set will be expressed in the concepts and language of the application and its users. It must then be transformed into a *technical specification*. The specification process [43], [44] must aim to produce a correct technical statement, *complete* in its coverage of the requirements and *consistent* in its definition of the implementation. It may include additional determinations or constraints that follow from a technical evaluation of the requirements in relation to what is feasible, available and appropriate in the judgment of the analyst and designer in agreement with the user.

It has long been the aim of computer scientists to provide formal languages for the expression of specifications so as to permit mechanical checking of completeness and consistency

[45]-[49], [91], but a widely accepted language does not yet exist. Given a machinable specification it is conceptually possible to reduce it mechanically to executable [50] and even efficient [14] code but these technologies too are not yet ready for general exploitation.

Thus, for the time being, the specification process will be followed by a *design* phase [49], [51]. The prime objective of this activity is to identify and structure data, data transformation and data flow [23]. It must also achieve, in some defined sense, optimal partitioning of system function [20], select computational algorithms and procedures, and identify system components, and the relationships between them. It is now generally accepted that iterative *top-down* [52] analysis and partitioning processes are required to achieve *successive refinement* [21] of the system design to the point where the identified objects, procedures, and transformations can be directly implemented.

3) Implementation: Following the completion of the design, system *implementation* may begin. In practice, however, design and implementation overlap. Thus, as the hierarchical partitioning process proceeds, analysis of certain aspects of the system may be considered sufficient for implementation, while others require further analysis. In a software project, time always appears to be at a premium. A work force comprising many different abilities is available and must be kept busy. Thus, regrettably, implementation of subsystems, components, procedures, or modules will be initiated despite the fact that the overall, or even the local design, is not yet complete.

As the implementation proceeds code must be *validated* [53], [54]. Present day procedures concentrate primarily on *testing* [55], though in recent years increasing use has been made of design *walkthrough* and code *inspection* [90]. These latter procedures are intended to disclose both design and implementation errors before their consequences become hidden in the program code. The ratio of costs of removing a fault discovered in usage as against the cost of removing the same fault if discovered during the design or first implementation phase is sometimes two or three orders of magnitude. Clearly, it pays to find faults early in the process.

In any case, testing by means of program execution is carried out, generally bottom up, first at the unit (module or procedural) level, then functionally, component by component. As tested components become available they are then assembled into a system in an *integration* process and *system test* is initiated. Finally, after some degree of independent certification of system function and performance, the system is designated ready for *release*.

The above very brief summary has identified some of the activities that are typically undertaken in a system creation process. Individual activities as described may overlap, be iterated, merged, or not undertaken at all. Design of an element, for example, may be followed immediately by a test implementation and preliminary performance evaluation to ensure feasibility of a design before its implications spread to other parts of the system. Clearly, there should be a set of overall controlled procedures to take a concept from the first pragmatic evaluation of the potential of an application for mechanization to the final program product executing in defined hardware or software and hardware environment(s).

4) Maintenance: Once the system has been released, the maintenance process begins. Faults will be observed, reported, and corrected. If user progress is blocked because of a fault, a temporary bypass of the faulty code may be authorized. In other circumstances a temporary or permanent fix may be applied in some or all user locations. The permanent repair or change to the program can then be held over for a new release of the system. In other cases, a permanent change will be prepared for immediate installation by all those running the system. The particular strategy adopted in any instance will depend on the nature and severity of the fault, the size and difficulty of the change required, the number and nature of program installations and user organizations, and so on. The aggregate strategy will have a profound impact on the rate of system complexity growth, on its life-cycle costs, and on its life expectancy.

The faults that are fixed in the maintenance process may be due to changes external to the system, incorrect or incomplete specification, design or implementation errors, hardware changes or to some combination of these. Since each user exposes the system in different ways, all installations do not experience all faults, nor do they automatically apply all manufacturer-supplied fixes or changes. On the other hand, installations having their own programming staff may very well develop and install localized changes or system modifications to suit their specific needs. These patches, insertions, or deletions may in turn cause new difficulties when further incremental changes are received from the manufacturer, or at a later date when a new release is received. The inevitable consequences of the maintenance process applied to systems installed for more than one user, is that the system drifts apart. Multiple versions of system elements develop to encompass the variations and combinations [56]. System *configuration management* becomes a major task. *Support environments* [33]–[35] that automatically collect and maintain total activity records become an essential tool in programming process management.

F. Life-Cycle Planning and Management

The preceding discussion, while presenting a simplified view of the life cycle, will have made clear the difficulty associated with cycle planning. In recent years this problem has received much attention [57], [58]. A variety of techniques have been developed to improve estimation of cost, time, and other resources required for software development and maintenance [59]–[64]. These techniques are based on extrapolation of past experience and tend to produce results in the nature of self-fulfilling prophecies. In general, it has not yet proved possible to develop techniques that estimate project requirements on the basis of objective measurement of such attributes as application complexity and size and the work required to create a satisfactory system. Techniques such as software science [65], [66] seek to do just this but to date lack substantiation [67] and interpretation. Major research and advances are required if software engineering is to become as manageable as are other engineering disciplines, though fundamentally the peculiar nature of software systems [28] will always leave software engineering in a class of its own.

IV. LAWS OF PROGRAM EVOLUTION

A. Evolution

The analysis of Section II associated with the life-cycle description of Section III, has indicated that evolution is an intrinsic, feedback driven, property of software. The metasystem within which a program evolves contains many more feedback relationships than those identified above. Primitive instincts of survival and growth result in the evolution of stabilizing mechanisms in response to needs, events and changing objectives. The resulting pseudohierarchical structure of self-stabilizing systems includes the products, the processes, the environments and the organizations involved. The interactions between and within the various constituents, and the overall pattern of behavior must be understood if a program product and its usage are to be effectively planned and maintained.

The organizational and environmental feedback, links, focuses, and transmits the evolutionary pressure to yield the continuing change process. A similar situation holds, of course, for any human organized activity, any artificial system. But some significant differences are operative in the case of software. In the first instance there is no room in programming for imprecision, no malleability to accommodate uncertainty or error. Programming is a mathematical discipline. In relation to a *specific* objective, a program is either right or wrong. Once an instruction sequence has been fixed and unless and until it is manually changed, its behavior in execution on a given machine is determined solely by its inputs.

Secondly, a software system is soft. Changes can be implemented using a pencil, paper, and/or a keyboard. Moreover, once a change has been designed and implemented on a development system it can be applied mechanically to any number of instances of the same system without further significant physical or intellectual effort using only computing resources. Thus the temptation is to implement changes in the existing system, change upon change upon change, rather than to collect changes into groups and implement them in a totally new instance. As the number of superimposed changes increases, the system and the metasystem become more complex, stiffer, more resistant to change. The cost, the time required, and the probability of an erroneous or unsatisfactory change all increase.

Thirdly, the rate at which a program executes, the frequency of usage, usage interaction with the operating environment, economic and social dependence of external process on program execution, all cause deficiencies to be exposed. The resultant pressure for correction and improvement leads to a system rate of change with a time scale measured in days and months rather than in the years and decades that separate hardware generations.

B. Dynamics and Laws of Program Evolution

The resultant evolution of software appears to be driven and controlled by human decision, managerial edict, and programmer judgment. Yet as shown by extended studies [68]–[76], measures of its evolution display patterns, regularity and trends that suggest an underlying dynamics that may be modeled and used for planning, for process control, and for process improvement.

Once observed the reasons for this unexpected regularity is easily understood. Individual decisions in the life cycle of a software system generally *appear* localized in the system and in time. The considerations on which they are based *appear* independent. Managerial decisions are largely taken in relative isolation, concerned to achieve local control and optimization, concentrated on some aspect of the process, some phase of system evolution. But their aggregation, moderated by the many feedback relationships, produces overall systems response which is regular and often normally distributed.

In its early stages of development a system is more or less under the control of those involved in its analysis, design, and implementation. As it ages, those working on or with the system become increasingly constrained by earlier decisions, by existing code, by established practices and habits of users and

TABLE I
LAWS OF PROGRAM EVOLUTION

I. *Continuing Change*

A program that is used and that as an implementation of its specification reflects some other reality, undergoes continual change or becomes progressively less useful. The change or decay process continues until it is judged more cost effective to replace the system with a recreated version.

II. *Increasing Complexity*

As an evolving program is continually changed, its complexity, reflecting deteriorating structure, increases unless work is done to maintain or reduce it.

III. *The Fundamental Law of Program Evolution*

Program evolution is subject to a dynamics which makes the programming process, and hence measures of global project and system attributes, self-regulating with statistically determinable trends and invariances.

IV. *Conservation of Organizational Stability (Invariant Work Rate)*

During the active life of a program the global activity rate in a programming project is statistically invariant.

V. *Conservation of Familiarity (Perceived Complexity)*

During the active life of a program the release content (changes, additions, deletions) of the successive releases of an evolving program is statistically invariant.

implementors alike. Local control remains with people. But process and system-internal links, dependencies, and interactions cause the global characteristics of system evolution to be determined by organization, process and system parameters. At the global level the metasystem dynamics have largely taken over.

Since the original observation [63], studies of program evolution have continued, based on measurements obtained from a variety of systems. Typical examples of the resultant models have been reported [69]-[72], [74], [76] including also one detailed example of their application to release planning [77].

It was repeated observation of phenomenologically similar behavior and the common interpretation of independent phenomena, that led to a set of five laws, that have themselves evolved as insight and understanding have increased. The laws, as currently formulated to include the new viewpoint emerging from the SPE classification, are given in Table I. Their early development can be followed in [9], [10], [72]. We note that the laws are abstractions of observed behavior based on statistical models. They have no meaning until a system, a project and the organizational metasystem are well established. More detailed discussion of their nature and of their technical and managerial implications will be found in [11], [77], [78] and [77], [79], [80], respectively.

The first law, *continuing change*, originally [3], [10], [79] expressed the universally observed fact that large programs are never completed. They just continue to evolve. Following our new insight, however, reference to *largeness* is now replaced by the phrase ... "that reflect some other reality ..."

The second law, *increasing complexity*, could be seen as an instance of the second law of thermodynamics. It would seem more reasonable to regard both as instances of some more fundamental natural truth. But from either viewpoint its message is clear.

The third law, the *fundamental law of program evolution*, is in the nature of an existence rule. It abstracts the observed fact that the number of decisions driving the process of evolution, the many feedback paths, the checks and balances of

organizations, human interactions in the process, reactions to usage, the rigidity of program code, all combine to yield statistically regular behavior such as that observed and measured in the systems studied.

The fourth law, *conservation of organizational stability*, and the fifth, *conservation of familiarity*, represent instances of the observations whose generalization led to the third law. The fourth reflects the steadiness of multiloop self-stabilizing systems. It is believed to arise from organizational striving for stability. The managements of well-established organizations avoid dramatic change and particularly discontinuities in growth rates. Moreover, the number of people and the investments involved, the unions, the time delays in implementing decisions, all operate together to prevent sudden or drastic change. Wide fluctuations may in fact lead to instability and the breakup of an organization.

The reader may find it difficult to accept the implication that the work output of a project is independent of the amount of resources employed, though the same observation has also been recorded by others [81]. The underlying truth is that activities of the type considered, though initiated with minimal resources, rapidly attract more and more as commitment to the project, and therefore the consequences of success or failure, increase. Our observations as formalized in the fourth law imply that the resources that can be productively applied becomes limited as a software project ages. The magnitude of the limit depends on many factors including attributes of the total environment. But the pressure for success leads to investment to the point where it is exceeded. The project reaches the stage of resource saturation and further changes have no visible effect on real overall output.

While the fourth law springs from a pattern of organizational behavior, the fifth reflects the collective consequences of the characteristics of the many individuals within the organization. It is discussed at length in [11]. Suffice it to say here that the law arises from the nonlinear relationship between the magnitude of a system change and the intellectual effort and time required to absorb that change.

TABLE II
SYSTEM X STATISTICS

Release 19 Statistics

Size	4800 Modules
	1.3 Assembly M-statements
Incremental growth	410 Modules
Modules changed[a]	2650 Modules
Fraction of modules changed	0.55
Release interval	275 Days

System Statistics

Age	4.3 Years
Change rate	10.7 Modules/day
Average incremental growth	200 Modules/release
Maximum safe growth rate	400 Modules/release

Most Recent Releases

Release	15	16	17	18	19
Incremental growth (Δ Mod)	135	171	183	354	410
Fraction changed	0.33	0.43	0.48	0.50	0.56
Change rate	12.5	0.12	9.6	9.9	9.6
Interval (Days)	96	137	201	221	275
Old mods, Changed/ Mod	7.9	8.6	10.0	5.1	5.4

[a]Modules that are changed in any way in release $i + 1$ relative to release i are counted as one changed module, independently of the number of changes or of their magnitude.

V. APPLIED DYNAMICS

A. Introduction

The previous sections have emphasized the phenomenological basis for the laws of program evolution, indicating how they are rooted in phenomena underlying the activity of programming itself.

The origin of the laws in individual and societal behavior makes their impact on the construction and maintenance of software more than just descriptions of the evolutionary process. The laws represent *principles* in software engineering. They are, however, clearly not immutable, as for example, are the laws of physics or chemistry. Since they arise from the habits and practices of people and organizations, their modification or change requires one to go outside the discipline of computer science into the realms of sociology, economics and management. The laws therefore form an environment within which the effectiveness of programming methodologies and management strategies and techniques can be evaluated, a backdrop against which better methodologies and techniques can be developed.

Their implications, technical and managerial, have been previously discussed in the literature [3], [9], [11], [79], [80]. In the present paper, we restrict the discussion to outlining an example of the application of evolution dynamics models to release planning.

B. A Case Study—System X

1) The System and its Characteristics: System X is a general purpose batch operating system running on a range of machines. The eighteenth release (R18) of the system is operational in some tens of installations running a variety of work loads. The nineteenth release (R19) is about to be shipped.

Table II and Fig. 6(a)–(g) present the system and release data and models available for the purposes of the present exercise. We cannot, however, provide here the details of statistical analysis and model validation [76], based on this data

and that from other systems that gives us confidence in our conclusions and predictions.

Examining the system dynamics as implied by models derived from the data and as illustrated by the figures, Fig. 6(a) shows the continuing growth of the system (first law) albeit at a declining rate (demonstrably due to increasing difficulty of change, growing complexity—second law).

Fig. 6(b) indicates that as a function of release sequence number (RSN) the system growth (measured in modules) has been linear but with a superimposed ripple (a strong indicator of feedback stabilization).

Fig. 6(c) shows the net incremental growth per release (fifth law).

For system architectures such as that of system X, the fraction of system modules that are changed during a release may be taken as a gross indicator of system complexity. Fig. 6(d) shows that system X complexity, as measured in this way, shows an increasing trend (second law).

Fig. 6(e) is an example of the repeatedly observed constant average work rate (fourth law).

Fig. 6(f) illustrates how the average work rate achieved in individual releases, as measured by the rate of module change (changed modules per release interval day (m/d) oscillates, a period of high rate activity being followed by one or more in which the activity rate is much lower (third law).

Finally, Fig. 6(g) plots the release interval against release sequence number. It has been argued that release interval depends purely on management decision that is itself based on market considerations and technical aspects of the release content and environment. Data such as that of Fig. 6(g) indicates, however, that the feedback mechanisms that, amongst other process attributes, also control the release interval, while including human decision taking processes, are apparently not dominated by them. As a consequence, the release interval pattern is sufficiently regular to be modelable, and is statistically predictable once enough data points have been established.

2) The Problem: Already prior to the completion (and re-

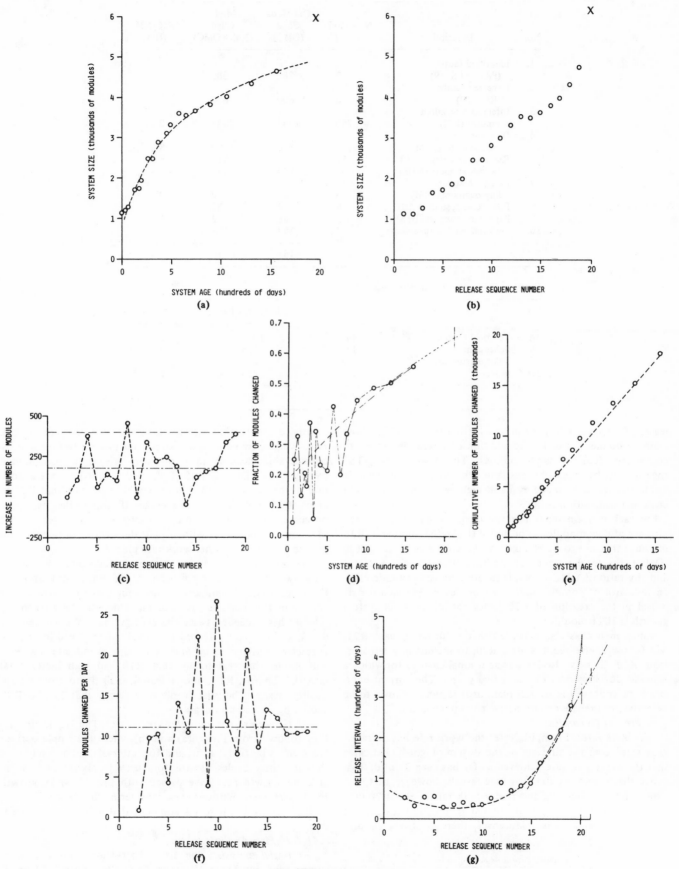

Fig. 6. System characteristics.

TABLE III
RELEASE 20 PLANNED CONTENT

Functional Enhancement

No.	Description	New Mods (NM)	Old Mods Chgd (OMC)	Mods Chgd (NM + OMC)	OMC/NM (IR)
1.	Identified faults (PRE. RLS. 19)	2	380	382	–
2.	Expected faults (RLS. 19)	0	600	600	–
3.	Interactive terminal support (ITS)	750	1783	2533	2.4
4.	Dynamic storage management (DSM)	170	1500	1670	8.8
5.	Remote job entry (RJE)	57	462	519	8.1
6.	New disk support (NDS)	17	124	141	7.3
7.	Batch scheduler improvements (BSI)	3	29	32	9.7
8.	File access system (FAS)	8	74	82	9.3
9.	Paper tape support (PTS)	12	80	92	6.7
10.	Performance improvements	2	157	159	–
		1021	5189	6210	

Detail of Interactive Terminal Support (ITS)

No.	Description	New Mods	Old Mods Chgd	OMC/NM
3A	Terminal support	444	1032	2.3
3B	Scheduling	127	293	2.3
3C	Telecom support	58	232	4.0
3D	Misc.	121	226	1.9
		750	1783	

lease) of R19, work has begun on a further version R20, whose main component is to be the addition of interactive access to complement current batch facilities. This new facility "ITS" together with other changes and additions summarized in Table III, are to be made available eighteen months after first customer installation of R19.

For each major planned functional change, the table lists the number of new modules to be added (NM), the number of R19 modules that are to be changed in the course of creating R20 (OMC), the total number of modules changed (NM + OMC), and the ratio of OMC to NM (the interconnectivity ratio (IR), an indicator of complexity). No modules are planned for removal in the creation of R20 hence the planned net system growth is 1021 modules.

Management has also accepted that a further release R21, will follow twelve months after R20, to include any leftovers from R20. It may also include additional changes for which a demand develops over the next two years. The current exercise is to endorse the overall plan, or if it can be shown to be defective, to prepare an alternative recommendation.

3) Process Dynamics:

a) Work rate: From Fig. 6(e) the work rate has averaged 10.4 m/d[1] over the lifetime of the system. Fig. 6(f) indicates that the maximum rate achieved so far has been 27 m/d. Evidence that cannot be detailed here reveals, however, that that data point is misleading and that a peak rate of about 20 m/d is a better indicator of the maximum achievable with current methodology and tools. Moreover, there is strong circum-

stantial evidence that releases achieved with such high work rates were extremely troublesome and had to be followed by considerable clean-up in a follow-up release, as also implied by Fig. 6(c). Thus, if R20 is planned so as to require a work rate in the region of 20 m/d, it would be wise to limit R21 to at most 10 m/d, the system average. If on the other hand, the process is further stabilized by working on R20 at near average rate, one could then, with a high degree of confidence, approach R21 with a higher work rate plan.

b) Incremental growth: The maintained average incremental growth for system X has been around 200 modules/release. Once again circumstantial evidence indicates that releases (for which, in this case, the growth rate (incremental growth per release) has exceeded twice the average) have slipped delivery dates, a poor quality record and a subsequent need for drastic corrective activity. Fig. 6(c) and Table II indicate that R19 will lie in this region and that R18 had high incremental growth. That is, R19, once released, is likely to prove a poor quality base. The first evidence emerges that maybe R20 should be a clean-up release.

c) Growth rate in modules for release: The same indication follows from Figs. 6(a) and (b) where the ripple periods are seen to be three, four, and five intervals, respectively over the first three cycles. In the fourth cycle, six intervals of increasing growth rate have passed with the R18–R19 growth the largest ever. Without even considering the planned growth to R20 (Point X), it seems apparent that a clean-up release is due.

4) R20 Plan Analysis:

a) Initial analysis: The first observation on the plan as summarized by Table III stems from the column (6) of IR

<hr>

[1] Modules per day = $\dfrac{\text{number of modules changed in release}}{\text{release interval in days}}$

factors. It has not been calculated for items 1, 2, and 10 since these represent activities that only rarely require the provision of entirely new (nonreplacement) modules. For items 4–9 the ratio lies in the range 8.2 ± 1.5, a remarkably small range for widely varying functional changes. Yet the predicted ratio for ITS is only 2.4. One must ask whether it is reasonable to suppose that the code implementing an interactive facility is far more loosely coupled to the remaining system than, for example, a specialist facility such as paper tape support? Is it not far more likely that ITS has been inadequately designed; viewed perhaps as an independent facility that requires only loose coupling into the existing system? Thus, when it is integrated with the remainder of the system to form R20, will it not require many more changes to obtain correct and adequate performance? From the evidence before us, the question is undecidable. Experience based intuition, however, suggests that it is rather likely that the number of changes required elsewhere in the system has been underestimated. Thus a high-priority design reappraisal is appropriate. If the suspicion of incomplete planning proves to be correct, it would suggest delaying R20, so that the planning and design processes may be completed. An alternative strategy of delaying at least ITS to R21 should also be evaluated.

b) Number of modules to be changed: The situation may of course not be quite as bad as direct comparison of the present estimate of the ITS interconnection ratio (IR) with that of the other items, suggests. In view of the 750 new modules involved, its IR factor could not exceed 6.4 even if all 4800 modules of R19 were effected by the ITS addition. Such a 100 percent change is, in fact, very unlikely, but the IR factor of 2.4 remains very suspect.

Moreover, even with the low ratio for ITS the sum of the individual OMC estimates for the entire plan exceeds the number of modules in R19. This suggests a new situation. Multiple changes applied to the same module must have become a significant occurrence. Even ignoring the fact that even independent changes applied in the same release to the *same* module generally demand significantly more effort than similar changes applied to independent modules, the total effort and time required must clearly increase with both the number of changes implemented and the number of modules changed. The presently defined measure "modules *changed*" is inadequate. The new situation demands consideration of more sensitive measures such as "number of module *changes*" and "average number of changes per module."

These cannot be derived from the available data. We may, however, proceed by considering a model based on the data of Fig. 6(d). Extrapolating the fraction changed trend, reveals that R20 may be expected to require a change of, say, 64 percent, or 3725 changed modules.[2] Comparing this estimate with the total of 6210 obtained if the estimates for individual items are summed, it appears that the average number of changes to be applied to R19 modules according to the present plan is at least of order two. We have already observed that multiple changes cause additional complications. Hence any prognosis made under the implied assumption of single changes (or of a somewhat lower interconnection ratio) will lead to an optimistic assessment.

[2] *Historical Note:* In the system on which this example is based the release including the interactive facility ultimately involved some 58 percent of modules changed. Moreover the first release was significantly delayed, and was of limited quality and performance. More than 70 percent of its modules had subsequently to be changed again to attain an acceptable product. Our estimate is clearly good.

c) Rate of work: The current plan calls for R20 with its 3725 module changes to be available in 18 months, that is 548 days. This implies a change rate of less than 6.8 m/d. This relatively low rate, following a period of average rate activity suggests that *work rate* pressures are unlikely to prove a source of trouble, even with multiple changes to many of the modules.

d) Growth rate: In Figs. 6(a) and (b), we have indicated the position of R20 as per plan, with an *X*. Both models indicate that the planned growth represents a major deviation from the previous history. Thus confirmation that the plan is realistic requires a demonstration that the special nature of the release, or changes in methodology, makes it reasonable to expect a significant change in the system dynamics. In the absence of such a demonstration, the suspicion that all is not well is strengthened.

e) Incremental growth: The current R20 plan calls for system growth of over 1000 modules. This figure which is five times the average and two and a half times the recommended maximum, must be interpreted as a danger signal.

We have already suggested that the low interconnection ratio for ITS suggests that the planners saw the new component as a stand alone mechanism that interfaces with the remainder of the system via a narrow and restricted interface. If this view proves justified, the large incremental growth need not be disturbing. But it seems reasonable to question it. With the architecture and structure that system *X* is known to have, such a relatively narrow interface is unlikely to be able to provide the communication and control bandwidth that safe, effective, and high capacity operation must demand. This is apparent from comparisons with, say, the paper tape or disk support changes or the RJE addition. The onus must be put onto the ITS designers to demonstrate the completeness of their analysis, design, and implementation.

Without such a demonstration one must conclude that the present plan is not technically viable. *Marketing* or other considerations may, of course, make it desirable to stay with the present plan even if this implies slipped delivery dates, poor and unreliable performance of the new release, limited facilities, and so on. But if such considerations force adoption of the plan, the implications must be noted, and corrective action planned. Ways and means will have to be created to enable users to cope with the resultant system and usage problems and the inevitable need for a major clean-up release. It might, for example, be wise to set up specialized customer support teams to assist in the installation, local adaptation and tuning of the system.

f) Release interval: Fig. 6(g) indicates two possible models for the prediction of the most likely (desirable?) release interval for R20 and R21. Linear extrapolation suggests a release period of under one year for each of the two releases. If this is valid, the apparent desire for a release after the 18 months is of itself unlikely to prove a source of problems. On the basis of evidence not reproduced here, however, the exponential extrapolation is likely to be more realistic and this yields an R20 release interval forecast of about 15 months and an R21 interval of some 3 years.

g) Recommendation—Summary: On the basis of the available data we have concluded that

1) to proceed with the plan as it stands is courting delivery and quality problems for R20;
2) a clean-up release appears due in any case;
3) failure to provide it will leave a weak base for the next

LEHMAN: PROGRAMS, LIFE CYCLES, AND LAWS OF SOFTWARE EVOLUTION

TABLE IV
MODIFIED RELEASE 20 CONTENT

Class	Reason	Items
Fault Repair	Clean-up of base	1, 2.
Hardware Support	Revenue Producing	6, 9.
Performance Improvement	Install—but do not announce. Will be available to counter-act ITS performance deterioration in R21'	7, 10.
ITS Related Components	To receive early user exposure	3c, 5, 8.

TABLE V
MODIFIED RELEASE 20 STATISTICS (FROM TABLE III)
IN ORDER OF PRIORITY

Item	New Mods.	Running Total	Changes	Running Total
1	2	2	382	382
2	0	2	600	982
6	17	19	141	1123
9	12	31	92	1215
7	3	34	32	1247
10	2	36	159	1406
8	8	44	82	1488
5	57	101	519	2007
3c	58	159	522	2529

release; at the very least the number of expected faults (Table III, item 2) is likely to prove an underestimate;

4) the absolute size of the ITS component and the related incremental system growth would represent a major challenge even on a clean base;

5) there are indications that the ITS aspect of the release design is incomplete;

6) change rate needs for R20 are not likely to prove a source of problems;

7) nor is the demand for attainment of a next release in eighteen months.

The following recommendations follow:

8) initiate immediately an intensive and detailed reexamination of the ITS design and its interaction with the remainder of System X;

9) from the integration records of R19 and by comparison with the records of earlier releases, make quality and error rate models and obtain a prognosis for R19 and an improved estimate for R20 correction activity; integration and error rate models have not been considered in the present paper but have been extensively studied by the present author and by others [85];

10) assess the business consequences of, on the one hand, a slippage of one or two years in the release of ITS and on the other, a poor quality, poor performance release with a slippage of, say, some months (due to acceptable work rate but excessive growth);

11) in the absence of positive indication of a potential for major deviations from previous dynamic characteristics or the existence of a genuine business need that is more pressing than the losses that could arise from a poor quality product, abandon the present plan;

12) instead redesign release 20 to yield R20'; a clean, well-structured, base on which to build an ITS release, R21';

13) tentatively release intervals of 9 months and 15 months are proposed for R20' and R21', respectively;

14) R21' should be a restricted release for installation in selected sites;

15) it would be followed after 1 year by a general release R22'.

h) Recommendations–Details: Assuming that the further investigation as per paragraphs 8 to 10 of Section V-B4g reinforces the conclusions reached, three releases would have to be defined. We outline here proposals for R20' and R21'. The third, R22' will be a clean-up but its content cannot be identified in detail until a feel for the performance and general

quality of R21' has developed. The detailed analysis is left as an exercise to the reader.

The inherent problem in the design of the ITS release is the fact that the component has a size almost twice the maximum recommended incremental growth. Moreover, with the possible exception of its telecommunications support (Table III, item 3c), none of the component subsystems would receive usage exposure in the absence of the others. Thus a clean ITS release cannot be achieved except by releasing the component in one fell swoop. Similarly, dynamic storage management (DSM) is exposed to user testing only when the ITS facility is operational. We may, however, investigate whether the telecommunication facility (3c) will be usable in conjunction with the RJE facility, item 5. If it is, there will be some advantage to be gained by releasing 3c and 5 before the remainder of ITS and DSM.

Strictly speaking, Fig. 6(c) suggests that R20' should be a very low content release dedicated to system clean-up and restructuring. But the six preceding releases were achieved with average change rates and, from that point of view, did not stress the process. Thus, if R20' is also an average rate release, it should not cause problems, and it would seem a low risk strategy to include R20' in all those items as in Table IV, that will simplify the subsequent creation and integration of the excessively large ITS release.

The list, in priority order, of the new proposal shows a maximum incremental growth (159) well under average. It is a matter of some judgment and experience whether it would be wiser to delay item 3c with 58 new modules and item 5 with 57 to R21' thereby achieving the very low content release mentioned above. With the information before the reader it is not possible to resolve this question since additional information, at the very least answers to the questions raised in Section V-B4g, would be required. However, the desire to minimize R21' problems suggests the adoption of the complete plan as in Tables IV and V.

In assessing achievable release intervals for these releases, we base our estimates only on the module change count and change rate. The constraints on the present example do not permit the full analysis which would consider models based on Fig. 6(g), and take into account additional data. At 10 m/d change rate, implementation of the complete plan appears to require 253 days, say 9 months, whereas exclusion of 3c and 5 would reduce the predicted time required to some seven months. This recommendation cannot be taken further without more information of both a technical and a marketing nature, and an examination of other interval models. But the need for a clean base for R21' suggests adoption of the maximum acceptable release interval. R21' will now include, at the very least, ITS (except 3c) and DSM. This involves at least 920 new modules, an excessive growth that cannot usefully be further split between two or more releases. Assuming a change fraction of, say, 70 percent (Fig. 6(d)), of a system that is expected to contain 5911 modules, we estimate a total of 4200 changed modules in the release, many with multiple changes. Since there will now have been seven near average change-rate releases, it seems possible to plan for a change rate of 15–20 m/d, yielding a potential release interval of under 9 months. That is, it would appear that, by adopting the new strategy, all of the original changes and additions could be achieved in about the same time, but much more reliably. More complete analysis, however, based on additional data, other models and taking into account the special nature of the releases might well lead to a recommendation to increase the combined release interval to, say, two years.

A further qualification must also be added. As proposed in the revised plan, R21' will still be a release with excessive incremental growth and is therefore likely to yield significant problems. The additional fact that the evidence indicates incomplete planning, reinforces concern and expectation of trouble ahead. It is therefore also recommended that R21' be announced as an experimental release for exposure to usage by selected users in a variety of environments. It would be followed after an interval of perhaps one year by an R22', a cleaned up system, suitable for further evolution.

i) Final comments: The preceding section has presented a critique of a plan, and outlined an alternative which is believed technically more sound. The case considered is based on a real situation, though in the absence of complete information details have had to be invented. But the details are not important since the objective has been to demonstrate a methodology. Software planning can and should be based on process and system measures and models, obtained and maintained as a continuing process activity. Plans must be related to dynamic characteristics of the process and system, and to the statistics of change. By rooting the planning process in *facts*, *figures* and *models*, alternatives can be quantitatively compared, decisions can be related to reality and risks can be evaluated. Software planning must no longer be based solely on apparent business needs and market considerations; on management's local perspective and intuition.

VI. CONCLUSION

This paper rationalizes the widely held view, first expressed in Garmisch [82], that there is an urgent need for a discipline of software engineering. This should facilitate the cost-effective planning, design, construction, and maintenance of effective programs that provide, and then continue to provide, valid solutions to stated (possibly changing) problems, or satisfactory implementations of (possibly changing) computer applications.

Following a brief discussion of the nature of computer usage and of the programs, the paper introduced the new SPE classification that addresses the essential evolutionary nature of various types of programs and establishes the existence of a determining specification as the criterion for nonevolution.

In the subsequent discussion of the concepts, significance and phases of the program life cycle, no details of life-cycle planning and management models, as such, have been included. In particular, we have not here discussed cost, re-

source, and reliability models [83]–[85]. Approaches to process modeling based on continuous models [73], [75] have also not been included, nor has the vital topic of software complexity [86]–[89].

Recognizing the intrinsic nature of program change, the laws that appear to govern the dynamics of the evolution process were introduced. Among their other implications, the laws indicate that project plans must be related to dynamic characteristics of the process and system, and to the statistics of change. By rooting the planning process in facts, figures, and models, alternatives can be quantitatively compared, decisions can be related to reality and risks can be evaluated. Software planning must no longer be based solely on apparent business needs and market considerations; on management's local perspective and intuition. To illustrate this, we have included a brief example of the application of evolution dynamics models to release planning.

Many of the concepts and techniques presented in this paper could find wide applications outside the specific area of software systems, in other industries, and to social and economic systems. Unfortunately that theme cannot be pursued here.

ACKNOWLEDGMENT

First and foremost, thanks must be extended to L. A. Belady, a close collaborator for almost ten years. Many others, particularly colleagues and associates at ALMSA, IBM, Imperial College, and WG 2.3 have contributed through their comments, questions, critique, and original thoughts. All of them deserve and receive the author's grateful acknowledgments and thanks for their individual and collective contributions. The author would like to single out Prof. W. M. Turski for the major contribution he made on his recent visit to London. Also, sincere thanks to Dr. G. Benyon-Tinker, Dr. P. G. Harrison, and Dr. C. Jones for their detailed and constructive criticism of an early draft of this paper and R. Bailey for his artistic support. Finally, the author would like to acknowledge the constant support of his wife, without which neither the work itself nor this paper would have been possible.

REFERENCES

[1] J. Goldberg, Ed., in *Proc. Symp. High Cost of Software* (Naval Post-grad. School, Monterey, CA). Menlo Park, CA: SRI, 1973, 138 pp.

[2] M. M. Lehman, "The environment of design methodology," Keynote Address, in *Proc. Symp. Formal Design Methodology*, T. A. Cox, Ed. (Cambridge, England), Apr. 1979. Harlow, England: STL Ltd., 1980, pp. 18–38.

[3] ——, "The software engineering environment," Infotech State of the Art Rep., "Structured software development," P. J. L. Wallis, Ed., vol. 2, pp. 147–163, 1979.

[4] W. A. Wulf, "Languages and structured programs," in *Current Trends in Programming Methodology*, R. T. Yeh, Ed. Englewood Cliffs, NJ: Prentice-Hall, 1977, pp. 33–60.

[5] L. A. Belady, Ed., *Proc. IEEE Special Issue on Software Engineering*, vol. 68, Sept. 1980.

[6] B. W. Boehm "Software engineering," *IEEE Trans. Comput.*, vol. C-25, pp. 1226–1241, Dec. 1976.

[7] W. M. Turski, *Computer Programming Methodology*. London, England: Heyden, 1978, 208 pp.

[8] B. W. Boehm, "Software engineering—As it is," in *Proc. 4th Int. Conf. Software Engineering* (Munich, Germany), pp. 11–21, Sept. 1979. (IEEE Cat. no. 79CH1479-5C.)

[9] L. A. Belady and M. M. Lehman, "Characteristics of large systems," in *Research Directions in Software Technology*, P. Wegner, Ed. Cambridge, MA: M.I.T. Press, 1979, part I, ch. 3, pp. 106–142 (sponsored by the Tri-Services Committee of DoD); and in *Proc. Conf. Research Directions in Software Technology* (Brown University, Providence, RI), Oct. 10–12, 1977.

[10] M. M. Lehman, "Programs, cities, students—Limits to growth?" Inaugural Lecture, May 14, 1974, *ICST Inaugural Lecture Series*,

vol. 9, pp. 211–229, 1970–1974; and in *Programming Methodology*, D. Gries, Ed. New York: Springer-Verlag, 1979, pp. 42–69.

[11] ——, "On understanding laws, evolution and conservation in the large program life-cycle," *J. Syst. Software*, vol. 1, no. 3, pp. 213–232, 1980.

[12] W. M. Turski, "Report on an SRC-sponsored visit to Imperial College," Dep. Computing, Imperial College of Science and Technology, Univ. of London, London, England, Oct. 1979, 2 pp.

[13] F. L. Bauer, H. Partsch, P. Pebber, and H. Wessner, "Notes on the project-CIP: An outline of a transformation system," TUM-INFO-7729, Tech. Univ. Munich, 67 pp, 1977.

[14] J. Darlington, "Programming transformation: An introduction and survey," *Comput. Bull.*, ser. 2, no. 22, pp. 22–24, Dec. 1979.

[15] H. A. Simon, *The Sciences of the Artificial*. Cambridge, MA: M.I.T. Press, 1969, 123 pp.

[16] R. A. Demillo, R. J. Lipton, and A. J. Perlis, "Social processes and proofs of theorems and programs," *Commun. Ass. Comput. Mach.*, vol. 22, no. 5, pp. 271–280, May 1979; and no. 11, pp. 621–630, Nov. 1979.

[17] C. A. R. Hoare, "Review of a paper by Demillo, Lipton and Perlis: 'Social processes and proofs of theorems and programs,'" *ACM Comput. Rev.*, vol. 22, no. 8, rev. no. 34897, p. 324, Aug. 1979.

[18] E. W. Dijkstra, "A constructive approach to the problem of program correctness," *Nordisk Tidsrift for Informations. Bahandling*, Sweden, vol. 8, pp. 174–186, 1969.

[19] C. A. R. Hoare, "An axiomatic basis for computer programming," *Commun. Ass. Comput. Mach.*, vol. 12, no. 10, pp. 576–583, Oct. 1969.

[20] D. L. Parnas, "On the criteria to be used in decomposing systems into modules," *Commun. Ass. Comput. Mach.*, vol. 15, no. 12, pp. 1053–1058, Dec. 1972.

[21] N. Wirth, "Program development by stepwise refinement," *Commun. Ass. Comput. Mach.*, vol. 14, no. 4, Apr. 1971, pp. 221–227.

[22] E. W. Dijkstra, "Notes on structured programming," in *Structured Programming*, O. J. Dahl, E. W. Dijkstra, and C. A. R. Hoare, Eds. New York: Academic Press, 1972, pp. 1–81.

[23] M. A. Jackson, *Principles of Program Design*. London, England: Academic Press, 1975, 299 pp.

[24] N. Wirth, "The module: A system structuring facility in high-level programming languages," in *Proc. Symp. Programming Languages and Programming Methods* (Sydney, Austral.), J. Tobias, Ed. Lucas Hts., New South Wales: AAEC, 1979.

[25] B. Liskov and S. Zilles, "An introduction to formal specification of data abstraction," in *Current Trends in Programming Methodology*, vol. 1, *Software Specification and Design*, R. T. Yeh, Ed. Englewood Cliffs, NJ: Prentice-Hall, 1977, pp. 1–32.

[26] C. Jones, *Software Development—A Rigorous Approach*, Englewood Cliffs, NJ: Prentice-Hall, 1980, 400 pp.

[27] M. Shaw, "The impact of abstraction concerns on modern programming languages," this issue, pp. 1119–1130.

[28] M. M. Lehman, "The funnel—A functional channel," Imperial College, Dep. Computing, Univ. of London, Res. Rep. 77/29, July 1977, 14 pp.; and *IBM Tech. Disclosure Bull.*, 1976.

[29] O. J. Dahl, E. W. Dijkstra, and C. A. R. Hoare, *Structured Programming*. New York: Academic Press, 1972, 220 pp.

[30] R. C. Linger, and H. D. Mills, "On the development of large, reliable programs," in *Current Trends in Programming Methodology*, vol. 1, *Software Specification and Design*, R. T. Yeh, Ed. Englewood Cliffs, NJ: Prentice-Hall, 1977, pp. 120–139.

[31] M. M. Lehman, "OS-VS2-MVS long range prognosis," Private communication, MML-104, 13 pp. Apr. 15, 1975.

[32] T. A. Dolotta and J. R. Mashey, "An introduction to the programmer's workbench," in *Proc. 2nd Int. Conf. Software Engineering* (San Francisco, CA) Oct. 1976. (IEEE Cat. no. 76CH-1125-4C, Oct. 1976, pp. 164–168.)

[33] A. F. Hutchings, R. W. McGuffin, A. E. Elliston, B. R. Trauter, and P. N. Westmacott, "CADES—Software engineering in Practice," *Proc. 4th Int. Conf. Software Engineering* (Munich, Germany), Sept. 1979. (IEEE Cat. no. 79CH-1479-5C, Sept. 1979, pp. 136–152.)

[34] J. N. Buxton, "Requirements for ADA programming support environment—STONEMAN," U.S. Dep. of Defense, Washington, DC, 44 pp., Feb. 1980.

[35] T. E. Bell, D. C. Bixler, and M. E. Dyer, "An extendable approach to computer-aided software requirements engineering," *IEEE Trans. Software Eng.*, vol. SE-3, pp. 49–59, Jan. 1977.

[36] M. W. Alford, "Software requirements engineering methodology (SREM) at the age of two," in *Proc. COMPSAC 78*, pp. 332–339, Nov. 1978. (IEEE Cat. no. 78CH1338-3C.)

[37] K. Heninger, "Specifying requirements for complex systems: New techniques and their application," in *Proc. Specification of Reliable Software Conf.*, pp. 1–14, Mar. 1979. (IEEE Cat. no. 74CH1401-9C.)

[38] R. T. Yeh, and P. Zave, "Specifying software requirements," this

issue, pp. 1077–1085.

[39] W. P. Stevens, G. J. Myers, and L. L. Constantine, "Structured design," *IBM Syst. J.*, vol. 13, no. 2, pp. 115–139, 1974.

[40] G. J. Myers, *Composite/Structured Design*. New York: Van Nostrand Reinhold, 1978, 134 pp.

[41] D. T. Ross, and K. E. Schoman, "Structuring analysis for requirements definition," *IEEE Trans. Software Eng.*, vol. SE-3, pp. 6–15, Jan. 1977.

[42] ——, "Structured analysis (SA): A language for communicating ideas," *IEEE Trans. Software Eng.*, vol. SE-3, pp. 16–33, Jan. 1977.

[43] T. DeMarco, *Structured Analysis and System Specification*. New York: Yourdon Press, 1978, 352 pp.

[44] B. W. Liskov and V. Berzins, "An appraisal of program specifications," in *Research Directions in Software Technology*, P. Wegner, Ed. Cambridge, MA: M.I.T. Press, 1979, Part 2.1, ch. 7, pp. 106–142 (sponsored by the Tri-Services Committee of DoD); and in *Proc. Conf. Research Directions in Software Technology* (Brown University, Providence, RI), pp. 276–301, Oct. 10–12, 1977.

[45] J. N. Buxton, and E. Randell, Eds., "Software engineering techniques," Rep. Conf. sponsored by the NATO Science Committee (Rome, Italy), Oct. 1969. (Brussels, 164 pp, 1970.)

[46] P. Van Leer, "Top-down development using a program design language," *IBM Syst. J.*, vol. 15, no. 2, pp. 155–170, 1976.

[47] Teichroew and E. A. Hershey III, "PSL/PSA: A computer-aided technique for structured documentation and analysis of information processing systems," *IEEE Trans. Software Eng.*, vol. SE-3, pp. 41–48, Jan. 1977.

[48] R. T. Yeh, "Current trends in programming methodology," vol. 1, *Software Specification and Design*. Englewood Cliffs, NJ: Prentice-Hall, 1977, 275 pp.

[49] T. A. Cox, Ed., *Proc. Symp. Formal Design Methodology* (Cambridge, England), 1977. Harlow, England: STL Ltd., 1980, 350 pp.

[50] F. W. Zurcher and B. Randell, "Iterative multi-level modelling—A methodology for computer system design," in *Proc. IFIP Congr. 1968* (Edinburgh, Scotland), pp. D138–142, Aug. 1968.

[51] L. Peters, "Software design engineering," this issue, pp. 1085–1093.

[52] G. H. Swaum, *Top-Down Structured Design Techniques*. New York: Petrocelli Books, 1978, 140 pp.

[53] E. Miller and W. E. Howden, Eds., "Tutorial: Software testing and validation technique," *IEEE Comput. Soc.*, 423 pp., 1978. (IEEE Cat. no. EHO-138-8.)

[54] J. B. Goodenough and L. M. Clement, "Software quality assurance testing and validation," this issue, pp. 1093–1098.

[55] J. B. Goodenough and S. L. Gerhart, "Toward a theory of test data selection," *IEEE Trans. Software Eng.*, vol. SE-1, pp. 156–173, June 1975.

[56] L. A. Belady and P. M. Merlin, "Evolving parts and relations—A model of system families," IBM Res. Rep. RC6677, 14 pp, Aug. 1977.

[57] M. M. Lehman and L. H. Putnam, Eds., "Software phenomenology, working papers of the (first) software life cycle management workshop (Airlie, VA), Aug. 1977. Fort Belvoir, VA: ISRAD/AIRMICS, Computer Systems Command, U.S. Army, Dec. 1977, 682 pp.

[58] V. R. Basili, E. Ely, and D. Young, Eds., "Second software life-cycle management workshop, 21–22 Aug. 1978 (Atlanta, GA)," 220 pp., Dec. 1978. (IEEE Publ. no. 78CH1390-4C.)

[59] C. P. Felix and C. E. Walston, "A method of programming measurement and estimation," *IBM Syst. J.*, vol. 16, no. 1, pp. 54–73, 1977.

[60] L. H. Putnam and R. W. Wolverton, "Quantitative management—Software cost estimating," in *Proc. Comp. Soc. 77, IEEE Computer Software and Applications Conf. (Tutorial)*, 326 pp., Nov. 1977. (IEEE cat. no. EH0129-7.)

[61] L. H. Putnam, "The influence of the time-difficulty factor in large scale development" in *Proc. Software Phenomenology Working Papers of the (first) Software Life-cycle Management Workshop* (Airlie VA), Aug. 1977. Fort Belvoir, VA: ISRAD/AIRMICS, Computer Systems Command, U.S. Army, Dec. 1977, pp. 307–312.

[62] B. W. Boehm, and R. W. Wolverton, "Software cost modelling—Some lessons learned," in *Proc. 2nd Software Life-cycle Management Workshop*, Aug. 21–22, 1978 (Atlanta, GA) pp. 129–132, Dec. 1978. (IEEE Publ. no. 78CH1390-4C.)

[63] F. N. Parr, "An alternative to the Rayleigh curve model for software development effort," *IEEE Trans. Software Eng.*, vol. SE-6, May 1980, pp. 291–296.

[64] S. C. Aron, *The Program Development Process, Part II The Programming Team*. Reading, MA: Addison-Wesley, 1980.

[65] M. Halstead, *Elements of Software Science*. New York: Elsevier, 1977, 127 pp.

[66] A. Fitzsimmons and T. Love, "A review and evaluation of software science," *Computing Survey*, vol. 10, no. 1, pp. 3–18, Mar.

1978.

[67] D. B. Johnston and A. M. Lister, "Software science and student programs," *Software: Pract. and Exp.*, vol. 10, no. 2, pp. 159–1960, Feb. 1980.

[68] M. M. Lehman, "The programming process," IBM Res. Rep. RC2722, p. 47, Dec. 1969.

[69] L. A. Belady and M. M. Lehman, "Programming system dynamics or the meta-dynamics of systems in maintenance and growth," IBM Res. Rep. RC3516, 30 pp, Sept. 1971.

[71] M. M. Lehman, "Programming systems growth dynamics," infotech State of the Art Lectures, no. 18, "Computer reliability," State of the Art Lectures, no. 20, pp. 391–412, 1974.

[72] L. A. Belady and M. M. Lehman, "A model of large program development," *IBM Syst. J.*, vol. 15, no. 3, pp. 225–252, 1976.

[73] J. S. Riordan, "An evolution dynamics model" in *Proc. Software Phenomenology, Working Papers of the (first) Software Life-cycle Management Workshop* (Airlie, VA) Aug. 1977," ISRAD/AIRMICS, Computer Systems Command, U.S. Army, (Fort Belvoir, VA), pp. 339–360, Dec. 1977.

[74] J. K. Patterson and M. M. Lehman, "Preliminary CCSS systems analysis using evolution dynamics techniques," in *Proc. Software Phenomenology, Working Papers of the (first) Software Life-cycle Management Workshop* (Airlie, VA), Aug. 1977, ISRAD/AIRMICS, Computer Systems Command, U.S. Army, Fort Belvoir, VA, Dec. 1977, pp. 324–332.

[75] M. Woodside, "A mathematical model for the evolution of software," *J. Syst. Software*, vol. 1, no. 3, 1980.

[76] C. K. S. Chon Hok Yuen, "A Phenomenology of Program Maintenance and Evolution," Ph.D. dissertation, Dep. Computing, Imperial College of Science and Technology, Univ. of London, London, England, to be published.

[77] M. M. Lehman, "Programs, programming and the software life-cycle," CCD-ICST Res. Rep. 80/6, 48 pp. Apr. 1980.

[78] ——, "Human thought and action as an ingredient of system behavior," in *Encyclopaedia of Ignorance*, Duncan and Weston-Smith, Eds., Oxford, England: Pergamon Press, 1977, pp. 347–354.

[79] ——, "Laws of program evolution—Rules and tools for programming management," Infotech State of the Art Conf., "Why software projects fail," pp. 11/1–11/25, Apr. 9–11, 1978.

[80] M. M. Lehman and F. N. Parr, "Program evolution and its impact on software engineering," in *Proc. 2nd Int. Conf. Software Engineering* (San Francisco, CA), pp. 350–357, Oct. 1976. (IEEE Cat. no. 76CH1125-4C.)

[81] F. P. Brooks, *The Mythical Man-Month—Essays on Software Engineering*. Reading, MA: Addison-Wesley, 1975, 195 pp.

[82] P. Naur and B. Randell, Eds., "Software engineering: Report on a conference sponsored by the NATO science Committee," (Garmisch, Germany), Oct. 7–11, 1968. Brussels, Belgium: Scientific Affairs Division, NATO, 1969, 231 pp.

[83] B. W. Boehm, J. R. Brown, and M. Lipow, "Quantitative evaluation of software quality," in *Proc. 2nd Int. Conf. Software Engineering* (San Francisco, CA), pp. 592–605, Oct. 1976. (IEEE Cat. no. 76CH1124-4C.)

[84] F. N. Parr and M. M. Lehman, "State of the art survey of software reliability," Dep. Computing, Imperial College, London, England, Res. Rep. 77/15, 102 pp.

[85] J. D. Musa, "The measurement and management of software reliability," this issue, pp. 1131–1143.

[86] T. J. McCabe, "A complexity Measure," *IEEE Trans. Software Eng.*, vol. 2, pp. 308–320, Dec. 1976.

[87] M. M. Lehman, "Complexity and complexity change of a large applications program," ERO Research Proposal, 32 pp, Mar. 1977.

[88] L. A. Belady, "Software complexity," in *Proc. Software Phenomenology, Working Papers of the (first) Software Life Cycle Management Workshop* (Airlie VA) Aug. 1977. Fort Belvoir, VA: ISRAD/AIRMICS, Computer Systems Command, U.S. Army, Dec. 1977, pp. 371–384.

[89] E. T. Chen, "Program complexity and programmer productivity," *IEEE Trans. Software Eng.*, vol. SE-1. pp. 187–193, May 1978.

[90] M. E. Fagan, "Design and code inspections to reduce errors in program development," *IBM Syst. J.*, vol. 15, no. 3, pp. 182–211, 1976.

[91] C. B. Jones, "The role of formal specifications in software development," in *Proc. Infotech State of the Art Conf. on Life-cycle Management*, 1980.

[92] H. Kopetz, F. Lohnert, and W. Merker, "An outline of project MARS—maintainable real-time system," Technische Universitat, Berlin, Germany, Bericht 79-09, 19 pp, July 1979.

Introduction

Van Horn, E.C. "Software must evolve." In: Freeman, H., Lewis, P.M., II, eds., *Software engineering*, Academic Press, New York, NY, 1980.

In the following paper, Earl C. Van Horn turns the idea of evolution from a passive observation about the life cycle of a system into an active strategy. His title tells the story: the title is not "Software does evolve", but "Software *must* evolve." He discusses evolution in several contexts:

- As a technical strategy: "Evolution—née maintenance—is a fundamental technique of software engineering. It is potent for managing complexity, and essential for helping clients understand their needs."

- As a career path: "Software evolution should be considered to be where the action is, and to offer challenge, prestige, and rewards."

- As a bottom-line validation: "The most precious thing in software engineering is the program whose correctness and usefulness has been confirmed by actual service. We must learn how to preserve, reuse, and improve these jewels, and must reward those who do."

Van Horn did his Ph.D. research in computer system design at M.I.T. in 1966. In that year he also published jointly with Jack Dennis the often-cited paper "Programming semantics for multiprogrammed computations" (*Comm. ACM*, 9, 3 (March 1966), 143-155). (The ACM conference session at which that paper was first presented was chaired by another author in this Tutorial, Anatol Holt.)

Van Horn's interest in evolving systems arose during his work at SofTech, Inc., in the early 1970's, when he was in charge of enhancements and corrections to an on-line circuit analysis program. He discovered that the program had been worked on by people at every level of skill, from senior programmers to summer students. There was little computer support for the modification process; good results depended on personal familiarity with the system—"the human cross-reference listing."

He began to introspect on the process: What was he being asked to do? What tools or management methods would help him? He was influenced by the ideas of Douglas Ross, a founder of SofTech, Inc., on incremental system development and the iterative review of specifications. (See, for example, Douglas Ross and Kenneth Schoman, Jr., "Structured Analysis for requirements definition," *IEEE Trans. Software Engineering*, SE-3, 1 (January 1977), 6-15.)

He developed his ideas further while working on software engineering methodology for Digital Equipment Corporation in the late 1970's, and he was ready to express them when he was invited to prepare a presentation for a workshop to be held at Albany, New York, under the sponsorship of Rensselaer Polytechnic Institute, the General Electric Company, and the National Science Foundation, in 1979. Philip Lewis, one of the organizers, told Van Horn on the telephone that the workshop theme was to be "Software engineering: a national issue." He knew immediately what his topic would be, and he gave Lewis the final title after less than a minute's thought.

After the presentation Van Horn worked through the summer in his spare time to create the written version that follows. His comprehensive bibliography highlights the fact that much has been published on the development phases of software and relatively little has been published on its operational phase. He told us: "I wanted to give the reader a sense of the managerial and engineering culture that gives rise to the problem, and why this culture exists." With this paper, Van Horn is helping turn that culture around.

SOFTWARE MUST EVOLVE

Earl C. Van Horn

Digital Equipment Corporation
Maynard, Massachusetts

INTRODUCTION

There is a tendency to think of a computer program as
something static -- something that does not change once it
correctly implements an intended function. In practice, however, programs are seldom static, particularly those that are
large and complex enough to be called software systems. As
long as a software system is used, one can expect a continual
flow of requests for its modification. Belady and Lehman
(1976) have codified this observation in their Law of Continuing Change:

> *"A system that is used undergoes continuing
> change until it is judged more cost effec-
> tive to freeze and re-create it."*

Moreover, the continual modification of a system often reduces its capacity to undergo further modification, so that
the day of freezing and re-creating arrives sooner rather than
later. The same authors have codified this phenomenon in
their Law of Increasing Entropy:

> *"The entropy of a system (its unstruc-
> turedness) increases with time, unless
> specific work is executed to maintain
> or reduce it."*

The re-creation of an existing system is always risky and
costly. The old system must remain in service, often for
years, while the new one is being created. If the old system
continues to be modified, the new one may be less satisfactory
than the old in some respects. If the old system is not modified, users may have to forego needed changes until the new
system is installed. When the new system is installed, errors
may be found in functions the old system performed correctly.
Although none of these problems are theoretically necessary,
their prevention is costly.

Is re-creation necessary? One way to avoid it would be to
repeal the Law of Continuing Change. It might be argued that

if our techniques for requirements analysis, design, and validation were only good enough, we would be able to get a software system right the first time, and not have to put up with continuing change. I do not believe this will happen very frequently in the foreseeable future, and in any case we cannot afford to wait. We must learn to live with the Law of Continuing Change.

Perhaps we can still avoid re-creation. If somehow we could learn to evolve systems rather than periodically re-create them, we could avoid the trauma of re-creation, or at least experience it less frequently.

There is hope that this evolutionary approach will succeed, because software evolution, i.e., the modification of existing software, has not received the research and engineering effort it deserves. I shall attempt to explain why software evolution has received so little attention, and shall mention some ways to aid and improve it. One way is to avoid the inappropriate connotations of the word "maintenance", which I am doing here by using the word "evolution". I want to encourage acceptance of evolution as the normal mode of software engineering, and encourage development of methods and tools for evolution.

A CRITIQUE OF "MAINTENANCE"

Maintenance Has Been Neglected

An important aspect of software engineering is concern for maintenance costs, that is, the costs of modifying a software product after it is placed in service. Maintenance costs can be a large fraction of the total cost of a software product, often larger than all other development costs combined [Boehm (1976); and Munson (1978)].

Nevertheless, little attention has been given to methods and tools for maintenance itself. Maintenance tends to be addressed indirectly, by creating better methods and tools for the other aspects of software development. To be specific, Figure 1 shows the typical stages in the sequential model of software development. All the activities in Figure 1 except maintenance have received considerable study, and the available literature reflects this. For example:

   o Most of the January 1977 issue of the *IEEE Transactions on Software Engineering* is devoted to requirements analysis. Formal languages, many of them processed by computer, are being developed to describe and analyze requirements [Teichroew and Hershey (1977); Ross (1977); Alford (1978); and Lamb et al. (1978)].

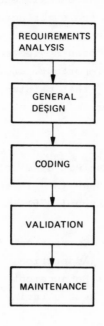

FIGURE 1. Sequential software development.

o Various methodologies and criteria for general design have been explained [Parnas (1972, 1979); Myers (1975); Jackson (1975); and White and Booth (1976)], and there are computer systems for describing and analyzing designs [Riddle et al. (1978); Hammond, Murphy, and Smith (1978); and Boyd and Pizzarello (1978)].

o There is advice on how to code for understand-ability [Kernighan and Plauger (1974)]. We are also encouraged to practice structured cod-ing [Dijkstra (1968)] and told of the benefits of top-down programming, chief programmer teams, and the like [Mills (1975); Baker (1972); and Brooks (1975)].

o Validation includes both testing and verifica-tion. There are techniques for test case gen-eration [Goodenough and Gerhart (1975); Clarke (1976); and Ramamoorthy, Ho, and Chen (1976)], symbolic execution [King (1975); Boyer, Elspas, and Levitt (1975); and Clarke (1976)], auto-mated test execution [Panzl (1978)], informal inspections [Fagan (1974); and Yourdon (1977)], and formal proofs of correctness [Gries (1976); and Good, London, and Bledsoe (1975)].

In contrast to the other topics listed in Figure 1, there is not a lot of literature on maintenance [Boehm (1976)]. What little there is tends to be descriptive rather than con-

structive, i.e., it discusses maintenance and how to manage
it, but not methods and tools for actually doing maintenance
[Munson (1978); and Swanson (1976)].

Why has maintenance been neglected? Maintenance costs
are acknowledged to be important, and researchers justify
their projects by saying that maintenance costs will be reduced, but few are eager to study maintenance directly.

What is Maintenance?

To understand the neglect of maintenance, let us first
understand what maintenance is. In an analysis slightly different from that of Swanson (1976), maintenance has four
purposes:

> Correction
>
> Adaptation
>
> Enhancement
>
> Restructuring

Correction is modification to fix bugs, that is, to make
the software function as intended. Whether or not the intended function is specified in writing, correction involves
only conformity to that function. It has nothing to do with
whether the intended function meets the client's real needs.

Adaptation is modification because of a change in supporting hardware or software. For example, if a file access
entry in an operating system has been changed to return more
error codes, modification to recognize the new codes would
be adaptive maintenance. For another example, a decision to
standardize on a particular data base management package would
initiate adaptive maintenance in those applications not currently using the package. Ideally, adaptive maintenance
should not affect user interfaces.

A large fraction of what is considered maintenance in
many organizations is enhancement, which is modification to
meet new or unrecognized user requirements. Enhancement can
be as simple as a change in a tax rate, or as complex as the
installation of a sub-system to monitor the progress of orders
in a factory.

Finally, maintenance can be done to restructure the software, i.e., to improve its internal structure while preserving
its external behavior. One reason for restructuring is to
make the current function easier to validate; for example,
one might rewrite an operating system's kernel so that it can
be proved secure. Restructuring can also make a system more
understandable, and hence easier to maintain in the future.

What's in the Word "Maintenance"?

All software maintenance is done for one or more of the
foregoing purposes, but no such activity is really maintenance. In standard English, "maintenance" means to restore
something to its original, satisfactory condition, but that

is not the objective of software maintenance [Mills (1976); and Munson (1978)]. Unlike spark plugs or house paint, software does not wear out. Consequently, software maintenance is never restorative, but is always aimed at producing something better than the original.

Software maintenance is in fact engineering, i.e., re-engineering of an existing product for one of the four purposes mentioned above. If the person who maintains your television set were to do the kind of "maintenance" that software maintainers do, he would be able to re-design the circuitry to correct an interference problem or add a split screen capability for viewing two channels at once.

The fact that software "maintenance" is not really maintenance is not in itself a serious problem. It simply means that the term "maintenance" is jargon for the modification of software already in service. Jargon is common in technical fields; if everybody knows what a term means, there should be no difficulty. In fact, most software people do understand that software maintenance is the activity explained in the preceding section.

But that is not the whole story. Although software people have dropped the standard denotation of "maintenance", they generally have retained its connotations. In English, "maintenance" connotes an activity that requires relatively less skill than the design of the object being maintained. For example, it takes a roomful of people with college degrees to design a television set, but one can learn to maintain a television set by taking a correspondence course. By connotation, a "maintenance man" is someone with relatively low skill, relatively low pay, and relatively low prestige. Of course, there is no reason why maintenance work is necessarily low in skill, pay, or prestige; for example, physicians are basically maintenance men for the human body. Nevertheless, the word does have those connotations.

THE IMPORTANCE OF SOFTWARE EVOLUTION

In order to avoid the inappropriate negative connotations of the word "maintenance", I shall instead use the word "evolution" to refer to the modification of existing software [Belady and Lehman (1976); and Belady (1979)]. It is easy to accept the idea that software evolution is important, challenging and rewarding -- certainly more so than mere maintenance.

The Growth of Code in Service

Today, software evolution is economically the most important aspect of software development. As mentioned previously, the cost of evolving a system after it is in service is

typically greater than all other life-cycle costs combined.
I suspect the majority of programmers are employed to evolve
software already in service, and no doubt a comparable portion of development computer resources are used for such
evolution. Furthermore, evolution can be expected to become
more important in the future, because the amount of code
available for evolution will increase as new programs are
placed in service faster than old ones are retired [Boehm
(1976)].

In the future, however, software evolution will be even
more important than the growth of code in service might indicate, because it is becoming more difficult for the first
release of a system to meet all of a client's needs. There
are two reasons for this.

The Growth of Functional Complexity

First, software systems are becoming more complex, because computer hardware is becoming faster and cheaper, and
because clients are demanding more functions, better interfaces, and more fault tolerance. This increasing complexity
will continually challenge the technology of software creation, so we must recognize that even our most sophisticated
techniques for design, coding, and validation may not be equal
to the task of getting a system right on the first try. We
must be prepared to develop a system in stages, all but the
first of which is an evolution of its predecessor [Basili and
Turner (1975)].

Creation of new software in stages is done today; the
stages are sometimes called base levels. Each base level is
both a technical and a management checkpoint. It proves feasibility of a portion of the design, and provides meaningful
measurement of progress in an activity that is notoriously
difficult to measure. Thus even the creation of new software
can best be treated as an evolutionary process, and the increasing complexity of applications will force us to rely on
this technique more.

The Evolution of Client Needs

There is a second, more fundamental reason why it is difficult to meet all a client's needs on the first try. Even
if we were able to meet a client's initially perceived requirements correctly (perhaps by evolution through base
levels), a client's first set of requirements is seldom his
ultimate.

Consequently, a new and complex computer application must
be developed in stages that the client can use and react to.
At the beginning of this process, the client will undoubtedly
understand his needs in terms of the automation of today's
manual activities. Once that automation exists, the client's

work flow, division of labor, costs, and even his products or services will change as a result of the new tool. In this new environment he will perceive further needs, and these will lead to changes and additions to his computer tool, which will in turn give rise to another environment, etc.

The most advanced requirements analysis technique cannot be relied on to discover the client's ultimate computer tool, because the client himself usually has no conception of this tool. Even if the requirements analyst has enough application knowledge to be able to imagine the ultimate tool, the proposal for it would no doubt be impossible to sell, because it would be so far from the client's experience.

Because of the complex interaction between a client's needs and his computer tools, and because it is usually too costly to create a new software system every time a client perceives new needs, the software for a new and complex application must evolve as the client's perception of his needs evolves.

Notice how the connotations of the word "maintenance" could be misleading if applied to the above activities. Maintenance (in the English sense) is necessary only because our physical products are not perfect. If a product is made of better materials or designed for longer service, it will require less maintenance. Maintenance is a necessary anomaly -- something one should not have to do.

How wrong it would be to conclude that software evolution is something one should not have to do. Evolution -- née maintenance -- is a fundamental technique of software engineering. It is potent for managing complexity, and essential for helping clients understand their needs.

SOFTWARE EVOLUTION TODAY

Nevertheless, the practice of software evolution leaves much to be desired. As mentioned in the discussion of "maintenance", there has been little research on evolution itself. There is lots of advice on how to design evolvable software, but little on how to actually do evolution.

Most of the tools available to evolvers are hand-me-downs from software creators. Although programming library systems are becoming more popular [Baker (1975); Glasser (1978); and Bauer and Birchall (1978)], and cross-references of linker symbols are common enough, there is rarely a system cross-reference that contains the names of include files and macros, for example. Information retrieval technology has not been vigorously applied to the problem of obtaining information about the structure, code, and documentation of an existing software system. Yet the quality of software evolution depends critically on how well the evolver understands the system he is evolving. We are not doing everything we could to facilitate that understanding.

Perhaps because of the negative connotations of "maintenance", software evolution is not well rewarded. It is not well paid, nor is it considered challenging or prestigious. Junior programmers are assigned to do evolution, partly because it is believed that a low skill level is required, and partly because senior programmers want to do creation and will change employers rather than do "maintenance".

Creation is considered to be where the action is. For example, I know an environmental technology firm that had trouble hiring good programmers to evolve their software. But when the firm decided to create a replacement for one of their systems, they had no trouble hiring good people to do that. One factor in the decision to undertake a creation project was that it seemed the only way to attract better programmers into the organization.

There is something like a Peter Principle [Peter and Hull (1970)] at work in software evolution. Once a programmer has become skilled at evolution, or even at evolving a particular system, he moves to the next creation project that comes along, leaving new people and marginal performers to tend to the evolution of existing systems.

With all these negative factors at work, is it any wonder that software evolution today is so costly and problematical?

SOFTWARE EVOLUTION TOMORROW

Evolvability as a Goal of Evolution

One way of improving software evolution is to use evolvability as a design criterion, and thus develop systems whose structure facilitates their evolution. Many current techniques, such as information hiding [Parnas (1972)], minimization of interfaces [Myers (1975)], and structured coding [Dijkstra (1968)], do make evolution easier, but they are applied mostly during software creation, and not often during evolution.

It is not enough merely to create evolvable software; we must preserve evolvability during evolution. In order to do this we must have the courage to restructure a system when the old structure is inappropriate. For example, if a new command language construct is best handled by providing an extra parameter to the lexical analyzer, we must make that change, even though it means changing and re-validating a dozen existing calls.

Software evolvers today are often under pressure to make changes quickly and with minimum risk to existing functions. Unfortunately these goals conflict with that of preserving evolvability by restructuring. Not every change will require restructuring, but when evolvers say that restructuring is necessary, they must be allowed to do it. Management must understand that an occasional delay in delivery of a change, and an occasional error introduced because of restructuring, are preferable to having patches accumulate like barnacles until excessive delay and risk accompany every change and a totally new system must be created. If occasional small delays and risks are accepted to preserve evolvability, the life of a system will be extended, perhaps indefinitely.

Once the techniques of evolution are in use, we can do more than simply preserve evolvability. If we know what constitutes an evolvable structure, and if we have the methods and tools to restructure a system, we can actually improve a system, i.e., we can evolve it so as to improve its evolvability. For example, if a system's data base manager and output spooler each has its own queue handler, the handlers could be replaced by a single queue handler. The common handler is more likely to be usable by the message dispatcher that will be added next year, and any queue handling improvements can be made and validated only once.

If evolvability can be improved by evolution, we need not be so concerned with having the very best structure when the software is created. Any flaws in structure can be healed as the software evolves.

Attitudes and Training for Evolution

As mentioned above, software creation is now considered to be where the action is, and to offer challenge, prestige, and rewards. Evolution is considered a necessary anomaly to correct deficiencies of creation. I advocate a reversal of our attitudes toward these two activities. Software evolution should be considered to be where the action is, and to offer challenge, prestige, and rewards. Creation should be considered a necessary anomaly to get the evolutionary process started.

It may take several years for this change of attitudes to occur, but it must occur. Evolution is too important to be left to junior people; it requires the best programmers available. In a large system with complex parts and interactions, there are often many ways in which a change can be made. Choosing the right way requires knowledge of the system, skill in applying design criteria, and judgment to know when a restructuring must be done. Furthermore, because the system is in service, the evolver has a great responsibility: the work must be done correctly and must not disrupt current operations.

There is, of course, no better place for on-the-job training than the crucible of evolution. But a newcomer should not evolve alone. Evolution should be done by a senior and junior person working as a team. The senior has responsibility and teaches, while the junior accepts assignments and learns. When the junior has learned enough, he can take a tour of duty in creation, where he has a chance to try out some design principles and gain a greater appreciation for trade-offs. Later he will return to evolution, this time as a senior person giving guidance to yet another newcomer.

Tools for Evolution

Emphasis on evolution should yield better tools to support it. Software development, which consists of both creation and evolution, should be considered a computer application just like banking or process control. Its requirements should be analyzed, and maximum feasible computer power should be applied to support it. The resulting support system should use the best information retrieval technology to help developers understand the system being developed. For example, a support system could:

(a) Provide interactive browsing in code and documentation, with the aid of cross-reference information,

(b) Display only the kind of information desired, such as procedure headings but not procedure bodies,

(c) Draw diagrams showing the high-level structure of the system, providing additional detail as requested,

(d) Provide a graphical, interactive design language, in which the design is related to the code, and

(e) Keep track of the changes made by different programmers at different times.

A support system for evolution would include many features of current integrated development approaches [Dolotta and Mashey (1976); Davis and Vick (1978); Osterweil, Brown, and Stucki (1978); Bratman and Court (1975); and Irvine and Brackett (1977)]. More details of what such a system would be like may be found in proposals for one called SEER [Van Horn (1978)] and for one being developed at the University of Connecticut [White and Booth (1979)].

The Evolutionary Development Process

In a world in which evolution is considered the normal mode of software development, one will seldom see the development process diagrammed as in Figure 1. Instead, the process will be thought of in terms of the evolutionary model shown in Figure 2. Each interval of implementation is followed by engineering evaluation for such factors as correctness, performance, and quality of design. The product will be returned to implementation if it is unsatisfactory or if it is only a base level.

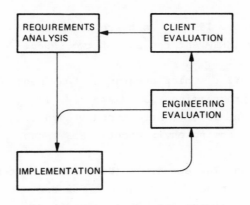

FIGURE 2. *Evolutionary Software Development.*

If a product passes the engineering evaluation, it is placed in service for the client. His evaluation is input to a requirements analysis activity, which will define the requirements for subsequent implementation. For each client the development process begins in the requirements analysis phase.

The time around the client loop can be anything from a few days to a year, and there may be several developments proceeding around the loop at different rates. An important function of a development support system is to help control multiple asynchronous developments. The time around the engineering loop may be as short as a day or two, but base levels should be introduced if necessary so that the engineering loop does not take more than a few months.

The familiar phases of general design, coding and validation can still exist, but they are details of implementation. The distinctions between them are less important than the distinctions shown in Figure 2. For example, coding and validation of a program can occur concurrently [Baker (1972); and Dijkstra (1976)].

CONCLUSION

For many years software people have bemoaned the fact that so little code is reused. But reuse is just evolution viewed from a different perspective: if software evolves, then the part that remains unchanged is reused. Methods, tools, and attitudes that favor evolution will therefore tend to encourage reuse, and so will help reduce duplication of effort.

The most precious thing in software engineering is the program whose correctness and usefulness has been confirmed by actual service [Belady (1979)]. We must learn how to preserve, reuse, and improve these jewels, and must reward those who do [Rawson (1978)].

REFERENCES

Alford, M. W. (Nov. 1978). Software requirements engineering methodology (SREM) at the age of two, *Proc. COMPSAC-78*, 332–339.

Baker, F. T. (1972). Chief programmer team management of production programming, *IBM Systems J. 11*, 56–73.

Baker, F. T. (June 1975). Structured programming in a production programming environment, *IEEE Trans. Software Eng. SE-1*, 241–252.

Basili, V. R., and Turner, A. J. (Dec. 1975). Iterative enhancement: A practical technique for software development, *IEEE Trans. Software Eng. SE-1*, 390–396.

Bauer, H. A., and Birchall, R. H. (Nov. 1978). Managing large scale software development with an automated change control system, *Proc. COMPSAC-78*, 13–17.

Belady, L. A. (Feb. 1979). Evolved software for the 80's, *Computer 12(2)*, 79–82.

Belady, L. A., and Lehman, M. M. (1976). A model of large program development, *IBM Systems J. 15(3)*, 225–252.

Boehm, B. W. (Dec. 1976). Software engineering, *IEEE Trans. Computers C-25*, 1226–1241.

Boyd, D. L., and Pizzarello, A. (July 1978). Introduction to the WELLMADE design methodology, *IEEE Trans. Software Eng. SE-4*, 276–282.

Boyer, R. S., Elspas, B., and Levitt, K. N. (June 1975). SELECT -- A formal system for testing and debugging programs by symbolic execution, *Proc. 1975 Int. Conf. Reliable Software, ACM SIGPLAN Notices 10*, 234–245.

Bratman, H., and Court, T. (May 1975). The software factory, *Computer 8(5)*, 28–37.

Brooks, F. P. (1975). "The Mythical Man-Month," Reading, Mass.: Addison-Wesley.

Clarke, L. A. (Sept. 1976). A system to generate test data and symbolically execute programs, *IEEE Trans. Software Eng. SE-2*, 215–222.

Davis, C. G., and Vick, C. R. (Nov. 1978). The software development system: Status and evolution, *Proc. COMPSAC-78*, 326–331.

Dijkstra, E. W. (March 1968). Go to statement considered harmful, *Commun. Assoc. Comput. Mach. 11*, 147–148.

Dijkstra, E. W. (1976). "A Discipline of Programming," Englewood Cliffs, N.J.: Prentice-Hall.

Dolotta, T. A., and Mashey, J. R. (Oct. 1976). An introduction to the programmer's workbench, *Proc. Second Int. Conf. Software Eng.*, 164–168.

Fagan, M. E. (Dec. 1974). "Design and Code Inspections and Process Control in the Development of Programs," Rep. TR 21.572, IBM System Dev. Div., Kingston, NY.

Glasser, A. L. (Nov. 1978). The evolution of a source code control system, *Proc. Software Quality and Assurance Workshop, Software Engineering Notes 3(5)*, 122-125.

Good, D. I., London, R. L., and Bledsoe, W. W. (March 1975). An interactive program verification system, *IEEE Trans. Software Eng. SE-1*, 59-67.

Goodenough, J. B., and Gerhart, S. L. (June 1975). Toward a theory of test data selection, *IEEE Trans. Software Eng. SE-1*, 156-173.

Gries, D. (Dec. 1976). An illustration of current ideas on the derivation of correctness proofs and correct programs, *IEEE Trans. Software Eng. SE-2*, 238-244.

Hammond, L. S., Murphy, D. L., and Smith, M. K. (Nov. 1978). A system for analysis and verification of a software design, *Proc. COMPSAC-78*, 42-47.

Irvine, C. A., and Brackett, J. W. (Jan. 1977). Automated software engineering through structured data management, *IEEE Trans. Software Eng. SE-3*, 34-40.

Jackson, M. A. (1975). "Principles of Program Design," New York: Academic Press.

Kernighan, B. W., and Plauger, P. J. (1974). "The Elements of Programming Style," New York: McGraw-Hill.

King, J. C. (June 1975). A new approach to program testing, *Proc. 1975 Int. Conf. Reliable Software, ACM SIGPLAN Notices 10*, 228-233.

Lamb, S. S., et al. (Nov. 1978). SAMM: A modeling tool for requirements and design specification, *Proc. COMPSAC-78*, 48-53.

Mills, H. D. (June 1975). How to write correct programs and know it, *Proc. 1975 Int. Conf. Reliable Software, ACM SIGPLAN Notices 10*, 363-370.

Mills, H. D. (Dec. 1976). Software development, *IEEE Trans. Software Eng. SE-2*, 265-273.

Munson, J. B. (Nov. 1978). Software maintainability: A practical concern for life-cycle costs, *Proc. COMPSAC-78*, 54-59.

Myers, G. J. (1975). "Reliable Software Through Composite Design," New York: Petrocelli/Charter.

Osterweil, L. J., Brown, J. R., and Stucki, L. G. (Nov. 1978). ASSET, A lifecycle verification and visibility system, *Proc. COMPSAC-78*, 30-35.

Panzl, D. J. (May 1978). Automatic revision of formal test procedures, *Proc. Third Int. Conf. Software Eng.*, 320-326.

Parnas, D. L. (Dec. 1972). On the criteria to be used in decomposing systems into modules, *Commun. Assoc. Comput. Mach. 15*, 1053-1058.

Parnas, D. L. (March 1979). Designing software for ease of extension and contraction, *IEEE Trans. Software Eng. SE-5*, 128-138.

Peter, L. J., and Hull, R. (1970). "The Peter Principle," New York: Bantam.

Ramamoorthy, C. V., Ho, Siv-Bun F., and Chen, W. T. (Dec. 1976). On the automated generation of program test data, *IEEE Trans. Software Eng. SE-2*, 293-300.

Rawson, E. B. (Feb. 1978). Standard software modules: Can we find the pot of gold?, *Digest of Papers COMPCON Spring 78*, 285-287.

Riddle, W. E., et al. (July 1978). Behavior modeling during software design, *IEEE Trans. Software Eng. SE-4*, 283-292.

Ross, D. T. (Jan. 1977). Structured analysis (SA): A language for communicating ideas, *IEEE Trans. Software Eng. SE-3*, 16-34.

Swanson, E. B. (Oct. 1976). The dimensions of maintenance, *Proc. Second Int. Conf. Software Eng.*, 492-497.

Teichroew, D., and Hershey, E. A. (Jan. 1977). PSL/PSA: A computer-aided technique for structured documentation and analysis of information processing systems, *IEEE Trans. Software Eng. SE-3*, 41-48.

Van Horn, E. C. (Nov. 1978). Software evolution using the SEER data base, *Proc. COMPSAC-78*, 147-152.

White, J. R., and Booth, T. L. (Oct. 1976). Towards an engineering approach to software design, *Proc. Second Int. Conf. Software Eng.*, 214-222.

White, J. R., and Booth, T. L. (July 1979). "Research in Advanced Support Systems for Software Development and Maintenance," Rep. CS-79-11, U. Conn. Computer Sci. Div., Storrs, Conn.

Yourdon, E. (1977). "Structured Walkthroughs," New York: Yourdon.

Introduction

Miller, J.C. "Structured retrofit." In: Parikh, G., ed., *Techniques of program and system maintenance*, Little, Brown and Company, 1982, 181-182.

The "Law of Increasing Complexity," as presented by Lehman in his paper in this Part, is

> As an evolving program is continually changed, its complexity, reflecting deteriorating structure, increases *unless work is done to maintain or reduce it.* (Emphasis added.)

The following paper, by J. Cris Miller, is the classic reference on how to put work into a system to combat its increasing complexity. It is reprinted from Parikh's pioneering collection *Techniques of program and system maintenance* (Little, Brown and Company, 1982). This is the story of how it came to be written.

In 1975-76, Miller and Parikh were working for a large midwestern retailer. Miller was in quality assurance, and Parikh was a senior programmer in applications, where less than 20% of the work was in new development. The undocumented, unstructured BAL and COBOL programs were almost impossible to maintain. The work was terribly depressing.

Management was weighing the alternatives: to rewrite the whole system or redo the worst parts. IBM was promoting "Improved Programming Technologies"—a collection of six techniques (structured programming, top-down development, development support libraries, HIPO, chief programmer teams, and structured walkthroughs). Improvements of 400% in development effectiveness and of 1600% in maintenance effectiveness were being touted. While these figures might have been overoptimistic, the potential of the new technologies was clear.

Miller had angrily denounced the articles in the December 1973 *Datamation* that announced a "revolution in programming." They seemed completely inapplicable to the world of existing software. But what if some means could be found to introduce the structured techniques into existing systems? Miller spent a month researching and interviewing in-house staff and in January 1976 issued the report "Improved Programming Technologies Retrofit: a study of the application of improved programming technologies to systems developed without improved programming technologies." Its premise was how to defer major rewritings of the system and extend its life. (Incidentally, management did decide to rewrite the system!)

Meanwhile, Parikh began to research maintenance. The first product was the report *Improved maintenance techniques* (Shetal Enterprises, Chicago, 1977, revised 1982). He then began to edit a book of readings, and commissioned Miller to contribute a short summary of his work. Miller had meanwhile changed jobs and was in the middle of a hectic consulting environment. Facing the deadline, Parikh decided to wait at Miller's house until he got this important article. Persistence paid off; he got the article at midnight.

Miller's paper was included among excerpts from Parikh's book, *Techniques of program and system maintenance*, which were published in *Computerworld* (December 10, 1979, IN DEPTH section) where Zvegintzov saw them. He too had been collecting material on maintenance. Zvegintzov contacted Weinberg, then chief scientist of Ethnotech, Inc., publisher of the first edition, and Weinberg introduced Zvegintzov to Parikh. Thus did the two editors of this Tutorial meet. When Parikh introduced Zvegintzov to Miller, they discovered that Zvegintzov had been a friend of Miller's younger brother in Berkeley 16 years earlier, and then lost touch. We bring you this story to illustrate what we meant in our Introduction to this Tutorial by a network and an invisible community.

In December 1979, Miller with Michael J. Lyons founded The Catalyst Corporation, Brookfield, IL, the first consulting company to specialize in the restructuring and redocumentation of existing systems, including the use of the Structuring Engine, a COBOL tool written by Miller to convert functional but unstructured COBOL into functionally equivalent structured COBOL. The Catalyst Corporation teaches and practices the Structured Retrofit which is described in the following paper. Further experience from The Catalyst Corporation will be found in two papers by Lyons and one by J.C. Miller cited in the annotated bibliography of this Tutorial.

Structured Retrofit

Jon C. (Cris) Miller

The structured methodologies are now fairly-well accepted for new systems development, although there are differences in interpretation from installation to installation. Their use has rarely been considered, and almost never accepted, in a maintenance environment. Structured Retrofit is the application of today's methodologies to yesterday's systems in order to support tomorrow's requirements.

The typical data processing department spends over half its staff on maintenance coding, maintenance compilations, and maintenance testing. What is needed is a departmental strategy which improves the probabilities of: quick satisfaction of random requests for maintenance, reduction in the number of programs designated incapable of cost-effective maintenance, and increases in the numbers of programs capable of supporting major enhancements without re-writes and extensive testing.

Consider creating a task force using:

1. chief programmer
2. librarian and development support libraries
3. programmer/analysts
4. top-down design
5. structured walk-throughs, and
6. structured programming

in a maintenance support capacity. The chief programmer leads the task force in seeking out candidate systems for Structured Retrofit. In advance, the team must have some scoring system for rating candidates. The system should include both subjective input from users and managers as well as objective data from the program's log. In this latter category, include the age of the program, the number of changes applied since its inception, and the time since last changed.

Each team member conducts some research, and presents the results to task force members in a walk-through fashion, as a basis for proceeding on program changes. Once the high-payoff candidates have been identified, the team members proceed to the next level of research, to be followed by another walk-through before making any changes to program code.

The priorities for changes within a program are:

1. standardization of visual properties (indentation, naming conventions, and paragraph prefixing, in particular)

2. use of libraries for inter-program communication (principally for record formats and standard formulas and algorithms)

3. isolation of I/O routines, with record counts, from in-line processing to one PERFORMable routine per file

4. elimination of PERFORM, GO TO, and ALTER ambiguities, uncertainties, and control pathology

5. elimination of overlapping PERFORM THRUs, and restriction of any residual THRUs to EXIT paragraphs

6. optimization (mechanically) of compiled code to improve program throughput, and

7. flowcharting (mechanically).

The validation mechanism is a file to file compare utility, which may be applied *at any time*. There is no need to complete all retrofit items, but merely to proceed as far as is cost-effective and time-effective. The methodology allows for resumption of retrofit activities at any time that its score on the priority system rises, from information supplied outside the task force.

There is one cardinal restriction: no member of the task force is authorized to make any change to eliminate any revealed error or to satisfy a request for program enhancement. This restriction eliminates time lost to user negotiation, and ensures that there is always a fall-back point, should the file to file compare utility reveal any insoluble problem. It also protects the user from losing an audit trail. The task force members do, of course, record any apparent bugs for review and authorized correction by the normal maintenance group.

The librarian, as in a development team, is the focal point of proven achievement, controlling the retrofit log, the test data used to validate the retrofit, and the mechanized documentation (library materials, flowcharts, and program listings). All migrate back to the normal maintenance area. The librarian may also have the task of researching the literature and marketing materials to find tools which speed up the retrofit activity.

This paper merely introduces the idea of a task force in a maintenance support function. It offers no objective data to support its position. The author contends, however, that existing software packages (library systems, convention enforcing programs, the SORT verb, report writers, structuring engines, and object code optimizers, as well as flowcharters) provide adequate tools for cost-effective retrofit. In closing, simply consider the potential savings from extending the mean time between conversions by months, years, or even decades by having code which can be reliably modified instead of scrapped. Remember that most code scrapped covers conditions undocumented in the old system, and forgotten in the specifications for its successor.

Introduction

Warnier, J.-D. "Reliability and maintenance of large systems." *DSSD (Data Structured Systems Development) User's Conference*/6, October 1981, Ken Orr & Associates, Topeka, KS.

The following paper discusses a long-term managerial and technical strategy for the evolution of systems. It is the third paper in the Tutorial to discuss the Warnier/Orr methodology. "Warnier/Orr" is a phrase based on the names of Jean-Dominique Warnier (pronounced VAH-NEE-AY), the author of this paper, and Ken Orr, whose company sponsored the User's Conference at which this paper was given. Two papers in Part II, by Parikh and Higgins, introduced the reader to the Warnier/Orr methodology as a key to understanding and to restructuring existing systems respectively. The following paper discusses the continued evolution and viability of systems designed with Warnier's methodology. It should be remembered that, though the Warnier/Orr methodology is an offshoot of Warnier's LCP/LCS methods, the methodology is not the same.

The four phases of Warnier's logical approach in developing a reliable large system are presented in the following simplified Warnier diagram:

Phases of Warnier's Logical Approach
{
LDR: Logical Definition of Results—Definition of end user needs

LCS: Logical Construction of (Data) Systems

LCE: "Logique de Conception de l'Exploitation"—Design of operations control

LCP: Logical Construction of Programs
}

According to Warnier, the maintenance problem is strongly linked to that of systems reliability. He describes the following three distinct functions, often confused by DP people:

- Correcting unreliable solutions.
- Integrating a new project (or application) into the existing system.
- Modifying existing systems and programs to satisfy the end-user's evolving needs.

Intriguingly Warnier's approach, when followed rigorously, totally eliminates the breakdowns of systems and programs. The reliable software largely eliminates the maintenance devoted to error corrections.

For enhancements and improvements of systems, he emphasizes that user-needs must be understood. Correct hierarchical diagrams developed during the LDR help understand user needs. The reliable logical file organization, determined by LCS, regardless of physical organization such as a data base management system or access method, helps the modification of existing systems and programs:

Logical design of operations or processes (LCE) ensures cohesion and correspondence between files, programs, and documentation.

Warnier also emphasizes the need for training in the four phases of his approach to accomplish development of reliable software. He also recommends user training in DP techniques, especially where logic is involved.

Warnier's rigorous, logical approach also allows smooth integration of a new application into an existing system. With this approach modification of an existing system becomes a systematic process. Warnier also warns regarding the proliferation of microcomputers:

I have grave misgivings when I see microcomputers invading schools and students being taught by teachers who are most interested in the technical aspects of the computer, but are not at all prepared to teach logical reasoning. As a result, we risk training a generation of brilliant handymen whose minds will be completely warped by bad habits learned since childhood. One will then see the lack of reliability of systems and her twin sister, maintenance, returning in force.

Warnier has been involved with data processing since 1956—first as an analyst and programmer and later as a teacher and writer. He was manager of a research group at the French computer company CII-Honeywell Bull until he retired at the end of 1981. The aim of his retirement, he told us, is: .

to diminish adminstrative work, to have more time to visit different countries where I am invited to help people using our logical approach, [and] to write new books: first, a programmed learning course on L.C.P., second, a book talking about the relationship between man and computer.

A variety of structured methodologies are advertised in manuals, books, and courses, and most claim to produce maintainable software. However, to our knowledge, none of the founders of these methodologies has probed as deeply as Warnier into the modification of systems and the integration of newly structured components into existing systems. In his books,

Warnier demonstrates the modifiability and modification of systems by examples and/or case studies. He has done pioneering work in "logical maintenance" of systems developed according to his methods. He argues that with his approach tedious maintenance disappears, and a highly specialized job of "systems modification specialist," requiring extensive training and a strong experience in computer science, emerges in its place. His work may be used as a model for developing "maintenance technologies" for other methodologies.

Warnier believes that software for the automation of some parts of the phases of his methodology can be built. His colleagues at CII-Honeywell Bull, Paris, are working on it.

Warnier's method has been successfully used in many countries in Europe, Asia, South America, and Africa. In North America, an offshoot of his method, Data Structured Systems Development, also called the Warnier/Orr Methodology, is becoming popular.

According to Warnier, the problems encountered are essentially management problems. It is necessary to get decisions from top management concerning the objectives of the firm and, consequently, the objectives of the DP system.

The other problem is teaching the people involved. There are two solutions for teaching DP people as well as end users:

- Teaching the students in schools and universities as is done in France and in many other countries: Japan, Spain, Portugal, and other countries in Europe, Africa, Asia, and South America.

- Teaching employees on the job by public or private organizations.

The logical concepts are not very difficult to learn, but teachers must have a good practical experience concerning the logical construction of systems and programs.

Warnier's other works that are available in English are

- Logical construction of programs. New York, NY: Van Nostrand Reinhold Company, 1974.

- Program modification. Boston, MA: Martinus Nijhoff Social Sciences Division, 1978. [The first book ever published on software maintenance.]

- Current developments in logical systems methodology. DSSD (Data Structured Systems Development) User's Conference/5, October 1980, Ken Orr & Associates, Topeka, KS.

- Logical construction of systems. New York, NY: Van Nostrand Reinhold Company, 1981.

RELIABILITY AND MAINTENANCE OF LARGE SYSTEMS

By JEAN-DOMINIQUE WARNIER
Cii Honeywell Bull

In the course of my talk, I would like to answer the following questions:

1. What does the term "large systems" mean?

2. How can the reliability of those systems be improved?

3. What degree of reliability can we obtain and what is the normal percentage of maintenance for the DP development function?

4. How can new projects be integrated?

5. How can existing solutions be modified?

Using some actual examples, we shall see how various firms and organizations have designed structured systems using the logical approach we have worked out, and we'll also talk about some practical problems we have encountered.

First of all, what does the term "large systems" mean? Many people seem to confuse hardware (computer) systems with the systems of data.

In small firms, a single hardware system is generally sufficient to ensure the storage, transmission, and processing of the entire set of data for the firm. In large firms or organizations, however, there are often several interconnected large computers, which are endpoints on a network of terminals, that do the data processing.

The magnitude of the problems to be solved in developing systems of data has continued to cause, even in these last few years, the installation of very complex systems, which are difficult to control. In my opinion, such systems of data run on very large computers are in a way the "diplodocus" of data processing. A diplodocus, by the way, is a species of dinosaur.

I am not against the use of large computers. But since man is inapt for solving problems involving enormous numbers of elements, it is necessary to subdivide large firms into smaller administrative units. Each of these units would, in turn, correspond to a logical data processing system. Each system could run on one computer, or on a part of a computer, or be shared among several computers.

There is no logical criterion to define the size of a unit and its corresponding data system. If each data system is strictly defined, in logical terms, connections between them are easily seen and modifications made without difficulty.

Logically speaking, having one "large systems" problem is equivalent to having several problems on systems of a more human scale. For this reason, I am going to talk about the set of data systems within big organizations or firms and not large systems in the common meaning of this term.

Once the different units making up a large firm are determined, and the corresponding systems are defined, it is necessary to ensure the reliability of their approved solutions. This must be done during the four large phases of the study.

- Definition of end-user needs: This phase is named LDR for Logical Definition of Results.

- Design of the structured set of data for each system: This phase is named LCS for Logical Construction of Data Systems.

- Design of operations control. This phase is named LCE: in French, the "Logique de conception de l'Exploitation" (i.e., operations).

- Construction of programs. This last phase is known as LCP, for the Logical Construction of Programs.

Each phase has perfected powerful tools for ensuring the reliability of the solutions chosen.

The logical approach that begins with the definition of end-user's needs (LDR) allows the integration of the present project's output requirements into the existing output requirements of previous projects. The purpose of this phase is to check that any new output is not simply a useless repetition of earlier output.

The tool used in this phase is a hierarchical diagram. Each required output has a hierarchical diagram defining exactly what is wanted. The diagram remains perfectly clear and brief, even if the question is very complex and contains so many combinations that they cannot be completely enumerated.

At the end of the LDR phase, all output is known and it is possible to schedule the workload and establish a calendar for a project. The reliability of that schedule is a major element of the system's reliability: an incorrect schedule often leads to defects that are the result of hasty work.

When a schedule is not followed, work within a unit is disturbed because the expected outputs are not available at the proper time. No schedule can be established and respected if the people involved are not correctly trained in the domain of logic as well as in their technical specialty.

When these conditions are met, a project involving 20 reports written in COBOL will require nearly 36,000 programming lines. The rate of delivered code for programmers who know LCS and LCP well is around 6,000 instructions per year per person. The workload would be split so that 25 percent of the time would be devoted to LCS and LCE, and 75 percent to LCP. In France, these figures represent a price tag of 7 or 8 dollars per instruction, taking into account the cost of analysis and programming plus fringe benefits and general administrative expenses.

Not enough emphasis is made on planning reliability. Even the best system, if delivered several months or years late, provokes serious disorders in the functioning of an administrative unit. Indeed, if such is not the case, then it is clear that the finished project was not at all useful.

Once the set of data for a unit's system has been defined, then it is possible to determine what part of that data is needed to obtain the required output. Designing the data system (LCS) may now begin. The object is to define all the files for subsets of the system that might be needed. The logical file definition is worked out in a hierarchical diagram. Later on, this diagram will be easy to complete or to modify. File items used for the project are distributed among the files. Relationships between files are rigorously defined. When the study is complete, each necessary data item will be stored once and only once, and all possible data regroupings verified to be easily obtainable. The reliability of the links between files is assured, as is the elimination of any duplicate data.

Developing the system of operational control (LCE) is next. This is a very important step, because it is in LCE that the systems documentation is organized and produced. Work on LCE has led to the automation by us at Honeywell Bull of large amounts of the LCS and LCP steps. When completed, this automation of systems documentation will considerably reduce the problems of managing the development of information systems having large numbers of programs.

Experiments using our approach to developing information systems over the last eight years have produced sizable, demonstrable reductions in the workload of analysts, programmers, and other EDP personnel, as well as notable decreases in computer and peripheral usage. For example, in one DP center over the last five years, the average systems failure rate has been only .47 percent. This compares well with the equipment manufacturer's guarantees of only 1.0 percent down-time on the equipment itself.

The remaining phase is designing the programs (LCP). Using LCP allows program verification before debugging on the computer. Moreover, using LCP checks the logical design with absolute certainty. The number of computer tests required averages less than two for each program (compiler excluded).

This procedure also avoids the danger of excessive usage of terminals in debugging programs. This might be less beneficial for computer manufacturers than for their customers but sentimentally I am on the side of the customers.

The maintenance problem is strongly linked to that of systems reliability. It is necessary, however, to explain what the word maintenance means, for DP people often confuse three functions that should be completely distinct. These functions are:

* correcting unreliable solutions;
* integrating a new project (or application) into the existing system;
* modifying existing systems and programs to satisfy the end-user's evolving needs.

Correcting Unreliable Solutions

When I am told that maintenance occupies eighty percent of analyst and programmer time, I call it catastrophic if that time is spent only correcting the systems. If, on the contrary, eighty percent of the time is used to integrate new projects into the existing system or to modify the system, I would say that an optimal design has been achieved.

In order to explain my position, I shall begin by discussing the first meaning of repair type maintenance, i.e., correcting unreliable solutions. Then I shall approach the problems of integrating new projects and modifying existing systems.

Firms and organizations have succeeded, using our methodology, in totally eliminating the breakdown of systems and programs. On the other hand, those who did not follow the methodology closely have had breakdowns accordingly.

Reliability and maintenance are strongly linked. When a solution is reliable, breakdowns disappear. Data processing should have the same requirements (or objectives) as aeronautics, i.e., to eliminate breakdowns completely.

If we can largely eliminate that part of maintenance devoted to correcting errors, more time would be available for enhancing our systems. But to be able to enhance or improve systems, we must be able to understand the user's needs better. Of the eighty percent of maintenance work performed, you have probably heard that three-quarters resulted from misunderstandings between end-users and DP people.

In defining end user needs (LDR) we have found that only correct hierarchical diagrams allow data processors to know what is required of them. The use of these diagrams greatly facilitates the maintenance process.

In dealing with the modification of existing systems and programs, it is the reliability of the logical file organization (determined by LCS) that certifies correct systems functioning. This is true regardless of the physical organization employed (i.e., data base system or access method).

With LCS, the lack of duplicate (redundant) data avoids discrepancies between different files. This is particularly important, for if the same data is stored in two or more files, one risks incomplete updating of the logical data base files. Such files often contain inconsistent data about the same subjects. The LCS methodology avoids this danger entirely.

Logical design of operations or processes (LCE) ensures cohesion and correspondence between files, programs, and documentation. Since programs run within the systems using LCE are organized using the same approach as LCP, this makes corrective maintenance largely unnecessary.

Finally, the reliability of the programming stage has been improved so much that the truly difficult programs simply do not occur. Most programming difficulties, in the past, stemmed from defective file design. Using LDR, LCS, and LCE clears the path for improved programming. At this level corrections hardly occur, as subsequent examples will show.

In conclusion, experience has taught us, particularly in large companies where system coordination is a greater problem than for small companies, that corrective maintenance can completely disappear. But all this is impossible without training DP people thoroughly in each phase of project development and management: LDR, LCS, LCE, and LCP.

Integrating A New Project (or Application) into the Existing Systems

Let's now turn to the discussion of the integration of a new project or application into existing systems. If the existing system has been constructed empirically, a study must be made of the interfaces between new project data and existing system data. This at least ensures the reliability of the new project, even though the old system is not necessarily improved.

If previous projects have been constructed logically, there will be no problem at the LDR phase of the new project. The major portion of the workload will appear at the LCS and LCE phases, as seen below.

Sometimes the LCS study reveals that all the necessary data is present in the old system. In this case, there will be no problem in designing the data (LCS phase). It will be sufficient to integrate the new programs into present operations control and then write those programs.

Sometimes, however, the LCS study reveals that none of the data present in the old system can be used for the new project. In that case, data design for the new project will be less obvious during the LCS phase. Once done, program integration will take place as in the previous example.

But more often than not, modifications that occur during the LCS phase will make it necessary to create new logical files and to change record format within some of the files. Every modification of the record's structure of an existing file requires an update of the structure of the file. Then we must look at the repercussions of this structure's modifications on all the programs using this file. A correct documentation allows us to identify all those programs. One could, in the beginning of the LCS phase, determine the problems to be solved and evaluate the workload for all the various possible cases.

Using a rigorous, logical approach allows us to obtain, after the modifications have been made and the documentation updated, a system as clear and well designed as the original. Such a system could receive as many successive modifications as necessary, and it will always be adaptable to new modifications. Moreover, when the hardware is changed, the portability of the system from a logical point of view, can be easily obtained.

The only problems that remain are technical ones. But the solutions to these problems are much easier to obtain with a good logical structured system's design.

Modifying Existing Systems

I would now like to discuss the modification of existing solutions. Very often, after a growing number of repairs and modifications, the design of the empirically worked-out projects tends to degrade, as does the system's documentation.

The point is soon reached where any new changes, suggested by a user still venturesome enough to make them, will be rejected by the DP people. And so an entire system can be put into question. Remarks such as, "We'll have to rewrite the payroll and production programs," are often heard.

This is really the problem of the large, empirically designed systems. One hesitates to modify the design of large systems because of implications with respect to historical changes. I am thinking particularly of the very large files of big insurance companies, banks, or organizations.

On the contrary, if the structure of the system to be modified has been logically designed, end-users know that the requested modifications are possible and will be accepted by the DP people.

The first step is to carefully describe the modifications to be made. For this, the data processors must consult the LDR documentation and modify the hierarchical diagram of the output, if necessary. Then they must look at the data input definition to decide the possible modifications. They must also review the output's patterns, computation, formula, and conditions. When this work has been approved by the users, with the help of DP people, the analysts then take charge of the problem.

The modifications generally concern the detailed organization of the programs and often their logical design. Each time those modifications require that we obtain new data for the DP system input, one must foresee some structures modifications of the system's data set. Consequently, part of the LCS work must be revised to meet new requirements and to examine the repercussions of the new files design.

Those modifications may require that some of the links between files be modified. They may also require a careful examination of the old programs using the newly modified files.

At this juncture, I would like to stress two points. First, tedious maintenance must disappear to make room for a highly specialized job, that of system's modification specialist. This job requires extensive training and strong experience in computer sciences. In all large firms, a technical help and a training support would be established. This would be the function of the logical system's engineers. This new specialization has been created in all the large firms using the methodology correctly, and particularly in the DP centers described in this paper. In those firms there is one or more logical system's engineers.

The second point concerns the growing importance of office automation as an extension of the organization's data system. A new class of people is emerging. These people have, or are going to have, the ability to create the programs they need themselves.

This is certainly a good development but it also entails some danger. Programs will be developed by individuals who do not have the proper training. It is strongly desirable, even necessary, that those who are not computer science specialists be trained in DP techniques, especially in the logical area.

I have grave misgivings when I see microcomputers invading schools and students being taught by teachers who are most interested in the technical aspects of the computer, but are not at all prepared to teach logical reasoning. As a result, we risk training a generation of brilliant handymen whose minds will be completely warped by bad habits learned since childhood. One will then see the lack of reliability of systems and her twin sister, maintenance, returning in force.

It would be better to solve the problem from the beginning. For instance, Japanese friends in Tokyo and Osaka have introduced the teaching of LCP in the teacher's colleges.

1st Example-The Quartermaster Corps

To exemplify my speech, I shall now present the results of a review of projects that was recently conducted in several large firms or organizations using our approach. The firms were involved in a wide variety of areas.

The Quartermaster Corps of the French army is in charge of supplying about 500,000 men with every sort of material, except weapons. The number of items included in the materials list is about 350,000, including food, clothes, and other nonmilitary goods.

A general, the central manager, commands the service. He is assisted by the chiefs of the different departments of the central command. Each military area has a regional command of the Quartermaster Corps. The regional command is managed by a general with the help of the regional chief officer. In each area there are several establishments in which the materials to be distributed to the forces are stored.

The personnel involved in the DP project comprised the following hierarchy: the end-users who are officers working in the different establishments of the regional or central commands; the officers in charge of the LCS phase; and the commissioned and noncommissioned officers in charge of designing, writing, and debugging programs (LCP phase).

The training for personnel of the Ministry of Defense, on whom the Quartermaster Corps depends, is organized like this: the noncommissioned officers have programming courses including LCP and COBOL or some other techniques. There are several centers for the army (land forces), air force, navy, gendarmerie, and other services. The DP officers are trained for varying lengths of time: full time for six months for captains and lieutenants; and for one or two years for majors, colonels, etc. A good deal of time is devoted to teaching LDR, LCP, LCS, and LCE. The end-users officers learn LDR and a little LCS.

Prior to 1977 the DP officers of the Quartermaster Corps had good logical training but no practical experience except in LCP. Some of the commissaries had been trained during a two-week period of instruction devoted to LCS. An agreement between the Quartermaster Corps and my group provided for aid to solve any problems encountered.

The project began in 1977. The problem was to remake the supply planning of the land forces. The DP material was a network with several Honeywell Model 66s, one by each military area to which many programmable terminals are connected.

At the end of the first phase of this project, the number of the outputs required by the end-users was about 200. The outputs (screen, listings) were divided as follows:

> one hundred for the central command;
> one hundred for each regional command.

In each regional command the required outputs were the same as for all the other units, i.e., designing the output for one regional command answered the needs of all the others.

In this project we encountered two difficulties common to all large firms. The first arose from the large number of end-users. There were dozens of people who could have been consulted in designing the LDR phase, but it was impossible to talk to everyone involved. It was better to consult a few specialists in solving the LDR problems. But those specialists were not the real end-users who defined the end-user's needs.

To avoid wrong requirements the specialists had to be concerned enough to ask opinions of as many end-users as possible and be given the means to conduct those consultations. This was done in the Quartermaster Corps.

The second difficulty encountered in large firms concerns the order in which the different sub-projects of the project must be designed. In our example, an emergency order had to be determined to order the sub-projects.

The project manager had given precedence to the output required by the central command. The LCS design had been very quickly implemented but the analysts noticed that the data necessary to obtain the output came from all the regional command systems.

At this point, the first part of the project was dropped temporarily and the part of the project concerning the regional command was worked up.

As soon as the software design of the output (LDR phase) had been done, the plan was drawn. The load was estimated at sixty man-years, fifteen for the data and system's LCS design and forty-five for programming (LCP). At the beginning of the project, five officers worked on the LDR and LCS phases, but very quickly this was reduced to only four, and then three, officers.

In 1978 we had a meeting with the general for the central command and the generals commanding the regions. They asked if it was possible to end the project by 1981. Because it was impossible to devote more than twelve programmers to this project, they decided that 1981 would be the deadline for the project's subset concerning the regional commands. This was achieved as anticipated. The portion of the project dealing with the central command will be finished in 1984. The reliability of our system for evaluating the workloads and time limits has been verified.

Since 1978, when the first subsets became available, the workload for repair-type maintenance has been nonexistent. On the other hand, some modifications to the requirements of the initial project have been made.

LCS is a powerful tool. This was particularly apparent as soon as the people in charge of this segment of the project had been trained sufficiently.

I spent about ten half-days consulting on the project, including two half-days with the command staff. The officer who managed the LCS work in the beginning is in charge of the programmer's team today. Another officer has worked out an operational research system to optimize the carrying of supplies. This subset of the project yielded some exciting results, but it is a little early to compute correctly the savings produced.

In the example above, the project "Supply Planning" is integrated into systems in which the other project had been empirically worked out. No difficulties have been observed with the new system, but problems concerning the prior nonstructured solutions remain.   The reliability of the old parts of the system are not good and the maintenance and repair represent a heavy workload.

2nd Example–Placoplatre

Placoplatre, a producer of plasterboard, was the first firm to use our logical approach.   Their DP people have been using LCP as far back as 1969, LCS since 1972, and LCE since 1975.   During that time, LDR has been applied by the end-users.

Currently, all existing projects at Placoplatre have been logically structured and all the programs constructed with LCP. You may have read something of this yourself because the **EDP Analyzer** has published two studies about the changeover to our methodology, one in 1974 and one in 1979.

Placoplatre is not nearly as large as the Quartermaster Corps.   The firm employs around 1,200 people, with gross sales in 1980 of 120 million dollars.   The head office and two plants are located near Paris; and two other plants are in the Alps at Chambery, and in Cognac.

Presently, a logical system of data has been worked out for four units: the head office, the Chambery plant, the Cognac plant, and the two plants in the Paris suburb, which are considered as a single unit.   The systems for all plants have the same structure and employ the same programs.   All the data systems function on one computer with several terminals.

In the early seventies, before the plant at Cognac had been built, there was one logical system for each plant.   When the Cognac plant was put into operation, a new logical system was created and the managers decided to put together into a single system the sets of data from the two plants in the Paris suburbs.   This important change, worked out at the highest level of the hierarchical design, has been achieved without any problems.

There are 480,000 COBOL statements for all the systems.   The number of DP people on the project, including the systems engineer, has been on the average of seven.   For more than eleven years, all the plannings has been evaluated on the basis of performance I have already outlined.   We find that such performance has been achieved in all the large firms that have used the methodology correctly.

The last system was converted in 1975. The next conversion will be achieved next year. Presently, the computer is a large Honeywell 2000, with terminals situated in the plants and in different commercial offices of the firm located in leading cities throughout France.

The analysts and programmers employed in this service in 1970 no longer work at Placoplatre. The turnover in personnel has been gradual but complete; however, this has not interrupted the smooth performance of the work because management has made a continual effort to avoid any discontinuity.

Difficulties have arisen in the LDR phase of the different projects because of the lack of training of several end-users. Courses are now regularly taught to remedy the situation. The DP people are most interested in solving this problem, and in trying to avoid mistakes at the LDR level that would destroy the reliability of the work in subsequent steps.

At the LCS level, no breakdowns have occured since March 1, 1976, and the repair-type maintenance workload has been negligible.

Different interfaces related to the modifications of existing solutions have been made. These consist for the most part, of some modifications of the file structures.

The most significant work arose from the realization of new projects, and the subsequent repercussions on the set of systems. During the last few years, the new projects often involved developing summary results from existing data bases. One planned enhancement, in our example, processed data concerning the company's suppliers.

Using the process control in the plants, we began to consider the relationship between data systems for production and those for administration.

One of the most interesting aspects of the Placoplatre system is the use of LCE for operating the programs.

No breakdowns have been observed since the system was put into effect on September 1, 1976. The operator's workload has decreased to such a degree that the greater part of their time is devoted presently to modifying programs. For the last five years, there have been few modifications to make, but it has often been necessary to integrate new projects into the system.

What has the Placoplatre experience been? At the programming level, there have never been any breakdowns, therefore the repair-type maintenance workload is nonexistent. At the LCP level, as at all other levels of the structured systems design, many modifications have been made because of the end-user's changing needs. All the workload has been shifted, advantageously, to make modifications asked by users.

For example, recently in a five-program sequence, three programs have been modified in important ways. In debugging those programs on the computer, one run per program after compilation, has proved sufficient. The three programs contained no errors.

One difficulty remains concerning the documentation. This is, for a short time only we hope, still done by hand. Unfortunately, when modifications are made at any level in the system, vast amounts of effort are sometimes wasted because of deficient documentation.

Placoplatre has taken an option on the software we are developing to automate the LCE system entirely, of which the documentation is a subset.

3rd Example–Gendarmerie Nationale

The next project I shall describe has been installed at the Gendarmerie Nationale. In France, the Gendarmerie Nationale depends on the Ministry of Defense and includes essentially; 1) three units in charge of protecting our president; 2) several units in charge of keeping order; 3) hundreds of squads consisting of a dozen men each. The squads are distributed throughout the French territory. The French territory is divided into ninety-eight departments. Every urban area of some importance is supervised by one or more squads who share responsibilities with the urban police in each town. The Gendarmerie numbers about 80,000 men.

Up to now the stolen car data was treated by hand in each department. To obtain better control, it was decided to create a national system with two Honeywell Model 66-10's, using an IDS-2 data-base management system.

The project anticipates gradually implementing 11,000 terminals located in the station houses and in the vehicles. The two Model 66's have 15 discs-units with 150 million bytes each. For the stolen car data system alone, 300 million bytes on-line are reserved. The work was begun early in 1979.

The system has been running since March 1, 1981. Five hundred terminals are in service and two hundred of these are in vehicles. These terminals allow access to the data base to find out immediately the condition of a suspicious vehicle.

To avoid further incident, every stolen car recovered must be updated in the data base before the car is returned to the owner.

The number of program statements for this project is about 25,000. The elapsed time has been evaluated at about eight man-years, two at the LCS-LCE level and six at the LCP level.

The efficiency of this project has proved to be nearly 50 percent worse than that observed elsewhere. The explanation for this was given to us by the project manager: he told us that they had tried to save time by neglecting certain steps at the LCS level. Fortunately, by effecting controls before starting to do any programming, errors were detected in time and corrected before the system was operational.

The system's reliability was proved completely as soon as the system was running. No wrong solution, at any level, has been detected in the last six months.

The system has been installed too recently for them to have had modifications problems. A new system to improve traffic circulation is about to be put into service. This will be the third structured system running at the French Gendarmerie.

Conclusion

Data processing reliability presupposes that at each step of the development process, a clear design is expressed unquestionably.

Data processing, which is an essential tool for communication, must itself be communicable. In general, direct communication between human beings tolerates shades of meaning and even vagueness, but communciation by means of data processing tools must be completely accurate and without nuances. Data processing makes it possible to communicate at levels where direct relationships between people become impossible.

When we aspire to absolute precision at the DP level we are entering into the realm of systems. The principal characteristic of a system is the cohesion of all the elements. Even the least grain of sand in the wheels of a complex system can cause it to stop or be destroyed. For these reasons the first quality of any system and especially of a DP system is reliability. And because reliability and clearness of their structures are essential, DP systems must be designed to be modified.

Part V: The death of software

In Hindu mythology, a trinity of Gods is responsible for the universe: Brahma creates the universe, Vishnu maintains the universe, and Shiva dissolves the universe. From the seeds of dissolution the universe is created again, and the cycle repeats itself (Figure V-1). In this model, death is a phase of the life cycle. It is a short phase, sometimes a bitter phase, but it is a phase that is integral to the cycle.

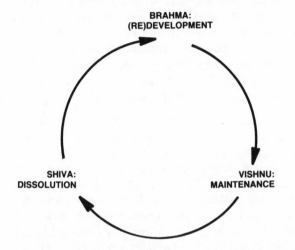

FIGURE V-1 LIFE CYCLE OF THE HINDU UNIVERSE

What role does death play in the life cycle of software systems? Judged by the papers collected in this Part, it is a confusing and frustrating role. Systems die when they should survive, and they survive when they should die.

Denning, in the first paper, argues that current educational practice misleads students about this matter. Methods of teaching programming suggest that programs have short lives; experience in the real world teaches just the opposite. Weinberg, in the second paper, shows that programmers, engineers, and users have widely differing ideas of what to keep, what to throw away, and what are the costs of their decisions. Spier, in the third paper, gives a hair-raising case history of how a program was incapacitated (but not quite killed) by a sequence of modifications. Finally, Brown ponders the question "Why does software die?" Ironically, this selection on software death gives as lively a picture of software as anything in the Tutorial.

The truth is that software, if it survives its infancy, is remarkably hard to kill. The questionnaire studies cited in the Introduction to Part I indicate that most applications systems are five or six years old, with a substantial proportion being over ten years old. We

shall cite evidence in a moment that portions of currently running code are older still.

Brown's paper in this Part cites two causes of software death:

- Failure to adapt to change.
- Murder, i.e., the software is overthrown by another, stronger, piece of software that does the same task.

The alert reader will recognize that, though these are threats to survival of a system, they are not alarming ones. The whole apparatus of software maintenance protects software against the first threat; the significant costs and incompatibilities of installing a new system protect against the second. If these are the only threats to their survival, then, like crabgrass or kudzu or cockroaches, software systems are here to stay.

We can add at least three more causes of software death:

- The software ceases to function.
- The hardware on which it runs is replaced.
- The function ceases to be used.

These threats are also surprisingly ineffective.

It is true that software does cease to function, or at least a sequence of ill-executed changes can cause it to function less well than it should. This is the topic of Spier's paper. However, management is exceedingly reluctant to abandon a program that works, even if it works badly. Spier's recommendation to rewrite was rejected:

> Firstly, the compiler was too widely used to be scrapped. Secondly, the management felt that if this compiler is impossible to maintain then any other compiler would be just as messy.

The threat of hardware incompatibility is equally weak. For one thing, manufacturers have, since IBM's introduction of the System/360 architecture, been wary of hardware incompatibility. For another, systems are now developed in higher level languages that can be "ported" to different hardware. And, finally, if the hardware is incompatible, it can be made to look compatible by emulation, as, for instance, the 360's and their successors are all capable of executing programs in the machine language of the 1401, the old workhorse of business data processing.

The last 1401 was built in 1965, for a total of more than 10,000. They were used by companies that were then the leading consumers of commercial data processing; most of these companies still are leading consumers. In 1981 at least one company, C-S Computer Systems, Inc., was advertising, in *Datamation*, software and services to translate 1401 machine language to COBOL. The business boomed in the early 1970's, presumably when many 1401's were decommissioned, and it started to boom again in the late 1970's when IBM announced the termination of hardware support for the 1401 and also, perhaps, when in-house staff with 1401 machine language expertise began to retire. Reportedly, business is still brisk. C-S Computer Systems even gets calls to examine modules which are in languages that the software owner cannot identify—but which are still being used. Here is hard evidence that software over fifteen years old is embedded in currently operating systems.

But what of software whose function is no longer used? Does it die? Al-Jarrah and Torsun's static analysis of some 230,000 lines of COBOL code found that 27% of the labels were never referenced ("An empirical analysis of COBOL programs," *Software—Practice and Experience*, 9 (1979), 341-359). Undoubtedly some of these labels were on "dead code," code which could never be executed. In a dynamic analysis of 22 commercial COBOL programs the same investigators ("Dynamic analysis of COBOL programs," *Software—Practice and Experience*, 11 (1981), 949-961) found that an average 20% of the program was never executed. Could this code be removed, and, if so, should it be?

Unused code is not, like unused physical resources, subject to vandals, thieves, or rust; it does not remove itself. In general, maintenance programmers do not remove it either. Part of their craft is to cut as little as possible. Programmers will not take responsibility for removing a function unless they are assured that there is no user of that function. In the case of dead code, a manager may take the fact of unexecutable code as good evidence that it is unnecessary, and may authorize its removal. In the case of a function (say, a report) which is produced but not used, a manager or auditor may poll the users and authorize its discontinuance, although this is no guarantee that the code will disappear. The most stubborn case is that of code that is executable but is not executed; therefore, its effect is invisible. Only a hero or a fool would authorize its removal.

But should such code be removed? All code, whether used or unused, increases the complexity of the system; complexity is what burdens the understanding of programs, and understanding is a major activity of maintainers. If the system is not purged periodically, it becomes unmanageable, and the careers of its managers become precarious. (As Parikh once said to one of his managers: "We're not controlling the system—it's controlling us.")

The conclusion is that software must be periodically and systematically purged. Just as in Hindu mythology the universe needs a purging God, Shiva, so a software system needs a purging manager. What to purge, when to purge, and how to purge are all open questions; they are raised repeatedly during our presentations. Again and again, we hear such complaints as: "We brought up the new accounting system, but several of the Divisions refused to change over to it."

A few answers are being heard, for instance John R. Ryan's paper "Software product quality assurance" at the 1982 National Computer Conference (*AFIPS Proceedings*, 51, 393-398), but this is truly an open area of software engineering research. Good guidelines on the death of software are the key to preventive software maintenance.

Introduction

Denning, P.J. "Throwaway programs." *Comm. ACM*, 24, 2 (February 1981), 57-58. See also letters in *Comm. ACM*, 24, 6 (June 1981), 402-403.

Peter Denning is a computer scientist and educator of international repute, famous for his work on the principles of operating systems design. He wrote the following paper during his 1980-82 term as President of the Association for Computing Machinery (ACM), the oldest professional society in the United States for computer people. With notable candor, he criticizes the educational community of which he himself is part:

> Programming education contains strong biases in the wrong direction. Few courses require students to find and use modules in libraries or in public files. (Lesson: Program from scratch.) Collaboration is strongly discouraged; students get no permanent sharable file storage on the computer. (Lesson: Programs are personal.) Once an assignment is handed in and graded, it serves no further purpose. (Lesson: Programs are throwaways.)

Generations of programmers have been nurtured in the assumption that programs are throwaways. In fact, programs are remarkably durable. We are currently living with a legacy of jerry-built software. We need operating systems that are hospitable toward saving and reusing program parts. Denning describes such facilities in the Bell Laboratories Unix system, and he suggested to us that we point the reader to an excellent recent paper by Brian W. Kernighan and John R. Mashey, "The Unix programming environment," *IEEE Computer*, 14, 4 (April 1981), 12-24.

Denning notes that his remarks are partly based on a paper by his Purdue University colleague, Douglas Comer ("Principles of program design induced from experience with small public programs," *IEEE Trans.*

Software Engineering, SE-7, 2 (March 1981), 169-174). We asked Comer how he came to write his paper. He said: "It's embarrassing—but I'll tell you."

He said that he had told his colleagues that, even though Purdue's Master's students were as well trained as any in the country, he wouldn't hire them as programmers: they were too immature. But how then do you teach maturity? Comer's solution, described in his paper, is

> [E]ach new programmer is given a small, public program as a first assignment. The programmer has a chance to learn what it means to maintain public software without jumping directly into maintenance of a large program like a compiler or operating system. More importantly, the programmers become conscious of others who depend on their work.

Other important papers on the education of maintainers are the pioneering article by Beil in Part I of this Tutorial and Fred Gruenberger's article, "So you're trying to teach computing" *(Datamation*, April 1977, 119-124).

We include with Denning's paper two letters commenting on it—partly to show that the President of the ACM is not immune from lively rebuttal, even when writing a President's Letter in the ACM's flagship publication, and partly to give the reader a taste of Robert Glass, sender of the first letter. Glass is not otherwise represented in this Tutorial, but he is a coauthor, with Ronald Noiseux, of *Software maintenance guidebook* (Prentice-Hall, 1981), which contains the best description to date of the work and character of maintenance programmers. He is also the author, under the pseudonym Miles Benson, of a lively series of books on computer projects that failed (Computing Trends, 6925 56th Ave S, Seattle, WA 98118).

Throwaway Programs

Peter J. Denning

Reprinted with permission from *Communications of ACM*, Volume 24, Number 2, February 1981, pages 57-58 and Number 6, June 1981, pages 402-403. Published by The Association for Computing Machinery, Inc.

Razors. Ball point pens. Diapers. Towels. Paper plates. Plastic forks. TV dinner trays. Fast food boxes. Pop bottles. Our world is full of disposable personal objects, transient things soon discarded.

Ten years ago began the debates about structured programming, which sought more correct, more understandable software through restricted program forms. These debates helped bring forth programming languages with strict syntactic structure—e.g., Pascal, Fortran 77, and lately Ada. They stimulated new texts on programming and new sets of rules for students in programming courses. But our students go on to be professional programmers whose software is unreliable and unportable; who often construct new programs from scratch rather than from existing programs; who keep such poor records that they cannot later reuse their programs. We continue to rely heavily on a small set of highly gifted software architects to keep our computer systems running.

Why is this? Why is so much software of poor quality? Not distributable? Why so little progress toward transportable software parts despite so much attention to program structure and project management? The seed of an answer is in a paper by Douglas Comer,[1] who has made the remarkable observation that the most useful public programs started out purely for the personal use of their authors.

Comer's insight is important when viewed in the context of our fondness for the personal and the disposable. As with other things in our daily lives, we have come to think of programs as personal objects. They are poorly documented and not intended for use by others. As a consequence they are difficult to reuse; they become throwaway objects, transient things soon discarded.

Toward Composable Software Parts

I regard the attitude "programs are personal objects" as the fundamental problem. That many programs turn out to be throwaway objects is an unfortunate consequence of this problem. This attitude is encouraged by our operating systems. It is ingrained in our approaches to teaching programming.

Much of our attention in recent

[1] See D.E. Comer, "Principles of program design induced from experience with small public programs," *IEEE Transactions on Software Engineering*, March 1981.

years has been directed toward *simplifying the task of writing single programs*. I include structured programming, advanced languages, interactive editors, program synthesizers, and debugging aids in the group of tools that assist in this goal.

We must now direct our attention toward *saving, sharing, reusing, and composing software parts*. Operating systems must become part of the solution of these needs. They are presently part of the problem.

In the 1950s and early 1960s, operating systems were intended as automatic control programs; their objective was to schedule work, to maximize efficiency, and to meter resource use. There was no "user interface." By the late 1960s operating systems began offering services that users could not supply for themselves. These included program libraries, file systems, and backup facilities. It is an unfortunate fact that much of the 1950s approach to the "user interface" survives to the present day. Job control languages are exceedingly difficult to use and often seem devoid of concept. Documentation about system utilities and services can hardly be understood by skilled systems programmers, much less by ordinary users. Many systems force users to save programs on cards or tapes; only a few have automatic backup and archiving.

In short, to foster a new attitude—that programs are potentially public, sharable, and transportable—we need operating systems that are hospitable toward saving and reusing program parts. I will cite Bell Labs' UNIX operating system to illustrate that the technology is at hand.[2] Most of the concepts in UNIX originated in experimental time sharing systems CTSS and Multics during the 1960s. They have now been refined for use on small machines.

Programming Environments

A programming environment is the set of facilities which permit a programmer to synthesize, connect, and execute program modules. Besides the usual editors, compilers, and debugging aids, a programming environment must also contain long term personal file storage; it must give access to libraries and to programs written by others; and it must provide a command interpreter to facilitate program invocation.

Bell Labs' UNIX is the most widely available example of a system with this type of programming environment. On logging in, a user is assigned a process containing the shell, a command interpreter that listens to his terminal. The shell interprets the first word on each line as the name of a program, which it invokes with the rest of the line as input parameters. Through the shell, the user has access to the directory hierarchy of the system, in which all files are kept. He may construct a personal tree of directories and files and he can specify the degree to which others can share these objects.

Central in the UNIX programming environment is the concept that *every program is a module with a single data-stream input and single data-stream output.* This is true of user programs as well as systems programs—including the shell program. By default, the input and output of a program are connected to the terminal. Simple shell notations permit the user to reconnect a module's input or output to arbitrary files in the system, and also to connect the output of one module to the input of

[2] See D.M. Ritchie and K.L. Thompson, "The UNIX time sharing system," *Comm. ACM 17*, 7 (July 1974), 365–375.

another. For example, typing

filename

invokes the file "filename" with its input being anything typed at the terminal and its output being displayed at the terminal. Typing

$filename < X$

invokes "filename" with file X as its input, typing

$filename > Y$

invokes "filename" with its output being stored in file Y, and typing

$filename < X > Y$

does both. Typing

filename1 | filename2

invokes both "filename1" and "filename2"; the second program's input is the first's output. These simple concepts permit programmers to easily construct and run more complex programs by connecting existing modules and files.

The shell permits users to store sequences of shell commands, called shellscripts, in files for later execution. This facility permits the user to construct more complex modules from simpler ones already available.

UNIX also permits a user to move freely among environments. For example, while editing a file, a user can escape to the shell, invoke the mail program, process his mail, and later return to the editing of his file. Or, a user can escape from processing his mail, use an editor to create a file, then return to the mail program and mail the new file. The user is not confined to any one environment; he can interrupt himself at any time and return later to finish the original task.

The simple set of concepts of UNIX forms a programming environment that encourages the user to employ the *whole system* in the solution of problems. He can connect any programs together at any time. He can save any new modules for later use. He can move freely among environments. He does not fear the operating system because he understands its basic principles. Because sharing is encouraged, he tends not to think of programs as personal or throwaway objects.

Programming Education

Programming education contains strong biases in the wrong direction. Few courses require students to find and use modules in libraries or in public files. (Lesson: Program from scratch.) Collaboration is strongly discouraged; students get no permanent sharable file storage on the computer. (Lesson: Programs are personal.) Once an assignment is handed in and graded, it serves no further purpose. (Lesson: Programs are throwaways.)

To reverse these biases, we need to provide students with programming environments embodying concepts like those in UNIX. But this is not enough. We also need new policies of instruction and grading that encourage students to avoid programming from scratch, to use software tools effectively, to construct modules intended for use by others, and to maintain documentation permitting reuse of their own software.

Why not institute grading policies that assign a higher reward for using existing software parts than for programming from scratch? Why not have projects in which students exchange modules, grades being assigned according to how well others are able to use or modify these modules? Why not require each student to maintain a manual of all software he has developed, and give him adequate file storage for his software during his academic career?

It will not be cheap to upgrade college and university facilities from their present conditions, to provide each student with interactive terminal access whenever he requires it, with sufficient personal file space, and with connection by network to other facilities. But it must be done. Here is an excellent opportunity for cooperation between industry and academia.

There is a danger that the rising interest in personal computers will perpetuate the software problem by encouraging students and other programmers to regard the entire computer as a personal object that seldom interacts with anything else. Most personal computer systems today have very primitive programming environments, little advanced beyond the operating systems of the 1950s. They introduce beginners to throwaway programs—most personal computers and programmable calculators discard programs by default when the power is shut down. Here is an excellent opportunity for cooperation between academia and industry.

acm forum

On Throwaway Programs

☐ As a practicing professional programmer of long standing, I am offended by the lead comments of the February President's Letter on Throwaway Programs. By what standard is it judged that "software is unreliable and unportable"? From what data is it concluded that "so much software [is] of poor quality"? I submit that there is no conclusive study to support these opinions; the literature contains many quotes of this kind, but none (to my knowledge) with any scientific underpinning. My own study [1] tends to show that software professionals need not be ashamed of their reliability performance.

Certainly, the major thrust of your editorial is correct. We *can* do better. We *can* move toward more generalized software parts, better programming environments, and more pragmatic education. (It is ironic that the parts approach to software development is at heart a bottom-up approach, and contrary to the top-down teachings of the 70s.) I am all for the substance of Denning's material, and I applaud his (and my) notion of "coöperation between academia and industry."

But please, he should not feel compelled to pick on the practicing professional to make his point. There are an awful lot of us "common people" in ACM, and we are pretty proud of what we do.

ROBERT L. GLASS
Computing Trends
Seattle, WA 98118

1. Glass, Robert L. Software versus hardware errors. *Computer* (IEEE), Dec. 1980.

☐ President Denning's letter "Throwaway Programs" in the February issue of *Communications* was excellent, but it might have been more aptly titled "The Case For Software Engineering." If one wants to build a bridge one does not hire a mathematician or a physicist, one hires an engineer. The problem that President Denning has taken aim at is caused primarily by using computer scientists to do a job which should be done by software engineers. In any field of endeavor the scientists are the pioneers; they conduct numerous "throwaway" experiments to find the lay of the land and to determine the basic laws that apply to the field. But once the laws have been determined it is the engineers who develop the tools and the methodology to apply the laws to practical real world solutions. Clearly real world solutions must be system oriented and cost effective, precluding the use of "throwaway" parts other than where clearly required.

An excellent example of this evolution in recent years is the nuclear field. Nuclear physics has evolved into nuclear engineering. This does not mean that there is no demand for nuclear physicists today. Rather the situation prevails that in practical field applications such as a nuclear power plant operation one hires a nuclear engineer and for teaching or research one hires a nuclear physicist.

We in the software industry seem to suffer from stunted evolution; we seem to be unable to make the transition. While the real world cries out for software engineers who are oriented toward system solutions and cost effective projects, we continue to crank out more and more computer scientists who treat their jobs as just another extension of their research oriented "throwaway" projects. We in ACM must bear our share of the blame for this. We continue to define and redefine and still redefine the computer science curriculum, but how much effort do we put into defining and establishing software engineering?

The core of a software engineering curriculum should be carrying a real world system project through its full cycle, starting with requirements definition, general design including test plan, detailed design including test procedures, system integration, verification and validation, release page preparation, and concluding with maintenance. The student should be required to produce full documentation for this and to undergo the appropriate reviews. To instill the importance of independent testing each student should do the test plan, test procedures, and verification and validation for a project other than his own.

Understandably this will be considerably more expensive than the "throwaway" projects of current computer science departments. But there is a ready solution to the problem: Establish a software house in conjunction with the software engineering department. This would not only solve the financial problem but have the added advantages of enhancing their projects with the real world constraints of schedule, cost effectiveness, and user interface.

J. W. FELLER
Control Data Corporation
Sunnyvale, CA 94086

Introduction

Weinberg, G.M. "Disposable programs spell prompt relief." *Computer Careers News* (July 28, 1980).

In the following paper, Gerald Weinberg takes Denning's "throwaway programs" one step further. Programmers habitually believe that their programs are one-time shots; users habitually want the programs rerun. This perceptual mismatch can be costly:

> It costs much more, in the end, to run a one-time program N times than to run an N-time program N times.

To avoid these disproportionate costs, Weinberg recommends that programmers and users agree on charge-back rates that reflect an agreed lifetime for the programs.

This paper originally was one of Weinberg's "Phase Two" columns, which appears regularly throughout the world. It was based on his consulting experience. At first, he thought everybody already knew that program costs must be based on program lifetime, but he discovered that not everyone did.

We have already introduced Weinberg in Part IV, so without further ado we yield to him the soapbox.

263

Disposable Programs Spell Prompt Relief

Gerald M. Weinberg

In many installations today, the number one problem is program maintenance. Although the total problem is far from simple, there are a number of relatively simple ideas that can be applied immediately to furnish "prompt relief." One such idea is the disposable program.

The idea of disposable programs is not new. Every programmer has written code that was to be used once and then thrown away, code such as: first-cut subroutines, as for simple, quick formatting of output; one-time reports; test drivers; research programs to probe some peculiar feature of the programming language, operating system, data base, or other "black box"; and engineering assist programs to help diagnose a hardware malfunction.

If you consider these five examples relative to your own experience, you will notice two categories:

KEPT—first-cut routines and one time reports.

DISPOSED—test drivers, research programs, and hardware testers.

That is, though all are thought of as single use programs, the KEPT routines tend to be held, somewhere, "just in case." Only the DISPOSED programs are actually discarded.

Can you recall an instance when you wished you had actually retained a discarded program? For example,

- A minor modification is made to a tested system, and you would like to be able to run the test driver—just one more time.

- A new version of the system software is installed, and you would like to see if it still has the glitches discovered by your research programs.

- The hardware once again begins to act peculiarly, reminding you of another situation you once diagnosed with a special routine.

Luckily, in the third case, the engineers usually manage to retrieve your old diagnostic code, which they slyly copied, "just in case"—yet another piece of evidence that engineers represent "a higher form of life" than programmers.

And can you recall cases of KEPT programs you devoutly wish you had destroyed when you had the chance? These are the programs you see and curse almost every day, as their user phones, pleading for "just one little change."

Hmmm? Perhaps we could immediately begin improving the maintenance situation by applying two simple rules about "one-time" programs:

1. If you are about to throw it away, keep it.
2. If you are about to keep it, throw it away.

Unfortunately, applying these two rules together creates an infinite recursion. All programmers would be instantly paralyzed. There must be a better way. (Or do you believe that instant paralysis of all programmers would be of great benefit to the human species?)

Can we discover a better set of rules? Let's explore the reasoning process that causes some temporary programs to be retained and others to be discarded. Consider the examples once again, you'll notice that the underlying principle seems to be: If the programmer is responsible for the decision, the program is discarded; but if the user is responsible, the program is kept.

The behavior of the engineers demonstrates *both* parts of the principle. In the old days, when programs were decks of cards, the engineers would scavenge the trash bins after the programmers had thrown away the diagnostics.

And why do programmers discard "temporary" programs, while users do not? I believe that programmers understand that retaining a program for possible use costs time, and money—even if the program is never used.

The programmer understands this principle because the programmer is the one whose time will be spent retaining the program. The user *doesn't* understand because the user seldom, if ever, perceives the cost and effort. To the user, a program is a program—somehow fixed once and for all.

Some enlightened users understand that if a program must be changed, there will be costs. Some know this by simple reasoning; others because they have been charged for modifications. But few users recognize that a program run a second time after lying dormant will also cost time and money.

There are many reasons why a program brought out of hibernation could incur costs:

1. The hardware environment has changed.
2. The system software environment has changed.
3. The size or format of the data has changed.
4. The human environment has changed.
5. Some part of the program or its supporting material has been lost or damaged.

Point 4 is perhaps the worst of the lot, and includes such situations as these: The original programmer has left for parts unknown. The original programmer can't remember the program. (even worse) In the belief that the original problem is clearly in mind, the original programmer embarks on the job of running it once more in a changed environment. The operators don't remember the procedures for the program. The people preparing the input don't remember what is required—and, of course, it's not documented clearly and completely because it was a one-time job. The user doesn't remember the job clearly—either what the parameters mean or what the output means.

So it does cost to rerun an "unchanged" program, and the longer the period of hibernation, the greater the cost. But you

Reprinted with permission from Gerald M. Weinberg, Weinberg and Weinberg, Rural Route 2, Lincoln, NE 68505. The article first appeared in *Computer Careers News*, July 28, 1980.

already knew this—we *all* know this. Then why, oh why, do we keep tumbling into the same trap?

I believe the answer lies in our unwillingness or inability to feed back the true costs of programming and program maintenance to our users. Among our service bureau clients, the problem seems to have been brought to manageable proportions by the following steps:

- When a program is commissioned, the lifespan and the number of executions must be specified.

- If there is uncertainty about either of these figures, contingent prices are given, reflecting the differing costs.

- The contract is written stating that the program will be destroyed after a certain time and/or number of runs, whichever comes first.

- The program remains the property of the service bureau, unless the customer takes ownership—in which case a much higher cost is placed on the job, in order to pay for preparing the program to be taken over by other than the original programmers.

- The customer is notified when the program is about to be destroyed, and is given the option (at a substantial and realistic price) of having the program rebuilt for further use.

- If the program is a "one-time" program, no notification is given, but the program is destroyed—literally—as soon as the customer agrees to accept the results.

When working with inexperienced users, it is not difficult to get these terms accepted. Neither is it difficult with very experienced users, who know quite well the realities of "one-time" programs that turn out to be "N-time" programs. Only the in-between users have difficulty accepting these conditions, for they believe they understand about programming,

but actually have no solid basis for understanding. These people require selling. In many cases, they quit one service bureau for another when presented with charges for keeping a "one-time" program alive. In the end, however, most of them come back with their tails between their legs. For one thing, they have learned the important lesson that: it costs much more, in the end, to run a one-time program N times than to run an N-time program N times.

After a few costly lessons, they are more than willing to sit down *in advance* and decide whether they want to invest in an N-time program or merely in a disposable program that will actually be disposed of.

In internal data processing situations, especially where there is no true charge-back for programming or program maintenance, these lessons are difficult to teach. There is no cost to the users of specifying a one-time program and then asking that it be run N times. Without cost, there is no motivation to learn.

Where there *is* chargeback, it is possible to do what good, professional service bureaus do. Without chargeback, you can sometimes achieve some relief by manipulating the one parameter you have available—time. You request the user to specify a one-time or N-time program and then give different time estimates for each. The one-time estimate is shorter, but carefully spells out the procedure that will be followed in destroying the program after its first user. At first, users will not believe this procedure will be enforced. After a few lessons, they will begin to understand and devote some energy to the decision.

Of course, some users will simply attack the computing center manager, or the programmer, with an ax, literal or figurative. Such are the perils of our profession. Besides, even an ax in the forehead is better than the pain in some lower anatomy caused by an immortal one-time program.

Introduction

Spier, M.J. "Software malpractice—a distasteful experience." *Software—Practice and Experience*, 6 (1976), 293-299.

In the following case study, Michael Spier recounts how "foolishness, compounded by ignorance and topped by incompetence resulted in a most incredible compound software bug." A sequence of modifications, each one understandable if not wise, all but crippled a functional compiler. When Spier was called in to fix the cumulated problem, it took him a significant amount of detective work to uncover the sequence of mistakes which had been made. He advised management to rewrite the compiler, possibly using a very early version of it as a starting base. They did not take this advice, but he does not recount whether the compiler was ever fixed, or by whom.

Spier has been in computing since 1957. In 1963 he designed and built the first commercial time-sharing system in Europe, for the French company Bull. From 1966 to 1972 he participated in designing and implementing the Multics time-sharing system at M.I.T. (For more on this system, see the paper by Van Vleck and Clingen in Part VI.) In 1972 Spier came to Digital Equipment Corporation. (He tactfully notes that the degraded compiler is not a product of his current employer.) Since 1981 he has been the manager responsible for the development of systems to automate manufacturing plants.

The paper was originally written for the journal in which it first appeared. The title of the paper is, in fact, a tasteful pun on the title of the journal. It was written (Spier told us) as a "counter example" to those who too dogmatically advocate a specific "method" (e.g., structured programming) as the automatic remedy to all software problems. He notes:

> The point being made is that software is a living entity which evolves in time; the goodness of software relates not just to the first coding but to its ability to live on gracefully, and reasonably correctly, as modifications are applied and as people meddle with its insides.
>
> Thus, in my opinion, there is more importance to the proper modular decomposition into small, physically distinct bodies of code than there is to some fancy structuring method if applied to a gigantic (and hence, unmanageable) single program. Within such modules, of course, it is necessary to apply all other known structuring methods.
>
> Also, there is need for wisdom and craftsmanship on the part of the programmer (no method will alleviate this need), and a need to bring forth the overall architecture and semantics of the program in some obvious way, for that wise programming craftsman to do a reasonable job.

Spier reports that he has received extensive reader correspondence about this paper, "indeed the most internationally diversified response of any paper I have ever written." He further states, "Thus I do hope it contributed to progress in Bombay, Moscow, Leningrad, and Riyadh, to mention just four of the more attention-drawing places where it found audience."

SOFTWARE—PRACTICE AND EXPERIENCE, VOL. 6, 293-299 (1976)

Software Malpractice—
A Distasteful Experience†

Software Malpractice—
A Distasteful Experience†

MICHAEL J. SPIER

Manager, Manufacturing Applications Systems Engineering, Digital Equipment Corporation
146 Main Street, Maynard, Massachusetts 01754, U.S.A.

SUMMARY

A sequence of events is described, leading to the severe deterioration of an initially well conceived and cleanly implemented compiler. It is shown how an initial "optimization" implanted a latent bug in the compiler, how the bug was subsequently activated through innocent compiler modification, and how the compiler then deteriorated because of the incompetent correction of the bug manifestation. This exceedingly negative case history is presented in the hope of conveying to the reader a better feeling for the complex problems inherent to industrial software production and maintenance. The difficulty in proposing any constructive (and complete!) software engineering methodology is known and acknowledged; the study of an episode such as described in this paper might help put the difficulties, with which we are confronted, into better perspective.

KEY WORDS: GOTO-less Programming, Program Correctness, Software Engineering Methodology, Software Production and Maintenance, Structured Programming.

PRE SCRIPTUM

We recognize nowadays that the more programs we write for applications of increasing complexity and sophistication, the more uncertain we become of our ability to write these programs such that they be as "good" as possible. It has become fashionable for our colleagues to propose various remedies—often dogmatic in nature—which are supposed to enhance the "goodness" of our programs. Thus, for example, we are encouraged to adopt "structured programming." Nobody *definitely* knows what it is—although popular myth has it that a total ban on GOTO statements will automatically impart beneficial "structure" to our code.

"Goodness", of course, is in the eyes of the beholder. I must confess to a nagging suspicion that some of the proposed remedies come from sources more concerned with classroom toy programs than with the realities of everyday software production. The suggested remedies are typically exemplified by means of some neat little exercise (*e.g.* enumeration of prime numbers, bubble sort, matrix inversion, eight queens problem),

---

† This paper describes a certain compound software bug which was encountered by the author at a certain point in his career. It must be emphasized that this case history relates neither to the author's present employment with Digital Equipment Corporation, nor to any DEC software product.

perhaps very suitable as a classroom illustration but a far cry from the real world programs where we hurt. It is nigh impossible to relate the sample program to the real one (*e.g.*, operating system monitor, airline reservation system, inventory control system, payroll program) such that the remedy might be evaluated in respect of its actual context of application.

What most proposed remedies have in common is their insistence on *how to write* the program. Little or no attention is paid to the remaining issues inherent to everyday software production. In reality, a program has to be designed, coded, debugged, verified for an acceptable level of reliability (I hesitate to use the word "correctness"), modified, improved both in the sense of functionality and in the sense of performance optimization, and all the while be kept at a stable level of lucidity in order to allow for its continued evolution.

The totality of issues which have to be taken into consideration is staggering. The development of a comprehensive software engineering methodology is a challenge whose immensity defies our bravest attempts. I suspect that too few of our academicians really grasp the larger implications of the problem, tending to polarize their attention on what in reality are insignificant issues (*e.g.*, the great GOTO controversy), while failing to see areas of difficulty which literally beg for attention (*e.g.*, how many of our experts in programming linguistics have ever designed a non-interpretive language where the symbolic debugging facility is an integral part of the language specification?)†

Old Chinese proverb say *"one picture worth thousand words."* It occurred to me that by describing an exceedingly negative—though, unfortunately typical—case study of how foolishness, compounded by ignorance and topped by incompetence resulted in a most incredible compound software bug, I might succeed in conveying a feeling for the problems that afflict the software industry.

I came across this bug a good many years ago. I doubt that the affected program, indeed the computer itself, are still in use. It happened well before I entered DEC's employment and is unrelated to DEC and its products. Still, he who sits in a glass house is wise not to cast stones. Thus the following has been fictionalized sufficiently to convey the essence of the story without pointing an accusing finger at any identifiable culprit.

THE STORY

Back in those days when core memory was scarce, random access disk storage was unknown and card readers and tape drives proliferated, there was a compiler. It consisted of 23 tape-to-tape subcompilation passes. The compiler was initially well designed and coded in as modular a fashion as could be expected under the circumstances.

Each pass was a distinct program, loaded from a library tape to overlay its predecessor in memory. A certain subset of memory was reserved as a common communications area between passes, containing both data and code. A software (*i.e.*, macro-) implemented CALL/RETURN mechanism existed. The CALL instruction would push the proper return address onto a software managed stack and transfer control to the designated subroutine. The RETURN instruction would transfer control to the locality indicated by top-of-stack, after having popped that datum from the stack to reveal the underlying return address. The stack resided in the common communications area; its size was barely sufficient to accommodate the collection of return addresses corresponding to the longest observed sequence of calls. There existed neither stack overflow nor stack underflow condition detection provisions.

† From a purely pragmatic point of view, I find little appeal in a miraculous new language, if the corresponding debugging tool talks back to me in octal or hexadecimal. If that is the only debugging tool available, then by sheer instinct of survival I would opt for machine language code, for else I would be penalized by having to learn the compiler's code generation idiosyncrasies.

Initial Coding

The compiler was modularly structured, having an iterative main program residing permanently in the common area:

```
main:    subroutine;
         prologue;
         while   (compilation is to proceed)
         begin
                 load   (next program overlay);
                 call   [current pass];
         end;
         epilogue;
end      main;
```

where a pass was of the general form

```
pass:    subroutine;
         perform necessary computation;
         return;
end      pass;
```

As can be seen, the above is the rudimentary representation of a well conceived program which, upon return from the current pass, would test certain common variables to determine whether or not the compilation should proceed. In the affirmative case it would bring in the next program overlay and call it.

Each logical database (*e.g.*, the symbol table) typically required two tape drives; an input tape containing the current version and an output tape onto which the updated version was copied. Two subroutines residing permanently in the common area were FLUSH and SWITCH, each parametrized for any given database. FLUSH guaranteed that the entire updated version of the relevant database was completely recorded on the corresponding output tape. SWITCH rewinded the relevant tapes and made the necessary common variable updates to effect the functional permutation of the pair of tapes.

Initial Foolishness

Then, a bright programmer made a stupendous intellectual discovery whereby he could instill additional (subjective) "goodness" into the compiler. He observed that FLUSH and SWITCH were of the form

```
flush:    subroutine;
          perform flushing;
          call        switch;
          return;
end       flush;
switch:   subroutine;
          perform switching;
          return;
end       switch;
```

and decided to optimize the compiler by removing all space- and microsecond- "wasteful" calls, which in his judgement were functionally superfluous. In a recent article, Knuth[1] encouragingly recommends this foolishness, and even provides the recipe for its realization, to quote [*ibid.* pp. 280–282]: *"If the last action of a procedure* p *before it returns is to call procedure* q, *simply GOTO the beginning of procedure* q *instead."* And indeed, that is exactly what our wise guy did

```
flush:    subroutine;
          perform flushing
          goto switch;
end       flush;
switch:   perform switching;
          return
```

not merely with respect to these exemplified subroutines, but systematically throughout the entire compiler. With admirable perseverance, that anonymous optimizer invested a tremendous amount of work (to him, perhaps, a labor of love)† in order to save a few words of memory and an unmeasurable amount of CPU time. The unmeasurably "optimized" compiler continued to perform its function as reliably as ever.

Further Foolishness

Another "improvement" took place. Passes were no longer CALL-ed. Given that the end-of-pass locality was known, and that a pass always RETURN-ed to a fixed location in the main program, that program underwent transformation:

```
main:    subroutine;
         prologue;
         while   (compilation is to proceed)
         begin
                 load    (next program overlay);
                 goto    [current pass];
loop:    end;
         epilogue;
end      main;
```

where a pass was now of the general form

```
pass_i:   perform necessary computation;
          goto        loop;
```

Following this "improvement," the compiler continued to perform reliably. In view of the fact that this new modification is fraught with subtle traps (as will be demonstrated in the following), yet did not affect the compiler's reliability in any discernibly adverse manner, I suspect that this too was the handiwork of our original optimizer, whose professional competence (as distinct from his level of wisdom) must be acknowledged with the greatest respect.

Ignorance

Time passed. Our genial optimizer went on to accomplish bigger and better things in life. The compiler was now being maintained by programmers who were well below the optimizing wizard's level of technical competence. The programming language evolved—as programming languarges invariably do—and new linguistic features had to be incorporated into the compiler. Additionally, the compiler was gradually being improved, for both object code optimization and enhanced error detection facilities.

A continuous compiler recoding effort was underway. Certain passes were modified. Other passes were split in two and recoded from scratch. The programmers performing this work had no clear understanding of the compiler's underlying coding conventions, especially in respect of the magnificent "optimization" job which was done earlier. They did, however, assume that any systematically replicated pattern of code presented a safe way in which to program by mimicry. This is a most reasonable assumption which any seasoned programmer makes intuitively and typically follows through with success. In this case, our brave programmers innocently added the straw that broke the camel's back.

The recoding and/or modification effort inevitably required the services of "optimized" subroutine pairs such as FLUSH and SWITCH. For example, the modified compiler now evolved to the point where under certain circumstances SWITCH was to be invoked independently of FLUSH. If certain errors had been detected, a state variable was set to indicate that actual code generation was to cease, while further syntactic and semantic analysis should proceed for diagnostic purposes. The time consuming FLUSH-ing was then deemed unnecessary, however, a *pro forma* SWITCH-ing still had to be done to satisfy file system requirements. In fact, the analogous skipping of predecessor subroutines happened with respect to various other

---

† "Don't underestimate the value of love in labors of love; redirect aesthetics but don't destroy them," Knuth, private communication.

such subroutine pairs. The technical problem confronting a program modifier was: "How is a label—such as SWITCH—attained?" The solution to the technical problem was obvious. Namely to look up existing code, and upon detection of a universal pattern of label reference to faithfully mimic that pattern. SWITCH and various other subroutines were all very clearly and systematically attained by a GOTO statement. Thus everybody invoked those subroutines *via* GOTO.

Unfortunately, the necessary underlying condition for the successful usage of the "optimization" technique described earlier is *that there exist at least one valid return address on the stack!*† The once reliable compiler started crashing when a sequence of GOTOs led to a single unmatched RETURN statement (*e.g.*, in SWITCH), provoking a stack underflow condition and sending control to the locality indicated by the value of the word which happened to immediately precede the base-of-stack locality.

Incompetence

This bug manifestation was extremely difficult to analyze. Not all CALLs were removed from the compiler. The optimizing wizard knew his business (proof: following his contribution, the compiler's reliability remained unaffected), and saw to it that each logical path contained a matching number of CALLs and RETURNs. Being unaware of this critical convention, the modifying programmers violated it by omission.

The stack was common to all passes. The actual violation of the implicit convention need not necessarily have happened when the stack was empty! Given that by virtue of the *Further Foolishness* LOOP was now attained *via* a GOTO statement, the possibility existed for a stack underflow in pass i to cause successor pass j > i to crash. The effect of the crash was clearly discernible; the cause of the crash may well have been located in an overlaid segment of code. These bug manifestations were highly capricious, depending upon the flow of control as dictated by specific input sequences.

Management became alarmed. Everybody went into frantic "debug mode," busily poring over memory dump listings. Eventually it was discovered that the crashes must be due to a stack underflow condition. Rather than analyze the problem to determine its cause, a quick and dirty solution was implemented to negate the problem's effect. The main program was modified in the following grotesque manner:

```
main:    subroutine;
         prologue
         goto   loop;
         while  (compilation is to proceed)
         begin

                 load   (next program overlay);
                 goto   [current pass];
loop:    call    cont;
cont:    end;
         epilogue;
end      main;
```

where every passage through MAIN would push onto the stack a dummy return address pointing to CONT (which is functionally equivalent to LOOP) such that any extraneous RETURN would effect a transfer of control to CONT rather than cause a stack underflow.

---

† Another necessary condition is that the subroutine "invoked" with a GOTO statement not have any formal stack frame allocation, if such allocation is performed by the CALL instruction.

The bug manifestations known to be caused by the stack underflow condition were definitely "fixed." A new bug manifestation came into being when an *insufficient number* of the erroneous control paths was exercised. Specifically, the erroneous control paths produced a *deficiency* of return addresses on the stack. The new version of MAIN produced a *surplus* of return addresses on the stack, exactly equalling the number of times that control passed through LOOP. The stack was barely sufficient to accommodate the collection of return addresses corresponding to the longest observed sequence of CALLs. When an insufficient number of erroneous control paths was exercised, the stack would now *overflow.* The new symptom was recognized, and "fixed" by increasing the size of the stack by a number of words equalling the number of compiler passes! These extremely distateful modifications were made by someone who must have been a most incompetent programmer. Understanding neither the error's cause, nor the sheer asininity of his solution, he went ahead and "fixed the bug" to the general satisfaction of his superiors.

The Sorry Ending

The bug manifestations related to stack mismanagement were definitely "fixed" to preclude compiler crashes. Compilation would always terminate. The compiler's output ceased to be correct always, given that control would sometimes undertake certain quantum jumps in logic. The compiler produced esoteric code, and programmers were busy repairing the compiler at syntax analyzer, expression evaluator and code generator levels.

At this point I was called in to lend a helping hand. It took me a significant amount of detective work to reconstruct the sequence of events described above. I recommended that the compiler be written off as a loss, and that an effort be launched to remake the compiler, possibly using a very early version of it as a starting base. The recommendation was rejected. Firstly, the compiler was too widely used to be scrapped. Secondly, the management felt that if this compiler is impossible to maintain then any other compiler would be just as messy. Hence, they reasoned, there was no point in committing themselves to an unknown evil when they had finally resigned themselves to living with the current one.

POST SCRIPTUM

A software product has a lifespan during which it must undergo constant change. The "goodness" of the product must be maintained throughout that entire period of existence, of which the initial implementation is but a part (and a minor one, at that). The desired qualitative excellence is unfortunately subject to continuous modification; more regrettably, it is subject to practically unavoidable quantitative restrictions.

Concerning these quantitative restrictions; *volume of code* plays an exceedingly important role when it comes to large-scale software projects. The language chosen must allow for the independent compilation of program modules of manageable size. Consequently, global code quality can no longer be controlled by the language processor alone. Hence, no single "super compiler" would provide remedy. A possible solution would be to have a multi-level language where the linking of precompiled bodies of code would be treated as a semantically meaningful *post compilation* phase.

Similarly, *runtime efficiency* is as important a factor, as is—alas—the insistence on *memory usage minimization,* especially with regard to the ever more sophisticated expectations of small-scale minicomputer users. It is the quantitative aspect of the desire for the fastest possible execution within the smallest possible memory partition, which significantly contributes to the qualitative deficiencies of our software. The problem exists, and no amount of indifference to it will make it go away.

We have seen how a misdirected effort to "optimize" the compiler snowballed into catastrophe. Lest the proponents of GOTO-less programming gloat and proclaim: "See, I told you! You replaced some CALLs by GOTOs and God has inflicted just punishment upon you," let us reflect on the true meaning of this episode. GOTOs are but a tool, to be wielded incompetently or in a proficient, workmanlike manner. The act of replacing CALLs with GOTOs had—in itself—not the slightest deleterious effect upon the compiler, because the perpetrator knew his business and performed with commendable expertise. His successors did what they did and caused a *potential* bug to be activated. Yet potential bugs of similar severity lurk in practically all advocated programming languages. Consider FORTRAN, where the sequence of calls $X - Y - Z - X$ triggers a well known linguistic deficiency. And just in case some ALGOL *aficionado* grins and says: "Aha! Why don't you use an intelligently designed language which supports reentrant procedures," I would suggest that ALGOL and its derivatives have their own potential traps, the most blatant of which is the allowing of default references from a nested block to some outerblock variable, a notorious source of bugs of omission which are typically caused by innocent typos.

Give a bare machine to a programming wizard, and he will be up and running within a few weeks. Cast "pearls"† to swine, and you are no closer to that undefined Utopian "structured programming." I believe that the problem transcends the purely technical domain, and that its solution must encompass the managerial domain as well.[3] Such solution must comprise the methodologies, rules and conventions which have to be respected in order to impart certain engineering standards upon the programming profession (remember, the only *real* cause for the fiasco described earlier was the violation of a single unstated rule!). We may have paid too much attention to the way in which we express our algorithm; perhaps it is time to focus more attention on the technical and human engineering contexts within which the algorithm has to exist.

REFERENCES

1. D.E. Knuth, 'Structured Programming with GOTO Statements', *ACM Computing Surveys*, 6, No. 4, 261-301 (1974).
2. E.W. Dijkstra, 'Structured Programming', in 'Software Engineering Techniques,' *1969 NATO Conference Report*, J.N. Buxton and B. Randell (Ed.), NATO Scientific Affairs Division, Brussels 39, Belgium, April 1970.
3. M.J. Spier, 'A Pragmatic Proposal for the Impovement of Program Modularity and Reliability', *Int. J. Comput. Information Sci.*, 4, No. 2, 133-149 (1975).

---

† I hope that Dijkstra[2] will excuse the pun.

Introduction

Brown, P.J. "Why does software die?" *Infotech State of the Art Report*, 8, 7, "Life-Cycle Management," 1980, 32-45.

The following paper by P.J. Brown, the last in Part V, is a treasury of ideas and tips on software maintenance. Why does software die? Principally, says Brown, because it fails to adapt to change. His message is

> If we are going to produce long-life software which will withstand all the changes... we must make it good and keep it good.

How can we do this? Brown first rejects several false solutions, then, in a long section titled "Preventive medicine," he examines a great range of good design and programming practices and shows how they relate to keeping a system adaptable. He concludes:

> Software that works may be expensive to produce, but software that works and *stays* working costs more still. The extra effort goes into building a structure that allows for change, in producing readable documentation, in making the software portable and above all in keeping bugs down so that they do not make a big hole in the maintenance budget.

Brown started his computing career with ICT (now ICL), the British computer company, in 1960. He also worked for two years on assembler and PL/I compilers for IBM. He received his Ph.D. in computer science from Cambridge in 1968 and has been with the Computing Laboratory at the University of Kent at Canterbury since that time. He is responsible for several software systems, some for university research use, some for outside buyers.

He was invited to present the paper at the Life-Cycle Management conference sponsored by Infotech Limited in London in 1980, where the audience voted it "best paper of the day." He told the editors:

> I chose to write the paper partly because I feel strongly that too many people are offering over-simplistic solutions to the problems of software writing and management: "Wave this magic structured wand and all your problems will go away." Another motivation was to provide a simple introduction to a wide range of issues.

> There was a lively question session afterwards. A strong point that came out was that those who really take the trouble to do things right certainly reap their rewards during software maintenance: the cost of maintenance of a well-planned and executed product can be an order of magnitude less than that of a shoddy one.

Some of the flavor of this question session was captured in "Life cycle management (analysis)," *Infotech State of the Art Report*, Series 8, Number 7, 1980, Pergamon Infotech, Maidenhead, Berkshire, England.

WHY DOES SOFTWARE DIE?

Computing Laboratory
The University
Canterbury, United Kingdom

Complexity is the prime contributor to the premature death of software. How can we effectively fight complexity, whilst increasing flexibility and portability? Causes of short-lived software are first reviewed. The paper examines the preventive measures involved in building flexible software structures for the design of long-lived programs and for reducing the high cost of keeping systems alive.

CAUSES OF DEATH

In order to understand how to make software live longer, it is fruitful to examine why software dies. Death of established software comes from one of two causes:

1. Failure to adapt to change.

2. Murder: the software is overthrown by another, stronger, piece of software which does the same task.

The relative danger of these two depends on the nature of the product. If the software is designed to meet one special need, then competition may be non-existent. The chance of murder is therefore negligible, but if, as a result of change, the software no longer satisfies its one purpose, it will immediately wither away. General-purpose software, on the other hand, is in a more competitive market, and there is a greater likelihood of murder; murder is all the more probable if the software is weakened because it has not responded to change.

Infant mortality

A frighteningly large proportion of software projects die between conception and maturity in the sense that no established final product results. The good practices needed to ensure that established software will have a long and prosperous life are just as important in avoiding death in infancy. Infant software faces all the dangers of adult software (plus a lot more besides).

Death due to change

The changes that can kill software can arise in several possible areas. There may be changes in the operational environment, which involves hardware, software and standards. The model of the outside world on which the software is based may change; a payroll program, for example, can be ruined by a radical change in tax laws. There may be changes in user attitudes and in the way they wish to communicate with software. There may be, indeed there will be, changes made to correct bugs in the software. Finally, there will be changes as a result of user requests for new facilities.

On top of all of these there may be cataclysmic changes caused by such events as natural disasters, wars, riots, bankruptcies or by highly-paid outside experts reorganizing the software. No amount of planning in the design of software will help avoid such happenings, so we shall exclude them from our consideration. Instead we shall consider in detail some of the changes for which preventive medicine may be possible.

Hardware changes

Much software is killed in the prime of life by a change of hardware. Typically the casualty is tied to one machine by virtue of being encoded in assembly language or a non-standard high-level language; the original machine is replaced by another, different, one and death is instantaneous. Even software that was supposedly based on a standard high-level language, such as COBOL, is not immune.

There has been so much slaughter of good software by hardware changes that more recently the pace of change in machine order codes has been slowed. New hardware is now much more frequently designed to be compatible with the old, though not as compatible as the salesmen would have us believe. The problem of hardware change remains a serious one.

Hardware differences are also important when software is so successful on one range of machines that it is decided to implement it on several other machines as well. If software is available on many machines it has an added strength and vitality that should help see it through to old age.

This gives further impetus to the desire to design software to be portable from machine to machine, so we shall discuss the subject of portability in some detail later.

Hardware changes less drastic than a machine replacement can still kill software. A new periph-

First published in the *Pergamon Infotech State of the Art Report*
'Life Cycle Management,' Pergamon Infotech Ltd., 1980.

eral device attached to an existing machine can have dramatic consequences. In the past, we have seen examples of this where a disk has been added to what was previously a machine based on magnetic tape. Changes of a similar magnitude are likely during the lifetime of any successful software. Failure to respond to such changes will not cause immediate death, but a gradual loss of friends among users, perhaps ending in eventual murder.

Software changes

All software systems have others that they depend on. Thus, an application program may depend on an operating system, a compiler, and probably on other supporting aids such as editors and documentation systems.

Even the operating system, which has nothing between it and the underlying hardware, still depends on its compilers, its utilities and its application programs, as without these it is useless.

For most of us, the biggest and most burdensome dependence is on the manufacturer's systems software. Unlike changes of hardware, which are infrequent but earth-shattering events, changes of software are frequent and often apparently minor. However, if you have an applications program and leave it alone for a year, you can almost guarantee problems: when you come to run it again it will fail because of some subtle 'small' change in the systems software. If you leave it for, say, three years, you can equally guarantee that not only will the software fail, but it will be almost impossible to trace all the minor systems software changes that have caused it to fail. Your software has died of neglect.

Thus, catering for software changes is a matter of constant vigilance and attention to detail. If you have not been careful, a small change in the systems software might completely invalidate the principles on which your software is based. In addition, every few years the vendor may issue a complete rewrite of his systems software, an event almost as far-reaching as a hardware change.

Our discussion of portability will consider software changes as well as hardware ones. In addition we shall discuss the subject of interfaces, which also has a bearing on software changes.

Changes in requirements

Consider a suite of programs that is used to aid document preparation. The following examples illustrate requirements changes that may occur during the program's lifetime:

1. **Change of parameter.** The standard page width is changed.

2. **Additional feature.** The program is required to work on texts in a foreign language, which uses a different character set and allows accents to be attached to each character.

3. **Change of algorithm.** The program is required to improve its algorithm for determining spacing and hyphenation.

4. **Change of user interface.** Users wish to communicate with the program interactively, whereas the software works in batch mode.

5. **Consolidation.** The software is to be combined with another software suite, which makes spelling checks and cross-reference listings, and has been written using different conventions.

To the software writer, the striking facet of such changes in requirements is that they represent bullets that may strike randomly at each and every aspect of his software. The parts of the software that are susceptible to hardware or software changes can, with care, be predicted in advance, and preventive action can be taken in the appropriate cases. Any attempt to lessen the effects of future requirements changes cannot be localized but must permeate the entire structure of the software.

Changes caused by errors

All software that is in practical use contains errors. Like changes of requirements, errors strike randomly at all parts of software, but fortunately the software writers have more control over errors than over requirements changes. We shall discuss control of errors later.

Errors are a deadly and merciless killer of software. Death can come in two ways. Firstly, if software is riddled with errors, users will abandon it, and it will thus die of neglect; this is a big cause of infant software mortality. Secondly, software may be killed by poverty, because the effort of correcting errors has become so expensive that it uses up all the maintenance budget. A particular danger is the error explosion.

It is well known that in correcting one error there is a relatively high chance of introducing a further error. Typically, correcting one error introduces 0.5 further errors, so the error correction process eventually converges. On some projects, however, correcting one error introduces 1.5 further errors. The result is a long and increasingly painful illness with inevitable death after a year or so.

Summary

If we are going to produce long-life software which will withstand all the changes we have outlined, we must make it good and keep it good. In order to keep software good we must protect it from the sudden fatal diseases that may strike it down in the prime of life, and from the steadily debilitating diseases which will increasingly affect it in its later years. But our aim is not just to keep our software alive, but to make it increasingly strong and vigorous - to make it a murderer rather than a victim. Our aim is also to keep our costs down; if it is too expensive to keep the patient alive, the management will have no scruples about euthanasia.

SIMPLE SOLUTIONS

For every difficult problem in life there are a hundred people, some sincere, others not, offering simple solutions. Thus we hear propounded simple ways to solve a nation's economic problems or the social problems of the inner cities, and as individuals we are offered simple ways to make a killing on the stock exchange, to impress our friends and neighbours, to win at gambling, or to maintain perfect health.

It is tempting to dismiss the lot as worthless, but many of them do actually contain some sound sense, even if the effects are somewhat oversold. People who have inflicted problems on themselves through some gross and simple mistake may indeed find the simple solution invaluable. To take a concrete example, assume a simple remedy for ill-health is based on following some prescribed diet. If your diet previously consisted only of deep-frozen suet pudding with chemical beer, then following the diet may have dramatic beneficial effects. If, on the other hand, your diet is already a sensible one and your problems of ill-health are deep-seated, then the new diet will not help at all.

So it is with the simple remedies for bad software. If your methods were previously hopelessly bad, a simple remedy may be a godsend to you; if you already run a decent outfit and your problems are the deep-seated ones found in any complex software, do not expect too much.

We shall examine a few of these simple remedies, in case they do help.

Simple remedy 1--the analogy

A popular line of argument goes like this. Some home-spun analogy is drawn between software production/maintenance and some other well understood sphere. It is shown that problems in the second sphere were solved at some time by a particular method. Therefore, runs the argument, all the problems of software can be solved in a similar way. 'Producing software is like riding a bicycle,' you may be told. 'If you go at a reasonable speed you won't fall off, but if you go slowly you will lose your balance.' Having heard this you are convinced that going at a reasonable speed will solve all your software problems, and when you get back to work all those nasty and complicated difficulties will be swept away by your speedy new broom.

Analogies are not valueless. An analogy between writing software and riding bicycles, building bridges or whatever, may enable us to see ourselves more clearly, and possibly to see where current trends are leading. But there is always some fundamental mismatch between the analogy and the real thing. Some factor will differ by an order of magnitude: it may be the cost of reproduction (which for software is tiny), the complexity, the pace of change, or simply the nature of the human beings who build and use the software.

Simple remedy 2--the general solution

Software design has been riddled with attempts to build general tools which cover the function of a host of special tools. Periodically there have been designs for general languages that cover all applications, general compilers that compile all languages for all machines, general interfaces (such as UNCOL), and general operating systems which cover commercial batch processing, airline reservation systems and educational BASIC. In the early 'seventies there was a big movement into 'extensible languages,' which were programming languages that could be moulded to meet any given need.

The success rate for all these projects has been low. This is because in any discipline there is a point beyond which generality is infeasible because of the overall complexity and conflicting requirements. Thus for transportation there are cars that are general enough to cover both city traffic and the fast open road, but there are not cars that can also fly and travel by sea. In software we are beginning to get a feel for where the sensible limits of generality lie, and to be very wary of new super-general projects. (Readers can judge for themselves whether our reference to transport is a good example or the epitome of the mistaken analogy we have previously chided.)

A movement which may well be a current example of over-generalization is the attempt to provide general software components. Granted, you can build general packages and general subroutines to do some well defined common tasks (particularly mathematical functions, sorting algorithms and the like), but is it sensible to think of building a large piece of software out of a host of prefabricated components?

Simple remedy 3--the new methodology

At any conference one finds a persuasive speaker extolling the merits of some new methodology that will solve all the problems of software production and maintenance. To many of these experts a pertinent question is: 'Why, instead of spending your time talking about your methodology, do you not set up a company which will use the methodology to produce software ten times cheaper than anyone else, and thus make a real killing?'

PREVENTIVE MEDICINE

Having said that simple remedies do not provide a complete answer to the problem of software production and maintenance, it is now time to examine more elaborate methods, which involve a good deal of work, but which provide an eventual payoff. Before going into details we shall examine a fundamental law that affects all software maintenance work.

Large and small programs

If we have two pieces of software, x and y, where y is similar to x except that each component is twice as large, then y will be four times as expensive to produce and maintain. We call this the square law. The square law comes about largely because communication problems multiply extremely rapidly as software gets bigger. These problems come, at one level, with the way pieces of software communicate with one another, and, at another level with the way that humans who write and maintain the software intercommunicate. Also of prime importance is the capacity of the human mind; some programs are just too complicated for humans to comprehend, and are therefore unmaintainable.

The key to successful maintenance of large software--and it is large software that interests us, because small software is easy--is to cheat the square law. The basic technique is to split a large program up so that it appears as two small programs. If these two programs were each half the size of the original, and were totally independent of one another, then, given the square law, the pair of them would be twice as easy to maintain as the original. If we could keep halving our maintenance costs in this simple way, life would indeed be perfect (except perhaps for those two-thirds of the world's programmers who would be made redundant as a result). In practice, however, it is simply not possible to chop programs into two independent halves. In fact, if an unskilled butcher does the chopping--and there are lots of such people about--the two halves will have elaborate interdependence and communication requirements. The result will be that the two halves will actually be more complicated than the original, and therefore more expensive to maintain.

The aim must be to find a way of splitting programs up which, while inevitably short of perfection, avoids butchery; the goal is to split a program up into two (or more) parts with controlled and simple interdependence so that the sum of the parts is perhaps 30% easier to maintain than the original whole. This splitting should continue until the parts, or modules as they are often called, are reduced to an easily managed size, at which point splitting is of no further advantage. It is this goal that the huge volume of literature on 'structured programming' is seeking to achieve.

Interfaces

The more a large program is split up, the more interfaces are needed between the constituent modules. Those experienced in software production and maintenance will often tell you that the design of interfaces is what software is all about.

Clearly in any large software system, where modules will continually be added, replaced or deleted during the maintenance period, some all-

pervading and systematic design of interfaces is vital. This standard interface must be general enough to cover all capabilities, and must be simple to understand, simple to use and, above all, simple to enforce. It is important to realise that a fixed interface will not always provide the best means of communication between any two particular modules; instead it should provide one standard way. Programmers will be tempted to extend or vary the interface in those cases where it turns out to be a bit clumsy, but such temptation should be resisted at all costs.

A good deal of work in programming language design is now concerned with making interfaces clean and explicit. An important part of this is the import and export of variables (and other entities). A variable that is exported is one that 'belongs' to a given module but is used by other modules, which import it. A good example of these ideas, and one which may have a huge impact on the software community, whether we like it or not, is the ADA language (004).

Structuring

A lot has been written about structuring software and indeed a whole Infotech report (003) is devoted to it.

There are many available structuring methods, but they are fundamentally quite similar and all aim to meet the following goals:

o To aid both the production of software and its maintenance

o To cover both the way the software is coded and the way it is documented

o To encompass some of the ideas in the classic book 'Structured Programming' (002).

We shall not try to describe here what has already been presented in detail many times, but will simply reiterate that the most important thing is to have some sensible methodology--the particular one selected is less important--and that this methodology should pervade all aspects of design and be reflected in the documentation. The key to producing an easily-maintained product is to make it a good product in the first place.

Information hiding

A concept that has a bearing on structure and division into modules is information hiding. The concept was introduced by Parnas (006) and is of special relevance to program maintenance. The idea of information hiding is that modules should be chosen so that the effects of each design decision are confined to a single module. To take our earlier example of the documentation program, the way that text is stored should only be known by one module. Similarly, if a particular sorting algorithm is used to produce indexes, concordances, etc., then the implications of this should also be confined to a single module. The advantage is, of course, that if the method of text storage and/or the sorting algorithm needs to be changed, then the effects are confined to single modules and do not, as often happens, subtly permeate the entire software design.

Program families

Another area with which the name of Parnas is associated is program families (007,008). A set of programs is a family if 'they have so much in common that it pays to study their common aspects before looking at the aspects which differentiate them.' Some examples of families are:

1. A set of similar programs that run on different machines.

2. A set of programs that perform identical tasks but have differing ways of entering data.

3. A set of programs that are issued in various cut-down versions to work, say, in small storage or with minimal run time overhead.

Many of us have found that if we are responsible for such families the maintenance task soon gets out of hand. Moreover, market conditions often dictate the creation of program families even if this was not the original design intention. (There is a similar situation with hardware families.)

Parnas advocates that a software family be designed from the very start to be a minimal usable kernel together with various extensions to build other family members. This not only helps when a family is the original design intention, but also when changes during the maintenance of a program cause the ad hoc creation of family members. Parnas gives a detailed example in (008), and this is an excellent starting point for those wishing to pursue the ideas in depth.

Parameterisation

Some provision for change can be allowed for in the way programs are encoded. In particular, constants (for example the size of a built-in array) should not be embedded deeply in the code, but should be assigned as parameters at the start. Most high-level languages allow for this by providing such facilities as 'manifest constants,' 'constant declarations,' or 'macros.' (Macros, if available, allow even more flexibility than just substituting values for constants.) Some software writers claim that programs should contain no explicit constants other than 0 or 1, as anything else is likely to need changing.

It is also vital, when encoding a program, to ensure that the formats of tables and the way they are accessed can easily be changed. It is absolutely certain that such formats will need changing during the life of successful software, and programs should be designed so that changes in the ordering or size of fields can be done by changing only the relevant data declarations. Otherwise a typical result would be a program that becomes

useless if, say, interest rates unexpectedly climb into double figures; such programs are a lasting rebuke to their writers.

Freezing

During the life-cycle of any software project there are times when the forces of change are so burdensome and so destructive to progress that the management freezes some or all of the software components. In determining whether to freeze, it is important to analyze the nature of the requests for change. This may indicate that the software is fundamentally wrongly designed, and is not satisfying its design goals; if so, freezing the rubbish may be a short-term palliative but in the long term will be useless. Instead a redesign is needed, painful as that may be. It is quite common for the bulk of requests for improvements in software to be concentrated in one module of it, and this is a strong indication that the particular module is a weak point and needs redesigning.

On the other hand an analysis of requests for change may show that they are all for extra bells and whistles--or for special facilities to combine frequently used sets of operations. If so, the software is in a healthy state and can be frozen if circumstances dictate. Indeed the designers should be much more worried if there are no requests for change.

Standards

Standards play a large part in making programs easy to maintain and to disseminate. There is a spectrum of standards starting at individual standards, and going through company and national standards to international standards. Standards can never be perfect. Among their defects are the following:

1. Standards change; typically international standards for programming languages change every six years.

2. Standards take a long time to become effective, and by then they may be obsolete. Users may then be forced to deviate from a standard because they need some new facility.

3. Some standards are too lax (e.g.; in the precision and accuracy of arithmetic) whereas others are too restrictive (e.g., they may drive away advocates of 'GOTO-less programming').

4. Standards sometimes do not gain acceptance, with the result that the 'standard' site is actually the odd one out.

As one proceeds across the spectrum towards international standards these defects get worse, but on the other hand the standard itself is potentially more valuable.

In spite of all the problems, standards, albeit defective, are better than no standards at all.

Portability

Software is portable if it can easily be moved from one environment to another. The change of environment may be a change of hardware or a change of systems software.

The easiest way to make software portable is to encode it in a standard high-level language. This is especially good if the language has a portable compiler. Programming languages such as PASCAL and BCPL, which (as yet) have no international standard, have achieved great success because they have portable compilers. If software written in, for example, BCPL needs to be moved to a new machine, then if that machine lacks a BCPL compiler, it is not a major job to port the compiler across, thus making the software written in BCPL portable. Another advantage of portable compilers is that it is much easier to exchange software from one compiler to another. This is not true for languages without portable compilers, as anyone who has moved a 'standard' COBOL program from one machine to another will know.

Because of the defects of standards it may not be possible to encode all one's software in existing portable high-level languages. To solve this problem, organizations often design their own language extensions and write a preprocessor to map these extensions into the standard language. The benefits of portability given by the standard are not lost but great flexibility is gained. Examples of this are RATFOR (005), which is designed to surmount the lack of structuring in FORTRAN IV, and GENTRAN (010), which is concerned with the portability of civil engineering software.

Systems software, particularly operating systems and compilers, present special problems in portability. For a discussion of these, and for a fuller discussion of other aspects of portability, see (001).

Like all the other measures to ease maintenance problems, portability costs time and money in the program production stages. It is no use simply issuing an edict that certain standards must be followed, and then expecting that there will be no problems when attempts are made to port the software in future years. Portability must be checked and verified at each stage of software production. To help this there exist verifiers such as PFORT (009), which help check whether a given program adheres to language standards. These verifiers are not, and cannot be, perfect, and there is no substitute for practical testing of portability at an early stage by actually moving the software, or certain modules of it, to a different environment. This is sure to reveal a host of nasty little problems which can then be cured before the software is developed further.

Documentation

It is imperative that the documentation of software have the same structure, the same standards and the same flexibility as the programming. Unfortunately this rarely happens in practice. This is often because too much emphasis is placed on the size of documentation and too little on quality and interrelationships between the parts. Documentation standards, which may, for example, specify a fixed form for the documentation of each subroutine, may aid comprehensiveness, but cannot help readability.

The most common error in documentation is to provide masses of detail, which could equally well be found from the program listing, but little on overall organization, on the reasons for design decisions, on how things can be changed, and on relationships between parts. Rarely does the author of the documentation put himself in the reader's position of trying to proceed in easy stages from total ignorance to a complete grasp of a complicated piece of software. A way to help remedy this defect is to subject documentation to a thorough scrutiny by ignorant readers at an early stage. This costs time and effort but helps ensure that gross inadequacies of documentation are found before the author leaves the company at some future date.

Obtaining good documentation is often a question of changing the attitude of those who produce it. Doing a good job is an interesting and challenging task, just like writing a good program. It is the producing of voluminous bad documentation that is a dull task.

Errors

When software has been encoded it is inevitable that it will contain semantic errors (i.e., errors that cause the software to do the wrong thing when it is run). These semantic errors may arise from programming slips or from design errors. Good design and perhaps verification methods can lessen but not eliminate such errors.

The best single action that can be taken to increase software's life is to eliminate these errors before the software is issued. This is done by writing a good suite of test programs. Consider the possible history of a single semantic error. One possible history is for the bug to be found during the production stage of the software. Another possible history is for the bug to be found two years later by a user in the field. This second case brings about the following sequence of events:

1. The user finds the bug. For each such bug the reputation of the software and its supplier drops a little.

2. The user reports the bug.

3. The supplier recreates the bug at his own

site. This is often difficult and expensive to do, because of communication problems, hardware differences, version numbers, etc.

4. The supplier tries to localize the part of the software that caused the bug. Sometimes this is easy, sometimes (e.g., because of a subtle corruption of storage) it is difficult.

5. The maintenance personnel dig out listings and documentation of the appropriate version of the offending module, and try to comprehend what is going on.

6. The bug is found and remedied.

7. A test program is written to show that the correction works.

8. The bug is also corrected in subsequent versions of the software, particularly in the next one to be issued.

9. The corrected software is issued to users, either immediately or at the next scheduled release date, depending on urgency.

On the other hand if the same bug had been detected at the production stage, soon after it had been made, then:

1. The offending piece of code should be easy to detect. It is quite likely to be the part most recently added to the system.

2. The workings of the offending code are still in the designer's/programmer's mind.

As a result the only actions needed are 6 and 7 above. Hence it is likely that the expense of correcting the bug is ten times less than correcting the same bug found later in the field.

Testing

Testing is a topic that has been the subject of entire conferences. We shall confine ourselves to a few points that we feel passionately about.

1. It is imperative to have a comprehensive test suite that is used not only at the first release of software but at every subsequent release too.

2. The only people who can write decent tests are the original designers/programmers, since they know the workings of the software and its weak points. If their testing work is supplemented by a separate Quality Assurance department, so much the better, but this is only a supplement.

3. It is tragically false economy if software is released without proper testing in order to meet a deadline. What it means is that maintenance will be many times more expensive and future deadlines will be even harder to meet.

4. It is vital that those who write the software actually use it. Incredibly, many software writers make no serious attempt to use their product. The result is a hopeless user interface, and a host of requests for changes when the software goes into the field.

5. All software should contain decent debugging aids, so that those responsible for correcting errors can find out what is going on. It is particularly important to be able to print out internal tables in a comprehensible manner. If the only debugging aid is a hexadecimal dump, bugs will cost much more to correct.

We believe that attention to these five points at the software design stage could have dramatically reduced the maintenance costs of a lot of current software, and would have greatly increased life expectancy.

CONCLUSIONS

In order to make software have a long and healthy life, it is necessary to put a lot of extra effort into the initial product. Software that works may be expensive to produce, but software that works and stays working costs more still. The extra effort goes into building a structure that allows for change, in producing readable documentation, in making the software portable and above all in keeping bugs down so that they do not make a big hole in the maintenance budget.

REFERENCES

001 Brown, P.J. (editor), Software Portability, Cambridge University Press (1977)

002 Dahl, O.-J., Dijkstra, E.W., and Hoare, C.A.R. Structured Programming, Academic Press, London (1972)

003 Hosier, J. (editor), Structured Analysis and Design, Infotech State of the Art Report, Infotech Ltd., Maidenhead, Berks (1978)

004 Ichbiah, J.D. et al., "Preliminary ADA Reference Manual," SIGPLAN Notices, Volume 14, Number 6 (1979)

005 Kernighan, B.W. and Plauger, P.J., Software Tools, Addison-Wesley, Reading, MA (1976)

006 Parnas, D.L., "On the criteria to be used for decomposing systems into modules," Communications of the ACM, Volume 15, Number 12, pages 1053-1058 (1972)

007   Parnas, D.L., "On the Design and Development
      of Program Families", IEEE Transactions on
      Software Engineering, Volume 2, Number 1,
      pages 1-9 (1976)

008   Parnas, D.L., "Designing Software for Ease
      of Extension and Contraction," Proceedings
      of the 3rd International Conference on
      Software Engineering, Atlanta, GA, pages
      264-277 (1978)

009   Ryder, B.G., "The PFORT Vertifier," Software--
      Practice and Experience, Volume 4, Number 4,
      pages 359-378 (1974)

010   Shearing, B.M. and Alcock, D.G., "Gentran,"
      Proceedings Colloque International sur les
      Systems Integres on Genie Civil, Liege (1972)

Part VI: The Management of Software Maintenance

A management problem is always half technical and half political. The manager of software maintenance must juggle a particularly tricky mix of techniques and politics and must reconcile a number of conflicts intrinsic to the role.

The first conflict is between the interests of the three groups that together control the operational software of the organization (Figure VI-1). The maintenance group is one of them; the users and the operations group are the other two. Each of the three groups has a different set of motivations, yet all must cooperate if the organization's work is to be done and the organization is to prosper.

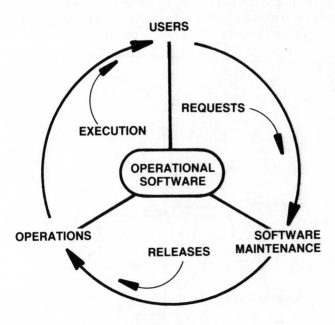

FIGURE VI-1 THE MANAGEMENT OF OPERATIONAL SOFTWARE

The users have the following motivations, in order of priority:

- The system must continue to perform its existing function ("today's business today").
- The system must change in order to track the changes of the organization ("tomorrow's business tomorrow").

A superficial observer might easily be misled about the ordering of this priority. In a successfully functioning organization, the users will always generate far more meetings, memoranda, and phone calls about a relatively small volume of new features of the software—thinking them up, pushing them, asking when they will be ready, getting information on them, and even thanking for them—than they will generate about the relatively large volume of existing capabilities. But note the proviso: *in a successfully functioning organization.* If an existing function fails, the user group will entirely forget about improvements until that function is restored. Nobody worries about bells and whistles when the engines are down. The operations and software maintenance groups tend to specialize on these two motivations of the users.

The operations group has a positive interest in stability and only a negative interest in changes, i.e., its concern with changes is to ensure that they do not disturb the stability of the system. Therefore the operations group performs the type of service associated with maintenance in physical systems—the archiving and back-up of storage, the rotation of physical units for preventive maintenance, and the recovery from random failures. By contrast, the software maintenance group has a positive interest in change (it pays their bills) and only a negative interest in stability, i.e., the concern of maintainers with stability is to ensure that stability does not prevent change.

Though software maintenance and operations groups have opposing interests in the matter of stability versus change, they share a common political conflict, i.e., each is a service group. A service group is always in an exposed political position. When successful, it is not directy credited, since (after all) it just "supports" the "real" work. When unsuccessful, however, it may incur direct blame.

There are two sure ways for the manager of software maintenance to fail in this exposed position: by trying to do a technically perfect job and by trying to please all the users all the time. In the first situation, the group is viewed as unresponsive and obstructive. In the second situation, the manager is like the lone defender of the Space Invaders video game (Figure VI-2); the invaders may not be fast or maneuverable, but they keep on coming, and in the end one of them will land a fatal shot. The fate of the manager is political disgrace, and the fate of the group is usually the ignominious imposition of "The Development Project" where highly paid outside consultants bleed the organization's computing resources by gestating an alternative system that will eventually be just as hard to maintain as the old one.

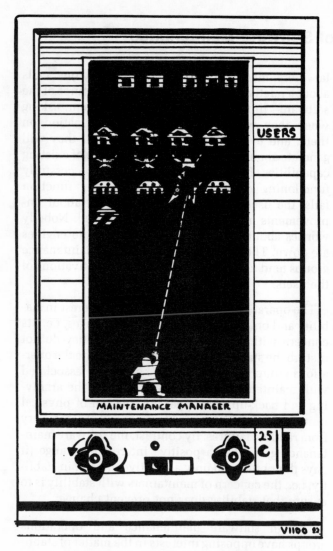

FIGURE VI-2 SOFTWARE INVADERS

criminated against unless special efforts are made to reward them explicitly.

These attitudes are slowly changing under several pressures. First, organizations that have used data processing for any length of time by now have an inventory of existing systems that constitutes a significant asset and therefore must be protected. Second, it is becoming clear that many "development projects" fall short of their goals precisely because their designers and implementors fail in a perception that is second nature to maintainers—how the new system must fit into the old.

These conflicts are natural and indeed healthy for the organization. Like the opposing tensions and compressions in a physical structure, they give the organization its form and functionality. The task of management is to make sure that each conflicting group has a territory in which to express its goals and that the groups have clear interfaces through which they can negotiate. It is not surprising, therefore, that all six papers in this Part deal with communication.

A third area of conflict, also shared by software maintenance and operations personnel, is between the perceived status of their jobs and the technical skills required of them. The closer a technician is to changing actual code, the higher the technical skill required.

(a) Users must understand what the system does.

(b) The operations group must understand (a) *and* how the system works.

(c) The software maintenance group must understand (a) and (b) and why the system works the way it does.

Nevertheless, maintainers are far too often considered second-class technicians whose job is to tidy up the fringes of the "original" work of development programmers. Managers report that it is hard to hire programmers if the job is advertised as maintenance, and members of the maintenance staff often feel dis-

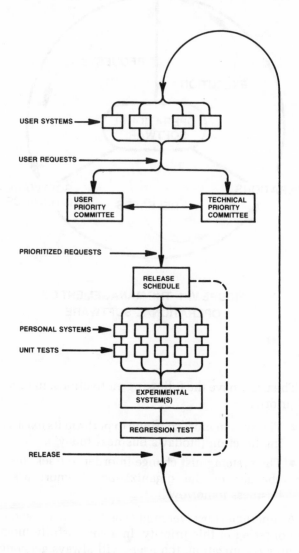

FIGURE VI-3 MAINTENANCE CYCLE INTERFACES

288

Figure VI-3 diagrams the interfaces through which a system must pass during the maintenance cycle, and it illustrates the technical context of the first four papers. At the top of the figure are USER SYSTEMS; these are multiple customer sites running the current release of the software. Each has local idiosyncracies such as local patches or different hardware configurations. In some cases the hardware may be completely different from site to site, as in the case of popular applications packages that run on many machines. Thus, the single "system" being maintained in fact appears in the field as multiple distinct versions.

Actual use of the systems (plus, in the case of an active sales organization, potential use by future clients) generates a stream of USER REQUESTS. This stream of requests is the maintenance manager's lifeblood; channeling it correctly is the key to success or failure.

The maintenance manager does not make the mistake of trying to decide among user priorities; such is the province of the USER PRIORITY COMMITTEE, where representatives of the user community trade political and economic arguments to support their own requests. Technical issues of cost, feasibility, and schedule are determined by the maintenance manager's staff in the TECHNICAL PRIORITY COMMITTEE. These two committees negotiate a list of PRIORITIZED REQUESTS and a RELEASE SCHEDULE in a process akin to budgeting. Any necessary arbitration must be provided by a level of management that bridges both user interests and the maintenance group.

The tasks necessary to satisfy the requests are split up among the maintenance staff so that, as far as possible, staff members can work independently. Thus, in Figure VI-3, staff members are shown as working on PERSONAL SYSTEMS. These personal systems may be split out from the total "system" in quite a different way than are the user systems. Consider, for instance, the maintenance of a library of mathematical routines; a maintenance programmer may work on a single algorithm in all its different machine implementations whereas a user has access to all the algorithms on a single implementation.

In due course the changes made on the personal systems are validated by UNIT TESTS and are integrated into an EXPERIMENTAL SYSTEM (or SYSTEMS) which are stand-ins for the user systems at the maintenance facility. REGRESSION TEST is a process of running all test cases that have *ever* worked to make sure that they *still* work. It is performed immediately before the scheduled RELEASE (distribution of the changed system to users) because of the user priority discussed earlier. Management will *not* yank a new feature from a new release because the feature itself only half works (in fact it is traditional that new features only half work), but management *will* yank a new feature if it prevents an old one from working. The new release becomes the new USER SYSTEMS, and the cycle continues.

The first three papers describe parts of this cycle in three heavily used systems. The fourth paper describes a communication system that smooths and directs the flow of messages required in such a cycle. The last two papers discuss the communications within the maintenance group necessary to promote morale in a difficult environment.

This introduction and the papers in this Part certainly do not dispose of all the problems of this challenging topic. Each book cited in the bibliography has something to add. Glass and Noiseux's *Software maintenance guidebook* has excellent material on people and maintenance and on planning for maintenance. Lientz and Swanson's *Software maintenance management* is an important source for how maintenance is actually staffed in a large sample of applications groups. McClure's *Managing software development and maintenance* is particularly good for the input and review that the maintenance group should have over an ongoing development project. Parikh's *Techniques of program and system maintenance* reprints nearly all of the most influential papers on maintenance management from the period 1969-1980.

Introduction

Bucher, D.E.W. "Maintenance of the Computer Sciences Teleprocessing System." *Proc. 1975 International Conference on Reliable Software*, 1975, 260-266.

The first two selections in this Part describe maintenance management for large commercial operating systems. Such environments provide examples of the maintenance problem in acute form, since operating systems (at least, successful ones) are large, long-lived, and are subjected to hard use by a wide variety of users. The management techniques that succeed in this environment must be robust. Reviewing these two papers and talking to their authors gave us an image of operating system maintenance groups as tight-knit teams with a long background of shared experience—very different from the common myth of maintenance programmers as novices operating in the dark.

The Computer Sciences Teleprocessing System, subject of the following paper, was designed in the late 1960's and went on-line in 1972. The current version has been upgraded to new hardware and vastly expanded in the area of data management, but its design is identifiably the same, and its languages are upwardly compatible. Don Bucher is a native of Canada, where he started in data processing in 1957. In 1964 he joined Computer Sciences Corporation, and in 1969 he joined the teleprocessing system project in the quality assurance function. Here, during the design and development phase of the system, he participated in developing a procedure for handling system changes which is still in place.

At the time Bucher wrote this paper, he was Manager of Quality Assurance. Since 1978 he has been in the Headquarters Marketing group of what is now a world-wide computing service. He therefore has an ideal perspective from which to view the management of the operational system all the way from the customers' wish-list down to the programmers' algorithms. He told us that the company is careful to keep technicians in contact with the commercial roots of the business, for instance by organizing an annual seminar for systems staff to meet the field representatives.

Bucher's paper also gives a capsule account of the documents, reviews, and testing procedures that contribute to the smooth management of a large system with a sensitive user base. This paper is a tutorial in itself! Readers interested in the technical goals of maintenance management might supplement this paper with "A quality assurance program for software maintenance," by John W. Center, which was given at NCC '82 (*AFIPS Conference Proceedings*, 51, 1982, 399-407).

MAINTENANCE OF THE
COMPUTER SCIENCES
TELEPROCESSING SYSTEM

D. E. W. Bucher
Computer Sciences Corporation

KEYWORDS AND PHRASES

maintenance, software, operating system, testing, project management, change control, Computer Sciences Teleprocessing System.

ABSTRACT

This paper describes the maintenance and enhancement of the Computer Sciences Teleprocessing System (CSTS) and its component processors. CSTS is the system offered by the INFONET Division of Computer Sciences Corporation to provide nationwide conversational and batch teleprocessing service. In the first section, the organization of the project personnel and major activities of project departments are described. The second section describes the process by which functional enhancements and error corrections are implemented. The final section describes testing techniques and procedures used during implementation.

The project staff is organized into implementation departments and service departments. Implementation departments develop new features of the system, corrections to errors, and improvements in system operation, especially in reduction of software overhead. Implementation departments are organized by system software functions such as operating system (device control, task management, and file management), language processors and data management systems, communications software, and applications. The service departments are system integration, performance analysis, product management and system test. The functions performed by these departments are described. Also described are the system evolution conferences and the periodic review of enhancements by a Change Advisory Board.

During the development of a new version of the system, effective tracking of the status of changed modules is essential. The data base and process used to track new features, error corrections and changed component modules are described. The flow of implemented changes through system integration and system test is delineated, as is the development and verification of change documentation for users, administrators and operations personnel.

The final section of the paper describes the design and documentation of test programs and the organization of test sets. Effective test operations are achieved by using self-checking tests as well as automated test operation and verification. Tests for compliance with functional specifications and for conformity to internal design are described.

INTRODUCTION

The prime factor affecting the reliability of software is the selection, motivation and management of the personnel who design and maintain it. Given an effective implementation team, the second factor is a service organization which provides timely and stringent test of the system during implementation or modification.

This paper describes the project organization that maintains the Computer Sciences Teleprocessing System (CSTS) [1] and the testing techniques used to ensure its reliability. CSTS is a general, time-sharing, conversational and batch teleprocessing service offered by the INFONET Division of Computer Sciences Corporation in the United States, and by affiliated companies in Australia, Canada, and South Africa. The system includes BASIC, COBOL, FORTRAN IV and V compilers, a text editor, three Data Management Systems and an extensive library of business, engineering and financial application packages.

CSTS was first offered for use in January, 1972 and currently operates on a network of eight operating systems. Each system consists of a UNIVAC 1108 central processor with a full 262,143 thirty-six bit word storage and 200 to 350 million words of disk storage.

During a typical prime shift, an average of seventy user tasks are executing at a center.

When the system went into production approximately 200 man-years had been expended to design and implement the software. During the three years of operation ending 1974, software maintenance consumed 30 man-years and system enhancements consumed 39 man-years per year.

Reprinted from *Proceedings of the 1975 International Conference on Reliable Software*, 1975, pages 260-266. Copyright © 1975 by The Institute of Electrical and Electronics Engineers, Inc.

The first section of this paper describes the organization of the project personnel and major activities of project departments. The second section describes the process by which functional enhancements and error corrections are implemented. The final section describes techniques and procedures used during implementation testing and final regression testing prior to a new release of the system.

PROJECT ORGANIZATION

The project staff is organized into implementation departments and service departments (see Figure 1). During 1970 and 1971, the period of greatest implementation activity, the staff size was approximately 120. The current staff is 69.

Implementation departments develop new features of the system, correct errors, and improve system operation. Implementation departments are organized by system software functions:

- Executive components (device control, task management, file management and system command language (GPS))

- Language processors and data management systems

- Communications software

- Applications library maintenance

This paper is concerned with the activities and support functions of the service departments. The service departments are:

- System integration

- Product management

- Performance analysis

- System test

The Performance Analysis department examines the production performance of the system, especially to determine causes and quantity of system overhead. For example, the Performance Analysis department investigates the frequency and causes of task swapping, and then recommends improvements to reduce such overhead while maintaining response time.

The Product Management department performs long-range planning and selects new applications relative to marketability, performance and revenue. The Product Management department also schedules and coordinates

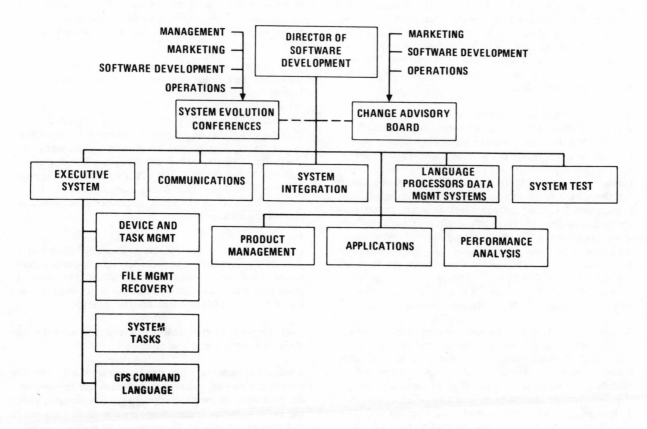

Figure 1. Project Organization

the development or purchase of new applications. Suggestions for potential major software are evaluated in conjunction with Marketing staff relative to:

- market size and potential revenue

- user profile and user requirements

- existing and potential competitor service and price

- required product capabilities and functions.

New software suggestions with positive potential are referred to a committee of senior executives for approval when a change in scope of the function or applications services of the system or additional funds are required.

The System Integration department maintains all source code (approximately 370 programs) and object module files which comprise CSTS, maintains system libraries, generates system boot tapes and administrates the operation of the R&D center on which the system is developed and tested.

The System Test department checks system modifications, and maintains and improves the test libraries. In addition, this department develops system change documentation and installation procedures for new system versions and releases the new system versions to operations. During the period of greatest implementation activity (1970 - 1971), a staff of 25 was engaged in testing. Currently, the department has a staff of 7.

In addition to these departments, a standing committee, the Change Advisory Board (CAB), reviews, evaluates, and schedules proposed enhancements to the system. This board includes members of the Software Development staff, Marketing, Finance and Operations. Marketing representatives provide input relative to the value of proposed changes to users. Members of the Software Development staff provide cost and schedule data, as well as specific implementation and functional specifications of the changes. Representatives from Finance and Operations provide information as to the effect of proposed changes on the production operation of the system and evaluate the effect on customer documentation.

Periodically, selected Marketing, Operations and Management personnel meet with a group of the Software Development staff for a System Evolution Conference. This conference is a combination of a technical symposium and planning session at which the long-range system and network evolution are discussed. The purpose of such conferences is to provide a forum where management and designers can exchange ideas about the projected teleprocessing market and changes to CSTS.

In summary, the project staff has been organized to provide control and effective division-wide communication in order to achieve system reliability and functional enhancement relative to user processing requirements.

SYSTEM DEVELOPMENT PROCEDURES

Three documents and a data base are involved directly with the maintenance and enhancement of CSTS. The processing of these documents and the monitoring of activities enabled by use of the data base are the keys to continuing evolution of the system.

The three documents are the Software Improvement Request (SIR), the Software Implementation Proposal (SIP) and the Software Problem Report (SPR). The data base that is used to control the flow of activity is called the CSTS Task List data base.

SIRs are submitted by field technical, marketing and operations personnel to request functional enhancements of the system. The SIRS are submitted to the operational unit's CAB representative who determines whether the SIR should be submitted to the CAB and ensures that the SIR is clearly defined and is complete. The CAB determines the validity of each SIR brought before it. If accepted by the CAB, the SIR is logged in the data base assigned to an appropriate member of the Software Development staff for analysis.

The analysis is documented through submittal of a SIP which contains an estimate of the implementation cost, a proposed schedule for implementation, as well as the specifications for implementation. The SIP is returned to the CAB for resolution where it can be accepted, rejected or modified, as appropriate. If approved by the CAB, the SIP is logged in the CSTS Task List.

An SPR is originated by any member of the INFONET staff to report an error. Like SIRs, SPRs are screened for accuracy and adequate information by the originator's representative on the CAB. If accepted as a valid problem, the SPR is logged in the CSTS Task List data base and assigned to a member of the appropriate implementation department for analysis. The resultant analysis indicates a target date for problem resolution, a proposed remedy for the problem and a temporary circumvention procedure until the error is corrected. Each modification to the system is submitted to the System Integration department as a package including the SIP or SPR responded to, module(s) changes, interface dependencies, external effects and proof of unit test. The change is logged in the CSTS Task List data base, closing the appropriate SIPs or SPRs. Logging the change notifies the System Test department that specific test activity should begin.

Note that the data base is used to monitor implementation, integration and testing of enhancements or changes to the system. Figure 2 represents a sample page of a CSTS Task List report. The data base was created and is maintained through the Data Management Language (DML) [2] processor of CSTS. Using the CSTS Task List reports, Software Development management can track progress of action items by system release, by implementation department, by implementor or by test status.

STATUS CODE - BLNK - REVIEW IN PROGRESS   F - FIX IN CURNT BLK TIME   N - NOT ENOUGH INFO   T - TIME AVAILABLE
                A   - ASSIGNED RELEASE   H - TABLE (HOLD F/FUTURE)   C - CORR, NO CSF   U - USER ERROR
                D   - DUPLICATE INVALID   Y - UNABLE TO REPRODUCE   R - REJECTED   X - REJ. CHG REQUEST REQD
                S   - OTHR FORM REF   P - PARTIAL FIX

FORM TYPE	FORM NO	DESCRIPTION	AREA	ASSIGNMENT	TEST STAT	RELEASE	CSF NO	CNTR ID-ORIGNATR	STATUS	MODULE AFFECT
P	2161.	OUT$ FILE KEYS	SYSTSK	RAYMOND		14.0		D-BRUEN	A	
P	2162.	IMPLICIT WALK DISPLAY IN GPS	GPS	HARRISON	D	12.0		D-BRUEN	A	
P	2163.	FORTRAN ENCODE/DECODE ENHANCMT	FR5	MATHE		14.0		D-MATHE	A	
P	2164.	FORTRAN ALPHA CONSTANT ENHANCMT	FR5	MATHE		13.0		D-MATHE	A	
P	2165.	FR5 ENCODE/DECODE FREE-FIELD	FR5	MATHE		14.0		D-MATHE	A	
P	2166.	FR5 TO SURFACE FL DATA OPTION	FR5	MATHE	JB	12.0	12559.	D-MATHE	F	FSCOLS
P	2167.	GPS CLOSE COMMAND	GPS	HARRISON	D	12.0		D-SANFOR	S	
P	2169.	LARGER FILE CAPABILITY	F/M-R	RATZ	PL	12.0		D-SEARL	A	
P	2170.	BOOT TAPE GENERATION	INTEGR	PAULSEN	OK	12.0		D-DRABEN	A	
P	2172.	ELIMINATE OLD LINKER	INTEGR	PAULSEN		14.0		D-BAGWAL	A	
P	2185.	DML-LINE STARTING WITH 2 COLON	DML	BROAD	JB	12.0	12665.	D-BROAD	F	PARSIT
P	2186.	DCT 500 PAPER TAPE HANDLING	RCC	DRABE		12.0		D-DRABEN		
P	2188.	AUTOMATIC DSKULK	GPS	HARRISON		12.0		D-HARRIS	A	
P	2189.	FR5 2-WORD TYPELESS VARIABLES	FR5	MATHE	OK	12.0	12632.	D-MATHE	F	FSARIS
P	2190.	FORTRAN CHARACTER TYPE	FR5	MATHE		13.0		D-MATHE	A	
P	2192.	IFMS/ALLOCSB REPORT 7 MSG MODS	APPL	ELSEN		4100		D-HOPKIN	A	
P	2193.	IFMS/TLSKED REPORT FORMAT CHAN	APPL	ELSEN		4.90		D-HOPKIN	A	
P	2196.	SPSS OPTION FOR FREE FORM I/P	APPL	ELSEN		74.3		D-TAYLOR	A	
P	2197.	SUPRES OUT$ DSPLAY-USAGE, SET	GPS	HARRISON		12.0		D-TAYLOR	A	
P	2201.	DEFINE-CHANGE-UNDERGO EQUATE	F/M-R	TROTTMAN		14 0		D-PERTH	A	
SPR	8678.	DML STATISTICAL OPERATION STAT	DML	BROAD		12 0		D-FORD	A	
SPR	8681.	WHEN FLE-CATLG DISPLYS ON/QBS	GPS	HARRISON				D-CLADIN		
SPR	8682.	SKULK DROP PRINTS FMD777 FLE	GPS	HARRISON		12.0		D-BLACK	A	
SPR	8684.	TERMINAL HNGS-DEVICES COMMAND	GPS	HARRISON				D-FORD		
SPR	8685.	ATTENTION DURING SKULK-GDE MDE	GPS	HARRISON		12.0		D-LINTOL	A	
SPR	8687.	DEVICES DROP FAILS DEALLOCATE	GPS	HARRISON				E-BLACK		
SPR	8688.	UNABLE TO USE 2 TAPE DRIVES	GPS	HARRISON				E-BLACK		
SPR	8689.	FAILURE TO GIVE PROMPT	GPS	HARRISON				E-BLACK		
SPR	8690.	GPS MISHANDLES VERSION SYNTAX	GPS	HARRISON				D-KEITLI		
SPR	8693.	LINK FAILS DIAGNOSE 512 PGES	LINKER	BAGWAL	OK	12.0	12319.	E-BAGWAL	F	LSQMOD
SPR	8694.	FUNNY OPEN READS CATLG TWICE	F/M-R	TROTTMAN		12.0		D-SEARL	A	
SPR	8694.	FUNNY OPEN READS CATLG TWICE	F/M-R	RATZ		12.0		D-SEARL	A	
SPR	8695.	MOVE OFFS FROM PAGE ZERO	F/M-R	PERTH		12.0	12709.	D-SEARL	F	FSLBDP
SPR	8696.	MARK LIBRARY AVAILABLE	F/M-R	PERTH	PL	12.0	12710.	D-SEARL	F	FSLBMC
SPR	8697.	FTN/FRS LOOPING-BACK SPACING	FR5	MATHE				D-ROSSER		
SPR	8698.	FTN/FRS GUARD MOD BACKSPACE	FR5	MATHE				D-ROSSER		
SPR	8700.	REFERENCES TO SYSVOL	D-T/M	RONALD	RR	12.0	12221.	-SHILLI	F	SSSTVL
SPR	8701.	FMD112 ON COPY	GPS	HARRISON	HW	12.0	12562.	D-FORD	F	CSCOPY

- -

FORM TYPE: P INDICATES SIP, R INDICATES SIR.

FORM NO: IDENTIFIER FOR THE SIP, SIR OR SPR.

DESCRIPTION: ABBREVIATED TEXT FROM THE FORM TITLE.

AREA: IMPLEMENTATION DEPARTMENT OR GROUP ASSIGNED.

ASSIGNMENT: PERSON ASSIGNED TO IMPLEMENT THIS ITEM.

TEST STAT: INITIALS OF PERSON ASSIGNED TO VERIFY THIS ITEM, "D" INDICATES DOCUMENTATION IS COMPLETE,
                     OR "OK" INDICATES VERIFICATION IS COMPLETE.

RELEASE: SYSTEM RELEASE NUMBER IN WHICH THIS ITEM WILL BE EFFECTIVE.

CSF NO: CHANGE SUBMISSION NUMBER LOGGED BY SYSTEM INTEGRATION.

CNTR ID-ORIGINATOR: NETWORK CENTER AND ORIGINATOR OF THIS ITEM.

STATUS: SEE REPORT HEADER.

MODULE AFFECT: SYSTEM MODULE CHANGED WHEN THIS ITEM HAS BEEN IMPLEMENTED.

Figure 2. CSTS Task List

Planning for a new system release begins with a review by department managers of specific target items. This review is based on schedule and available resources. Marketing and Operations managers provide priority considerations for target items. The proposed content of the release is determined and the CSTS Task List data base is revised if appropriate. Department and individual assignment lists are generated using DML. As implementation progresses the data base is updated to reflect completed items. Because all system components are implemented and maintained using CSTS in production mode, the utility of enhancements and stability of the system is improved. The designers and implementors are motivated to provide effective command syntax, to develop processors with a high degree of utility, and to conduct extensive unit tests because they use and "live with" the evolving system.

Using SIPs, the System Test department prepares functional specification documentation for the release. Separate documents are prepared describing changes significant to users, system administration and operations. These documents are used in designing modifications to the test library. The System Test department staff assignments are made for both documentation and testing and the assignments are entered in the data base.

In developing a new system release, project management must first define a significant group of enhancements to the system, then schedule implementation and testing and finally control the evolution of the system in order to meet the schedule and ensure system stability.

Project management establishes a schedule of milestones for the release. These milestones include:

- Major design revisions to be completed at an early date

- Changes which are significant to system stability (implementation of such items is scheduled for early completion)

- Date by which all processor code changes are due

- Regression test period

- Documentation delivery

- Delivery to operations

Review of these milestones, the rate of submission of system module changes and the rate of submission of SPRs measured against revised components provides project management with the information necessary to reallocate resources as required to avoid unstable modules in the system or schedule slippage. The resources allocated are both human and hardware, involving production time on CSTS for development and for test sessions.

TESTING TECHNIQUES

Test cases for major components of the system may be classified as external, internal or diagnostic. External tests are designed to verify conformity of the component to its functional specifications. Internal tests are designed to verify that a module has been implemented as specified in its design documentation. In preparing internal tests, subroutine calling sequences (number, type and value range of arguments), storage capacities and flow paths are checked. The purpose of internal tests is to ensure that all flow paths are exercised. Diagnostic tests are designed to deliberately violate functional or design specifications. Each diagnostic that can result from misuse of a new capability is displayed at least once. The System Test department attempts to develop difficult situations unforeseen by the implementors. Diagnostic tests are developed by analyzing both functional and design specifications. These tests may be considered as that subset of the external and internal tests which will not execute (or be processed) as valid input by the processor under test.

A preeminent design principle in all test cases is that they be self-checking and produce as little output as possible. For example, the FORTRAN tests call a standard subroutine used to verify the accuracy of all types of expression results. In the event of an error, this subroutine displays the statement number at which the error occurred, the variable or array (and subscripts) in which the result is found, the actual and expected results.

In many cases, output files must be generated during a test to be used as a checking mechanism. Such files are originated and verified manually to become the standard of comparison. The output of subsequent tests is compared with the standard file by a scanning utility routine which reports discrepancies between the files. The scan routine will resynchronize the files when extra or deleted records occur relative to the standard file and may eliminate comparison of records with specific values such as date and time of execution. Self-checking techniques are valuable in increasing the producitivity of the System Test staff, especially in conducting massive regression tests. These techniques allow the test staff to design extensive stringent tests or to execute many such tests without having to manually check a high volume of hard copy output in order to verify the results.

Another prerequisite of a test case is that it must be self-documenting. Each test file includes a preface or commentary which contains:

- Test identifier (file name)

- Component tested

- Subroutine(s) used or other execution dependencies

- Description of test point

- Method of test

- Input/output required.

Figure 3 illustrates the commentary preface to a COBOL test. Because this commentary exists as a preface to the test files, hard copy documentation need not be published. Instead, the documentation may be obtained from the test files, as required.

A library exists in the CSTS R&D system for the test cases (files) of each major component or processor of the system. For example, separate libraries exist for each language processor test set, the file management and recovery test set, the command language test set and the communications test set. Each library contains a cross-reference file in which test points are correlated with specific tests. Examination of this file allows selection and access of tests for specific test points or features.

The test set for FORTRAN consists of 180 programs which contain a total of 75000 statements. The test set for DML consists of 76 programs which contain a total of 5000 statements. File management and recovery are tested by the File Management Loading Facility (FMLF) processor. Input to FMLF consists of parameters such as file sizes, file attributes, access methods and input/output operations to be performed. During the FMLF process, each input or output operation is logged in a printable output file. Each operation is verified, and if

```
IDENTIFICATION DIVISION.
PROGRAM-ID.        CLX521.
AUTHOR.            COMPUTER SCIENCES CORPORATION.
INSTALLATION.      650  N.  SEPULVEDA  BLVD.
           LOS  ANGELES,       CALIF.
DATE-WRITTEN.      OCTOBER, 1970.
DATE-COMPILED.
REMARKS.

            TEST ID -- CLX521      COMPONENT TESTED -- COBOL

            SUBPROGRAMS USED --  NONE

            USED BY --  NONE

            FUNCTIONS TESTED --      STANDARD   UNKEYED
                                        SEQUENTIAL   I/O

            DESCRIPTION --  CLX521  IS  A  PROGRAM  DESIGNED
                TO  TEST  ONE  FEATURE  OF  STANDARD  UNKEYED
                SEQUENTIAL  I/O.   THE  PROGRAM  CREATES  A
                PDM  FILE  USING  THE  PDM  MOVE-MODE
                UNSPANNED  CAPABILITIES  OF  FILE  MANAGEMENT
                AND  THEN  READS  THE  FILE  USING  PDM
                LOCATE-MODE  AND  LOGICAL  RECORD  SERVICES
                (LRS).

            OPERATING INSTRUCTIONS --   COMPILE  AND  EXECUTE

            INSTRUMENTATION --  N/A

            ENVIRONMENT --  N/A

            INPUT --     1-  PDM  LOCATE-MODE  FILE  (LC521A)  -
                             DISK
                         2-  LRS  FILE  (LC521A)      -   DISK

            OUTPUT --    1-  PDM  MOVE-MODE  FILE    (LC521A).  -
                             DISK

                         2-  TEST  RESULTS  REPORT   (LC521B)  -


ENVIRONMENT DIVISION.
CONFIGURATION SECTION.
```

Figure 3. COBOL Commentary Preface

an error occurs, appropriate data is dumped to the log file for analysis. There are 70 test cases used as input to FMLF. Multiple FMLF processes provide ease of heavy input/output load testing of the system.

Because the test sets for CSTS have existed for some years, and are in constant use, much of the documentation is contained within the test libraries for ease of maintenance. The system itself provides a convenient storage and maintenance facility. An excellent model for the organization and content of complete test set documentation is NBS FORTRAN Test Programs [3].

Test operations may be classified as specific test session, mini-test sessions, general regression sessions, and total regression sessions. A specific test session is one in which a specific new feature (SIP) or specific problem (SPR) correction is tested. A mini-test session is conducted by invoking a driving command program which executes a wide variety of tests in approximately five minutes to prove the general viability of the system or a major component of the system. Such tests are frequently used by the System Integration department to prove that a new version of the system is viable for an extended test session. A general regression session is conducted by invoking a driving command program which will prove whether a processor has reached production status. For example, a new FORTRAN compiler is built in a development library. Access to that library is available to the FORTRAN test set library. A general regression test consisting of twenty programs can be compiled and executed in fifteen minutes. If this test is successful the compiler is placed in the system library for general development use. Before the compiler is delivered to Operations, the total regression test is executed. The total regression test comprises a set of driving command programs which compile and execute all tests in the library.

Analysis of test results and of the quantity and rate of generation of SPRs provides project management with a view of development status and system stability independent of implementation status reports. Management is able, with this information, to distribute resources relative to both implementation schedule and system stability.

The maintenance of test sets is, as with the system itself, keyed to the existence and schedule of SIPs and SPRs. Analysis of a new system feature (SIP) results in design of a new test file, modification of an existing test or revision of the expected results of an existing test. SPRs written by persons other than the System Test staff are considered as deficiencies in the test set. Tests are modified or created to reproduce reported problems and are used to verify error corrections. Early development of new tests is important. Throughout the life of the project, test set design and implementation has been planned, scheduled and effected in parallel with system development. System components are tested as soon as they are integrated. Subsequently, extensive regression tests are conducted as the system evolves. The frequency of regression testing is balanced with development requirements relative to consumption of hardware resources. Testing is necessarily a policing function in that the objective is to detect deficiencies in design, documentation and implementation. The testing staff provides a service to assist developers in assuring the high quality of their product. Cost-effective testing is achieved by care in analyzing test results to ensure that valid errors are accurately described in SPRs and that adequate data are provided for diagnosis.

The key to production of a reliable system release is control:

Control of release content, specification and schedule,

Control of implementation,

Control over testing, and

Control over resource reallocation to solve the inevitable schedule and stability problems.

The principles and techniques described have proven effective in the maintenance and improvement of CSTS.

BIBLIOGRAPHY

1. CSTS Concepts and Capabilities, E00175-01, March 1973. INFONET Division Computer Sciences Corporation.

2. Blackwell, I. and Schwarts, J. DML-An Interactive Data Management Language, Proceedings of IFIP Congress 74.

3. Holberton, F.E. and Parker, E.G. NBSJR 73-250 NBS FORTRAN Test Programs, Version 1 and Version 3, June 1973, Final Report, U.S. Department of Commerce.

Introduction

Van Vleck, T.H., Clingen, C.T. "The Multics system programming process." IEEE Computer Society, *3rd International Conference on Software Engineering*, 1978, 278-280.

The second selection also deals with an operating system—the Multics system offered by Honeywell Information Systems, Inc. Multics was conceived in 1964 as a joint project of M.I.T., General Electric, and Bell Telephone, and it first came on-line to users in 1969. From its inception it was programmed in a higher level language (PL/I) and offered to the user a time-shared virtual machine with a single-level virtual storage (i.e., any object, whether variable, array, file, or device, is addressable as if it were directly available to the program). All these long-range decisions were taken because the original planners grasped how far an operating system has to travel and how long it lasts; the system was built to evolve.

Both Van Vleck and Clingen worked on Multics from its early days. Tom Van Vleck came from M.I.T., joined the programming team in 1966, and stayed until 1981 when he moved to Tandem Computers, Inc. Charles Clingen came from General Electric and joined the team in 1967. His first job was the design-level review of the resource demands of the virtual storage system. In 1968 he became manager of the General Electric software group in Massachusetts, and in 1978 he became Director of the Multics Development Center.

Their paper deals with communication processes within the maintenance programming group, within the span of Figure VI-3 between PRIORITIZED REQUESTS and RELEASE. The technical quality of the system is maintained by the severest test of all—peer review. A programmer presents the technical design of a proposed change to a meeting of the Multics Change Review Board. Van Vleck told us that any system programmer can sit on this Board—but you have to be prepared to sit through the complete meetings. The meetings are held jointly at two development sites, in Massachusetts and Arizona, with design discussions held via electronic mail. Clingen told us that there is a policy to "force" communications among individuals on the project, for instance by distributing all design documents to all members.

This helps to bring new programmers up to speed, a real challenge for projects whose life-span is longer than the assignment of an individual worker.

A change is programmed online by a programmer or a small team of programmers on a development system. The flexibility and security of the time-sharing operating system enables the changed code to be exercised without contaminating the operational version. The change is then reviewed by colleagues and is unit tested. As soon as it has passed unit test, it is installed as part of a running system at a development integration site, either in Massachusetts or in Arizona. The time between installation on the EXPERIMENTAL SYSTEM and RELEASE can be used by the operations group at the test sites to validate the operations procedures of the new feature, for instance the "bring-up" instructions. Clingen characterized this sequence as "a continuous flow of development against a planned future release."

Van Vleck sent us this list of "key concepts" for controlling this complex process:

- Document before implement. Design in writing.
- Consensus and review.
- Incremental integration of changes, early exposure.
- Lots of machine resources, powerful tools.

The paper reprinted here does not deal with the political processes of prioritizing requests or of procuring resources. Clingen told us that marketing pressure characteristically comes in two forms: from prospective customers the cry is for "More features!" and from actual customers it is for "More reliability!". The resources for the maintenance and development group are fixed by a budgeting process which weighs current demands from the marketing side against a technical assessment of their cost and feasibility.

For another remarkably frank look at the management of Multics, read "A managerial view of the Multics system development" by Corbató and Clingen, in *Research directions in software technology*, edited by Peter Wegner, The MIT Press, 1979.

THE MULTICS SYSTEM PROGRAMMING PROCESS

T. H. Van Vleck and C. T. Clingen

Honeywell, Cambridge Information Systems Laboratory

ABSTRACT: Features of the Multics system programming process lead to high programmer productivity with a small programming staff and a finished system with high software reliability. Other workers' predictions of increasing difficulty of system maintenance with time have not been observed; reasons for this are suggested.

Introduction

Multics began as a research time-sharing system and evolved into a full-scale commercial operating system over a period exceeding 10 years. Its initial design included a collection of advanced features which proved to be efficient for software development and for running production. Figure 1 is an overview of the development history.

Figure 1. Multics Development History

This paper describes the process of system programming for Multics and shows how unique properties of the process lead to unique properties of the operating system, such as ease of use, ease of maintenance, and high reliability.

Generation of Requirements

Requirements for system changes and improvements arise from two sources: marketing provides direction about future customer requirements, and current customers request new features and extensions and also find bugs. A special class of customer that plays a significant role in the definition of new requirements is the system programmer community. Since they use Multics every day, they are especially responsible for the discovery of performance problems and inconsistencies both in the user interface and internal to the system.

Design Process

Usually, a Multics system programmer begins a project by writing a brief technical memorandum describing the problem to be solved, and seeking consensus at the level of problem definition from the other members of the programming staff. Often, the attempt to identify the problem encounters differences of opinion, and these lead to refinement and iteration.

Once the problem is satisfactorily defined, the designer writes a technical memorandum describing his proposed solution, and again seeks consensus. Often, this requires a series of committee meetings, chaired by the designer, and open to all members of the development staff.

When the design is understood, the programmer writes a formal Multics Change Request (MCR). An MCR summarizes the change to Multics, the reasons for the change, and its implications. If system documentation is affected by the change, drafts of the changes are supplied with the MCR. The MCRs are batched and submitted to each member of the MCR Board.

The MCR Board is a small group (10) of programmers, which includes the most experienced and knowledgeable people on the staff. The board meets weekly. Prior to each meeting, board members scrutinize MCRs for technical correctness and consistency with the overall design of the system. A majority vote is required to pass an MCR. Very few MCRs are rejected; proposals which fail to get a majority, or which any board member finds incomplete, insufficiently general, or with possible hidden consequences, are postponed for a week. The discussion of a controversial MCR often leads to its being rewritten or withdrawn for further study. Decisions made by the board are based only on technical grounds; considerations of schedule, manpower and budget belong to another arena.

The Board serves as a guardian of system conventions and as an education mechanism. Since no change can be installed without an approved MCR, programmers take care to conform to system conventions and to document their changes carefully, in order to have the MCR pass quickly. The reasons for rejection or postponement of an MCR serve to educate the programming staff, including the board members, in the sometimes subtle consequences of system conventions and standards. The board often attempts to generalize specific questions into new technical policies; if such a step is successful, the new policies are added to the system programming standards manual.

Although bug fixes do not require technical memoranda, even the simplest one-line change requires an MCR. This rule leads to some additional paperwork, but ensures that intended functions are not mistaken for bugs, and helps educate the whole team about the kinds of bugs that may exist elsewhere in the system.

An important attribute of the design process is that it forces a high level of technical peer review of all system changes by those most qualified to judge implementation: the system programmers. Although this review proceeds at the rate of over 500 MCRs per year, the additional overhead involved is compensated for by designs of high quality and interfaces that maintain a high degree of internal consistency over the years.

Implementation

For most projects, the designer is also the programmer, debugger, and documenter. This practice eliminates a troublesome layer of communication and responsibility determination. This approach is feasible due to the ease of the actual programming and debugging task in the Multics environment. High programmer productivity

Reprinted from The Third International Conference on Software Engineering Proceedings, 1978, pages 278-280. Copyright © 1978 by The Institute of Electrical and Electronics Engineers, Inc.

has been established as a Multics tradition; this has come about partly by selecting talented and dedicated people, and partly by providing them with powerful tools, including PL/I.

Because most of the system is written in PL/I, programmers are not concerned with the difficult problem of managing the sharing of machine registers at every point in the program. The PL/I storage management mechanism coupled with the Multics virtual memory relieves the programmer of much of the traditional responsibility for space management as well.

The library of program development, debugging, and maintenance tools which evolved as part of the system makes it easy for individual programmers or small teams to tackle large projects. Editing, compiling, and unit checkout are routinely done online, as is documentation. In fact, there is even a system programmer facility that formats and prints an MCR form given text input and a list of boxes to check. Other system programming tools simplify the coordination of multiple independent changes to the same module, assist in determining which statements in a program are most costly, and help keep track of the interconnections of system modules.

Changes requiring a new version of the central supervisor are tested on a dedicated hardware configuration connected to the system programming site by inter-computer network. An experienced system programmer can generate and test a new version of the supervisor in about ten minutes, by using file-transfer and system-generation tools. The development machine is also used to perform integrated testing of large projects and to analyze the effect of changes on system performance. Performance analysis is routinely carried out at the system level, by means of standard benchmarks; at the module level, by means of the system's built-in instrumentation; at the program level, by means of subroutine call trace facilities; and at the statement level, by means of compiler generated statement usage counters.

The use of a high-level system programming language, together with the other system programming tools, facilitates design iteration, since the cost of rewriting a module completely is lowered. The amount of code discarded during the building of Multics is many times the size of the current supervisor. Some critical modules of the system have been redesigned up to a dozen times, with gains in simplicity and performance each time. In many cases, performance analysis of a module led to a deeper understanding of its function, and enabled us to rewrite the module to simplify the most important case, improving performance without sacrificing generality.

Use of a high-level language also reduces the necessity for internal module-level documentation, since the program itself, especially if well commented, can be used as documentation. Standard Multics practice for programs that produce operator messages is to insert complete documentation for the message, including its meaning and the appropriate response, into the source of the module producing the message. This information appears as a comment to the compiler, but is extracted by standard library maintenance tools and transformed into a manual describing the messages produced by the system.

Program Auditing

When a Multics system programmer has completed a change, he submits his modules to a knowledgeable colleague for review. Thus, not only is the design reviewed by the design discussion process and the MCR Board, but the actual implementation is also subjected to expert scrutiny.

The auditor is responsible for pointing out problems with general structure, documentation, conformance to system standards, and correct operation. The MCR Board sometimes attaches special comments to an MCR to remind the programmer and auditor of important things to check. The auditor can, and often does, suggest changes in the structure of a program, the names of variables, and the comments, as well as in items that actually affect the execution of the program. Several

rounds of auditing may be necessary before programmer and auditor agree that the program is ready to install.

Integration and Exposure

Audited changes are installed on a Multics system that serves as a primary exposure site. Since most of the bookkeeping is done online, new software is installed more or less continuously, usually within a day or two after auditing, at a rate of about 50 programs a week. Once a new module is installed, its source code becomes the official version used by any other programmers making changes to the same programs; Multics provides tools that allow the easy automatic merging of multiple independent software modifications.

A standard performance benchmark is run whenever a new version of the central supervisor is installed. In a sense, this is a fourth level of review of a new implementation, this time based upon overall performance characteristics as opposed to human perusal. If any unanticipated performance problem has been introduced, it is easy to de-install the new software and go back to performance analysis, while the code is still fresh in the programmer's mind. The maintenance tools that keep the system source and object libraries up to date have the ability to revert a change quickly, if problems develop in either function or performance. Corrections are made to the system by modifying the source and installing a new version; there are no patches.

Since the exposure site is used by many different projects, mostly for purposes other than Multics system programming, installing a module that later has to be pulled is avoided whenever possible. Sometimes, it is easier to fix the bug and make a second submission, rather than pull and reinstall a submission that may consist of many programs. Problems of this sort are rare relative to the rate of system change.

Formal Release

Formal releases of Multics to field sites are made once or twice a year. To a large extent, this strategy is a result of the mechanism used for production of software manuals, which are not published incrementally, but consist of batches of changes to the previous version. A formal release also requires additional software quality assurance and regression testing, with an even wider variety of user programs than that found at the exposure site. Sites receiving the formal releases report high software reliability.

Table 1. Source line count by library.
(Include files expanded, comment only lines omitted.) (Release 6.0, December 1977)

	PL/I		non-PL/I	
	prgs	lines	prgs	lines
bos	0	0	40	33,433
hardcore	512	158,488	145	70,645
language	331	144,773	45	18,809
network	109	36,636	21	4,811
obsolete	5	574	0	0
standard	388	126,140	36	4,136
tools	685	240,227	123	25,470
unbundled	917	425,007	83	68,723
total	2947	1,131,845	493	226,027

Observations

In 1971, Belady and Lehman[1] suggested that as large software systems evolved in time, their maintenance would become increasingly difficult, due to communication and coordination problems. This effect has not been observed with Multics: the rate of system change has remained constant or increased, while the staff has remained about the same size. Several reasons may account for our experience.

First, it may be simply that the size of the group is so small that these effects are swamped by noise. Although there are about 30 system programmers, their areas of specialization have little or no overlap, and so the actual group size requiring coordination is usually more like four or five. The value of the advanced features of Multics is shown by the fact that a relatively small programming group handles maintenance and bug fixing, quality assurance, and continued extension in response to customer needs for all aspects of the system, which now consists of over 3,500 modules (about 1 million lines of source code).

Second, the standard practices required of Multics system programmers may combine to postpone collapse. Belady and Lehman suggest that the use of structured programming methods and a high-level language will decrease the likelihood of collapse. Our use of PL/I provides a documentation benefit, and also shortens the time required for an individual change. The modular organization of the Multics supervisor limits the number of cases of inter-program communication via shared global objects, held to be one of the roots of system collapse.

Third, the ability and willingness of the Multics group to rewrite rather than patch tends to limit the number of problems with "bugs in the fix" which are thought to lead to additional maintenance effort. About 2/3 of the programs comprising Multics were modified during 1977: some of these changes were one-line fixes, while others were complete rewrites of existing functions or totally new modules.

Table 2. Percentage of Library Compiled by Year.

	70	71	72	73	74	75	76	77
bos	0.0	0.0	0.0	0.0	0.0	5.0	47.5	47.5
hardcore	0.0	0.0	0.0	0.0	0.0	0.0	28.1	71.9
language	0.0	0.0	2.1	6.8	4.4	21.4	0.8	64.6
network	0.0	0.0	0.0	0.0	0.0	0.0	0.0	100.0
obsolete	0.0	0.0	0.0	0.0	0.0	0.0	0.0	100.0
standard	0.0	0.2	2.3	5.5	7.4	15.5	24.0	45.0
tools	0.1	0.8	2.3	7.0	7.9	20.3	17.0	44.6
unbundled	0.0	0.0	7.4	0.6	3.9	1.8	9.4	76.9

Finally, the strategy of integrating and exposing system changes on an incremental basis and making formal releases at a much slower rate seems to obtain the best features of both strategies. Rapid exposure release discovers unexpected consequences of each change quickly, so that corrective action can be taken before other efforts are interfered with, while slow formal release allows additional time for software stabilization and user documentation.

REFERENCES

1. Belady, L. A. and M. M. Lehman, "Programming System Dynamics, or the Meta-dynamics of Systems in Maintenance and Growth," IBM Research Report RC3546, Sept. 1971.

2. Corbató, F. J., C. T. Clingen, and J. H. Saltzer, "Multics -- the first seven years," Proc. SJCC, May 1972, pp 571-583.

3. Corbató, F. J., "PL/I as a tool for system programming," Datamation 15, May 6, 1969, pp. 68-76.

4. Corbató, F. J., and C. T. Clingen, "A Managerial View of the Multics System Development," Proc. Conf. on Research Directions in Software Technology, MIT Press, Cambridge, Ma. 1978.

5. Corbató, F. J., "Sensitive Issues in the design of Multi-Use Systems," MIT Project MAC MAC-M-383, Dec., 1968.

6. Mullen, R. E., "Automated Merging of Software Modifications," Proc. Honeywell Software Productivity Symposium, April 1977.

7. Saltzer, J. H., and J. W. Gintell, "The Instrumentation of Multics," Comm. ACM, Vol. 13, no. 8, Aug. 1970, pp 495-500.

Introduction

Ford, B., Bentley, J., Du Croz, J.J., Hague, S.J. "The NAG Library 'Machine'." *Software—Practice and Experience*, 9 (1979), 65-72.

We turn now from operating systems to applications systems, specifically to the maintenance of a huge library of mathematical routines by NAG, the Numerical Algorithms Group Ltd, a British non-profit organization. We chose the following paper because of its concise presentation of the many different dimensions that a maintenance group must handle.

Any system that is distributed to multiple users can be cut several ways:

- Functions (e.g., this routine solves polynomials or this routine maximizes functions).

- Releases (e.g., this is the system as issued on January 1, 1982).

- Versions (e.g., this version runs under IBM's OS/MVS or this version runs under Multics).

In addition, a function is not treated by NAG as just a computer language module; it contains at least source code, object code, technical documentation, user documentation, sample runs, and test cases. NAG organizes this material as a library of texts, partially in machine-readable form, with its own indexes, introductions, instructions, and linking materials. Customers receive a "slice" matching their needs.

Finally, as the reprinted paper shows, the organizational staff consists of a mixture of specialists, some volunteer and some professional, some oriented more toward mathematics and some oriented more toward computing.

The "machine" in the title is the organizational and technical structure that manages these complexities. (The term "machine" must be taken as a typical British understatement, as one might call the moon-walk project "a trip" or the whole of World War II "a bit of a show.") The machine portrayed in the figure on the third page should be compared to our Figure VI-3. The keys to running such a machine are to keep a clear idea of who is being served and with what products, to use software tools effectively, and to observe the "operational principles" recommended in the paper: *Consultation, Collaboration, Coordination, Planning, Standards, and Mechanization.*

Brian Ford has a Ph.D. in applied mathematics; he called the inaugural meeting of the NAG project in 1970 and became Director of NAG Ltd. when it was formed as an independent company in 1976. Steve Hague became NAG's first full time employee in 1971 and is Deputy Director of the company. Jeremy Du Croz is the Library Development Manager, responsible for co-ordinating contributions to the NAG Library and for its assembly, maintenance, and support. Janet Bentley joined NAG in 1975 for a research project on portability of numerical software; in 1978 she became NAG Library Service Coordinator, becoming a liaison between NAG and its users.

The book *Practice in software adaption and maintenance* edited by Ebert et al. (North-Holland Publishing Company, 1980) contains twenty-one papers on the problems of publishing and/or bringing up software packages on a variety of systems. It contains the paper by Hague and Nugent, "Computer-based documentation for a multi-machine library," which describes plans for further computerization of the NAG Library.

SOFTWARE—PRACTICE AND EXPERIENCE, VOL. 9, 65–72 (1979)

The NAG Library 'Machine'

B. FORD, J. BENTLEY, J. J. DU CROZ AND S. J. HAGUE

Numerical Algorithms Group, 7 Banbury Road, Oxford OX2 6NN

SUMMARY

If a reliable, high quality numerical algorithms library is to be developed then it is essential that we recognize the need for collaboration between different technical communities in the development of the library. This paper suggests an ultimate design for the library and describes the implications of that design for the people involved in the development of the library.

KEY WORDS Numerical algorithms library Library design Library development Contribution Validation Assembly Implementation Distribution

INTRODUCTION

Since its inception the Numerical Algorithms Group (NAG) project has pursued four aims:

1. To create a balanced, general purpose numerical algorithms library to meet the mathematical and statistical requirements of computer users, in FORTRAN and Algol 60.
2. To support the library with documentation giving advice on problem identification and algorithm selection, and on the use of each routine.
3. To provide a test program library for certification of the library.
4. To implement the library as widely as user demand required.

There are at present 150 members of NAG who are part of the NAG Library 'Machine'. Generally each person has a specific interest or function within the library development process. They may be

contributors, who contribute library contents and write test programs and documentation. They are academics or government scientists who are selected for their individual ability in an area of numerical mathematics.

validators, who certify that the work of the relevant contributor is of the required standard. They are of comparable stature to the contributor in their field of numerical mathematics.

translators, who translate the algorithms into other languages, usually Algol 60 and Algol 68.

implementors, who implement the Library on a particular machine range

or one of the 23 full-time staff employed either in the Central Office or as machine range coordinators.

The Group appreciated in 1970 that collaboration between different technical communities, whose members would inevitably be geographically dispersed, was necessary if a library was to be produced. The library would be reliable and of high quality if each phase of the activity was performed to defined standards, in a prescribed manner, in pursuit of specified objectives. A Central Office of full-time staff was established to process,

0038-0644/79/0109-0065$01.00

© 1979 by John Wiley & Sons, Ltd.

Received 2 February 1978

monitor and maintain the contents of the Library and to coordinate the manpower that created and implemented the software.

The disciplined employment of the energy, interest and ability of each individual member of NAG in the creation, development and maintenance of the Library is the key to the NAG Library 'Machine'. Although we choose to describe NAG as a machine, the group is in reality a living flexible organization—'a tank with a heart'.

In the paper we shall suggest an ultimate structure for the Library; outline the major components of the Library Machine and review their functions; underline the operational principles of the Machine; and finally comment on its performance.

LIBRARY DESIGN

We require a library structure designed to satisfy the requirements of all users of the Library.[1] The spectrum of users, in their knowledge of numerical analysis, of programming and of problem formulation and solution, will be very broad.

Types of software

In general, however, we can satisfy the majority of their requirements by three types of Library software.

Type	Function	Example
Problem solvers:	one routine call to solve the problem	solution of set of simultaneous real linear equations
Primary routine:	each routine contains one major algorithm	LU factorization
Basic module:	basic numerical utility designed by the chapter contributor for his own and his fellow contributors' use	extended precision inner product

Communication of information

A consistent approach should be employed throughout the Library for communication of information, between its constituent parts and in particular to the user. Wherever possible, information should be passed through calling sequences. The design of calling sequences, the ordering of parameters within them and the naming of routines and variables should be systematic throughout the Library. A common error-mechanism should be used everywhere.

At least three operational requirements can be recognized in the design of each calling sequence:

—convenient and correct use by the programmer,
—satisfaction of the needs of the algorithm,
—use of the data structures of the numerical area.

These requirements underlie the preparation of interfaces for the three types of user software.

—problem solvers: minimum calling sequence,
—primary routines: longer calling sequence, if necessary to permit greater flexibility and control,
—basic module: optimized calling sequence reflecting perceived needs of all contributors yet recognizing demands of efficiency of use.

The three types of Library software could ultimately provide the three tiers of a steady-state library structure. At the present time a number of chapters within the NAG Library do not fit into such a design.

This illustrates a dilemma faced by library designers in general. The state-of-the-art in many branches of numerical software continues to develop, and notions about optimal library design also may change. A library currently in use represents a very significant investment in effort, guided by the state of affairs and of thinking several years ago. The library designer who wishes to keep abreast of developments must not lightly disregard this investment.

Contents of Library

The contents of the Library must evolve as research and development permit. Hence we require a library structure which enables the library contents to change with the minimum inconvenience to users.

It is convenient to divide the contents of the Library in accordance with areas of numerical mathematics. Further subdivision will be required following the natural substructure within each mathematical area. The number of algorithms included will reflect the user demand for problem solution and the resolution of problem type within each area.

THE 'MACHINE'

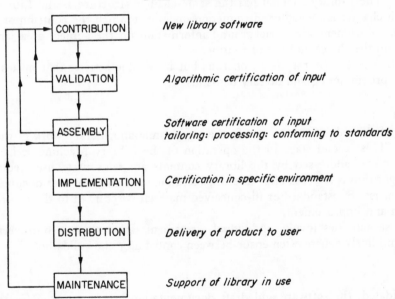

CONTRIBUTION — *New library software*

VALIDATION — *Algorithmic certification of input*

ASSEMBLY — *Software certification of input*
tailoring: processing: conforming to standards

IMPLEMENTATION — *Certification in specific environment*

DISTRIBUTION — *Delivery of product to user*

MAINTENANCE — *Support of library in use*

Contribution

The primary function of a contributor is to identify the major types of problems met by users in his area of interest and to provide the 'best' algorithm in the library for each type. The algorithms are selected following a stringent performance evaluation of contending methods. The test program and data sets are retained by the contributor.

Ideally we require routines which will run, virtually without change, to prescribed efficiency and accuracy, on all the machines to which we carry the Library. We need adaptable algorithms[2] which can then be realized as transportable subroutines.[3]

The contributor uses an agreed subset of the language.[4] As has been shown,[5] this approach can largely overcome the problem of language dialects, yet permit a reliable and robust subroutine[6] to be developed.

The aim of the contributor is to write a single routine, which can be tailored to perform to the required accuracy and efficiency on each machine.

As a basis for the development of all NAG software, a simple model has been developed of features of any computer that are relevant to the software. This conceptual machine is described in terms of a number of parameters (e.g. base of floating point number representation, overflow threshold). Each parameter may be given a specific value to reflect a feature of a particular computer (e.g. SRADIX[7] is 16 for IBM 360 and is 2 for CDC 7600).

Hence the contributor writes his single routine for the conceptual machine. The routine is then tailored for each distinct configuration by selection of the values of the parameters. In this way the individual demands of accuracy and efficiency for the routine are met for every machine range.

For each routine the contributor provides an implementation test which will be used by implementors to demonstrate the operational efficiency and accuracy of the routine in each environment.

Many users welcome an example of the use of each routine. It is convenient to provide such an example in the user documentation. The contributor writes this example program and provides an example data set, if necessary, together with the results for inclusion in the Library Manual. The contributor prepares draft documentation to support his work. Each routine is then described in an individual document which bears the same name as the routine. The Library Manual has the same chapter structure as the Library. At the head of each chapter is a chapter introduction document which the contributor must also prepare. This document gives background information on the subject area, and recommendations on the choice and use of routines.

Contribution to the Library is an onerous but invaluable activity that makes extensive algorithmic, programming and literary demands.

Validation

The task of the validator is to certify the algorithmic and literary work of the relevant contributor. This second stage in the operation of the Library Machine seeks to ensure that the problems addressed by the library contents are relevant to user requirements; that each algorithm is selected after due consideration; and that the user documentation is clear and concise. Substandard or ill-conceived material is returned to the contributor for modification and improvement.

As all these activities involve individual assessment rather than incontrovertible fact; discussion and lively debate often ensue between contributor and validator.

Assembly

Once validated, the software and draft documentation are sent to the Central Office, whose staff are responsible for assembling and processing both the code and the documentation ready for general distribution at each new release (Mark) of the Library.

As the Library is the work of many individuals, there is inevitably inconsistency and confusion in interpretation and in satisfaction of agreed standards. Hence in assembling the codes and documentation provided by contributors it is essential that we check for compliance with these standards. Wherever possible, these are machine proven, but there are certain standards which need to be checked by hand; for example, we must ensure that the relevant chapter design is being followed and that the user interface chosen for routines satisfies the demands of the general Library structure.

Processing tools available in the Central Office for machine processing of contributed software include the following:[8, 9, 10, 11, 12]

PFORT verifier
DECS
POLISH
BRNANL
APT

Processing of the contributed software by the Central Office, whether automatic or manual, is designed to achieve the following functions:

—diagnosing a coding error either of an algorithmic or linguistic nature;
—altering a structural property of the text, e.g. imposing a particular order on non-executable statements in FORTRAN;
—standardizing the appearance of the text;
—standardizing nomenclature used, e.g. giving the same name to variables having the same function in different program units;
—conducting dynamic analysis of the text, e.g. by planting tracing calls;
—ensuring adherence to declared language standards or subsets thereof;
—changing an operational property of the text, e.g. changing the mode of arithmetic precision;
—coping with arithmetic, dialect and other differences between computing systems.

As further certification of the efficiency, accuracy and effectiveness of the contributed codes, Central Office staff run the routines, together with implementation and example programs, on three different systems (ICL 1900—48 bit floating point word, IBM 370—32/64 bit word and CDC 7600—60 bit word).

Once certified, the routines are used to prepare an updated version of the 'Contributed Library'. This new version, known as a new Mark of the Library, is released once a year and consists of the last generally released version of the Library supplemented by the newly-certified routines and any other improvements or corrections. For example, at Mark 6, 64 new routines were added to the 298 routines in the Library at Mark 5. The implementation and example program suites, and the NAG Library Manual, are supplemented in a similar manner.

Implementation

One of the tasks of the Central Office is to coordinate all the implementations of the NAG Library. The number of such implementations depends upon precisely what you count; at the crudest level the Library is available on 13 distinct major machine ranges and is being implemented on 8 more. But taking into account

—minor variations in hardware,
—different precision versions,
—different compiler versions;

the numbers of distinct compiled Mark 5 libraries are:

	FORTRAN	Algol 60
Already available	30	11
	(+2 at Mark 4)	
In course of implementation	10	5

There is a good deal of scope for reducing the total amount of work spent in implementation if we take advantage of common features of the various machine ranges. For example, for FORTRAN double precision implementations, a production version of APT (developed in the NAG Central Office) automatically performs most of the conversion from the single precision 'Contributed Library' to a double precision version. This is then the common starting-point for all double precision implementations.

These divide into two subgroups: the 'IBM 360 like machines' with hexadecimal arithmetic and the machines with binary arithmetic.

Implementation tree (FORTRAN)

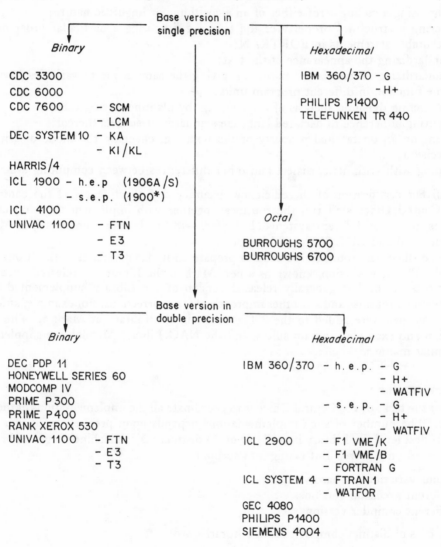

314

The predicted source texts for each of the machines in the two subgroups have common requirements. All of the byte machines require special modified subroutines in the Special Function chapter. By historic accident, many of the machines with binary arithmetic (e.g. Honeywell, Modcomp IV, Xerox 530 and Univac 1100 (with FTN compiler)) have FORTRAN compilers which do not include a Double Precision Complex facility. The feature is simulated by Double Precision arrays, with an extra leading dimension of 2, and the amended source text used on these machines.

Coordination of implementations requires the Central Office
—to supply the initial software,
—to advise about any anticipated difficulties (e.g. machine code)
—to help solve any problems which arise,
—to ensure that the implementation is of an acceptable standard (e.g. by examining the computed results).

Each implementation starts from its 'Predicted Library' tape prepared by the Central Office.

The tape holds

—the 'Predicted Library' source text in the relevant precision or precisions,
—the example programs each with their input data and results (all in the relevant precision(s)),
—the implementation programs, each with their input data and results (all in the relevant precision(s)).
The function of the implementor is to read the material into filestore, and then systematically to compile and to test the routines, example programs and implementation test programs. The activity is essentially one of file handling, file management and file comparison. Sophisticated programs have been developed for automatic comparison of results.

Distribution

Each implementor prepares a certified library distribution tape. This contains a precompiled version of the implemented Library, the source text of the routines from which it was prepared, and the example programs plus the input data and results computed during its certification. The structure and format of the tape are chosen to be optimum for the given implementation. The contents and form of the tape are described in a Library Support Note, which also advises the Library site staff how to read the software off the tape into filestore.

OPERATIONAL PRINCIPLES

1. Consultation: enables the Library to address problems met by users, and the Library Machine to serve the needs and requirements of all its parts.
2. Collaboration: gives access to the required expertise and knowledge.
3. Coordination: permits individual parts of the Library to be developed independently, within a unified structure.
4. Planning: permits overall design of individual chapter contents.
5. Standards: ensure the effectiveness and reliability of the product developed.
6. Mechanization: minimizes the cost of development, distribution and maintenance, and is the most reliable method of software processing.

6

CONCLUSIONS

A 'machine' such as the one we have described must, of necessity, involve staff with different abilities, backgrounds and interests. It has to combine its academic staff, responsible for library contents, and its commercial staff required for servicing the library. In our organization this involves both volunteers, responsible in the main for providing up-to-date contents and indeed new language versions, and the full-time employees responsible for the coordination and maintenance of the library machine.

For the project to be successful there must be rigour, to ensure that quality and reliability are achieved and maintained, and yet there must be flexibility, to enable cooperation and to optimize the service for each and every implementation. We depend upon enthusiasm to broaden the coverage provided by the Library, and yet we require experience in order to achieve a balanced, general-purpose numerical library service.

REFERENCES

1. B. Ford and J. Bentley, 'A library design for all parties', in *Numerical Software—Needs and Availability* (Ed. D. A. H. Jacobs), Academic Press, London, 1978.
2. B. Ford, S. J. Hague and B. T. Smith, 'Some transformations of numerical software' (in press).
3. S. J. Hague and B. Ford, 'Portability—Prediction and correction', *Software—Practice and Experience*, **6**, 61–69 (1976).
4. B. G. Ryder, 'The PFORT verifier', *Software—Practice and Experience*, **4**, 359–377 (1974).
5. J. Bentley and B. Ford, 'On the enhancement of portability in the NAG project—a statistical survey', in *Portability of Numerical Software* (Ed. W. Cowell), Berlin, Springer–Verlag, 1977.
6. W. J. Cody, 'The construction of numerical subroutine libraries', *SIAM Review*, **16**, No. 1, 36–46 (1974).
7. B. Ford, 'Preparing conventions for parameters for transportable numerical software', in *Portability of Numerical Software* (Ed. W. Cowell), Berlin, Springer–Verlag, 1977.
8. J. J. Du Croz, S. J. Hague and J. L. Siemieniuch, 'Aids to portability within the NAG project', in *Portability of Numerical Software* (Ed. W. Cowell), Berlin, Springer–Verlag, 1977.
9. S. J. Hague, 'Software tools', in *Numerical Software—Needs and Availability* (Ed. D. A. H. Jacobs), Academic Press, London, 1978.
10. B. G. Ryder, *The FORTRAN Verifier: User's Guide*, Bell Telephone Laboratories, Technical Report No. 12.
11. J. Dorrenbacher, D. Paddock, D. Wisneski and L. D. Fosdick, '*POLISH, a FORTRAN program to edit FORTRAN programs*', Dept. of Computer Science, University of Colorado at Boulder, Ref.: No. CU–CS–050–74 (1974).
12. L. D. Fosdick, '*BRNANL, a FORTRAN program to identify basic blocks in FORTRAN programs*', Dept. of Computer Science, University of Colorado at Boulder, Ref.: No. CM–CS–040–74 (1974).

Introduction

Cashman, P.M., Holt, A.W. "A communication-oriented approach to structuring the software maintenance environment." *ACM SIGSOFT, Software Engineering Notes*, 5, 1 (1980), 4-17.

The authors of the previous selection used the term "machine" for the whole organizational structure of a maintenance group. The authors of this selection view the channeling of communications through such a "machine" as a significant problem of maintenance management, and they have designed and built a software tool, MONSTR™, which is the first software maintenance tool that specifically recognizes the cyclic and political aspects of the communications of Figure VI-3.

Cashman and Holt came to their tool the hard way. Paul Cashman is a systems analyst at Massachusetts Computer Associates, Inc., who is involved in the design and management of the National Software Works (NSW). NSW is an operating system funded by the U.S. Department of Defense that links disparate computer systems (DEC-10's, Multics, IBM 360's, and UNIXes) so that a user can mix programs and data from any system. NSW aims to repair the incompatibility problems that plagued the Department of Defense's experimental ARPANET network (and still plague commercial networks); just because two computers can communicate does not mean that they can use each other's messages.

The intercomputer incompatibilities for which NSW was designed were mirrored by interorganizational incompatibilities between those developing and using NSW. Much of the problem was too much communication, too little directed; ARPANET electronic mail provided means for everyone to talk to everyone else, but it provided no guidance on who should talk (and, more pointedly, respond) to whom. At this point Cashman called in Anatol Holt.

Holt is a computer scientist from the earliest days. With a B.S. and an M.S. in Mathematics from Harvard and M.I.T., respectively, he joined William Turanski to create a "Generalized Programming System" on the Univac I under the leadership of John Mauchly. After Turanski's death in 1960, Holt completed his Ph.D. in linguistics at the University of Pennsylvania. During the 1960's and 1970's he worked for Applied Data Research, Inc., the software firm, and its research subsidiary, Massachusetts Computer Associates, Inc. Under the sponsorship of the U.S. Air Force, he guided the Information Systems Theory Project, which sought to define communication among and between both people and machines. After two years as Director of Boston University Academic Computing Center, he joined ITT's Programming Technology Center in 1981. Holt's interest in computers is only incidental to his interest in human communication. "Steam engines are to thermodynamics as computers are to X," he told us. "That X is what I am looking for."

The tool that Cashman and Holt designed—MONSTR, or MONitor for Software Trouble Reporting—is based on a simple observation: the utility of a message is based on its path as well as on its content. To give a specific example, a Software Trouble Report is a very different document if a user knows that a member of the systems staff is required to respond than if it is just launched into a void. Similarly, a programmer's analysis of a technical problem is a very different document if it is written in response to a customer's Software Trouble Report than if it is generated on the programmer's own initiative. MONSTR makes explicit these and many other similar considerations.

The following paper describes the design aims of MONSTR. For more on its utility in reducing confusion and increasing productivity and morale in maintenance, read "Early experiences with MONSTR: a software maintenance management tool," by Kathleen Knobe in the *Proceedings of COMPCON 81*, the IEEE Computer Society's International Computer Conference, 1981. Further discussion of the concepts underlying systems like MONSTR can be found in "Designing systems to support cooperative activity: an example from software maintenance management," by Holt and Cashman, in the *Proceedings of COMPSAC 81*, the IEEE Computer Society's Fifth Computer Software and Applications Conference, 1981.

A Communication-Oriented Approach
to Structuring the
Software Maintenance Environment

Paul M. Cashman
Massachusetts Computer Associates, Inc.

Anatol W. Holt
Boston University Academic Computing Center

1. Introduction

Software maintenance is an expensive proposition. SM routinely accounts for 50% - 80% of total life cycle costs of a software system, and in some cases exceeds 99% of the life cycle cost [17]. The problems of SM are especially acute when the systems being maintained are the software systems known as embedded computer systems. Characteristically, these systems are large (50-100,000 lines of code), long-lived (10-15 years or more), must perform with a very high degree of reliability, and must be constantly updated to meet changing requirements [4]. The importance of reducing the cost of SM is recognized in the requirements for the Ada programming environment (the "Pebbleman" document):

"As software maintenance has become the main cost-factor in the lifecycle of computerized systems, specific efforts should be made to reduce this factor... The human factor aspect of the work itself, as well as the properties of the environment in which maintenance takes place, should be investigated in order to derive improved methods, procedures, and tools for maintenance." [15]

In general, there are three main complementary approaches to the problems of software maintenance:

1. The computer science approach: This approach aims at reducing the number and severity of software bugs, and making programs easy to modify as requirements change. The emphasis in this approach is on the creation and use of such things as structured technologies, specification and design languages, verification techniques, abstract data types, and improved programming languages.

2. The toolkit approach: This approach emphasizes the use of more and better tools: symbolic execution packages, test data generators, resource monitors, source-level debuggers, etc. The belief is that with more sophisticated tools, programmers may detect bugs earlier and fix them more easily.

3. The environmental approach: The profusion of sophisticated tools is negated by the fact that many tools a project would like to use do not run on the project's machine. Also, the tools do not have uniform user/tool and tool/tool interfaces. This has led in recent years [11] to the environmental approach, which takes one of two forms. One form is to have an environment into which

Reprinted with permission from *ACM SIGSOFT, Software Engineering Notes*, Volume 5, Number 1, 1980, pages 4-17. Published by The Association for Computing Machinery, Inc.

existing tools can be placed. The National Software Works [13] is an example of this approach. The other form is to build an environment from scratch, tools and all. Examples of this approach are FASP [19] and Gandalf [5]. (Approaches 2 and 3 might be termed the "software engineering" approach, in contradistinction to the "computer science" approach.)

We contend that these approaches, although valuable, are insufficient in themselves. In this paper we will present the communication-oriented approach to structuring the environment for software maintenance. This approach concentrates on processes which must be supported, rather than concentrating on capabilities, tools, or other static structures. The approach structures the maintenance environment so as to reflect the communication problems between different agents (which can be people or programs) involved in the process of SM.

The communication-oriented approach complements the use of advanced techniques and tools, and provides an environment where the SM process can easily be monitored by managers. It is a logical extension of the environmental approach, in that it tends toward concentrating more control over the possible actions of project members in the hands of the project manager. (Although this sounds very dictatorial, remember that the purpose of such control is to prevent project members from destructively interfering with one another, and to encourage beneficial mutual cooperation.)

In section 2, we discuss the activities which constitute SM, the taxonomy of problems which arise during the SM process, and the failure of traditional approaches to address the managerial problems encounted during SM. Section 3 presents MONSTR (MONitor for Software Trouble Reporting), a system which embodies our approach to SM. The concepts and facilities of MONSTR are outlined, and MONSTR is shown to be a framework in which sophisticated software tools could be used in a well-controlled manner. Our conclusions are presented in section 4.

2. The Process of Software Maintenance

2.1 Components of the SM process

The term "software maintenance" encompasses a number of activities, all of which must be supported in a true SM environment:

1. Reporting the problem. Software is changed for two main reasons: to correct bugs (system behavior which violates system specifications) or to add new features (extending the specifications). In either case, someone (such as a system user or tester) must report the need for the change to someone else (system operator, maintenance supervisor).

2. Analyzing the problem. This may involve asking the person who reported the problem for more information.

3. Specifying the solution. This may involve getting agreement between a number of people on the best solution.

4. Implementing and unit-testing the change.

5. Validating the change. This is to insure that the change was made, that the change is correct, and that nothing else in the system has been modified except that which was agreed upon.

6. Updating the repository. Often the "clean copies" of system components are kept in a restricted-access library or repository.

7. Disseminating the new configuration. In general, the maintainers do not have unrestricted access to the actual operational system(s). They must either get permission to update such systems, or turn over the new components to people who do have permission to modify the operational system(s).

8. Assigning responsibility to people for activites 1-7. This is essential for controlling access to protected files and for tracking the progress of changes.

9. Determining the status of changes. A manager may want to know what has been done concerning a particular bug, or who is responsible for the next processing step. A user may ask when he can expect to see a new configuration with certain improvements.

This list of activities is by no means complete, but it is comprehensive enough to show that the people who perform these activities must communicate with one another. This is a rather obvious point, but one well worth considering.

In many small projects it is easy to overlook the communication aspects of the software maintenance process. This is because the project members are members of one company and are located in one place. Communication is informal, and the manager considers it sufficient to keep an "audit trail" (a record of who changed what, for what reason, and when the change was made). If the manager wishes to know what a programmer is doing, the manager can just walk down the hall and ask.

In embedded computer system projects, the communication aspects of the project are critical. The activities of many people - scores or hundreds - must be coordinated. Many contractors may be involved; at the very least there is an independent verification and validation contractor in addition to the software contractor. The project members may be geographically dispersed, communicating via a computer network such as the Arpanet. The operational configurations may be in many different locations, used by different groups with idiosyncratic ways of allowing access to the configurations. Clearly, a software maintenance environment must address the communication problems which arise in the context of embedded computer system projects.

2.2 A taxonomy of SM communication issues

What kinds of communication issues exist in the SM process? Following [16], we can examine certain abstract communication "disciplines" in the light of the questions these disciplines must answer.

1. Synchronization questions: How do you prevent two people from updating the same module at the same time? If one person owes a response to another person by a certain deadline (in order for the response to have any effect), how is this deadline enforced? When may an operational configuration be updated?

2. Naming and identification questions: Does a software system component have a fixed or configuration-dependent name? What bug report is this? What is the name of the problem it addresses? How are people and organizations named? Is a person's name different when that person changes roles (e.g., a tester becomes an analyzer or an implementor)?

3. Authentication questions: Was the allowed change made, and only the allowed change? Was the configuration updated correctly? Was a cancellation notice sent by someone authorized to cancel?

4. Authorization questions: Who is allowed to make a given change to a given module? Who may enter new modules in the repository? Who may update an operational configuration? Who may classify a bug report, or set its priority?

5. Routing questions: To whom should this bug report be sent? To whom should this new component be sent? How is a bug report routed to the right person? Over what route should it be sent?

6. Cancellation questions: Who may cancel a bug report? At what point, if ever, is a cancellation rendered meaningless? To whom should a cancellation be sent at any given moment?

7. Delegation questions: If one organization is held responsible for disseminating bug reports to other organizations for fixing, how is responsibility ultimately determined?

8. Valuation questions: How are priorities translated into deadlines? If a priority is set incorrectly by one person, can it be reset by another? What are the implications of this?

2.3 Communication in the traditional SM environment

Most of the above questions are traditionally considered to be "project management" questions. The issues they raise are handled by management directives, with the implicit assumptions that (a) project members are motivated to follow the directives; and (b) project members have near-perfect recall and comprehension, so they remember and understand how to apply the directives. Since the directives are hard to enforce, the manager implicitly relies on physical features of the project environment, such as file and directory protections, physical separation of "clean" and "working" copies of code, etc. These protection mechanisms prevent foul-ups in the worst cases of carelessness or bad intention; however, they do not insure that necessary communication between project members actually happens.

In a typical SM environment, the necessary communication is accomplished by mechanisms outside the environment: through face-to-face (or telephone) conversations, or through electronic mail. Mail (i.e., electronic mail) is customarily used to keep a record of agreements, decisions, policies, etc. In a geographically distributed project, the impossibility of face-to-face and expense of telephone conversations combine to make mail the primary means of intra-project communication. The experience of the Arpanet has proved the utility of network mail, and many sophisticated mail tools (e.g. DEC's MS [3], BBN's HERMES [18]) have been devised.

No matter how sophisticated the mail tool may be, there are still flaws in its use for project communication:

1. Mail is a general-purpose medium for communication, and mechanisms must be imposed upon it in order to constrain project communication to follow rules created by management or worker consensus. However, even if such mechanisms are imposed, they may still be circumvented if project members have access to a general mail tool (as they almost always will).

2. The mail system cannot guarantee that a message has been accepted by the recipient (i.e., the recipient agrees to take responsibility for having read the message). The result of this is that two conversational partners will always be uncertain as to the state of each other's knowledge. A formal "acceptance boundary" between organizations is a sine qua non for correcting this problem.

3. Use of the mail system causes a split between communicating and discovering when and to whom to communicate.

4. If different companies are involved in a project, the mailboxes of the participants are protected in such a way that no tool may access all of them (other than the system mailer). A single problem can cause many messages to be generated. This, combined with the differing protections on mailboxes, makes it exceedingly hard for a tool to trace the treatment of a particular problem.

The mail system, then, cannot meet the needs of a medium for intra-project communication. Yet it remains "the only game in town." The result is the effect observed by Kafka [10]:

"It occasionally happens that one department ordains this, another that; neither knows of the other, and though the Supreme Control is absolutely efficient, it comes by its nature too late, and so every now and then a trifling miscalculation arises."

Unconstrained project communication leads to these effects:

1. There is no control of the SM process. "Control" effectively depends on the motivation and comprehension of the project members.

2. Managers have difficulty seeing into the SM process. The project members are like molecules in a gas: it is impossible to say what each one is doing at any instant, and the system behavior may only be described statistically.

3. Access to restricted copies is not effectively restricted. If communication were constrained, it would be possible to grant permissions to access files on a per-file basis. For example, if a change is proposed to files X, Y, and Z, once the change is agreed to the project communication system could authorize access to clean copies of X, Y, and Z (perhaps even export them to the programmer's workspace).

Of currently existing advanced programming environments, only CADES [9] recognizes the importance of structuring project communication by programmatic means. Most other environments simply extend traditional operating system ideas of file access protection. In traditional environments a project manager sets up a static structure of rights and permissions for files, tools, and devices. It is possible [14] to manipulate these permissions dynamically to approximate the effect of an integrated communication-permission system. This is cumbersome and leads to errors when done by a person. What is needed is a protocol-driven system. Such a system is given a description of the allowable paths of communication, the meaning of messages sent over each path, and a description of the project's structure. It then constrains project communication to move along those paths and those paths alone. In the next section, we describe such a protocol-driven maintenance system.

3. MONSTR - A Communication-Oriented Maintenance System

MONSTR (MONitor for Software Trouble Reporting) is a communication-oriented maintenance system currently being built [1] by the authors. Since MONSTR is protocol-driven, it can be tailored for use by a specific project. MONSTR's first use will be in and by the National Software Works project. The nature and structure of this project exacerbate the difficulties a project can have if the communication aspects of the SM environment are ignored.

3.1 Background of MONSTR

NSW is a distributed operating system for the Arpanet. It consists of a core system (interprocess communication (IPC), manipulation of rights, batch job submission, resource catalog) and a group of tool-bearing hosts (TBHs). Each TBH has an implementation of the IPC and file-handling facilities, and an interface between locally provided tools and the NSW.

NSW is a distributed project. There are two government sponsors, two companies building the core system, three TBH contractors, one company (in two locations) serving as a system operator and validation contractor, and one company serving as tool manager. The contractors are located in Los Angeles; Rome, NY; Cambridge and Wakefield, MA; and Nashua, NH. Six different Arpanet hosts provide computer resources. There are four levels of system configuration, from the Debug System (most volatile) to the User System (most stable).

When the NSW evolved to the point where it was necessary to remove the responsibility for the operation of the User System from the developers, an ad hoc protocol was devised for communicating software trouble reports (STRs) between system users, operators, and developers. STRs and other classes of management transactions (eleven in all) were transmitted via the Arpanet mail. Each project member (the number of project members hovered around 20) had a mailbox. In addition, mailboxes were set up to correspond to NSW project organizations: PG (Policy Group - the sponsors); OPS (operators); PDC (Product Development - validation); ACC (Architecture Control - system integration); TM (Tool Manager); DMCs (Development and Maintenance - responsibility for specific components).

It was not long before the faults of the mail system and the ad hoc, unenforced protocol made life unbearable for many project members and managers. It was impossible to track the scores of bug reports through the maze of mailboxes. Project schedules slipped because managers could not get a unified view of who was working on which STRs. People disagreed over who was responsible for a given STR at a given time. The profusion of messages made developers feel that the STR protocol was a needless paper mill. Users went for months without being apprised of bug fixes or desperately needed new features [12].

We note here the inability of the approaches mentioned in the Introduction to address the problems affecting this project. The programmers were using high-level languages (PL/I and BCPL, mostly) and had such tools as a source-language debugger for BCPL, source-comparison programs, optimizing compilers, and concordance generators. The project was not floundering due to an egregious lack of quality in the software; in fact, less than 15% of the STRs dealt with severe problems. (The other 85% dealt with annoyances, such as unclear error messages, or deficiencies - small but valuable extensions - or operational problems.) The project's difficulties were due to lack of effective, controlled communication. What was needed was not maintenance tools, but a maintenance system. In April, 1979, the authors began to specify MONSTR as an answer to these communication problems.

3.2 Concepts of MONSTR

MONSTR is a protocol-driven system. It is supplied with a description (in the form of a state-transition diagram [6,7,8]) of the communication paths which may be used by project members during the process of software maintenance. This description may be thought of as a road map. Just as a real road map shows physical routes between geographic locations, a protocol description shows communication paths between organizational locations. MONSTR allows organizations to be autonomous, i.e., intra-organizational communication is unconstrained. Inter-organizational communication is, however, constrained by MONSTR to follow the specified protocol. The protocol may, of course, be changed.

Given the existence of the protocol, STRs may be tracked exactly. At any given time, MONSTR can tell whether the STR is inside an organization (and which one), or if it is in transit between organizations (and which ones). MONSTR can answer questions about the protocol (e.g., if an STR is in a given state, what can happen next? What kinds of messages may be sent, and to whom?). The exact history of an STR can be kept and displayed, either from its inception to the present, or in the reverse order.

MONSTR generates identifiers for STRs and STR-related messages immediately upon their entering the system. This eliminates confusion arising from the mail system's inability to generate system-wide names. A MONSTR STR identifier indicates the type of message (STR, cancellation of an STR, modification to an STR, confirmation of a cancellation) and its history, if it has one (split off from another STR, created by merging STRs together). The names of states, persons, and organizations are supplied to MONSTR by a person acting as system configurator.

MONSTR sees a project as consisting of a number of project-specific organizations (vide the NSW organizations above). STRs and related messages are transmitted by MONSTR from one organization to one or more other organizations. People are grouped into organizations, and log on to MONSTR as members of these organizations.

MONSTR addresses the problem of determining organizational responsibility for an activity by requiring that a person explicitly tell MONSTR that s/he accepts responsibility for a message. Note that acceptance, in this sense, is different from simply reading a message. The acceptor accepts on behalf of the whole organization, but the acceptor's name appears in all status probes or history traces.

It often happens that the problem described in an STR is really better attacked as a number of subproblems, or in working on one problem, other related problems are uncovered. In these cases, we want to have a group of STRs, each of which can be separately tracked. Furthermore, we want to preserve the "family" relation among them. Therefore, MONSTR allows STRs to be split. The original STR may be kept in existence or not, depending on the view of the person doing the splitting. Each split-off STR then takes on an independent existence and moves through the project as per the protocol.

The converse of splitting is merging. STRs are merged if they are felt to be manifestations of a single underlying problem, or if they can best be handled by a single fix. STRs can be merged to form a new STR or they can be merged into an existing STR.

The "family tree" of an STR can become complex. MONSTR allows querying of an STR's ancestry (all the STRs which, through splits and merges, make up the STR) and posterity (all the STRs descended from the given one by splits and merges).

STRs may be modified or canceled. In both cases, there is new information about the problem described in an STR, and this information must go directly to the organization currently responsible for processing the STR. (In that sense, the cancellation or modification message moves outside the normal protocol channels.) A modification notice requires no response, but a cancellation does. It may be that the person who canceled the STR is mistaken: there may be a real problem in need of correction. Therefore, MONSTR will not cancel an STR until and unless the receiver of the cancellation notice signifies agreement by invoking a "propagate cancellation" command. This command informs all organizations expecting a response to an STR that that response will not be forthcoming: the STR has been canceled.

3.3 Facilities of MONSTR

The commands offered by MONSTR to people wishing to report bugs or process STRs are outlined below. (MONSTR system generation and protocol modification commands are not shown.) The descriptions are excerpted from the MONSTR User's Reference Manual [2].

3.3.1 Logging in and out

LOGIN	Log in to MONSTR, identifying yourself as a member of an organization.
MOVELOG	Log out as a member of one organization and log in as a member of another organization.
LOGOUT	Log out of MONSTR.

3.3.2 Basic processing

HELP	See a description of a MONSTR command, the syntax of an STR identifier, or the ways in which an STR may be classified or retrieved.
CREATE	Create an STR.
DISPATCH	Dispatch an existing STR to the next organization as jointly determined by the protocol and the intentions of the person doing the dispatching.
IN-BOX	Display the IDs of all STRs which are now waiting to be accepted by an organization.
READ	Type out (or direct to a file) all or part of an STR, with an option to accept delivery.
ACCEPT	Accept delivery of an STR.
RESPOND	Respond to an STR.
REMIND-ME	Set a reminder timer on an STR.
WHAT-REMINDERS	Display IDs of STRs with uncancelled reminder timers.

3.3.3 Status and content probing

STATUS	Display the state of an STR.
WHAT-NEXT	Show all possible outputs from the current state of an STR.
HISTORY	Show all state changes and transformations for an STR.
ANCESTRY	Expand an STR ID to show the IDs of all STRs which are its ancestors by splitting, merging, modifying, and cancelling.
POSTERITY	Print the "expanded" IDs of all STRs which have a given STR as an ancestor.
SUMMARIZE	Print the title and summary of an STR.
CLASSIFY	Attach values to the STR (e.g., priority for fixing, affected component, etc.) for associative retrieval.
RETRIEVE	Display the IDs of all STRs whose classifications match user-specified criteria.

3.3.4 Transformations of STRs

SPLIT	Split an STR into two or more STRs.
MERGE	Merge two or more STRs into a single STR.
MODIFY	Send a modification notice to whoever is currently processing an STR.
CANCEL	Send a cancellation notice to whoever is currently processing an STR.
PROPAGATE-CANCELLATION	
	Effect the cancellation of an STR.

3.3.5 System status reporting

RECENT-SUBMISSIONS	Display the IDs of all STRs created since a given time.
REPORT	Print (or direct to a file) a report on all active STRs, sorted according to user-specified criteria.

3.4 MONSTR as the framework for a software maintenance environment

MONSTR is a good starting point from which to develop a software maintenance environment. Because it is a protocol-driven system, the SM manager must precisely define the protocol which MONSTR uses. In doing so, the manager defines the roles, responsibilities, and activities necessary for SM to be done in the context of his or her project. (This definition is in itself a valuable, often neglected activity.) MONSTR then becomes a medium for controlled communication among project members who are carrying out their role-defined responsibilities.

Given that MONSTR insures that communication flows only in managerially authorized channels, it should be possible then for MONSTR to grant access to restricted resources (e.g., files) for use by specific role-players for specific periods of time. This access-granting would naturally be part of the protocol. By way of example, consider this simple protocol: organization A receives STRs from users and transmits them to organization B. For each STR, B analyzes the problem (using B-controlled resources) and sends a patch proposal to A. (A patch proposal states which files are affected and the estimated time to install and test the patch. The affected files are ones controlled by A.) A evaluates the patch proposal and, if it is satisfactory, tells B to go ahead. This authorizes B to access only those files (under A's control) which B named in the patch proposal. When the patch is installed, B informs A. (In a real protocol there would be many feedback loops, which we omit from this example.)

If MONSTR were mediating this interaction, A's acceptance of B's patch proposal tells MONSTR that A has authorized B to read and write certain files under A's control. No other A-controlled resources may be accessed. Consequently, MONSTR could cause the named files to be placed in B's workspace. At the same time, MONSTR remembers the authorization. There is no need for B to be granted access to the entire portion of file space which includes the files to be modified. When B tells A the patch is installed, MONSTR moves the modified files back into A's domain, thus rescinding B's access to them. MONSTR can, of course, automatically keep track of who changed what file, why, when, and how - the usual configuration management record-keeping.

This scenario presumes that there is a protection mechanism which is directly or indirectly at MONSTR's call. It also presumes that the tools used by the project members cannot circumvent that mechanism. This shows that MONSTR, as described in sections 3.2 and 3.3, is not a perfected SM environment. However, because it concentrates on a crucial aspect of SM which is generally ignored by other environments, MONSTR is in a good position to be extended into a true SM environment.

MONSTR can be extended to talk to other programs which perform specific maintenance and information-gathering functions. In the above example, MONSTR could direct a file transfer program to move files to and from the repository. Other auxiliary programs might include:

* an STR "syntax checker," which reads an STR and checks that all references to other STRs are valid (i.e., the STRs exist);

* a configuration management record-keeper, which, upon interrogation by MONSTR, provides the version numbers of all components running at the time a problem occurred;

* an STR "clerk" which extracts pertinent log file entries and appends them to the STR.

We note that the communication-oriented approach is, by its very nature, applicable to many other problems besides the creation of an SM environment. One example of this is the creation of a software production environment. Since maintenance is simply an extension of the production process, a "production protocol" may be devised and enforced by a MONSTR-like system. Another example is the coordination of people involved in compiler validation. Validation reports, test cases, compiler code, certifications, etc., must be exchanged among people in different parts of the country. The communication problems in such a situation can overshadow the actual validation activity, just as the communication problems of the NSW project eclipsed the more tractable technical problems.

3.5 MONSTR as an instance of a tool type

MONSTR is an example of a class of tools we have called contact tools - i.e., tools whose purpose is to mediate contact among a set of concurrently active, cooperating agents. These agents are necessarily using shared resources. Contact tools do not have a user, but rather a set of interrelated users. By the very nature of their cooperation, these users must communicate with each other. (Note: the concurrency does not arise solely because two or more users are using the contact tool simultaneously. Rather, concurrency must be understood in the time frame of the resources being used. In the case of MONSTR, a single STR will be worked on by many different people over the course of days or weeks. These workers are working on the STR concurrently.)

Tools, as one most often thinks of them, are committed to a single user for the furtherance of his purposes, and thus may be contrastively called solitary tools. Traditional program preparation tools such as editors, compilers, and debuggers are all solitary tools. On the other hand, operating systems, airline reservation systems, and MONSTR are examples of contact tools.

The design of contact tools characteristically raises issues of synchronization, naming, and the other disciplines enumerated in section 2.2. The communication-oriented approach to the building of various environments (for maintenance, production, configuration management, etc.) gains special power from the ability to design and build special-purpose contact tools as skeletal structures in which to embed tools of the solitary kind. Although successful contact tools have been built, they have not been recognized as such, and the communication aspects of many problems have largely gone unrecognized. The communication-oriented approach aims to reveal the underlying communication issues in any activity.

4. Conclusions

There are traditionally three complementary approaches to the problems of software maintenance. The computer science approach concentrates on making programs bug-free and easier to modify. The toolkit approach concentrates on building tools to detect and correct bugs easily. The environmental approach concentrates on building aggregates of tools with uniform user/tool and tool/tool interfaces. We introduce a new approach: the communication-oriented approach. This approach emphasizes the need to support the software maintenance process, rather than emphasizing capabilities, tools or static structures. The approach is to structure the environment so as to reflect the communication problems between different agents (which can be people or programs) organizations involved in the SM process. The SM process is shown to consist of a number of activities, the carrying out of which requires communication between participants. Various kinds of communication issues in SM are isolated, and the traditional approaches are shown by example to be incapable of dealing with them.

We describe MONSTR, a maintenance system designed using the communication-oriented approach. MONSTR accepts "coupled" state-transition graphs which describe desired protocols, and then constrains project communication to move strictly in accordance with these protocols. The status and history of a software trouble report can be easily and exactly determined. MONSTR can answer questions about the protocols. The protocols may be changed at any time to reflect reorganization of the project.

We analyze MONSTR's appropriateness as the framework for a true SM environment. Because MONSTR constrains communication to flow only in managerially approved channels, MONSTR can authorize access to specific resources (such as files) by certain role-players for specific times.

Finally, we note that the communication-oriented approach is applicable to many seemingly different problems, such as the problems of devising a software production environment or a compiler validation system. These problems have a common characteristic: the need to coordinate the activities of many people who must communicate in a variety of ways. The communication-oriented approach addresses problems of organization which are missed by traditional computer science or software engineering approaches.

5. References

[1] Cashman, Paul M. MONSTR: The NSW Tool to Monitor Software Trouble Reporting. Massachusetts Computer Associates document CA-7907-0911. September 1979.

[2] Cashman, Paul M. MONSTR User's Reference Manual. Massachusetts Computer Associates document CA-7911-0101. November 1979.

[3] Digital Equipment Corporation. TOPS-20AN User's Guide (Chapter 4: Local and Network Mail). Order numbers AA-5221A-TM, AD-5221A-T1. May 1979.

[4] Fisher, David A. "DoD's Common Programming Language Effort." IEEE Computer, pp. 24-33. March 1978.

[5] Habermann, A.N. Lecture before Boston SIGPLAN. September 20, 1979.

[6] Holt, Anatol W. Roles and Activities. Unpublished monograph, Boston University Academic Computing Center. May 1979.

[7] Holt, Anatol W. "Net Models of Organizational Systems, in Theory and Practice." In Ansatze zur Organisationstheorie Rechnergestutzer Informationssysteme (C.A. Petri, editor), pp. 39-62. GMD MBH, Bonn, report 111. 1979.

[8] Holt, Anatol W., R. Shapiro, H. Saint, S. Warshall. Final Report for the Information Systems Theory Project. Applied Data Research, Princeton, NJ report 6606. February 1968.

[9] Hutchings, A.F., R. McGuffin, A. Elliston, B. Tranter, and P. Westmacott. "CADES - Software Engineering in Practice." Proceedings of the Fourth Int. Conf. on Software Engineering, pp. 136-152. September 1979.

[10] Kafka, Franz. The Castle. Kurt Wolff Verlag, Munich. 1926.

[11] Lehman, M.M. Preface to the Proceedings of the Fourth Int. Conf. on Software Engineering. September 1979.

[12] Machado, R., and N. Peterson. NSW Applications Experiment: Final Technical Report. TRW Defense and Space Systems Group, Redondo Beach, CA. September 1979.

[13] Millstein, Robert E. "The National Software Works: A Distributed Processing System." Proceedings of the ACM 1977 Annual Conference, pp. 44-52. September 1977.

[14] Muntz, Charles A. "Using NSW to Manage a Distributed Task." Presentation at the NSW Contractors Meeting, May 1979.

[15] "Pebbleman revised" (Department of Defense Requirements for the Programming Environment for the Common High Order Language). January 1979.

[16] Petri, C.A. "Kommunikationsdisziplinen." Gesellschaft fur Mathematik und Datenverarbeitung MBH, Bonn, report ISF-76-1. March 1976.

[17] Proceedings of the Irvine Workshop on Alternatives for the Environment, Certification, and Control of the DoD Common High Order Language, pp. 139-148. June 1978.

[18] Rude, R.V., and Charlotte Mooers. BBN-HERMES Reference Manual. Bolt Beranek and NewMan, Inc., Cambridge, MA.

[19] Stuebing, Henry. "FASP - the Facility for Automated Software Production." Proceedings of the Irvine Workshop on Alternatives for the Environment, Certification, and Control of the DoD Common High Order Language. June 1978.

Introduction

Zvegintzov, N. "Four common complaints—tips boost maintenance programmer morale." *Computerworld* (March 30, 1981), Special Report section.

Finally, we turn to two selections on maintenance programmer morale. Both deal with the human, rather than the technical, content of communication within the maintenance group. According to audience response at our presentations, morale is now the foremost problem cited by maintenance managers, followed by the maintainability of new systems, and the purging of old.

This selection was written by one of us as a contribution to a Special Report section of *Computerworld* on people productivity. One reader, Kathi Chappuis of the International Labor Organization, pointed out that the article does not stress sufficiently the necessity of acknowledging the maintenance staff's importance to the organization; often staff feel used but not appreciated. The same point was made by Eleanor Maurer of Blue Cross of Northern California in a presentation at the 1982 National Computer Conference.

Four Common Complaints
Tips Boost Maintenance Programmer Morale

By Nicholas Zvegintzov
Special to CW

Many management information systems (MIS) managers tell me that the programmers who maintain and upgrade existing programs are essential, but that they often exhibit morale problems. The most common complaints about maintenance programming are:

- It deals with trivial problems.
- It's hard work.
- It's never finished.
- It doesn't seem to go anywhere.

Good morale relies on having an important job to do, having the tools to do it, seeing it done and getting credit for it. So these complaints strike at the very nature of morale. Let's see how to answer them — not with insincere promises that things will be different tomorrow, but with answers that build maintenance staff morale on today's reality.

Maintenance deals with trivial prob-

other report — but that's what professional expertise is all about. That's what we're paid for, to find trivial solutions to hard problems, not to find hard solutions to trivial problems.

Maintenance is hard work? Sure it is. Don't deny it — glory in it. Remember the findings of Daniel Couger and Robert Zawacki in their book *Motivating and Managing Computer Personnel* — DPers are higher than all other professionals in their need for challenge and growth. If they want challenge and growth, they must go where the hard work is. At the same time, make sure that they have the tools they need, so that they know they're doing real work and not needless drudgery.

The key is *order*. The more disorder in the system, the more the drudgery. So be on the look-out for tools and techniques which add, reveal, impose or restore order, software tools which cross-reference, document or diagram existing code, "fourth-generation"

> 'Remind the maintenance programmer that the health of the organization is in its response to change, just as the growth of the tree is in its outermost ring. Sure, the methods are often trivial for a computer expert . . . but that's what we're paid for, to find trivial solutions to hard problems.'

---

lems? Hardly! Maintenance deals with the business changes which are the life-blood of the organization. Banking regulations change to allow new business which blends savings, checking and credit card transactions — so the demand deposit accounting system must change. A new marketing subsidiary is acquired — so the sales information system must change.

Remind the maintenance programmer that the health of the organization is in its response to change, just as the growth of the tree is in its outermost ring. Sure, the methods are often trivial for a computer expert — another edit, another table, another sort, an-

language tools which reduce the amount of code to do the same functions, and restorative methods which upgrade spaghetti code to structured code.

And don't be reluctant to badger salesmen and consultants about your needs. When they promise miracles tomorrow with new systems, ask them what they can do today with existing systems.

Maintenance is never finished? Well, yes and no. Each individual change is finished, but the maintenance programmer deals for years with the "same" system. But remember that the programmer gets a paycheck for years from the same organization. So continuity isn't all bad, sometimes it's job security!

Nevertheless, too much security can lead to stagnation and premature burnout of a valuable employee. Recognize and use the programmer's desire to see the system better as well as bigger. The programmer should be able to see perceptible improvement as well as a sequence of small changes.

Have a systematic policy of making the system simpler, stronger, more structured, easier to understand. When making substantial changes to any module, take the opportunity to upgrade the code, to remove out-dated branches, correct sloppiness and error, to systematize and document. Make sure that resources are available (say, 10% of programmer time) to upgrading and replacing old code with clean code that is functionally equivalent.

Remember that what you are maintaining is not code, but the business function served by the code. Programmers are like house-owners, if they're going to live with the system for a while, they appreciate the opportunity to make it a better place to live.

And, finally, they complain that maintenance doesn't go anywhere. This complaint comes in two flavors: it doesn't go anywhere career-wise, and it doesn't go anywhere in professional advancement.

The first complaint is in your hands to deal with. Maintenance work (and operations, too) is an attractive career path for the organizationally minded technician. The maintenance programmer has an unrivaled opportunity to learn both the existing procedures of the organization and its fast-breaking business and policy twists. It is an excellent basis for management advancement.

Remember that the star who develops an entirely new system often gets, as the next assignment, the job of maintaining it, so his career is still one step behind that of the star who goes into maintenance in the first place. (Of course, there are still organizations which are in their first generation of computing, and therefore still need development stars above all, but such organizations are becoming fewer as DP moves into its maturity.)

> 'The maintenance programmer has an unrivaled opportunity to learn both the existing procedures of the organization and its fast-breaking business and policy twists. It is an excellent basis for management advancement.'

The other half of the complaint is that maintenance programming doesn't go anywhere professionally. You hear this from staff who are more technically than organizationally oriented. Such staff are valuable to you and must be fairly answered. They point out that the articles in professional journals, the proposals from high-paid consultants, and the promotional literature from software houses is all about the techniques and opportunities and rewards of developing new systems.

Who speaks for maintenance? Turn this question around. Ask them, "If you want green grass, would you rather be in a pasture with a thousand cows or in the field where you are a pioneer?" It's easy to write programs and journal articles alone in an ivory tower, and it's easy to leaflet a business with brightly colored brochures of new products.

What's hard is to handle and understand the big, powerful, ornery systems that pay the bills in the real world. That's where the professional challenge is today. Remember that a recent poll of leading educators by Shetal Enterprises of Chicago, publisher of "Software Maintenance Newsletter" found that colleges don't teach maintenance because nobody knows enough about it yet.

Maintenance is still a frontier in software engineering.

Summing up, the main morale points for maintenance staff are:
- It's the life-blood of the business.
- Of course it's hard work.
- It's not meant to be finished — it's meant to be used.
- It's where the action is.

If none of this works, well, you may have selected the wrong types for maintenance work.

Introduction

Bronstein, G.M., Okamoto, R.I. "I'm OK, you're OK, maintenance is OK." *Computerworld* (January 12, 1981), IN DEPTH section.

The final paper turns to the internal dynamics of communication among maintenance staffers and their managers.

Both authors are at Amdahl Corporation and deal with the software that supports the design development and manufacturing of the corporation's products. Gary Bronstein is Director of Engineering Development Systems and Robert Okamoto is Manager of Design Automation. In 1979 they were disturbed by the priority conflicts inherent in having maintenance and development in a single organization. But if there were separate organizations, would anyone want to work in maintenance?

At this point Bronstein and Okamoto happened to attend an American Management Associations class which covered the topic of "How to sell ideas to your boss." It was pointed out that different approaches must be taken with different types of people. They reflected: "If there are these different types of people, can we match people better with their jobs, or can we recruit better for jobs such as maintenance?" They also gave a great deal of thought to the socio-economic reward system for maintenance. From this they began to evolve the maintenance environment described in the following paper.

Both authors have done maintenance programming. They respect the skills involved and the close relation of those skills to the functionality of the organization's software, and therefore to the well-being of the organization itself. If the staff are to appreciate their own value (as recommended in the last selection), the boss must appreciate it first.

I'm OK, You're OK, Maintenance is OK

By Gary M. Bronstein and Robert I. Okamoto

Structured methodologies and techniques, contrary to popular opinion, are not driving maintenance programming out of existence. As an industry, we continue to spend more on the maintenance of old programs than we spend on the development of new ones.

We believe that maintenance programming is a rewarding profession and have built an effective maintenance organization at Amdahl Corp. by avoiding many of the pitfalls of traditional maintenance groups.

Engineering software at Amdahl is responsible for the software required to design, develop, test, manufacture and maintain Amdahl's computers. This includes computer-aided design, diagnostics, control systems for the console processor and a variety of software tools for the production and distribution of software and hardware.

Several years ago, software development and maintenance were performed by the same groups. This often produced conflicts in priorities between development and maintenance. To resolve these conflicts, we decided to create two kinds of groups — "development" groups and "support or maintenance" groups.

Traditional Assumptions

There were those who thought this division of responsibilities between groups would not work. Their reasons were what we would call the following traditional assumptions about maintenance or support programming:

• Maintenance is not challenging, rewarding or creative.

• Maintenance requires neither skill nor experience.

• Nobody who was competent would do maintenance for very long.

Their conclusion was that everyone would want to do development and nobody would want to do support.

These assumptions begin to explain why software deteriorates and why maintenance costs are so high. From these assumptions, one can conclude that most maintenance is done by entry-level programmers in an environment where maintenance is considered the most menial of programming tasks.

The attitude that maintenance is "technological janitor work" is part of what Don McNeil termed "The Myth of Software Maintenance" [CW, Feb. 18]. As he went on to say, "It also produces rotten software."

The traditional assumptions conflicted with our analysis of the work itself. Maintenance programming means supporting the needs of existing software users. The work entails a variety of activities, skills, challenges and rewards.

Correction, Enhancements

The two basic classifications of work are correction and enhancement. Correction is the process of isolating and repairing code that does not perform to the original or established specifications. Enhancement is the addition, modification or complete redevelopment of code to support changes in specification or operational environment.

Although the definitions of correction and enhancement are straightforward, the execution of the work is extremely difficult and complex.

Correction activities are often conducted in a Sherlock Holmes atmosphere. Clues are sparse or nonexistent. The environment of problems as they occurred is usually altered or destroyed. A lack of written material or clues forces one to verbally investigate and extract bits of information.

As data and assumptions are pieced together, prime suspected routines are first identified and then scrutinized. Test cases are often run in an attempt to recreate the crime. Finally, the faulty code is isolated and corrective measures are taken.

Enhancement is similar to development in its phases, but the emphasis is different. Both activities require:

- Analysis.
- Design.
- Implementation.
- Testing and Acceptance.

Analysis is the dominant phase in enhancement. Does the enhancement extend the current design or must the design be modified or scrapped? What is the remaining life of the product and how much money should be invested in the enhancements? Are there alternate solutions available? What are the changes? How is other software affected?

What results from this analysis is usually a small project relative to the size of the program being modified. The remaining phases of design, implementation, testing and acceptance are just as important as they are in development, but they are proportionately smaller phases.

We have discussed the activities of maintenance work and the associated challenges. What rewards come from the work itself?

The triumph of a maintenance programmer over a program bug and the successful modification of an undocumented program illustrate the reward that comes from solving a tough maintenance problem.

An important difference between maintenance and development is the time frame. Production program failures tend to be "line stoppers." Enhancement or modification requests result from undesirable shortcomings in the software. The reward is frequent and feedback immediate as programs run and users are happy.

In maintenance, a programmer often supports more than one product. Or for backup and continuity, a team of programmers supports several products. The reward is variety in products, environments and end users.

Finally, maintenance activities are done on behalf of people. Somebody has a problem that is either keeping him from getting his job done or is making his job more difficult. Helping to remove these impediments for other people can be very rewarding.

Our New Assumptions

The work of maintenance is certainly not a sandbox for neophyte programmers. To put maintenance in its proper perspective requires a new set of assumptions. Among them:
- Maintenance is challenging, rewarding and creative.
- Maintenance requires considerable skill and experience.
- There are competent people who enjoy maintenance and pursue it as a career.

We do not mean that development and maintenance programmers are interchangeable. We mean, instead, that one kind of programming activity should not be considered inferior or superior to another.

Maintenance and development are activities requiring different people and skills. An important part of building an effective maintenance group is to understand those differences and to recruit and organize based upon the requirements of the maintenance job.

The Maintenance Programmer

The ability to make good, sound judgments depends on the experience and technical expertise of the maintenance programmer.

The maintenance programmer must be able to identify with the needs of the end user. This means understanding the operational environment and what the user is trying to accomplish with the software. The maintainer must also put on a development hat. To best understand existing software, it is important to understand the style, habits, idiosyncrasies and thought processes of the responsible developer.

The maintenance programmer must be technically versatile. The ability to work with different equipment, programming languages, styles, tools, users, environments and documentation is required.

Psychic Functions

In addition to the technical skills, the maintenance programmer must have the right balance of what experts refer to as psychic functions or communication styles. Psychologist Carl Jung identified four basic psychic functions inherent in everyone. These functions are thinker, feeler, sensor and intuiter. These same functions are called communication styles by others and are labeled analyzer, affiliator, activator and conceptualizer respectively.

The styles reflect profiles of attitudes, assumptions and actions resulting from people experiencing things differently.

For example, the analyzer makes judgments about the relationship of things and places high value on facts, figures, data and reason. The analyzer would normally be described as analytical, organized, rational and thorough.

The affiliator places value on personal relationships. Adjectives appropriate for the affiliator are perceptive, patient, adaptable and supportive.

The activator is concerned about what is "actual" at this moment. The time frame is the here and now. Descriptions of the activator are assertive, objective, energetic and resourceful.

Finally, the conceptualizer is concerned primarily about the nature of things in terms of their significance and meaning. The conceptualizer places high value on ideas, concepts and theories. Adjectives describing this style are imaginative, creative, idealistic, original, abstract and innovative.

While there can be pure analyzers and pure affiliators, most people are a combination of styles (see figure). The activator supports the imposed time constraints. The analyzer must control the work — organize, define, resolve and implement. The affiliator is the supporter, the hand-holder, the one who can patiently listen, the one who is flexible and perceptive.

The characteristics of the three styles will sometimes conflict. It is on these occasions that the experience and skills of the maintenance programmer determines which must prevail.

Our experience has shown that technical skills and the communication style profile required of the job are important in selecting people for positions. Matching the job and communication styles required is a tool in our recruitment and selection process.

An additional important factor contributing to the success of the maintenance programmer is the environment in which the work is accomplished.

Maintenance Environment

Maintenance programming has existed in a social and technical environment that is a direct outgrowth of the traditional assumptions we have encountered. In this environment, maintenance programmers have been unworthy or "not OK." They have generally been paid less and received less recognition. Little attention has been paid to their orientation, training and professional growth within a maintenance group. They need only follow in the footsteps of the developer.

Similarly, the need for maintenance programmers to apply standards and methodologies has been ignored. There are few tools to deal with the special problems they encounter.

An attractive environment for maintenance programming is required if a stable, experienced group is to exist. That environment should support and reward people for excellence in what they do well and what they enjoy doing.

In our environment, we have not made distinctions between development and maintenance programmers in either compensation or titles. There have been employee-initiated transfers in both directions between development and maintenance organizations.

A recent survey of the informal power structure of the organization disclosed that each group thought it had the most informal power. This seems to say that no group considered itself "second class."

More Training

Maintenance demands more orientation and more training than other programming activities — especially for entry-level programmers. One factor is the greater variety of work. Another is the fact that the programs being maintained were developed by others and many have been subsequently modified before reaching their current state.

Formal classes can deal with part of the Babel of different computers and different languages. In the classroom, one can also learn the latest in methodologies to help in the enhancement or redevelopment of code. But only an extended apprenticeship with an experienced maintenance programmer can lead to an understanding of past practices and programming styles. It is this understanding rather than a criticism or value judgment about past practices that produces today's correction or enhancement.

These are some problems facing the maintainer:
• Maintaining programs written without standards.
• Lack of documentation and source.

• Different computers and languages.

We recognize that these problems are decreasing, but they are not going to disappear. Since the problems will always be there, maintenance tools are being conceived and constructed to deal with some of them.

Higher level language code can be de-compiled from object files or assembler. This can be a great asset where a maintainable source file no longer exists. Structure charts and flowcharts can be constructed where no current charts exist. Cross-referencing of variables including aliases aids in the change process. There are other tools and there will be more.

Communication Styles

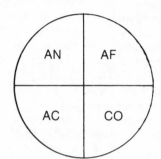

AN-Analyzer
AF-Affiliator
AC-Activator
CO-Conceptualizer

A salesperson must be able to communicate effectively in all styles. His style profile might look like this.

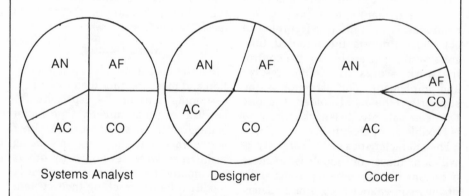

Systems Analyst   Designer   Coder

People good at various phases of programming might have profiles like these.

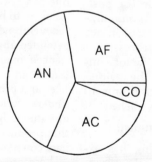

An effective and satisfied maintenance programmer often has this communication style profile.

342

The total maintenance programming environment is the major determinant in the quality and cost-effectiveness of maintenance. We have taken steps to create an environment in which "OK" maintenance programmers are highly productive in what they do well.

A great deal has been said and written about the high cost and unreliability of maintenance. As an industry, we have spent considerable effort to improve the software development process as a means of improving the maintenance situation.

However effective the improvements might be, their effect is muted if the personnel performing maintenance are not competent, motivated, productive employees. Finding such people and forming effective maintenance groups has been severely hindered by the traditional assumptions that maintenance programming is inferior, unrewarding work that must be endured only as an apprenticeship to doing something else.

Improving the maintenance situation requires the assumption that maintenance programming is as challenging and rewarding as any facet of the programming profession. It also requires an environment which deals with both the rational and emotional needs of maintenance programmers.

The rational part of the environment recognizes the unique needs of the maintenance programmer for tools, methods and training. We are convinced that resources spent on the maintenance process will have as great an impact on software cost and reliability as anything we have done for the development process. But changing technology alone will not accomplish the goal.

The organization must create a psychological environment in which it is "OK" to be a maintenance programmer. Those programmers must be recognized and rewarded for the things they do well. They must perceive that their function is as important to the organization as any other function.

So let us praise maintenance programmers. They have long been overlooked for their importance to the programming profession.

Gary M. Bronstein is director of engineering systems development at Amdahl Corp., Sunnyvale, Calif.

Robert I. Okamoto is manager of design automation at Amdahl.

Epilogue: Songs for unsung heroes

Maintenance professionals have been named the "unsung heroes" of software. These are the people who are called in the middle of the night, usually to handle a condition that has never occurred before. These are the people who are assigned, as a coding chore, to fill a hole that goes far deeper than a system's code. These are the people whose presence is only appreciated when they are absent or when they are replaced by less skilled personnel. This Tutorial will serve its purpose if it has brought to you a little of their reality.

A collection such as this reflects the strength and weakness of the literature that it surveys. A reviewer of an early version commented that Part IV (on the evolution of software) seemed a philosophical tangent; that Part V (on the death of software) seemed to add little; and that Part VI (on management) lacked general guidelines that management could put into practice.

This criticism has some merit. The best work done so far on a global theory of maintenance is collected in Part IV, but much work remains to be done. The maintenance community's confusion on an important issue is reflected in Part V: everyone agrees that software must be purged, but they find it hard to do. In Part VI we assume that maintenance managers are pragmatic people who learn more from a summary of real policies in a real environment than they do from a more abstract survey.

The same reviewer, however, has many positive comments:

> Because I come from industry, I am especially happy with the real-world emphasis of most of the authors, and because I am trained academically I am happy to see maintenance become something other than a seat-of-the-pants operation. This can only help to improve the state of computing in the future. . . [The Tutorial] will be of use in both academic and industrial environments, and if it receives wide enough circulation, may help to alleviate one of the most pressing problems in computer science, that of maintaining software.

We stand behind the authors and behind our selection of their papers. We feel that maintainers write as the people they are—practical people battling to bring order to a system that continually threatens to go beyond the border of comprehension or over the precipice of complexity. They write like unsung heroes.

Other readings

We believe that this Tutorial provides a well-structured approach to maintenance, but it is not complete. In some directions, it must be supplemented by other reading; in other directions, the topic itself is barely understood. The territory is open for you, the readers, to pioneer.

In particular, we have deliberately avoided tramping over ground well covered in other collections. The following four books are complementary collections of readings:

Parikh's *Techniques of program and system maintenance* (the first American book on software maintenance) collects much of the maintenance literature of the period 1969-1980, particularly its management aspects.

Miller and Howden's IEEE Computer Society Tutorial *Software testing & validation techniques* is an important source of papers on error control, which absorbs about 20% of the maintenance effort.

Capers Jones's IEEE Computer Society Tutorial *Programming productivity: issues for the eighties* includes many papers on programmer understanding and program representation, a topic on which Jones is a leading expert.

Finally, *Practice in software adaption and maintenance*, edited by Ebert, Lügger, and Goecke, collects papers, some of them quite technical, on adapting multiversion software systems to different operating systems.

Complete references for these books, and for other publications on maintenance, can be found in the Annotated Bibliography at the end of this Tutorial.

Open questions

This Tutorial, and the other referenced literature, only scratches the surface of the maintenance topic. Huge areas remain unexplored. Here are a few examples.

Structured methodologies are supposed to produce reliable systems, within budget, that satisfy user requirements. The proponents of these methodologies often add that the resulting systems are "easily maintained." But how do they know this? If they do know it, do they tell you how to maintain their systems while preserving the original structure of the systems?

Documentation. How much do maintainers need? On what media? How can they keep it up to date?

Resources. At least half of all programming is maintenance, as has been true for many years. Is this proportion too high or too low? Why? What would you do about it?

The shape of changes. In a typical organization, what proportion of changes is large and what is small? In what proportion of changes is the changed code scattered throughout the system versus clustered in a single unit? (Is there a typical organization?)

Redevelopment. How do you save the functionality of a system while replacing its structure and/or components?

The psychology of maintainers. How do you increase the motivation, skill, and professionalism of maintenance staff?

Conclusion

We could ask many more questions, but these are enough. These are not quiz questions with answers at the end of the book; this is the end of the book. After you close it, the hard part begins.

Annotated Software Maintenance Bibliography

Girish Parikh

This short bibliography presents a selection of readings on software maintenance and related topics. It is designed not as a comprehensive listing but as a guide to the reader into the growing literature on the subject. The introductions and reprints in this Tutorial provide many more references.

Periodicals

Software maintenance techniques. David A. Higgins, publisher, EduCo Corporation, 6777 Wadsworth, Suite 102, Arvada, CO 80003. To our knowledge, this semiannual publication is the only periodical devoted entirely to software maintenance.

Software productivity digest. Edited by Girish Parikh, Shetal Enterprises, Dept IEEESM, 1787 B West Touhy, Chicago, IL 60626. Publication is expected to start in 1983. Software maintenance will be regularly featured.

Among general computing journals, *Computerworld* and *Datamation* have been the most supportive of maintenance over the years. Six papers selected for this Tutorial first appeared in *Computerworld* (both of Parikh's papers, Zvegintzov's "Four common complaints," and the papers by Higgins, Miller, and Bronstein and Okamoto). Only one paper in this collection is from *Datamation* (Zvegintzov's "The Eureka Countdown"), but five from there were included in Parikh's *Techniques of program and system maintenance*, which we did not want to duplicate.

Books and papers

Baker, B.S. "An algorithm for structuring flowcharts." *J. ACM*, 24, 1 (1977), 98-120. This paper describes an algorithm which transforms a flowgraph into a program containing control constructs such as **if then else** statements, **repeat (do forever)** statements, multilevel **break** statements (causing jumps out of enclosing **repeat**s), and multilevel **next** statements (causing jumps to iterations of enclosing **repeat**s). The algorithm can be extended to create other types of control constructs, such as **while** or **until**. The program appears natural because the constructs are used according to common programming practices. The algorithm does not copy code, create subroutines, or add new variables. Instead, **goto** statements are generated when no other available control construct describes the flow of control. The algorithm has been implemented in a program called STRUCT which rewrites Fortran programs using constructs such as **while, repeat,** and **if then else** statements. The resulting programs are substantially more readable than their Fortran counterparts. [From the abstract.]

Belady, L.A., Lehman, M.M. "A model of large program development." *IBM Systems J.*, 15, 3 (1976), 225-252. Discussed are observations made on the development of OS/360 and its subsequent enhancements and releases. Some modeling approaches to organizing these observations are also presented. [From the abstract.]

Bergland, G.D. "A guided tour of program design methodologies." *IEEE Computer*, 14, 10 October 1981), 13-37. Excerpted in Martin and McClure, 1982. After describing, applying, comparing, and evaluating four major methodologies—hierarchical functional decomposition, data flow design method, data structured design (Jackson), and programming calculus (Dijkstra)—this guided tour concludes with an interim procedure for use until the "right" method appears. Bergland illustrates the maintenance consequences of the structured approaches.

Boehm, B.W. "Software engineering." *IEEE Trans. on Computers*, C-25, 12 (December 1976), 1226-1241. Excerpts are included in Parikh, 1982. This excellent paper provides a definition of software engineering, a state of the art survey and likely future trends. It overviews the technology available in the various phases of the software life cycle, including maintenance, and in the overall area of software management and integrated technology management approaches. It includes 104 references.

Burns, K. "Using automated techniques to improve the maintainability of existing software." *DSSD User's Conference/6—Maintenance*, Topeka, KS, October 8, 1981, 33-39. A project completed by Sage Software Products, Inc. is described as a case problem. The two concepts for measuring maintainability are included—programmer span of control and maintainability index. Burns refers to and describes the "retrofit process" as used by the company.

Canning, R.G., ed. "That maintenance 'iceberg.'" *EDP Analyzer*, 10, 10 (October 1972). This report reveals that about 50% of the programming expenses of most business users of computers goes toward maintenance and enhancement of existing programs. Included are case studies of three corporations. Some causes of maintenance changes and the problems associated with them are described. A plan for more maintainable systems is given which consists of designing for changes, tools for design changes, configuration policies, control and audit, organizing for maintenance, and converting to more maintainable systems.

Canning, R.G., ed. "Easing the software maintenance burden." *EDP Analyzer*, 19, 8 (August 1981). This report begins by describing three different approaches taken by three companies for creating more maintainable systems. It then draws material from three books on maintenance (Lientz and Swanson, 1980; Parikh, 1982; and Glass and Noiseux, 1981). Finally, it covers off-loading of maintenance work onto end users and onto package vendors.

Clapp, J.A. "Designing software for maintainability." *Computer Design* (September 1981), 197-202, 204. This excellent article includes the following topics: What is software maintenance? How does maintenance differ from development? Planning for maintenance, and the future of maintenance. Included are sections on "Software maintenance planning factors" and "Resources for software maintenance."

Clark, D.M. "Maintenance programming." *Computerworld* (July 28, 1980), IN DEPTH section. This article is one of the gems in the sparse but urgently needed literature on how to do maintenance.

de Balbine, G. "Better manpower utilization using automatic restructuring." *AFIPS Conference Proceedings*, 44, 1975, 313-327. Also in Parikh, 1982. This excellent paper describes results achieved by restructuring existing FORTRAN programs into a "structured" FORTRAN superset S-FORTRAN, by using a proprietary package that operates as a "structuring engine." Examples of more easily understandable restructured programs are included.

Ebert, R., Lügger, J., Goecke, L., eds. *Practice in software adaption and maintenance. Proceedings of the SAM Workshop*, Berlin, April 1980. Amsterdam, The Netherlands: North-Holland Publishing Company, 1980. Twenty-one papers, some quite technical, are presented on the problems of publishing and/or bringing up software packages on a variety of systems. An excellent bibliography is included.

Freedman, D.P., Weinberg, G.M. *Handbook of walkthroughs, inspections, and technical reviews*. Boston, MA: Little, Brown and Company, 3rd edition, 1982. Excerpted in Parikh, 1982. This excellent handbook includes material on maintenance reviews for technical as well as for managerial people.

Gilb, T. *Software metrics*. Cambridge, MA: Winthrop Publishers, Inc., 1977. [This publisher has been acquired by Little, Brown and Company, Boston, MA.] Lund, Sweden: Studentlitteratur AB, 1977. (In print only with the latter.) Many practical techniques are provided for estimating reliability and efficiency.

Gilb also presents his own MECCA method and details the experiences of leaders in the field such as TRW Systems and Lockheed. See also several Gilb reprints in Parikh, 1982.

Glass, R.L., Noiseux, R.A. *Software maintenance guidebook*. Englewood Cliffs, NJ: Prentice-Hall, Inc., 1981. Presented is information for professionals who perform technical and managerial functions, as a perspective for the software engineering student to understand the spectrum of software activity with a focus on maintenance.

Jones, T.C. "Measuring programming quality and productivity." *IBM Systems Journal*, 17, 1 (1978), 39-63. Also reprinted in Jones, 1981. This engineering article includes a discussion of the usefulness of separating quality measurements into measures of defect removal efficiency and defect prevention. Regarding maintenance costs, Jones states: "The smaller the change the larger the unit cost is likely to be. This is because it is necessary to understand the base program even to add or modify a single line, and the overhead of the learning curve exerts an enormous leverage on small changes. Additionally, it is often necessary to test the entire program and perhaps recompile much of it, even though only a single line has been modified."

Jones, [T.] C. *Tutorial—Programming productivity: issues for the eighties*. IEEE Computer Society, 1981. A compendium of 35 papers with Jones' reflections.

Lientz, B.P., Swanson, E.B. *Software maintenance management—a study of the maintenance of computer application software in 487 data processing organizations*. Reading, MA: Addison-Wesley Publishing Company, Inc., 1980. Results of a questionnaire survey provide the best source of data on maintenance practices and management attitudes.

Linger, R.C., Mills, H.D., Witt, B.I. *Structured programming: theory and practice*. Reading, MA: Addison-Wesley Publishing Company, 1979. "If a professional programmer was to read only one book on 'structured programming,' this should be it," writes Weinberg in *Understanding the professional programmer* (Little, Brown and Company, 1982). "The style and content of this book set the tone for professional programming of the future," he adds. The book includes the chapter "Reading structured programs."

Liu, C.L. "A look at software maintenance." *Datamation* (November 1976), 51-55. Also in Parikh, 1982. Liu provides an excellent introduction to the world of maintenance.

Lyons, M.J. "Structured retrofit—1980." *Proceedings of SHARE 55* (1980), 263-265. As an introduction to the evolving structured retrofit techniques pioneered by J.C. Miller, these topics are presented: What is maintenance?—scoring, restructuring, formatting, validation, structured programming engines, COBOL structuring engine standards, formatters, and optimizers.

Lyons, M.J. "Salvaging your software asset (tools based maintenance)." *AFIPS Conference Proc.*, 50, 1981, 337-341. According to Lyons, "structured retrofit is an effective alternative to rewrites and purchased software." Structured retrofit uses a software tools-based methodology for combatting decay and high costs of maintenance. The critical tool in structured retrofit is the COBOL structuring engine.

Martin, J. *Applications development without programmers.* Englewood Cliffs, NJ: Prentice-Hall, 1982. An intriguing book from an industry guru. Martin looks several years ahead. He covers "packaged" routines that deliver application software to order. The topics include language for end users, data base user languages, application generators for end users, end user driven computing, and APL. He also briefly covers how the maintenance load can be reduced by redeveloping software using application generators.

Martin, J., McClure, C.L. *Maintenance of computer programming.* Carnforth, England: Savant Institute, 1982. A book by industry guru Martin with "Maintenance" in the title gives credibility to this neglected topic. The contents include designing for maintenance, use of fourth-generation language, user-driven computing, prototyping, information engineering, application packages, performing the maintenance function, planning for future maintenance, and strategic planning and migration. Also included is a nine-page package software contract.

McClure, C.L. *Managing software development and maintenance.* New York, NY: Van Nostrand Reinhold Company, 1981. Presented are project management methods showing how to control rising software costs by applying the principles of software engineering to software development and maintenance activities.

Miller, E., Howden, W.E. *Tutorial: software testing & validation techniques.* IEEE Computer Society, 1978. Areas covered include program structure analysis, test coverage, quantification, and methodologies for planning and controlling the test process. Contains 44 reprints.

Miller, J.C. "Structured retrofit—1981." *Proceedings of SHARE 57* (1981). This progress report on structured retrofit, presented by the pioneer of the concepts, includes case histories, reasons for retrofit software, and the lessons learned externally and internally.

Mosteller, W.S. *Systems programmer's problem solver.* Boston, MA: Little, Brown and Company, 1981. A wealth of material for a systems programmer. An applications maintenance programmer can also benefit from the book. The informal, anecdotal style makes it informative and interesting reading.

Parikh, G. "Improved maintenance techniques." In the series *Programmer Productivity Reports*, PPR1, 1977, revised 1982, Shetal Enterprises, Chicago, IL. Excerpted in Parikh, 1982. This report describes how to use structured techniques in maintenance. It delineates the application of top-down development, librarian, team operations, walkthroughs, structured programming, and HIPO to maintain existing systems and programs.

Parikh, G. "How to document program changes and enhancements internally." In the series *Programmer Productivity Reports*, PPR5, 1978, Shetal Enterprises, Chicago, IL. A simple technique based on the commenting feature of a programming language provides instant identification of program changes. For further reference, it also includes identifications of the external specifications for the changes. The technique can be easily adapted for almost any programming language on any computer system. Its use generally does not take any additional core storage. Examples from real world COBOL and BAL programs are included.

Parikh, G. "A powerful structured tool: the Warnier-Orr diagram." In the series *Programmer Productivity Reports*, PPRW, 1980, Shetal Enterprises, Chicago, IL. This report introduces the versatile Warnier/Orr diagram. It includes the diagram's use in maintenance, primarily to document existing software.

Parikh, G. *How to measure programmer productivity.* Chicago, IL: Shetal Enterprises, 1981a. An overview of the state-of-the-art and evolving programmer productivity measurement techniques. Includes the chapter "Productivity in maintenance and conversion" and an extensive annotated bibliography.

Parikh, G. "Measuring programmer productivity in a maintenance environment." *Proceedings of SHARE 57*, Chicago, IL, 1981b. This paper, based on experience and research, overviews the state of-the-art and evolving techniques of measuring programmer productivity in a maintenance environment. The quantitative and qualitative aspects of programmer productivity are covered. The factors affecting maintenance programming productivity (e.g., management attitude, training, organization of the maintenance function, documentation, software tools, experience, application knowledge, programming language, and structure of software) are considered, and suggestions are made for evaluating performance.

Parikh, G. *Techniques of program and system maintenance.* Boston, MA: Little, Brown and Company, 1982. Contains a programming and management overview of software maintenance, compiled from the vast body of computer literature, and some original material. Includes an extensive annotated bibliography and an index.

Perry, W.E. *Managing systems maintenance.* Wellesley, MA: QED Information Sciences, 1981. Describes systematic methods for effective maintenance. Includes over 40 forms and checklists.

Reifer, D.J., Trattner, S. "A glossary of software tools and techniques." *IEEE Computer*, 10, 7 (1977), 52-60. This paper provides a comprehensive listing of the software tools and techniques. It describes the three major stages of a typical software life cycle (conceptual and requirements, development, and operations and maintenance), and the six categories of software tools (simulation, development, test and evaluation, operations and maintenance, performance measurement, and programming support). A table relates the life cycle areas for the major categories of software tools, and a matrix relates the specific tools/techniques listed in the glossary to categories of software tools of which they are a part. The glossary of aids briefly describes seventy tools/techniques. It includes 61 references.

Shneiderman, B. *Software psychology: human factors in computer and information systems.* Cambridge, MA: Winthrop Publishers, Inc., 1980. [This publisher has been acquired by Little, Brown and Company, Boston, MA.] This excellent book includes material and references on program comprehension.

Swanson, E.B. "The dimensions of maintenance." IEEE Computer Society, *2nd International Conference on Software Engineering*, 1976, 492-497. This excellent paper presents the "dimensionality" of the maintenance problem for practitioners and researchers. "Some measures are suggested for coming to grips with this dimensionality, and problems of utilization associated with these measures are explored." This paper introduced the much quoted classification of software maintenance into corrective, adaptive, and perfective.

Warnier, J.-D. *Program modification.* Boston, MA: Martinus Nijhoff Social Sciences Division, 1978. Shows how to make modifications without losing the basic qualities of the original program constructed according to Warnier's method LCP (Logical Construction of Programs).

Weinberg, G.M. *The psychology of computer programming.* New York, NY: Van Nostrand Reinhold Company, 1971. A classic study of computer programming as a human activity. The author challenges the myths and half-truths of the profession. He offers surprising and challenging ideas about the roles and relations of human beings within the programming environment. The relaxed, anecdotal style makes the book delightful to read. It includes many case histories, and an annotated bibliography.

Weinberg, G.M., Wright, S.E., Kauffman, R., Goetz, M.A. *High level COBOL programming.* Cambridge, MA: Winthrop Publishers, Inc., 1977. [This publisher has been acquired by Little, Brown and Company, Boston, MA.] Excerpted in Parikh, 1982. This book contains many gems for a maintenance programmer. It is significant that a whole chapter is devoted to maintenance, the subject almost always neglected in such books. It also includes material on critical program reading.

Yau, S.S., Collofello, J.S., MacGregor, T. "Ripple effect analysis of software maintenance." *Proc. COMPSAC78*, IEEE Computer Society's Second International Computer Software and Applications Conference, 1978, 60-65. A technique is described for tracing the "ripple effect" of a maintenance change, i.e., the effects on the function and performance of a program of a single change as its results are carried throughout the program.

Yau, S.S., Collofello, J.S. "Some stability measures for software maintenance." *IEEE Trans. Software Engineering*, SE-6, 6 (1980), 545-552. The ripple effect of a maintenance change on the function and performance of a system are further described. A measure for the stability of a program, i.e., its resistance to such ripple effects, is defined.

Yourdon, E. *Techniques of program structure and design.* Englewood Cliffs, NJ: Prentice-Hall, 1975. Excerpted in Parikh, 1982. In addition to some material on maintenance, this book includes a section on converting unstructured programs to structured programs by use of the duplication of coding, the state variable, and the Boolean flag technique. It also includes material on testing.

Yourdon, E. *Managing the structured techniques.* New York, NY: Yourdon Press, 2nd edition, 1979. Excerpted in Parikh, 1982. The book is an excellent management summary of structured programming, structured design, structured analysis, chief programmer teams, and other productivity techniques. It contains some enlightening flashes on maintenance.

Zvegintzov, N. "What life? What cycle?" *AFIPS Conference Proceedings*, 51, 1982, 561-568. The traditional systems life cycle model does not portray the life of a system, nor is it a cycle. An alternative model is described that portrays the modification cycle of the system and the detailed activities of making a change. Implications are drawn for maintenance, development, and the education of software engineers. [From the abstract.]

Name Index

Names of authors whose papers are included in this Tutorial, and the page numbers of their papers, are in bold.

Mrs. Shobha Sanade and Mr. Siva P. Raparla helped compile the "Name Index" on an IBM Personal Computer using the word processing software Spellbinder™.

Rich, C., 150, 163
Riddle, W.E., 221, 232
Riordan, J.S., 215
Ritchie, D.M., 260
Robinson, L., 82, 163
Ross, Douglas T., 168, 179, 214, 217, 220, 232
Roubine, O., 82, 163
Rude, R.V., 332
Ryan, John R., 256
Ryder, B.G., 286, 316

Saint, H., 332
Saltzer, J.H., 305
Saxena, A.R., 144
Schnellman, George, 60
Schoman, K.E., 168, 179, 214, 217
Schwarts, J., 299
Seeds, Harice, 60
Shapiro, R., 332
Shaw, A.C., 82
Shaw, M., 214
Shearing, B.M., 286
Shneiderman, B., 62, 111, 114, 350
Shore, J., 81, 144
Shostak, R.E., 163
Shrobe, H.E., 150, 163
Siemieniuch, J.L., 316
Siewiorek, D.L., 144
Simon, H.A., 214
Smith, B., 150, 163
Smith, B.T., 316
Smith, M.K., 221, 231
Spier, Michael J., xi, 267, **269-75**, 275
Spitzen, J.M., 163
Stabley, Donald, 55, 60
Stanat, D., 144
Steinbeck, 101
Steinbrenner, K., 37
Stevens, W.P., 214
Stewart, Charles, v
Stockton, C.G., v
Stone, W. Clement, 62, 63
Stucki, L.G., 228, 231
Stuebing, Henry, 332
Suzuki, N., 163
Swami, Bhashyananda, v
Swanson, E. Burton, 1, 2, 5, 9, 10, 29, **31-37**, 37, 187, 222, 232, 289, 348, 350
Swaum, G.H., 214
Sweeney, John, 60

Teichroew, D., 214, 220, 232
Teitelman, W., 150, 163
Thayer, T.A., 174, 179
Thompson, K.L., 260

Tompkins, G.E., 29, 37
Torsun, 256
Tranter, B., 332
Trattner, S., 350
Trauter, B.R., 214
Trombka, B., 144
Turanski, William, 317
Turner, Albert J., 115, 123, **125-31**, 131, 224, 230
Turski, W.M., 213, 214

Van Horn, Earl C., xi, 187, 217, **219-32**, 228, 232
Van Leer, P., 214
Van Vleck, T.H., xi, 267, 301, **303-05**
Vick, C.R., 228, 230

Walston, C.E., 214
Walton, Richard, 60
Warnier, Jean-Dominique, xi, 83, 85, 86, 87, 88, 89, 93, 102, 187, 237, 238, **239-54**, 350
Warshall, S., 332
Wegbreit, B., 163
Wegner, Peter, 213, 214, 301
Weinberg, Gerald M., v, xi, 5, 10, 62, 165, 187, 189, **191-96**, 197, 233, 263, **265-66**, 348, 350
Weiss, D.M., 81, 82, 144
Wells, R.E., 163
Wessner, H., 214
Westmacott, P.N., 214, 332
White, J.R., 221, 228, 232
Wile, D., 163
Wirth, N., 131, 214
Wisneski, D., 316
Witt, B.I., 62, 348
Wittig, Barbara, v
Wolverton, R.W., 189, 214
Woodside, M., 215
Wright, S.E., 62, 350
Wright, W., 144
Wulf, W.A., 144, 213
Wurges, H., 81, 144

Yau, S.S., 350
Yeh, R., 163, 214
Young, D., 214
Yourdon, Edward, v, 8, 10, 221, 232, 350

Zave, P., 214
Zawacki, Robert, 335
Zelkowitz, M.V., 96
Zilles, S., 81, 214
Zurcher, F.W., 214
Zvegintzov, Diana, v
Zvegintzov, Nicholas (Brand, Jonathan), v, xi, 5, 61, 62, 63, **65-68**, 68, 115, 133, 179, 233, 333, **335-36**, 347, 350, **355**
Zvegintzov, Serge, v

Topic Index

Editors' Biographies

Photo courtesy of DELTAK. Inc.

Girish Parikh

Nicholas Zvegintzov

Girish Parikh, President of Shetal Enterprises, Chicago, consults, writes, teaches, and lectures in the fields of software maintenance and software productivity, including programmer productivity. Of his fourteen years in Data Processing, he admits to spending half in actual maintenance work. Over half of his programming years was spent in contract programming, consulting, and service bureau environments. He has applied the structured techniques in development and maintenance, has studied them continuously, and has written about them, especially about their use in a maintenance environment. He has a B.E. in Civil Engineering from Gujarat University, India.

Parikh is the author/editor of *Techniques of program and system maintenance* (published by Little, Brown and Company, 1982), the forthcoming *The guide to software maintenance* (also from Little, Brown), the *Programmer productivity reports* and *How to measure programmer productivity* (both published by Shetal Enterprises) and the newsletter *Software Productivity Digest*, expected in 1983.

Parikh has published in a variety of computer periodicals including *Computerworld*, *Data Processing Digest*, and *Data Management* and has presented seminars on software maintenance and programming productivity. He is a lecturer at DePaul University and teaches graduate courses on Software maintenance and Software methodologies. He has developed a series of video courses, *Measuring programmer productivity* with DELTAK, inc.

From Parikh's coeditor, Nicholas Zvegintzov: "Girish Parikh is one of the most remarkable people I know. When I am mad at the world—sometimes even at *him*—he cools my agitation with his own affectionate calm. His wife Hasu has served me many delicious and surprising dishes from traditional Gujarat recipes and thereby given me a whole new view of the value of programming with existing systems. Thank you both!"

Nicholas Zvegintzov consults, writes, and teaches in the field of software maintenance—the modification and upgrading of existing software systems to meet changing needs. As a management consultant, he provides support on the following topics:

- Control, evaluation, and upgrading of operational software systems.
- Installation of an effective software maintenance methodology.
- Motivation, morale, professionalism, and productivity in maintenance groups.
- Techniques, tools, and tactics for the maintenance programmer.

He came to the study of software maintenance after a decade spent in university research and a decade spent in applications programming.

Zvegintzov graduated from Oxford University in 1962 with a B.A. and M.A. in Experimental Psychology. From 1962 to 1969 he conducted research in computer science and artificial intelligence at the University of California, Berkeley, and at Carnegie-Mellon University, Pittsburgh. From 1969 to 1979 he programmed, designed, upgraded, and documented applications systems. Since 1979 he has worked full-time as a consultant in the field of applications software maintenance.